Postdigital Dialogues on Critical Pedagogy, Liberation Theology and Information Technology

Praise for *Postdigital Dialogues on Critical Pedagogy, Liberation Theology and Information Technology*

Postdigital Dialogues on Critical Pedagogy, Liberation Theology and Information Technology *is reminiscent of what Paulo Freire called "talking books", which bring two powerful authors into a direct and fluidly exchange. As such, it exemplifies the very power of dialogue, illustrating the inextricable relationship of knowledge as both a social construction and collective endeavor. The result is a beautiful treatise that, although focused on Peter McLaren, allows the multiplicity of questions and responses to boldly weave a powerful story, from where essential political issues crucial to our liberation and the survival of the planet can emerge. In this sense, McLaren and Jandrić convey a beautiful dance of ideas, woven intricately over the years from each man's consciousness, scholarship, and lived experiences as radical intellectuals, political freedom fighters, and transformative advocates in the world.*

Antonia Darder, Endowed Chair of Ethics & Moral Leadership, Loyola Marymount University

In Postdigital Dialogues on Critical Pedagogy, Liberation Theology and Information Technology, *Peter McLaren and Petar Jandrić have provided us with a pathbreaking volume traversing the realms of Marxist theory, critical pedagogy, and Liberation Theology combined with the most creative, far-reaching applications of critical social theory likely to be found anywhere. Those applications extend to the realms of modern technology, global capitalism, ecological crisis, U.S. imperialism, and of course the state of modern education in the United States and elsewhere. This is nothing short of a landmark contribution to literature spanning the fields of history, sociology, global studies, philosophy, and education. McLaren's iconic work is also biographically highlighted here, starting with an introductory section (written by Jandrić) that brilliantly traces the personal and intellectual development of the world's leading critical pedagogical theorist. A highly-recommended collection of essays for anyone interested in state-of-the-art revolutionary theorizing that outlines a much-needed path out of the modern crisis.*

Carl Boggs, author of *Fascism Old and New*

In an age when critical pedagogy and a new language for rethinking politics is crucial, Postdigital Dialogues on Critical Pedagogy, Liberation Theology and Information Technology *is a crucial book to read, study, and give to others.*

Henry Giroux, author of *The Terror of the Unforeseen*

This is a truly inspiring convergence of revolutionary ideas to offer signposts for redemption in this baleful "New Fascist" era.

Peter Mayo, author of *Higher Education in a Globalising World* and *Hegemony and Education under Neoliberalism. Insights from Gramsci*

This is a wide-ranging, provocative, and insurrectional series of transnational dialogues that becomes an immediate classic within the much beloved tradition of the "Talking Book" in critical pedagogy. #tospeakatrueword #planetarity #fuckglobalwhitesupremacy!

Richard Kahn, Professor of Education, Antioch University Los Angeles

Peter McLaren stands among the doyens of critical pedagogues, having done much to take the field forward over decades, and this book – of correspondences with Petar Jandrić – goes far in revealing the breadth of that endeavour. To read this book is to eavesdrop on an extraordinary conversation, at once intimate and enriching. Chock-full of insights, this volume exemplifies a lifetime of passionate, humane and radical scholarship, as McLaren ranges effortlessly across education, social theory, religion, the digital age, ecology and the Anthropocene. The cast includes Jesus, Marx, Freire, Rand and Trump and it is clear where McLaren stands in each case. This book is both immensely enjoyable and educational and I shall want to read it again.

Ronald Barnett, Emeritus Professor of Higher Education, University College London Institute of Education

Peter and Petar, the wonderful namesakes, have written a book consisting of epiphanic dialogues in their idiosyncratic and rousing styles. The book is an introduction to the authors' recent thinking, an emic view to the work and research themes of two critical scholars, and also a demonstration of how the discourse of critical pedagogy has over the years expanded from the classroom and public pedagogy to comprise various themes in the changing relationship between technology, education, and society.

Juha Suoranta, Tampere University, Finland

In this thought provocative book, Peter McLaren and Petar Jandrić push again the borders of existing thinking on radical critical pedagogy. In our current times of transhumanism, this book offers its readers new spaces for hope and revolutionary praxis. By connecting faith and postdigital sciences this dialogical book goes beyond addressing issues of capitalism to suggesting a way to reclaim the future of humanity.

Maria Nikolakaki, Associate Professor, University of Peloponnese, Greece

What started out as a multiyear dialogue between world-renowned educator Peter McLaren and communications technology scholar-activist Petar Jandrić has morphed here into a must-read reflection on revolutionary critical pedagogy and liberation theology as an indispensable reservoir of theories, ideas, insights and practices to draw on for those who want to confront the ravages of a predatory global capitalism.

Wide ranging and exciting, of the greatest political urgency, this work will inform and inspire contemporary emancipatory struggles around the world.

William I. Robinson, Professor of Sociology, University of
California at Santa Barbara
Author of *Into the Tempest: Essays on the New Global Capitalism*

This ground-breaking work by two eminent scholars a generation apart in age addresses crucial questions as to whether digital technologies and rapid communication can help free us from a seemingly never-ending capital accumulation designed only to benefit the few. Using ideas from critical pedagogy and liberation theory it asks whether there is hope that new technologies can help the many become more complete and equal human beings in a world no longer devoted to profit and exploitation.

Sally Tomlinson is Emeritus Professor at Goldsmiths London University and
an Honorary Fellow in the Education Department University of Oxford

This book is both a homage to, and a kind of radical intensification of, the educational dialogue. McLaren and Jandrić's exchanges not only excavate the value of critical pedagogy in contemporary times of techno-capitalism, but also expose the richness of their surrounding intellectual communities. The result is a hopeful work that develops liberation theology for the postdigital era.

Jeremy Knox, University of Edinburgh

In proposing a revolutionary critical pedagogy as a tool informing the struggle for a liberated future McLaren and Jandrić have done a great service in recapitulating past critical theories and indicating a way forward towards a future beyond a digitised capitalism. I highly recommend their conversation as a critical thought provoking and emotion eliciting exercise.

Helen Raduntz, Adjunct Research Fellow, University of
South Australia

Peter McLaren and Petar Jandrić's Postdigital Dialogues on Critical Pedagogy, Liberation Theology and Information Technology *boldly confronts, in illuminating conceptual analyses, a multitude of contemporary challenges to the creation of new human relations, relations that are not rooted in the value form of labor but rather in human production for humans – production that affirms every other being as a necessary facet integral to one's own essential and total being. Grappling with such pressing issues as the formation of consciousness in an ecosystem saturated by technology, the re-emergence of authoritarianism and fascist social structures, and the stakes in attempts to reconcile the spiritual and the material, McLaren and Jandrić range far and wide, but through sharp dialectical reasoning, they always bring the analyses back to capitalism as a totality that must be abolished. In their far ranging discussions, McLaren and Jandrić vigorously deploy "theory" in the particular sense articulated by Theodor W. Adorno: as that which "seeks to give a name to what secretly* holds the machinery together," that which "seeks to raise the stone under which the monster lies brooding."

Deborah Kelsh, The College of Saint Rose

This book is an invitation to join McLaren and Jandrić on a rigorous yet lively, challenging yet rewarding walk across a sprawling range of pressing political, scientific, educational, and yes, even theological issues of our time. The walk is rigorous in the depth and nuance of the research and argumentation; it's lively in the way the dialogues are situated again and again in the ongoing political antagonisms of our era; its challenging as it weaves together diverse thinkers together in unorthodox ways; and its rewarding not because it leaves the reading having finally "got it," but rather because it leaves us with an entirely new set of questions to explore, and the resources necessary to explore them.

Derek R. Ford, Assistant Professor of Education Studies,
DePauw University

In this excellent book, Petar Jandrić and Peter McLaren have created a perceptive commentary on the possibilities and perils of our postdigital world.

Richard Barbrook, Senior Lecturer in Politics at the University of Westminster,
founder member of Class Wargames and director of the
Digital Liberties cooperative.

Peter McLaren and Petar Jandrić have written a necessary book for these times. Book that no social militant can stop reading.

Fernando Lázaro (Argentina), Educador Popular, Docente Universidad
Nacional de Luján Militante social CEIPH

Also available from Bloomsbury

On Critical Pedagogy, 2nd Edition, by Henry Giroux
Pedagogy of the Oppressed: 50th Anniversary Edition by Paulo Freire
Education For Critical Consciousness by Paulo Freire
Pedagogy of Hope by Paulo Freire

Postdigital Dialogues on Critical Pedagogy, Liberation Theology and Information Technology

Peter McLaren and Petar Jandrić

BLOOMSBURY ACADEMIC
LONDON • NEW YORK • OXFORD • NEW DELHI • SYDNEY

BLOOMSBURY ACADEMIC
An imprint of Bloomsbury Publishing Plc
50 Bedford Square, London, WC1B 3DP, UK
1385 Broadway, New York, NY 10018, USA

www.bloomsbury.com

ISBN: HB: 978-1-3500-9995-1
PB: 978-1-3501-4466-8
ePDF: 978-1-3500-9996-8
ePub: 978-1-3500-9997-5

Typeset by Deanta Global Publishing Services, Chennai, India
Printed and bound in Great Britain

To find out more about our authors and books visit www.bloomsbury.com
and sign up for our newsletters.

I dedicate this book to my wife Wang Yan, a powerful and fearless soul who has brought great love and comfort to me in the winter of my life.
Peter McLaren

I dedicate this book to my partner Ana and my son Toma, who made me into what I am today and now fearlessly live with consequences.
Petar Jandrić

Contents

Postdigital Revolutionary Critical Pedagogy in and for the Anthropocene

Acknowledgments

This book is based on a continuous exchange of correspondences between Peter McLaren and Petar Jandrić in the period between 2011 and 2019. These exchanges—conversations, texts, and e-mails that were later embellished with quotations and references—resulted in numerous publications in several formats and languages. Over the years some of the articles were republished in several places—yet they never remained the same. With each subsequent version, we added more granular insights and interpretations, including new material. As a result, the correspondences became more dialogical and multiversal, as they became reshaped by interactions and feedback loops from a variety of intellectual communities such that we can no longer claim these dialogues to be ours. Instead, they belong to the intellectual collective, which was created throughout the intervening years during which time all of humanity was facing down the specter of new species of capitalist terror, a terror that has only become more molecular and invasive. The dialogues also reflect the spirit of our times and the affordances of available communication technologies. As Jeremy Knox observed in his review of one of our works, "What better way to highlight the intertextual challenges of presence, authenticity and authorship, without even so much as a mention of the digital" (Knox 2019: 128). We extend our sincere gratitude to all readers, editors, reviewers, students, and others who engaged with our works over the years. Special thanks for this book go to Sarah Hayes, who masterfully wrote up Petar's biography; Peter Hudis for his Foreword; and Michael Adrian Peters for his Afterword. Finally, we dearly thank our families, who suffered our sudden withdrawals from our surroundings while we frantically typed on our phones and computers.

While much of this text has already been published, more than half is new material. Chapters in this book roughly follow the chronology of our correspondences and published articles. Between 2011 and 2014 we focused on technology, and between 2015 and 2019 we shifted our attention to liberation theology. Within these broad areas, however, the resulting material resembles a freshly baked pastiche—we significantly cut and pasted within the published texts, and, recognizing aporias and oversights, redressed those omissions with new material. As a result, this book is very different from any of our publications to date. With thanks to various publishing houses that supported our work, we include the following genealogy of some of these texts.

Peter McLaren: Portrait of a Revolutionary

This chapter is reproduced verbatim from Jandrić, P. (2018a). Peter McLaren: Portrait of a Revolutionary. *Rassegna Di Pedagogia*, 76(1–2), 139–58.

Revolutionary Critical Pedagogy Is Made by Walking: In a World Where Many Worlds Coexist

In 2014 we published the original article: McLaren, P., & Jandrić, P. (2014a). Critical revolutionary pedagogy is made by walking—in a world where many worlds coexist. *Policy Futures in Education,* 12(6), 805–31. An abbreviated version of this article was published in Croatian language as: McLaren, P., & Jandrić, P. (2014b). Kultura borbe protiv neoliberalnog kapitalizma. *Zarez,* 398–99(16), 8–9. A year later, the article was again reshaped and published as McLaren, P., & Jandrić, P. (2015a). Critical revolutionary pedagogy in and for the age of the network. *Philosophy of Education,* 14(1), 106–26, with the abstract translated into the Ukrainian language.

For Peter's book *Pedagogy of Insurrection: From Resurrection to Revolution,* we expanded the article with some insights into liberation theology: McLaren, P., & Jandrić, P. (2015b). Revolutionary critical pedagogy is made by walking—in a world where many worlds coexist. In P. McLaren (Ed.), *Pedagogy of Insurrection: From Resurrection to Revolution* (pp. 255–98). New York: Peter Lang. After two years, that version was further expanded into a chapter in Petar's book: McLaren, P., & Jandrić, P. (2017a). Revolutionary critical pedagogy is made by walking—in a world where many worlds coexist. In P. Jandrić, *Learning in the Age of Digital Reason* (pp. 159–94). Rotterdam: Sense. Finally, Petar's book was translated into Croatian language where chapter is published as: McLaren, P., & Jandrić, P. (2019b). Revolucionarna kritička pedagogija ostvaruje se u hodu: u svijetu gdje mnogi svjetovi supostoje. In P. Jandrić, *Znanje u digitalnom dobu. Razgovori s djecom jedne male revolucije.* Zagreb: Jesenski i Turk.

In this book we present a slight update of the version published in *Learning in the Age of Digital Reason.*

The Critical Challenge of Networked Learning: Using Information Technologies in the Service of Humanity

This chapter is reproduced and slightly expanded from McLaren, P., & Jandrić, P. (2015c). The critical challenge of networked learning: using information technologies in the service of humanity. In Petar Jandrić & Damir Boras (Eds.), *Critical Learning in Digital Networks* (pp. 199–226). New York: Springer.

From Liberation to Salvation: Revolutionary Critical Pedagogy Meets Liberation Theology

This chapter is reproduced almost verbatim from McLaren, P., & Jandrić, P. (2017b). From Liberation to Salvation: Revolutionary critical pedagogy meets liberation theology. *Policy Futures in Education,* 15(5), 620–52. To achieve coherence, however, parts of the original chapter have been relocated into other chapters of the book.

Karl Marx and Liberation Theology: Dialectical Materialism and Christian Spirituality in, against, and beyond Contemporary Capitalism

This chapter is based on McLaren, P., & Jandrić, P. (2018a). Karl Marx and Liberation Theology: Dialectical materialism and Christian spirituality in, against, and beyond contemporary capitalism. *TripleC: Communication, Capitalism & Critique*, 16(2), 598–607. Upon request, an abbreviated version of the *TripleC* article was also published as: McLaren, P., & Jandrić, P. (2018b). Peter McLaren's Liberation Theology: Karl Marx meets Jesus Christ. In J. S. Brooks and A. Normore (Eds.), *Leading Against the Grain: Lessons for Creating Just and Equitable Schools* (pp. 39–48). New York: Teachers College Press. For this book, the original *TripleC* article has been substantially expanded. A new section, based on McLaren, P., & Rikowski, G. (2001). Pedagogy for revolution against education for capital: An E-dialogue on education in capitalism today. *Cultural Logic*, 4(1), has been added to the beginning of the chapter.

Paulo Freire and Liberation Theology: The Christian Consciousness of Critical Pedagogy

This chapter is based on McLaren, P., & Jandrić, P. (2018c). Paulo Freire and Liberation Theology: The Christian consciousness of critical pedagogy. *Vierteljahresschrift für wissenschaftliche Pädagogik*, 94(2): 246–64. A new section, based on McLaren, P. (1997b). Paulo Freire's Legacy of Hope and Struggle. *Theory, Culture & Society*, 14(4), 147–53, has been added to the beginning of the chapter.

Reclaiming the Present or a Return to the Ash Heap of the Future?

This chapter is reproduced almost verbatim from McLaren, P. (2019a). Reclaiming the present or a return to the ash heap of the future? *Postdigital Science and Education*, 1(1), 10–13.

Scattered throughout the Book, we also reproduced small parts of following articles:

Jandrić, P. (2014b). Deschooling virtuality. *Open Review of Educational Research*, 1(1), 84–98.

McLaren, P. (2019). God and governance: Reflections on living in the belly of the beast. *Postdigital Science and Education*, 2(1), 311–34.

McLaren, P., & Jandrić, P. (2019a). Revolutionary critical rage pedagogy. In M. F. He & W. Schubert (Eds.), *Oxford Encyclopedia of Curriculum Studies*. New York: Oxford University Press.

Foreword

Peter Hudis

Technology is an integral part of the development of the productive forces. To exclude from it the greatest productive force—living labor—cripples and emasculates science itself. Under capitalism, the separation of the intellectual powers of production from manual labor, the incorporation of all science into the machine, means the transformation of the intellectual power into the might of capital over labor, the engineer and technician against the worker. In a word, it means the transformation of man into a mere fragment of a man, just when the narrow technical needs of the machine itself demand variation in labor, fluidity, and mobility—all rounded, fully developed human beings using all of their human talents, both natural and acquired.

Raya Dunayevskaya (1958)

These words, contained in the foundational text of Marxist humanism, Raya Dunayevskaya's *Marxism and Freedom: from 1776 Until Today* (1958), capture the spiritual and intellectual content of these wide-ranging discussions between Petar Jandrić and Peter McLaren. Their focal point—the impact of contemporary digital technologies—addresses the central question of our time: will humanity become completely imprisoned by the objects of its own creation, or will it break from the increasingly abstract forms of domination that define everyday life by creating *new human relations* that frees technology and social life of its capitalist value form.

The direction of world politics and economics does not provide us with any rosy scenario when it comes to such questions. The unrelenting logic of capital accumulation, alongside the failure of innumerable efforts to break from it by left-wing governments in both the West and non-Western world, has given capital a new lease on life, posing an enormous threat to the existence of civilization as we have known it. The dire direction in which we are headed is reflected in an array of intellectual accommodations to the given, from postmodernism to posthumanism. So overwhelming is today's technological irrationality that some leftist theorists go so far as to embrace our presumed transformation into cyborgs as a virtue.

None of this accommodationism is found in these discussions with the world's leading figure in critical pedagogy. McLaren and Jandrić avoid such detours and dead-ends by holding to the most fundamental dimensions of Marx's thought—its *humanism*. The crux of the matter is the *absolute contradiction* between the nature of technology at any given stage and the value form of its operation. As Marx repeatedly reminds us throughout his work, there is no such thing as a machine or instrument of production "as such." Their significance and meaning are disclosed by their embeddedness in a specific set of social relations. The latter inevitably take on an indirect, abstract form in capitalism, since it is governed by the drive to augment wealth in monetary form as an end in itself. This is true of all forms of capitalism, whether "free market" or state capitalist, whether calling itself "democratic" or taking the form of a single-party state dictatorship. Societies governed by the law of value are characterized by an absolute contradiction between the wealth and knowledge embodied in technological formations and their inherent destructiveness in consuming virtually every formation in its drive for ever-more (abstract) monetary value. Given this, is there any way out?

There is no capital without labor. There is no technology without intellectual as well as manual labor. And there is no human labor without the capacity for free, conscious, and purposeful creation. Capital's drive to pump out ever-more value in less amounts of time *necessitates* that it elevate scientific and technological power at the expense of the human subject. At one and the same time, however, it relies on this human subject to reproduce the value of the accumulated capital, without which the system cannot continue. This is why the growth of automated and high-tech production and services has not lessened but instead *extended* the length of the working day. And despite the claims of accelerationists and others, there is no evidence that it will lessen in the future, even as capital becomes more dependent on precarious, part-time, and temporary low-paid labor (it is increasingly common for workers to hold two or three part-time jobs at once). Various political and contingent factors always play a role here, but the decisive one remains the logic of capital itself. This is repeatedly obscured by those who treat changes in digital technology independent of the value form of their operation.

McLaren and Jandrić's work retains the space for hope and reimagining the human, not simply on utopian or apocalyptic grounds, but by seeking to retain what Marx held together: an ability to decipher capital's most abstract and alienated forms of domination while never taking his finger of the pulse of human relations. In doing so, this book can aid us in envisioning the "fully developed" human being.

Introductions

Peter McLaren: Portrait of a Revolutionary

Petar Jandrić

I have been reading Peter McLaren since I first learned about critical pedagogy as a graduate student in Scotland. In 2011, I finally met Peter at the II International Conference on Critical Education in Athens and requested an interview. Little did I know what was coming next! After a few years of cowriting, we ended up with so much text that it needed to be divided between several publications, and even then we would accumulate more text. Since then, Peter and I continued cowriting and meeting in person at least once per year. What started as a typical case of a young scholar interviewing a leading figure in his field has turned into warm friendship and collaboration, which has now resulted in numerous publications covering two main themes: (digital) technology and liberation theology and their potential contributions to a pedagogy of liberation.

With each cowritten article I learned more about Peter's work and its deep connections to his personal life, a life that has been fraught with its own tempests and teapots, and one in which Peter has been made to pay a price, personally and academically, not once, but many times over. When Peter was feeling blue, I would discover a poem or image in my inbox and feel its deep connections with his latest academic insights; when Peter married Wang Yan (Angie), we engaged in deep discussions about the pedagogy of love. As I dove deeper and deeper into Peter's work, I increasingly felt that it would be really important to connect it with his life. I was not ashamed to ask, and Peter never hid anything. Yet, these isolated facts were far from a whole-rounded picture—a picture I desperately wanted to have yet could not find in existing sources. For a man who has participated in revolutions and revolutionary activities throughout much of his adult life, who has been jailed as a teenager, teargassed and beaten by Turkish riot police, chased by armed drug cartels, attacked in the press, and is known as a maverick and iconoclast, I have discovered another side of Peter. A man who prefers long walks in his neighborhood, who openly engages in regular chats with his students and colleagues about navigating through the academic maze, who spends solitary hours playing blues licks that he learned by listening to Robert Johnson, Lightning Hopkins and Muddy Waters, and who spends hours corresponding with his diverse, international community.

As soon as people started connecting my name with Peter's, I recognized the tendency to mystify Peter and his life. Interestingly enough, such mystifications arrive more or less equally from the left and from the right: a unique combination of Peter's specific demeanor and his humble nature makes him a great target for both hate and worship. However, Peter is far beyond positive and negative mystifications: I've often seen him dismiss the first with a gentle push toward critique and dismiss the latter without offending the offender. However, the importance of Peter's work has long ago superseded his personal capacity for responding to each and every interpretation of his work. With more than fifty published books, numerous articles, and tens of thousands of registered quotations, Peter has become a living legend in the contemporary critical pedagogy movement—and in the most productive years of his life!

When Winfried Böhm invited me to write an article, which later turned into this chapter, the need to understand Peter's work through his life and career has meticulously blended with the need to demystify Peter's persona. Based on our numerous conversations supported by his Wikipedia entry (Wikipedia 2019a), I classified Peter's work into two overreaching phases. Each phase is divided into three stages, which are framed either by significant events in Peter's life or by significant developments in his work. In this way, I arrived at the following classification:

The Reconciliatory Phase

> 1948–1973: Early childhood and wild years
> 1974–1984: From rookie teacher to acclaimed writer and perspective academic
> 1985–1993: From perspective academic to one of the leading architects of critical pedagogy

The Revolutionary Phase

> 1994–2001: From cultural studies and postmodernism to Marxist humanism
> 2001–2013: From Marxist humanism to revolutionary critical pedagogy
> 2013–: Peter McLaren's liberation theology

In the Reconciliatory Phase, Peter was mostly interested in evolutionary development or "correcting" education. In a typical biographer's maneuver, the story begins with Peter's school years, 1948–1973: Early childhood and wild years. The second stage, 1974–1984: From rookie teacher to acclaimed writer and perspective academic, has also imposed itself without any effort—it covers Peter's five years as a middle school teacher, the success of his best-selling book *Cries from the Corridor* (McLaren 1980), and the period of his doctoral studies. The third stage, 1985–1993: From prospective academic to one of the leading architects of critical pedagogy, is marked by Peter's collaboration with Henry Giroux at Miami University of Ohio. During that time, Peter deeply engaged in cultural studies and postmodernism and significantly contributed to foundations of North American critical pedagogy.

In the Revolutionary Phase, Peter turned his attention from education to broader social issues and switched his evolutionary perspective into open revolutionary anti-capitalism. The fourth stage, 1994–2001: From cultural studies and postmodernism to Marxist humanism, starts with Peter's move to the University of California, Los Angeles, and his turn from postmodernism to class struggle and Marxism. The fifth stage of Peter's work—2001–2013: From Marxist humanism to revolutionary critical pedagogy—is not marked by a change of job or location. However, in 2001, Peter actively started to employ Paula Allman's phrase revolutionary critical pedagogy (Allman 2001), which denotes his shift toward social struggle at large. At the moment of writing these words, the last stage—2013–: Peter McLaren's liberation theology—is in full swing. Those of us who regularly work with Peter can only admire at the torrent of new ideas he produces on a regular basis.

These phases and stages should be understood merely as "necessary evils" or tools needed to make some order in Peter's complex life and work. However, borders between them cannot be cut cleanly. While Peter did occasionally revoke some of his earlier works, he always placed overgrown ideas into a broader context and used them as tools for conscientization and critique. Spanning over a rich lifetime, Peter's work presents a complex curve of development. Sometimes it approximates a straight line, but sometimes it makes significant curves and diversions. For better or worse, the only ideas and values about which Peter is truly dogmatic are his love and care for humanity.

This chapter is based on numerous sources. After almost a decade of cowriting with Peter, I managed to read a significant part of his rich opus. Peter's life and work have been a subject of numerous critiques, which I explored at every opportunity. In preparation for this chapter, Peter kindly supplied various documents such as his latest curriculum vitae and the list of his publications. Last but not least, Peter did a lot of work in this chapter: approved the classification of his career into phases and stages, provided useful insights and comments, and made many corrections. Most importantly, Peter's direct engagement with this chapter offers a wealth of information that cannot to my knowledge be found in any other sources. Endorsed by Peter himself, this chapter is a scholarly biography with elements of personal autobiography—an unusual combination, which is hoped to produce a balanced, honest, warm, and personal view to Peter's life and career until present.

1948–1973: Early Childhood and Wild Years

Peter Lawrence McLaren was born on August 2, 1948 in a conservative working-class family in Toronto. Peter was the only child. Yet, surrounded by his many cousins, children of his father's sister and his mother's four sisters and two brothers, he was never lonely. Peter's mother Frances Teresa Bernadette McLaren was first a homemaker and then a telephone operator. His father, Lawrence Omand McLaren, was a World War II veteran who climbed up a career ladder from a television salesman to general manager of Phillips Electronics for Eastern Canada. At the age of 50, however, he became a victim of ageism. This forced him into a series of progressively low-paying jobs, which, combined with his poor health, led to his premature retirement and death. Peter's mother was Catholic, his father was brought up Presbyterian, and Peter was raised in the Anglican tradition, explored different spiritual paths including Buddhism, shamanism, Theosophy, spiritism, and Umbanda, until his conversion to Catholicism in his early thirties.

As a teenager Peter was interested in literature, poetry, literary and art criticism, philosophy, and social science. In middle school, Peter won a writing award for producing a science fiction story; in high school, he was making 35 mm movies and wanted to become a film director. Under the influence of his high school teacher Dennis Hutcheon, Peter became interested in theology and contemplated becoming a priest, and Harold Burke, another English teacher, motivated him toward theater. Yet, the exciting temptations of the late 1960s counterculture led him on a different path. At the age of 16, Peter became disillusioned with school, which he nevertheless attended with considerable success. Witnessing his father's unfortunate life after the layoff, he vowed that he would never work for a large corporation.

After completing high school, Peter hitchhiked to San Francisco and Los Angeles and joined the budding countercultural scene. He participated in anti-Vietnam war protests, met with Black Panthers, Timothy Leary, and Allen Ginsberg, started playing blues guitar, and experimented with drugs. He stayed at flophouses with fellow hippies and nearly every night he, along with his fellow travelers, were interrogated by the FBI who were seeking to arrest draft resisters. At a time, he recalls,

> I spent considerable time with a variety of colorful and creative individuals whose lives bounced paradoxically between expressive rituals of emancipation and pathological rituals of self-destruction. Drugs became a part of many lives. For many, drugs seemed to serve as a symbolic medium to penetrate the contradictions between freedom and constraint in a society nourished by the myth that progress through technology is the only objective reality. Timothy Leary, the high priest of LSD, handed me a note at a concert: DIPLOMA, it read. YOU ARE NOW FREE. (McLaren 2016: 35)

During that period, Peter started writing short stories and poetry. With some help from Allen Ginsberg, Peter began to prioritize creative potentials of his written work over the delights of the flesh: "While Timothy Leary and I tripped together on LSD, Allen Ginsberg told me to stop taking psychedelics and to concentrate on my writing" (in Davis 2015). Upon his return from California, Peter was jailed and systematically beaten by Toronto police. As he recalls later, there he "learned a major political lesson. . . . [Peter] had begun to realize that a new generation was being born and life was not going to be easy, especially if you lived your life against the grain" (in Davis 2015).

In 1968 Peter enrolled at the University of Toronto to study Chaucer, Beowulf, Middle English, and Old English. He also took a course with acclaimed sculptor, Robert Downing, who used to drive Peter around Toronto in his sports car where they smoked marijuana and discussed the various sculptures around the city. Peter realized he had no real talent as a sculptor. As a freshman student, he was a part-time member of the Yorkville Village hippie community where he was invited to parties and gatherings of the underground Toronto arts community—Peter still vividly remembers a party where a young woman performed The Dance of the Seven Veils—and gained firsthand insight into the dynamics of the double-speak of hippie (counter)cultural production: "All pretending that we were creating a new society free from the normative shackles of conventional morality and lifestyle, but basically we were looking for drugs, sex and rock and roll and our twenty minutes of fame" (McLaren 2015a: 132). To test his willpower, Peter spent the entire night in Mount Pleasant Cemetery high on LSD, reciting his favorite poem, "Lament," by Dylan Thomas (2010), while attempting Zorba the Greek dance moves around the tombstones, which appeared to dance along with him. It was the dance moves of the life-size stone Angels that impressed him the most. Upon reflection, Peter thinks this episode was related to his own inability to distance himself from self-destructive aspects of the 1960s drug culture.

Peter dropped out of the University of Toronto, as some of his close friends were getting addicted to heroin, and he wanted to escape from their influence by moving to Kitchener, Ontario, where he decided to complete his English degree at the University of Waterloo. In 1973, Peter earned a Bachelor of Arts in English Literature, specializing in Elizabethan drama, at the University of Waterloo. Some Vietnam War draft resisters who were touring Canada helped to educate Peter further about the war and the history of US imperialist politics. Peter moved back to Toronto to enter what was then called Toronto Teachers College, which had replaced the Normal School in 1953. Peter was certified to teach kindergarten to grade 8. Shortly thereafter, teacher education in Ontario was transferred to the universities. Because he received a certificate rather than a university degree, Peter enrolled in extra courses during his doctoral program so that the same year he received his PhD, he also received a B.Ed. degree. Peter had already been awarded an M.Ed. degree from Brock University prior to enrolling in his PhD program at the Ontario Institute for Studies in Education, University of Toronto.

1974–1984: From Rookie Teacher to Acclaimed Writer and Prospective Academic

As a freshly minted teacher, Peter spent a year teaching in an affluent neighborhood. Yet he wanted to serve where he was most needed, so he moved to the impoverished, multicultural, multiracial, high-density Toronto inner-city suburb community known as the Jane-Finch Corridor. In Jane-Finch Peter learned pedagogies and teaching strategies developed by fellow teachers that he felt were largely coping strategies to get through the day. Yet he wanted to reach beyond "surviving" his challenging environment, and he embarked on a series of pedagogical experiments for the benefit of his students. As a young teacher, Peter learned an important lesson that teaching is not a job, but a calling—and for the rest of his career, he would cherish warm and personal relationships with his students.

The poverty he witnessed in the Jane-Finch Corridor had a profound emotional effect on Peter, and he lamented the lack of pedagogies in the school that could help students address issues of poverty, racism, and violence in the local community and beyond. As a response, Peter wrote an honest and brutal account of challenges facing the Jane-Finch community. Published in 1980, his book *Cries from the Corridor*

(McLaren 1980) became one of top ten best-selling books in Canada. The year that *Cries from the Corridor* was published, Peter was accepted as a doctoral student at the Ontario Institute for Studies in Education, University of Toronto. He developed a close relationship with his Doctoral Chair, Richard Courtney, who was one of the world's foremost authorities on children's drama. He was also a professional actor. Professor Courtney earned his academic position on the strength of his books and reputation and his Fellowship in the Royal Society of Arts. But he held only one academic degree—a bachelor's degree from Leeds, and less productive and less influential professors looked down upon Professor Courtney because they held doctoral degrees. While Peter worked his way through the PhD program under the tutelage of Courtney, he was elected by the governing board of Massey College as a Junior Fellow.

While at Massey College (modeled after England's Oxford and Cambridge universities), Peter attended High Table dinners and lectures by famous academics. Junior Fellows were required to wear a long black robe and on occasion to try to converse in Latin, German, or French (Peter was an utter failure in second languages). This piqued his interest in ritual. It was also the year he converted from the Anglican Church to the Roman Catholic Church. The year he successfully defended his thesis, "Education as a ritual performance," Peter was elected a Fellow of the Royal Society of Arts, Manufactures and Commerce in England. Members of the Royal Society had included notable historical members such as Benjamin Franklin, Karl Marx, Adam Smith, Charles Dickens, William Hogarth, and Guglielmo Marconi. Even though Peter earned significant recognition as a scholar by the time he graduated, Peter considered himself fortunate to be appointed to the position of Special Lecturer in Education at Brock University as a one-year sabbatical replacement (replacing a professor who had been charged by the Royal Canadian Mounted Police for a computer program copyright violation).

Peter began to develop Paulo Freire's ideas in working with teacher educators, and the reception by his students was mixed. Although the Dean had promised to extend his contract for a year, Peter was dismissed after his contract expired. He applied for jobs all across Canada, but many university search committees considered Peter to be a potential thorn in their side due to his outspoken political views and his vociferous admiration for Freire's work and the writings of Henry Giroux, who had been fired by the President of Boston University for his development of critical pedagogy and whose tenure battle received national attention in the United States in 1983. Eventually Giroux was offered a teaching position at Miami University of Ohio.

1985–1993: From Perspective Academic to One of the Leading Architects of Critical Pedagogy

In 1985, Peter joined Miami University's School of Education and Allied Professions and spent the next eight years working with Henry Giroux. Upon his arrival, Peter continued his PhD research on the educational value of rituals, which culminated in the award-winning book, *Schooling as a Ritual Performance: Toward a Political*

Economy of Educational Symbols and Gestures (1986), later republished in several editions and languages. Peter's research interests during this period reflected his undergraduate studies in (Elizabethan) drama, film, theater, arts and his graduate studies in curriculum, ethnography, and anthropology. He was especially interested in ethnic, gender, sexual, political, and religious identity formation within school settings and oppositional cultural politics, which uncovered the ideological underpinnings of schooling. As he recalls,

> My work became less directed at the classroom per se, and more focused on issues such as political, cultural and racial identity, anti-racist/multicultural education, the politics of white supremacy, resistance and popular culture, rituals of the school as vehicles for both resistance and conformity; the formation of subjectivity, and liberation theology. I was becoming focused on the larger relevance of critical pedagogy. In other words, I felt that critical pedagogy was habitually elusive when it came to hands-on solutions but fiercely relevant when addressing life's permanent conditions of exploitation. I realized that there were teachers who could write about the classroom and in doing so provide more practical insights than I could but that I could make a contribution in rethinking the conceptual and political terrain of critical pedagogy in the educational literature. (in Pozo 2003)

Peter and Henry helped to bring the works and ideas of the critical pedagogue Paulo Freire into North America, while Peter's two edited books for Routledge, England, reintroduced Freire's works to educators and social workers in the United Kingdom. Their collaborator and friend, Donaldo Macedo, translated Freire's main works; Peter and Henry wrote introductions, afterwords, and explanations. But they did not merely popularize Freire; instead, they actively built upon Freire's work and laid ground for the North American tradition of critical pedagogy as we know it today. Peter's major works from this period include the *Critical Pedagogy, the State, and Cultural Struggle* (Giroux and McLaren 1989), *Paulo Freire: A Critical Encounter* (Leonard and McLaren 1993), *Critical Literacy: Politics, Praxis, and the Postmodern* (Lankshear and McLaren 1993), *Politics of Liberation: Paths from Freire* (Lankshear and McLaren 1994), and *Between Borders: Pedagogy and the Politics of Cultural Studies* (Giroux and McLaren 1994).

Working with Henry Giroux, Peter delved deeply into cultural studies and the linguistic turn in philosophy and critical theory that came to be known as postmodernism. As his work moved further and further from the classroom, his thinking became more and more sophisticated, and he became probably the harshest critic of his own bestseller *Cries from the Corridor* (McLaren 1980).

> Reading it from the perspective of a critical theorist confronts me with my own ideological and pedagogical shortcomings; it places me face-to-face with my own situation as a young teacher in discourses that unconsciously worked against my own emancipatory intention. It is painful for me to read many of these vignettes because I recognize that I was not immune to many of the criticisms that I now

lay at the feet of unjust schooling practices and the workings of a racist, sexist, and culturally imperialistic social formation. (McLaren 2016: 32)

In 1989 Peter significantly expanded *Cries from the Corridor* (McLaren 1980) with an innovative, nuanced, and granular theoretical commentary and turned his popular bestseller (which was once sold in subway stations and bus terminals) into an academic bestseller entitled *Life in Schools: An Introduction to Critical Pedagogy in the Foundations of Education* (McLaren 2016); as of 2016, the book is in its sixth edition. According to Wayne Ross,

> across its six editions the basic structure of the book remained relatively consistent, although the content has changed and expanded in notable ways. The progressive radicalization of McLaren's thought can be traced across each edition of the book. . . . Life in Schools has always reflected an emancipatory politics, critiquing the abuses of capitalism, racism, sexism, homophobia, cultural imperialism, and asymmetrical power relations, but the left-leaning postmodernism and politics of reform that informs parts of the earlier editions has been swept away. (Ross 2016)

In his late 30s and early 40s, Peter was a young prospective academic on an exciting mission. Shoulder to shoulder with other great figures such as Henry Giroux, Paulo Freire, Donaldo Macedo, Joe Kincheloe, and others, Peter has built the movement of critical pedagogy in North America as we know it today. In 1989, while still an Associate Professor of Education, he was awarded the distinction of being named Renowned Scholar-in-Residence at the School of Education and Allied Professions, Miami University, as the youngest person in the university to hold this title. While teaching at Miami, Peter built concepts and ideas, which had been waiting for mainstream recognition for decades.

1994–2001: From Cultural Studies and Postmodernism to Marxist Humanism

In 1993 Peter was recruited by the Graduate School of Education and Information Studies, University of California, Los Angeles, where he remained for the next twenty years. At first he continued working with Henry Giroux within reconciliatory traditions of cultural studies and postmodernism. Examples of such work include *Critical Pedagogy and Predatory Culture: Oppositional Politics in a Postmodern Era* (McLaren 1995) and *Rethinking Media Literacy: A Critical Pedagogy of Representation* (McLaren et al. 1995). In his preface to *Critical Pedagogy and Predatory Culture,* Paulo Freire writes:

> Peter McLaren is one among the many outstanding "intellectual relatives" I "discovered" and by whom I in turn was "discovered." I read Peter McLaren long before I ever came to know him personally. . . . Once I finished reading the first

texts by McLaren that were made available to me, I was almost certain that we belonged to an identical "intellectual family." (Freire 1995: x)

However, as he began to realize the theoretical and practical limits of the reconciliatory traditions, Peter's thought has turned more and more toward Marxism.

In 1997 Peter publishes the first book that explicitly refers to revolution in its title: *Revolutionary Multiculturalism: Pedagogies of Dissent for the New Millennium* (McLaren 1997a). A few years later, he publishes the famous *Che Guevara, Paulo Freire, and the Pedagogy of Revolution* (2000), which is generally recognized as his revolutionary manifesto. This book is interesting both for its academic content and writing. A student of English literature, and an award-winning author since his childhood, Peter had now taken an important leap forward: he wrote a mature academic text with all the qualities of a popular bestseller. In the back matter of *Che Guevara, Paulo Freire, and the Pedagogy of Revolution*, Rodolfo D. Torres writes:

> In this lucid and theoretically informed reappraisal of the legacies of Che and Freire, Peter McLaren has made a significant contribution to a renewed Marxist theory. Where critiques of capitalism seem to be out of fashion, this volume engages the lives of two great revolutionaries in the context of "globalization" and increasing class inequality. (in McLaren 2000)

And in its introduction, Joe Kincheloe provided Peter with a nickname that will remain with him forever:

> The beginning of the twenty-first century … is probably a good time to proclaim Peter McLaren the poet laureate of the educational left. No one operating in critical education has Peter's capacity to turn a phrase, to focus our attention on the relationship between pedagogy and injustice, or to make us chuckle while moving us to see anew. (Kincheloe 2000: ix)

The unique quality of Peter's writing was also recognized in his other works. Thus, in his preface to the third edition of *Schooling as a Ritual Performance: Towards a Political Economy of Educational Symbols and Gestures,* Henry Giroux writes: "as a writer, he [McLaren] combines the rare gifts of the astute theoretician with that of the storyteller in the manner celebrated by Walter Benjamin" (Giroux 1999: xxiii).

Looking back, it is now easy to recognize that Peter's Marxist humanism had been developing since his childhood. However, his appraisal of the two iconic figures on the left has finally made this revolutionary turn "official." Peter's turn provoked many reactions, which are probably best summed up by Freire's wife Nita:

> What makes a blond man of the "North," a respected professor and intellectual, want to write about two men from the "South," accustomed to and engaged in the centuries-old, daily round of oppression and exclusion of the people of Latin America; two men united by similar aspects of courage and daring in historical time but, principally, in the space of solidarity, generosity, and humility? (Araujo Freire 2000: xiii)

In 2001 Paula Allman publishes the book *Critical Education Against Global Capitalism: Karl Marx and Revolutionary Critical Education* (Allman 2001) where she introduces the expression "revolutionary critical pedagogy." Peter immediately adopts the term, which marks the beginning of a new phase in his work.

Peter's awards slowly grew in number, significance, and geographical coverage. Alongside numerous visiting professorships and keynote talks all over the United States, in 1999 he received the *Trofeu O Lacador* Award presented by the Religious Society of Seu Sete De Male for his support of Afro-Umbandista religion in Porto Alegre, Brazil. In 2000 he received the *Amigo Honorifica de la Comunidad Universitaria de Esta Institucion* from *La Universidad Pedagogica Nacional* in Guadalajara, Mexico. Furthermore, Peter's work has for the first time become a topic of dedicated publications such as the Special Issue of the *International Journal of Educational Reform* entitled "The Revolutionary Pedagogy of Peter McLaren" (2001).

2001–2013: From Marxist Humanism to Revolutionary Critical Pedagogy

Now in his 50s, an acclaimed member of the small group of founding fathers of North American critical pedagogy and a respected professor at one of the top universities in the United States, Peter had the theoretical background, the life experience, and the opportunity to develop a mature theory of revolutionary critical pedagogy. This development builds on Peter's earlier Marxist works such as *Marxism against Postmodernism in Educational Theory* (Hill et al. 2002); Peter's interest in wider social questions such as neoliberalism reflected in *Critical Theories, Radical Pedagogies, and Global Conflicts* (Fischman et al. 2005), *Critical Pedagogy: Where Are We Now?* (McLaren and Kincheloe 2007), *Revolutionizing Pedagogy: Education for Social Justice within and beyond Global Neo-liberalism* (Macrine, McLaren, and Hill 2009); and particularly on Peter's interest in theory and practice of capitalism reflected in *Teaching against Global Capitalism and the New Imperialism: A Critical Pedagogy* (McLaren and Farahmandpur 2004), *Capitalists and Conquerors: A Critical Pedagogy against Empire* (McLaren 2005a), *Red Seminars: Radical Excursions into Educational Theory, Cultural Politics, and Pedagogy* (McLaren 2005b), *Critical Pedagogies of Consumption: Living and Learning in the Shadow of the "shopocalypse"* (Sandlin and McLaren 2009), *The Havoc of Capitalism: Publics, Pedagogies and Environmental Crisis* (Martin et al. 2010), *Academic Repression: Reflections from the Academic-Industrial Complex* (Nocella, Best, and McLaren 2010), and *The Global Industrial Complex: Systems of Domination* (Best et al. 2011).

During this time, Peter spends a lot of time in Latin America—with Chavistas in Venezuela, with workers and unions in Mexico and Colombia, and with Zapatista supporters. In 2005 a group of scholars and activists in Northern Mexico established *La Fundacion McLaren de Pedagogía Critica* to develop a knowledge of McLaren's work throughout Mexico and to promote projects in critical pedagogy and popular education. In 2006 the *Catedra Peter McLaren* was inaugurated at the Bolivarian University of Venezuela. In 2011 *Instituto McLaren de Pedagogía Crítica* was established in Ensenada, Mexico. During his many trips to Latin America, Peter met key people such as Hugo Chávez and Lopez Obrador and significantly contributed to an exchange of ideas and practices between the Americas. During this period, Peter was also one of the first critical pedagogues whose work was translated into Russian. Later, he was invited to lecture on Western Marxism and critical pedagogy in China. Peter's career has now become global, and his writings have been extensively translated to Spanish, Mandarin, and more than twenty other languages.

Peter has now become a textbook reference, and his critical pedagogy is taught at universities all over the world. Books about Peter's work include *De la pedagogía crítica a la pedagogía de la revolución. Ensayos para comprender a Peter McLaren* (Pruyn and Charles 2005), *Teaching Peter McLaren: Paths of Dissent* (Pruyn and Charles 2007), *Peter McLaren, Education, and the Struggle for Liberation* (Eryaman 2009), and *Crisis of Commonwealth: Marcuse, Marx, McLaren* (Reitz 2013). Peter has given hundreds of interviews and public appearances. In order to make his works more accessible, Peter has edited a widely cited collection of interviews: *Rage and Hope* (McLaren 2006).

Peter was never a stranger to awards, yet now they started piling up significantly. He was presented with the 2002 Inaugural Paulo Freire Social Justice Award by the Paulo Freire Democratic Project at Chapman University, California. In 2004 he received an honorary doctorate at the University of Lapland, Finland. In 2007 the Soka Gakkai International USA presented him with the Liberty Award. In 2010 he received a doctorate, *honoris causa*, from the University of Salvador, Buenos Aires, Argentina. In 2012 he received the title Honorary Chair Professor at Northeast Normal University in mainland China. Peter was invited as an honored guest by the Tarahumara (Rarámuri) indigenous group in the state of Chihuahua, Mexico, and visited the Purépecha community in Cherán, a town in the state of Michoacán, Mexico. The civic council of Cherán, which had created its own armed militia and fought for the status of an autonomous community, honored Peter with the Defense of the Forest Award. Members of the community had been murdered by illegal loggers (members of the drug cartels who were diversifying their economic base) who were routinely stealing truckloads of lumber from the indigenous lands. The resistance to the killings and kidnappings was led by women. Peter has become a Fellow of American Educational Research Association (AERA) Class of 2012. Peter also received an honorary doctorate from the University of Chilecito in Argentina in 2015. Last but not least, his books received far too many awards for an academic chapter.

Peter's work has never been popular with the powers-that-be. However, his move toward critical Marxist humanism and then to revolutionary critical pedagogy has increased his problems with the mainstream. In 2006, Peter topped #1 on Andrew Jones' blacklist of progressive educators "Dirty Thirty" (Fassbinder and McLaren 2006) aimed at harassing leftist professors at US universities. Occasionally, before a talk, Peter would receive anonymous death threats on his phone or at his hotel. Seeking a less stressful working environment, and the challenges of working behind the infamously conservative "Orange Curtain" in Orange County, California, Peter was offered a Distinguished Professorship at Chapman University, in the small city of Orange, which he accepted after twenty years teaching at UCLA.

2013–: Peter McLaren's Liberation Theology

Peter has remained at Chapman University since 2013. Chapman's founding religious denomination is the Disciples of Christ that recognizes the integrity of a variety of spiritual paths and supports an ecumenical environment. Peter is married to Wang Yan from Northeast China—a brilliant young Chinese woman, who is interested in deepening the relationship between critical pedagogy and improvisation. Inspired by his numerous visits to Latin America, his childhood fascination with religion, and his conversion to Catholicism, Peter started developing more palpable links between the tradition of liberation theology and revolutionary critical pedagogy. This work culminated with his masterpiece *Pedagogy of Insurrection: From Resurrection to Revolution* (McLaren 2015b) and the series of follow-up dialogic articles expanding on its ideas (McLaren and Jandrić 2017b, 2018a, b, c).

Peter's liberation theology builds on his childhood interest in theology, his theoretical achievements in Marxist humanism and revolutionary critical pedagogy, his worldwide practical experiences (most notably in South America), and various other streams of his life and thought. Within this framework, Peter produced some of his most mature and sophisticated insights, and once again went against the grain to inspire and shock the (academic) mainstream with catchy, powerful claims that Jesus was a communist, that the Kingdom of God equals Marx's imagined socialist society, and that science and religion should unite against its common enemy of capitalism. Underlined by a strong emancipatory and liberatory message, these claims startle people on all sides of the political spectrum. However, their critics miss a crucial point of Peter's current work: at the present historical moment marked by a strong dominance of the right, and a desperate fragmentation of the left, Peter's liberation theology develops new modes of revolutionary organization and offers new hope for humanity.

These days, the list of various recognitions for Peter's work is far too long for a book chapter—since 2013, he received more than thirty awards and honorary positions in countries including but not limited to Greece, Venezuela, Colombia, Turkey, Mexico, the United States, Ukraine, China, Argentina, and the United Kingdom. Peter now firmly belongs to world's intellectual *crème de la crème*, and his public appearances such as the recent debate with the Nobel laureate Vernon Smith (McLaren and Smith 2017) are followed with great attention in all strata of the society. Unsurprisingly, such success has also brought into light many enemies. In 2016, following his marriage with Yan Wang, a right-wing blog accused Peter of being a traitor to the white race. Anonymous hackers voiced over one of Peter's interviews, in the Russian language, and replaced his verbal comments with an entirely false English translation. Yet, with his unique combination of humility and openness to the other, Peter has always risen above primitive insults and abuse.

Peter's role at Chapman University in Orange, California, where he is Distinguished Professor in Critical Studies, includes serving as Co-Director of The Paulo Freire Democratic Project and International Ambassador for Global Ethics and Social Justice. He extensively publishes, edits, teaches, and speaks all over the world. In 2018 he presented an edited book *Radical Imagine-Nation: Public Pedagogy & Praxis* (McLaren and SooHoo 2018), and in 2019 he published an autobiographical comic book *Breaking Free: The Life and Times of Peter McLaren, Radical Educator* illustrated by Miles Wilson (McLaren 2019b). His work is now subject to a growing number of dedicated publications such as the Special Issue of *Policy Futures in Education* entitled "Pedagogies of Insurrection" (Bojesen 2017). Peter is now more productive than ever, and we can only guess what he will come up with next—but we can rest assured that it will be ground-breaking, emancipatory, and fit for the contemporary historical moment.

Epilogue

The story of Peter McLaren may seem like a primer of the American Dream—a kid from a humble working-class family, who pulled himself up by his bootstraps to become one of the most respected living theorists in his field. The story of Peter McLaren may seem like a primer of an extraordinary talent, which, in spite of all obstacles and difficulties, has managed to surface and shine. The story of Peter McLaren may seem like a primer of gradual intellectual growth of a humble but perseverant scholar and human being. The story of Peter McLaren may seem like a primer of an artistic soul, which significantly contributes to the discourse of the social sciences. The story of Peter McLaren may seem like a primer of an extraordinary person, who did some extraordinary things and yet remained humble, warm, and open to people from all walks of life.

These stories may capture Peter's career, yet they all miss the spirit of Peter's personality and work. During our friendship, which now spans for almost a decade, I was privileged to witness what I believe is the soul of his work. Peter never was, or wanted to be, a primer or a leader. He is a researcher, gifted with extreme curiosity, and a warm human being, who wants to help others overcome oppression in order to reach their full potential. Peter is an inspiring fellow traveler—always creative, but never leaves people behind; always in a position of intellectual and moral power, but never in position of political power. With his long silver hair, tattoos, indigenous clothing and jewelry, an inevitable leather bag, and the proverbial John Lennon glasses, Peter has remained faithful to his countercultural origins and connected to the world that brought him into being. For all his academic contributions and personal traits, Peter was made into an icon of the contemporary left and a living monument of contemporary critical pedagogy—a position he never sought, but always carried with a combination of pride and humility.

Peter has tremendous respect for political heroes such as Che Guevara, yet he is not one of them. Peter has only the best words for his intellectual brother and friend

Paulo Freire, yet he never took up a political position. Peter has created his own type of hero: an intellectual hero, a hero of humility and respect for everyone, who inspires and gently pushes everyone he meets to do the best of their ability for the benefit of humankind. Peter is deeply critical of his own work, never satisfied with his current achievements, and always in the quest to improve further. Peter does not invite people to reproduce his work, but to use his work to live with the world. As he now approaches the most intellectually productive years of his life, I do hope to share a part of this journey with Peter McLaren and extend our friendship and work far into the future.

2

Petar Jandrić: Portrait of a Hunter Gatherer

Sarah Hayes

My first encounter with Petar Jandrić was curiously based on pure chance. In 2012 Petar sent out a call for submissions for chapter contributions for a book he was editing, through a mailing list for anarchist academics. It caught my eye, because it took a refreshingly critical approach toward technologies, echoing my own philosophical position. Seven years on, I can reflect on how sorry I would have been . . . had I not seen, and responded to, that call for chapters. The invitation was warm, friendly, and widely inclusive. In short, it was entirely characteristic of the Petar I have come to know so well and who literally throws his arms wide to the world for others to join him in his writing and in his life. Petar does not just invite submissions to a book, or for a Special Issue. He is a hunter of philosophical ideas, and a gatherer of people, and has a special gift for finding ways of sparking dialogue in the process. Petar nurtures those whom he gathers, improves their work, turns them into friends, and brings together (at times with breathtaking speed . . .) a powerful and valuable publication. He holds onto those people and (whether they realize it or not), they remain connected as part of his extended family. Also, in keeping with Petar's open manner of sharing, his call for submissions revealed a lot about him as a person, his interdisciplinary background, and his ethos. Though originally educated as a scientist, Petar's route through higher education had striking similarities to mine, prompting me to think . . . I have to meet this guy!

Working at Aston University in Birmingham, United Kingdom, at the time, I responded to Petar's email with a chapter, but I also suggested we set up an Erasmus-funded visit in autumn 2012, for me to visit his institution so that we could exchange ideas on future writing projects. In the meantime, I read some of his articles about Wikipedia and education (Jandrić 2010) and about critical education and communication technologies (Jandrić 2011) and I began to get a sense that we might have a much longer writing partnership than a five-day visit! Meeting Petar in person was pure delight. He welcomed me to his institution, his country, his home, and his family. I ran a session with his students and I met with his senior managers, but mostly we talked in cafés and bars (where much of our work together has been initiated since). I recall an evening in his flat, meeting Petar's partner Ana for the first time, and a crowd of Petar's former university friends turning up unexpectedly to join us, to the shock of the cat. What began as a tentative exploration of shared interests in the politics surrounding technology quickly developed into a warm friendship and many collaborations leading to numerous coauthored and coedited publications.

As I write this portrait, thousands of miles away from Zagreb, I realize how little distance has ever mattered in our writing. Petar has a knack of emailing as if there have been no gaps in space or time between our projects (and often there isn't!). However, contemporary higher education is unrelenting, all-consuming, and impossibly busy. I am aware that in our seventh year of working together, it is only now that I have this meaningful space to take the opportunity to contemplate Petar's background in detail. Often the celebrated writing of academics has actually been constructed in stolen moments from weekends, from time with family or when on holiday, because academic labor in universities has now swelled to include an enormous number of duties (Hayes 2019). It is, though, a real pleasure to write this portrait of Petar, to connect his work deeply to his personal life and to his cultural context. It is also a privilege to be invited to do so (and to share a little of our own story) in this exciting book where Peter and Petar discuss their powerful journey through radical dialogues, revolutionary critical pedagogy, digital technology, liberation theology, close friendship, and a pedagogy of love in our postdigital age.

Early Years: Science, Philosophy, Music, and Art

In conversations with Petar, I have learned of his unconventional upbringing as a child of young parents, both students at the time of his birth. Convention is of course relative to culture, and I would not suggest that my own upbringing in the United Kingdom was particularly conventional. My parents did not study at university, whereas Petar found himself attending the graduation of his mother, who studied physics, when he was just four years old. Stepping back to the early 1980s, Petar's mother had seen her career take off in informatics and engineering. Later she moved to become a manager of a large insurance company and then a university professor, making important practical and theoretical contributions to the field. Petar's father is a cultural worker in fields including, but not limited to, visual arts and theater and a curator in the Croatian Natural History Museum. A strange combination of influences from the sciences and arts played out in the relationship of his parents. This has some parallels that have surfaced in Petar's life with his partner Ana, who is an artist. Petar studied physics and alongside his scientific work, he came to view the universe as both infinite and limited, especially when observed through scientific approaches alone. Time spent in pubs and at exhibition openings, together with many part-time student jobs in the cultural sector, meant that he also felt at home in galleries, museums, theaters, and concert halls.

At first the natural sciences as a field of study claimed priority in Petar's life, but alongside this relatively cloistered academic route, Petar (like Peter) found his own personal, expressive outlets. Music and playing in punk (and later jazz) bands, as well as engaging in theater groups, contributed to his ongoing fascination with culture and growing interest in philosophy (which began in his late teens). Petar reasoned that if he studied physics, he could always read philosophy in tandem. He had always wanted to be a philosopher, but it wasn't until later, during his masters and PhD research, that he began to recognize how he might connect his passions for both science and philosophy. If he had known (a little more than a decade later) that he would be the editor in chief of a pioneering Springer journal, *Postdigital Science and Education,* and would have written numerous coauthored works with key academics of our times, he would, I am sure, have been exceedingly pleased with the direction in which life was going.

The 1990s: Emerging from a Dark Place to Build a Future

Petar has never dwelled on the painful, ugly, and dangerous years of the war in Croatia during the 1990s. A teenager at the time, he has managed to escape the cynicism that enveloped many of his contemporaries who survived the chaos and bloodshed. At the same time, Petar takes the view that we can only prepare our students for citizenship in a world where all institutions are imperfect and unfinished. Assuming a critical perspective (McLaren and Jandrić 2014a and 2015c) means, for Petar, continually challenging myths that perpetually arise to reinforce unnatural borders between people. The values that Petar gleaned from his engagement with critical pedagogy, and his mission—to break down all barriers to communication between people—that began as a teenager as a response to the havoc of war, are paralleled in Petar's writings on antidisciplinarity (Jandrić 2012) and postdisciplinarity (Jandrić 2013, 2014a, and 2016).

As Croatia began to slowly emerge as a new country, the shattering effects of the war left an environment where many people were unable to connect university with opportunity. Petar therefore sought different avenues through travel, that included hitchhiking, sleeping in squats and tents, and experimenting with drugs. He was motivated by a desire to connect with what the West appeared to offer, which at that time was mainly concerts, art galleries, museums, festivals, alternative cultural events sponsored by underground communities that included talks by renegade European intellectuals. During this period, Petar became a part of various European countercultural punk, Goa, psychedelic trance, and theater (mostly anarchist) communities, which he now occasionally supports through his engagements at the Anarchist Bookfairs and other events. And as the infrastructure to establish the first Internet connection in Croatia was put into place in 1990, a digital route to the unknown opened up that Petar was eager to explore.

2000–2009: From Zagreb to Edinburgh and New Critical Theories

Having studied physics, it should come as no surprise that Petar was not new to computers. After a short stint in jobs related to physics, he began working for an educational center at the Croatian Academic and Research Network in 2004 where he had developed e-learning projects that supported various IT courses on a national level. Since then Petar has participated in many EU and non-EU projects, and alongside this work, has supported the program and organization of the Amadeo Theatre and Music Company, which his father opened in Zagreb's Upper Town in the summer of 2000. Petar has never separated his cultural interests from his academic work, which makes his writing particularly authentic and vibrant. He conducts many engagements in his native Croatian language and translates books he has written in English. For Petar, preserving linguistic diversity through nourishing his national language takes pride of place in his work as well as contributes to his many other counterhegemonic practices as a public intellectual and cultural worker grappling with the many challenges spawned by our global capitalist society.

Petar's far-reaching work experiences in e-learning soon led him to believe that he was approaching the limits of his personal development in the field. Through this work he met pioneers and early adopters of e-learning, many of whom would later end up as CEOs of large private educational companies and as deans, ministers, and various other leadership positions in Croatia. As Peter McLaren points out in this book: "I believe that information is power. We need to know how institutions operate, how people inside of them behave. This is crucial." Petar has gained an in-depth understanding of the ways in which institutions operate. This has often been echoed in our conversations, as we have discussed our own institutions, power relationships, and global change in higher education, all of which have recently proliferated across ubiquitous new media platforms.

In the mid-2000s Petar met Ana and again discovered the joys of traveling together with a like-minded partner (with the added perks of more comfortable sleeping accommodations and fewer bug and rodent infested hotels). He also discovered a wider world related to e-learning, that stretched from philosophy though media studies to critical theory. At the age of 29, he experienced a fortuitous moment. He met Hamish Macleod at a conference. From this encounter he realized that, although he was earning enough money to afford a reasonably comfortable life, something was missing—he had reached an intellectual glass ceiling. His fast progression in the field of e-learning also meant that he was encountering barriers to his progress, especially when based in a non-European Union country. Turning his back on the possibility of further promotion, he applied for a student loan, sold his dented, rust-splotched car that had seen better days, and left Croatia in 2006 to move to Edinburgh. Ana followed a year later, and both of them worked on a plan that allowed them to study together for their master's degrees and survive on a very lean daily budget. I later learned from Ana that she had studied at the Edinburgh College of Art, the same institution that I had graduated from two decades before. After graduation, Petar worked in Edinburgh University's National e-Science Centre related to CERN and directed by the United Kingdom's first e-Science Envoy, Professor Malcolm Atkinson. Later he was hired to support learning technology at the Glasgow School of Art, while at the same time undertaking his PhD in Croatia. During this labor intensive time, he still managed to write study guides and to teach online on "zero-hours contracts" at various UK institutions such as the International Correspondence Schools in Glasgow and the University of East London.

Petar's choices of employment had always entailed either data or art, but now he began reading critical theory from the Frankfurt School and beyond, and his love of philosophy resurfaced. In Edinburgh, and with the help and support of people such as Hamish Macleod and Ian Martin, Petar discovered critical pedagogy and other radical educational traditions, which had a huge impact on his thinking. This became a real point of departure for him, along with forays into the critical philosophy of technology (Feenberg 1991). With the help of Hamish, he grew to know others at Edinburgh University, including Christine Sinclair, Siân Bayne, Jen Ross, Jeremy Knox, Michael Gallagher, and other friends and colleagues who have worked closely with him ever since (Jandrić, Sinclair and Macleod 2015; Jandrić, et al. 2017). This was Petar the hunter gatherer emerging from relative anonymity and taking his first major steps (as the Beatles say, "with a little help from my friends") toward becoming a leader in the field. During this time of burgeoning possibilities and opportunities, Ana had been anxious to return to Croatia, and Petar's learning technology role at Glasgow offered little route for progression. So, almost inevitably, Petar returned to Croatia and was offered a lecturing role at Zagreb University of Applied Sciences. Ana, in turn, took up an academic position at the University in Split.

2010–: Creating Dialogues

A new phase began when Petar received strong support from his Dean, Slavica Ćosović Bajić, to develop projects that pragmatically suited his interests at the time, and to freely develop his research. Petar's reputation began to grow as an expert consultant in projects that involved design work as well as the implementation of technological systems (in various places such as schools, the public sector, and banks), and the sometimes technocratic and mechanical dimension of this work was mitigated through other intellectual pursuits such as writing and publishing more philosophically oriented works. This emphasis on the affective and existential domain helped Petar maintain his psychological equilibrium, while at the same time, forging a dual identity that distinguishes Petar from many other contemporary critical theorists. His work became intellectually engaging and yet was focused on practical experiments. Understandably it was praxis philosophy that caught his attention. Petar brings to critical pedagogy a much-needed praxiological perspective from growing up in the former Eastern Bloc where the imagination was more often placed in the service of survival and fighting scarcity, rather than in an academic ivory tower that afforded professors more opportunities to detach their work from the quotidian struggles that had practical import. He is very much appreciated in the field of education for refreshing advances in critical pedagogy with new adaptations that reflect changes brought by the Internet.

When I first visited Petar in Zagreb in 2012, he had just published *Critical e-Learning: Struggle for Power and Meaning in the Network Society* (Jandrić and Boras 2012) and was working on *Critical Learning in Digital Networks* (Jandrić and Boras 2015). We discussed the forms of discriminatory practice that have persisted over decades toward those who install, support, or train others in the use of technologies. We had each noticed, in our different contexts, how the increasingly competitive nature of research in marketized universities sets colleagues against each other in the most debilitating ways. In the case of learning technologists and information technology support professionals, lecturers and senior managers often (and perhaps inadvertently) ascribe a form of lower-class status to these coworkers. Referring to them as "techies" and making assumptions that the support role they currently occupy is where they will remain, reflects a form of occupational discrimination that is not dissimilar from judgments made based on race, gender, or religion.

Frequently such "professionals" struggle through this adversity and progress into academic roles (Hayes 2018). This is a transition both Petar and I have made, but these colleagues may also lack confidence to do so, when persistently treated as if they are of a lower status. Perhaps this treatment of people who develop systems is simply one part of a wider epoch of digital reason, which we now all inhabit and which has significantly altered the order of things (Peters and Jandrić 2018a). In our writing together, Petar and I have always argued that people and institutions need to find ways to look beyond the constraints of corporate capitalism toward free knowledge creation and publication for everyone (Hayes and Jandrić 2014; Jandrić and Hayes 2018; Jandrić and Hayes 2019; Peters, Jandrić and Hayes 2019). In these and other articles we have written, about neoliberal rationality reinforced through policy discourse, we concur with Couldry that "its workings get embedded in daily life and social organization" (Couldry 2010: 12). These norms and values have become internalized and institutionalized and have become embedded in academic culture over time, so that neoliberalism crowds out other rationalities and ways of organizing labor and collaborative space. Here Petar has made a significant contribution to disrupting such norms. He is also proud of his practical projects, many of which have made real contributions to a better world.

As Petar began to consolidate his international and local contacts and establish many new ones, he embarked on a period of interviewing many renowned academic authorities about technology and critical pedagogy. In 2011, meeting Peter McLaren for the first time in Athens, Petar requested an interview and there began the start of a collaboration and deep friendship for years to come, yielding many publications. Petar also had the pleasure in 2013 of becoming a father, when Ana gave birth to Toma. Only a little later, Petar began also working closely with Michael Peters both on publications for Michael's journals and on many coauthored articles and books. Petar's firsthand experience of e-science and big data now came back into play, as he wrote on these topics with Michael. Together these works and many others make substantial contributions to knowledge, for instance, on the state of the university: *The Digital University: A Dialogue and Manifesto.* (Peters and Jandrić 2018a), the "Peer Production and Collective Intelligence as the Basis for the Public Digital University" (Peters and Jandrić 2018b), and "Neoliberalism and the University" (Peters and Jandrić 2018c). I had the pleasure of writing with Petar and Michael on the topic of education and "technological unemployment" (Peters, Jandrić and Hayes 2019) and now in a new edited book on this topic bringing together, once more, many of Petar's wider network of collaborators and friends (Peters, Jandrić and Means 2019).

Meanwhile, Petar continued to undertake interviews with major theorists documenting unique and powerful dialogues that together unsettle and disturb the all too comfortable "truths" that neoliberal universities can come to perpetuate. These dialogues are brought together into a unique book *Learning in the Age of Digital Reason* (Jandrić 2017). Aware of my interest in the writings of George Ritzer, Petar invited me to join him in conducting his interview with George in autumn 2016 (Ritzer, Jandrić and Hayes 2018). When I reviewed *Learning in the Age of Digital Reason* (Hayes 2018), I found that Petar had creatively introduced his eminent academic interlocutors as if they had gathered for an impromptu party, finding themselves in unlikely conversations with each other, alongside activists, artists, media theorists, and historians. His interlocutors do not separate the past in any way from our digital present, with a debate with Larry Cuban launching the party and critiquing the persistent economic rationale in policy for education over recent decades. An exchange with Andrew Feenberg on critical pedagogy and philosophy of technology followed, picked up by Michael Peters with insights into the social character of knowledge and dialogic approaches for integrating human knowledge on learning and digital media. The breadth of these interviews (including dialogues with Richard Barbrook, McKenzie Wark, Henry Giroux, Peter McLaren, Siân Bayne, and many others) is both a testimony to Petar's talents, charisma (and perhaps dogged persistence too . . .) in not only engaging these powerful thinkers in such meaningful dialogue but also connecting these accounts in a longer critical narrative—a celebration, that cannot be ignored, of just what collective knowledge actually means. As the host of the party, Petar could not have made his guests feel more valued!

This equally applies to offline and online worlds—for Petar does not really distinguish between the two. In 2016 I found myself joining Ana and Petar at Croatia's biggest international open-air rock festival INmusic, following the very successful hosting by Petar's institution of the first Association for Visual Pedagogies Conference AVPC 2016: Visual Pedagogies and Digital Cultures (AVPC 2016). It was a great way to follow up one of the most dynamic, inclusive, and energetic higher education conferences I have attended. The contributions of activists and friends involved in social movements that Petar encouraged, alongside more traditional academic presentations, are powerful reminders of how few spaces exist where we can hear this combination of voices. Petar and I, both separately and together, have sought to disrupt a traditional academic ethos, which privileges only certain forms of writing, speaking, and behavior.

When in 2018 Petar launched the new Springer journal, *Postdigital Science and Education*, he brought many of us with him too, in roles on the editorial board or as associate editors (Jandrić et al. 2018). However, the collaborative approach Petar has taken with *Postdigital Science and Education* does not stop there. Seeking further ways to disrupt the managerialized (and also dull . . .) publication conventions of many education institutions and academic publishers (Peters and Jandrić 2018b), Petar repeatedly encourages large groups to write collective pieces such as "Postdigital Dialogue" (Jandrić et al. 2019) and "Between the Blabbering Noise of Individuals or the Silent Dialogue of Many" (Arndt et al. 2019). As such, Petar does not subscribe to any particular movement; instead he gathers people and he moves them forward in dialogue. At the same time, Petar is a cutting-edge researcher situated at the intersections of critical pedagogy and social and environmental justice with issues such as posthumanism, artificial intelligences, and big data.

Epilogue

The story of Petar Jandrić has no settled conclusion (well at least not yet). When holding all of the credentials for promotion, Petar usually steps out firmly in another direction. . . . In 2006 that direction led him to Edinburgh, where he discovered he could still work at ease in the uneasy spaces between the practical and the theoretical. More recently, he was encouraged to take a high administrative position in higher education, but once more he resisted such accolades to instead generate further critical dialogues. This has its price in terms of salary, ongoing hybrid roles, and uncertainty. Is it a fear of responsibility then, or a fear of control that generates these decisions not to occupy those proverbial exalted academic spaces? Petar would say that, in a sense, he has already found his place—a place of not belonging.

Like a hunter gatherer, Petar constantly occupies temporary settlements, develops new projects, tours the world giving talks and gathering more interlocutors. Moving between the academic, the practical, and the artistic, he readily admits that he is often dressed too formally or not formally enough. He is forever caught between the scientific and the social, yet in these tensions he has also written some of his most powerful and creative critical theories. Petar readily acknowledges those who have influenced his writing and shared his journey. In our case, neither of us recalls when we ceased to use track changes in our coauthored work. We simply developed an ongoing dialogue and the warmest of friendships that began back in 2012 and is still developing. Sometimes our writing is more Petar, sometimes it is more me, sometimes it develops with others. As such, this is a journey that is far from complete and one I hope will continue for a very long time.

Revolutionary Critical Pedagogy Meets Digital Technology

3

Revolutionary Critical Pedagogy Is Made by Walking: In a World Where Many Worlds Coexist

Revolutionary Critical Pedagogy in and for the Twenty-First Century

PJ: Your early work has been strongly influenced by postmodernism. For more than a decade, however, it has slowly but surely entered "the Marxist-humanist trajectory" spanning from authors with various Marxist tendencies and the neo-Marxism of the Frankfurt School to the original works of Marx (McLaren, McMurry, and McGuirk 2008). The shift from postmodern Peter to Marxist Peter has been elaborated fairly extensively—for instance, in conversations with Marcia Moraes and Glenn Rikowski published in *Rage and Hope* (McLaren 2006). Please summarize it in few sentences.

PM: Good question to start our conversation. Let me try to provide a succinct response. One of the foundational social relations that interdicts a student's access to resources necessary to see the world critically is, I believe, class exploitation. An exploitation that despoils communities and dispossesses workers of their humanity. Education opposes schooling. Education is that which intrudes upon our instincts and instruments of mind and augments them; it pushes our thoughts along the arcs of the stars where our thoughts can give rise to new vistas of being and becoming and to new solidarities with our fellow humans. Our responsibilities for creating critical citizens should be proportional to our privilege. Today a good education is no longer seen as a social responsibility but as picking carefully from an array of consumer choices provided by a number of new companies and corporations. We now offer endless arrays of remedies for new kinds of learning disabilities. Just take your pick. As early as the 1980s, I was asking myself: How do we react to the cries of help from the youth of today, whose full-throated screams meet the immemorial silence of the numbingly predictable and increasingly ossified pedagogical tradition? An answer to this question mandated a move away from the ironic distantiation, self-indulgent detachment and posture of Byronic heroism assumed by the vulgar divas of the academy who clearly chose identity politics over class politics and in so doing became complicitous in the very relations of inequality they officially rejected.

PJ: Departing from the Frankfurt School of Social Science, contemporary critical theories of technologies have developed into various directions (including, but not limited to, the elusive fields of postmodernism). Some of these theories ended up quite far from their Marxist roots; nowadays, they seem stuck at the place that you left more than a decade ago. Can you elaborate your return to Marxism as a theoretical base for reinvention of critical education in the context of information and communication technologies?

PM: Well, I can't promise you that much in terms of communication technologies since I have never focused on technologies of communication in the sense of computer or digital technologies, the Internet and such. But I will share what I have picked up along the way that may seem pertinent to revolutionary critical pedagogy as I have been developing that field along with other critical educators over the years. And if you feel that any of my ideas make contact with something useful to your own political project, Petar, feel free to use this correspondence as you see fit. Around the time I studied for my doctorate, I was becoming familiar with some works by Rosa Luxemburg, Karl Kautsky, György Lukács, Raymond Williams, Anthony Wilden, and other scholars who introduced me to the works of Jacques Lacan, Gregory Bateson, Terry Eagleton, Leon Trotsky, Louis Althusser, Paul Willis, John Molyneux, Jean-Paul Sartre, Simone de Beauvoir, David Harvey, Ellen Meiksins Wood, Alex Callinicos, Henri Lefebvre, and David McNally. I read them in a parallel universe to the doctoral readings assigned to us, which were mostly overpopulated by pragmatists like Dewey (whom I enjoyed) and Richard Rorty (whom I didn't), and some readings in hermeneutics such as Paul Ricoeur (whom I enjoyed the most). Most of it could be found among the dull pantheon of curriculum theorists and learning theorists that we were required to read for our classes. While I don't wish to expostulate about the classes offered in our doctoral program, because some of them proved important, I was much more interested in the Frankfurt School than the education theorists, much more interested in semiotics than in writers on organization theory or on the various ways of structuring your classroom and writing up behavior objectives for each class you taught. But then I surprised my fellow students—and myself—by moving into anthropology and comparative symbology and settled on the work of Victor Turner and performance theory for my doctoral dissertation.

When I moved to Miami University to work with Henry Giroux, I read in cultural studies, the Harlem Renaissance, Stuart Hall, Larry Grossberg, Paul Willis, Michael Lebowitz, Stanley Aronowitz, John Holloway, Hélène Cixous and French feminist thought, Julia Kristeva, literary theory, Gilles Deleuze and Félix Guattari, Jean-François Lyotard, Jacques Derrida, Ernesto Laclau, Chantal Mouffe, Michel Foucault, Gayatri Spivak, and the usual suspects. I was following the fashion at the time and picked up some important insights along the way. After that it was sociolinguistics with Mikhail Bakhtin, Basil Bernstein, Noam Chomsky. Along the way I discovered works by Teresa Ebert and Mas'ud Zavarzadeh and the Red Collective, Moishe Postone, Slavoj Žižek, Cornelius Castoriadis, Boaventura de Sousa Santos, Ramón Grosfoguel, bell hooks, Marxist educators Paula Allman, Mike Cole, Dave Hill, and

Glenn Rikowski, and later, after 1995, I decided to concentrate on the works of Karl Marx, Paulo Freire, Raya Dunayevskaya, Peter Hudis and Kevin Anderson, C. L. R. James, Frantz Fanon, and Karil Kosik. That is until I became interested in decolonial studies and liberation theology around 2013, concentrating mostly on the works of Leonardo Boff and José Porfirio Miranda. Whatever I was studying involved to some extent the theme of capitalist development that was variously described at that time under the epithets "postindustrialism," "post-Fordism," or "postmodern capitalism." And then of course the term neoliberal capitalism has gained ascendancy up to the present.

While I didn't really study technology, I had read some work by Marshall McLuhan and some more contemporary work by Manuel Castells. I was interested in reading about information age capitalism and information technologies and how computers and telecommunications were used by capital to create capital mobility across national boundaries that eventually culminated in the national security state of widespread societal surveillance. And how this has helped the United States achieve full spectrum dominance as a military power. While I had some misgivings about the technological determinism of McLuhan, I understood that media is driven by profit and television programs often serve as infotainment filler for the advertising. I was pretty much convinced that television worked like a drug, and I was absolutely convinced that you couldn't write poetry on a computer—it's too left-brained. Even today, I can't even *read* poetry on a computer. Even though my many visits to Latin America convinced me that we have not in any way left the smokestack era of factory production, I became interested in the various ways that capital has penetrated the entire society by means of technological and political instruments in order to generate a higher level of productivity and in order to monitor and reconstitute its response to the self-organization of the working class through these new technologies. Of course, innovations in the context of knowledge production and communication in the new information society do not merely serve as instruments of capitalist domination and police state invigilation. They can be employed in creating alternative and oppositional movements in the larger project of transforming capitalist society into a socialist alternative.

I read Orwell's *1984* (1949) in my teens, discovered Debord's *Society of the Spectacle* (1994) [1967] in my early twenties, and of course later on I found Foucault's (1995) work on Jeremy Bentham's panopticon to be important, and a few years ago Bernard Harcourt came out with *Exposed: Desire and Disobedience in the Digital Age* (Harcourt 2015), which examined the role of pleasure in our surveillance culture and how digital media shape the directions of our desiring. But Marx was the theorist that most captured my interest.

PJ: There has been a lot of water under the bridge since Marx developed his theories. Please address some contemporary challenges to his dialectical thought.

PM: I am critical of autonomous Marxists such as Hardt and Negri, who, in books such as *Empire* (2001), argue that the multitude, who have amassed the necessary "general intellect," are now in place as a web of resistance to capitalism—and they have done so simply by refusing to reproduce capitalism, without any unifying philosophy of praxis. Marxist-humanist theorist Kevin Anderson correctly sees this as a rejection of transcendence in favor of immanence (i.e., a rejection of Hegel). He writes:

> This gaping flaw in Empire is rooted in the type of philosophical outlook they have embraced, one that radically rejects all forms of what they term transcendence in favor of staying on the plane of immanence, i.e., taking elements within the given social reality as one's point of departure . . .
>
> But we do not have to choose between such one-sided alternatives. Consider Hegel's standpoint, as summed up by Theodor Adorno of the Frankfurt School: "To insist on the choice between immanence and transcendence is to revert to the traditional logic criticized in Hegel's polemic against Kant" (Adorno, *Prisms*, p. 31). In fact, Hardt and Negri regularly attack Hegel and the Enlightenment philosophers as conservative and authoritarian, while extolling pre-Enlightenment republican traditions rooted in Machiavelli and Spinoza. What they thereby cut themselves off from is the dialectical notion that a liberated future can emerge from within the present, if the various forces and tendencies that oppose the system can link up in turn with a theory of liberation that sketches out philosophically that emancipatory future for which they yearn.
>
> Marx certainly overcame the pre-Hegelian split between immanence and transcendence. The working class did not exist before capitalism and was a product of the new capitalist order, and was therefore immanent or internal to capitalism. At the same time, however, the alienated and exploited working class fought against capital, not only for a bigger piece of the pie, but also engaged in a struggle to overcome capitalism itself, and was in this sense a force for transcendence (the future in the present). (Anderson 2010: 11–12)

Here we see, as with Habermas, a rejection of all forms of radical transcendence and a refusal to conceptualize dialectically an alternative to capitalism. As Anderson notes, doing so inspires a fear of utopianism, or worse, authoritarianism and colonial hubris. For Habermas, Hardt, Negri, and to a certain extent Holloway (although I very like his work about Zapatismo), there appears to be a fear of the Promethean side of Marx's humanism that, Anderson notes, points toward transcendence of the given. Thus in the case of Habermas, we return to a reformist liberalism, while Hardt and Negri are moving toward a poststructuralist radicalism.

The solution, as Anderson proposes, is to "stare negativity in the face" (to cite Hegel) and work within a variegated dialectic that takes into consideration race and ethnicity, gender, sexuality, and youth. We cannot simply refuse to take state power, as John Holloway and others recommend, since the state with its pernicious logic of domination will continue to exist until we have created a new social order, one that consists of freely associated labor on a world scale.

The Neighborhood Has Just Become More Interesting

PJ: Nowadays, concepts such as "postindustrialism," "post-Fordism," "postmodern capitalism," and "information society" are often merged into an overarching concept of

Manuel Castells's (2001) and Jan van Dijk's (1999) "network society." One of the main differences between the industrial society and the network society lies in the structure of production: the first is predominantly based on production of physical artifacts, while the latter is predominantly based on production of knowledge. This brings up the notion of knowledge economy, where hordes of information workers produce added value from juggling invisible and intangible bits and bytes. However, production of artifacts is also on the rise—as you previously said, "we have not in any way left the smokestack era of factory production." What is your take on the main contemporary changes in the structure of production?

PM: That's a key question, Petar. The knowledge society is premised on communication, on dialogue, on creating knowledge presumably for the well-being of humanity. The knowledge economy, on the other hand, is interested in appropriating communication technology for the purpose of producing information that can be centralized, monitored, and controlled partially through the systematic deskilling of workers and their stupidification through the ideological weapons of rote learning and what Freire calls "banking education." In fact, the knowledge-based economy is really an illusion. When we can eliminate underemployment, then perhaps that term will have some real salience. We already have a highly educated workforce with plenty of skills. What we need is a massive redistribution of wealth in the form of more jobs while at the same time working toward a socialist alternative to capitalism. So let's not be misled by all this talk about immaterial labor. Social exchanges are not equal, immaterial labor is not free of capitalist alienation and exploitation. Computers have not made us free and independent producers. I often ask myself why we are even co-operating with generating high-caliber human capital for corporations?

Glenn Rikowski recently put it thus: "To become capital or to humanize our souls?" (McLaren and Rikowski 2000). That is certainly the key question for these times. I'd like to summarize some important points here made by Rikowski. Human capital, as Marx pointed out, has become a condition of life in capitalist societies. The human being is a form of capital and capital is a form of human life. While it is believed that competitive advantage comes from knowledge and innovation, knowledge workers are being exported all over the globe just like manual workers. The knowledge economy geared to employers' needs has narrowed the aims of education by marginalizing critical inquiry and skills. In fact, Rikowski goes so far as to note that education and training are actually a part of the knowledge economy, as higher education students from overseas bring in huge export earnings.

Capital, as Rikowski describes it, is a form of social energy, and is not self-generating. It depends upon our labor power, which creates surplus value, and then various forms of capital develop from this surplus value. Labor power produces immaterial as well as material commodities. Labor power is the most explosive commodity in the world market today, Rikowski points out, and education and training set limits upon the social production of labor powers, preventing the development of those powers that can break the chains imposed by the value form of labor—that is, by the augmentation of value, the creation of surplus value. In order to change ourselves, to reinvent ourselves, to decolonize our subjectivities forged in the crucible of capitalism, we need to transform the social relations that sustain our capitalized life-forms. That should be the larger purpose of education, not adjusting ourselves to, or reinscribing ourselves within, the value form of labor.

PJ: Jan Van Dijk juxtaposes "the network society" with its predecessor—"the mass society"—and links them with characteristics of the supporting media. Predigital media of mass society, such as radio and television, support one-way communication between centers of power and peripheries; the network society is associated with multidirectional digital social and media networks, and "individuals, households, groups and organizations linked by these networks" (van Dijk 1999: 24). Another important difference between the two generations of technologies lies in their scope. Back in the 1980s, my home was packed with many different one-purpose devices: radio, television, cassette player, vinyl record player, Walkman, telephone, photo camera, video camera. . . . Technologies of the network society, on the contrary, are conceptually universal, and the computer is "a medium of the most general nature" (Carr 2011).

Mass society had been based on many technologies designed for specific and limited purposes, while network society is based on adaptations of one technology for many different purposes. Yet, one technology seems to successfully cut across both generations—what can we learn about today's Internet from our historical experiences with television?

PM: I have always appreciated the work of Joyce Nelson, especially her book *The Perfect Machine* (1991), which reveals the ideological collusion between the television industry and the nuclearized state in their quest for the perfect technological imperative: efficiency. Nelson undresses the relationship between the advance of television and defense contractors and the arms industries such as General Electric, DuPont, and Westinghouse. She reveals how the military-industrial complex and the American entertainment industry operated as two sides of the same coin—that coin being to gain ascendancy in the struggle for geopolitical hegemony. But to do so by capturing through a cathode ray tube the glorious effulgence of a nuclear detonation, with its orgiastic uproar surging into the form of a mushroom cloud like a giant pulsating phallus that brings about such breathtaking, awe-inspiring destruction. Livers, spleens, heads, and torsos are not simply thrown into the air like party favors at a birthday celebration, but immediately incinerated. Now that's the apotheosis of efficiency! But the effects of the radiation on the survivors of Hiroshima and Nagasaki were censored by government forces in the United States. How could American viewers forget the television appearance of President Eisenhower when, like a benign, smiling sorcerer, he waved a neuron wand over a Geiger counter that activated a remote-control bulldozer, beginning construction on a Colorado nuclear power plant. (It's not easy to remember the future and I wonder how many Americans back then could imagine that many decades later, The Rocky Flats Plant site located near both Denver and Boulder, which manufactured trigger mechanisms for nuclear weapons from various radioactive and hazardous materials from 1952 until 1989, would be sued by community residents when sixty-two pounds of plutonium was discovered stuck in the exhaust ducts of the plant.)

Back in the 1950s, teleplays (live dramas) were considered too serious and were replaced by sitcoms with canned laughter and shows emphasizing right behavior versus unlawful behavior—with the familiar infantilizing good versus bad motifs offering a televisual moral compass for youth coming of age in the postwar years. The Soviet nuclear arsenal was also propagandized during the Cold War as a real threat to every American home, and television provided instructions on how to protect your family in the event of nuclear war. Nelson also examined the creation of political candidates and presidents through the medium of television, and how the United States was able to colonize the world culturally through popular television shows.

I grew up in the 1950s, and we were one of the first families to own a TV because my dad started selling TVs when he returned from fighting the Nazis after World War II. Little did my father know that he was peddling the instrument that refracted the collective technological unconscious of our culture through gateways of fear and guilt—a technological unconscious rooted in the nuclear unconscious that began after the bombing of Hiroshima and Nagasaki.

PJ: Your understanding of television as a technological unconscious rooted in the nuclear unconscious fascinates me! I never thought about these links before.

PM: Television is the eye of our unconscious, like the Eye of Sauron in *The Lord of the Rings* (Tolkien 2012)—through its ideological programming, it colonizes our subjectivity, works through massaging our organs of irrationality. It replaces the messy flesh of our bodies (which we secretly wish to discard) with the flesh of our dreams—it remakes us by revalorizing the masculine self of conquest and control and allows us to live what is unmanageable and uncontrollable outside our heads inside our heads where we can stage-manage an essentially chloroformed reality. We look to technology as we would to religion, for our salvation. It is the mirror in which we hope to find our perfection reflected back at us through our acquisition of universal knowledge, knowledge lost when we were supposedly thrown out of the Garden of Eden by God. David Noble has written on this theme with considerable insight and aplomb (see, for instance, his book *Digital Diploma Mills* [2001]).

I mention the nuclear unconscious here, reflecting on an article done decades ago by Dean MacCannell (1984), who shed some light on the founding of the American comprehensive high school, in particular, the connection between the founding of the comprehensive American high school and the Cold War. I mentioned this in a previous exchange with Glenn Rikowski published in my book, *Rage and Hope* (McLaren 2006) and in a few articles. MacCannell's insights are innovative in uncovering the historical roots of racist schooling in the United States and linking this with the nuclear unconscious that marked the United States at that time. MacCannell links the politics of the Cold War and US nuclear strategy—specifically post-Hiroshima strategic foreign policy—to what he calls the "nuclear unconscious" that was instrumental in structuring urban education in the 1950s and 1960s. He sees educational policy as connected in an unconscious way to the doctrine of deterrence and the concept of limited survivability.

Here, according to MacCannell, it is important to understand the relationship of "hidden demographic-psychoanalytic desire" to the "postnuclear" arrangement of US society during the Cold War (MacCannell 1984: 40). I won't go into the theoretical grounds of his argument, which are wonderfully fleshed out in his essay, but suffice it to say that he draws on Talcott Parsons, Heidegger, and Lacan in examining the idea of the creation in the United States of a unified national culture that works through a type of abstract administrative totalization that requires unity and justifies imperialism. His work is interesting in the way it examines structural oppositions in society and how they are administered within regional and urban systems within the nation-state. And how these structural oppositions and macrosocial arrangements—and especially the way that they are managed—have become spaces where the unconscious has been displaced, having lost its ability to speak, and where subjectivity has been retotalized. Against the double oppositions that theorists such as Greimas have taught us to appreciate, those that create new categories, MacCannell adeptly recognizes that society's "implosive reduction of all previously generative oppositions: male/female, rich/poor, black/white are collapsing into a single master pattern of dominance and submission, and there is no semiotic or institutional way of breaking the pattern" (1984: 38).

PJ: As you said a few pages earlier, "the dull pantheon of curriculum theorists and learning theorists" never speaks about this shaping of education through the nuclear unconscious or the Cold War—and without an understanding of this history, it is impossible to develop an understanding of today's ideology. Please say more!

PM: Directly after World War II, the dominant thinking among US military strategists was that cities of over a million people were the only targets of sufficient economic value to warrant the use of atomic weapons. The United States believed that the Soviets would strike first and many cities would be wiped out. Yet it was also believed that a sufficient number of people outside the cities would survive an attack and rebuild US society—and as we shall see, this would be white people. Rural white folks and those living in smaller cities outside the large metropolitan areas (with a population greater than 100,000) were those that were slated for saving the reigning values of free enterprise after a Soviet first strike. According to MacCannell, the city becomes a "nuclear defense weapon" in that the "defense role of the city is not just to receive the hit, it is to *absorb* the hit, so that damage minimally spills over to surrounding 'survival areas'" (MacCannell 1984: 40, italics original). The cities would therefore be "cured" of their officially designated social problems (crimes, disease, and high mortality rate). The idea was that the city would absorb the attack so that damage minimally spilled over into surrounding "survival areas" made up of predominantly white populations. To try to defend the cities by "hardening" them (McCannell 1984: 34) would only intensify the attack, and it might spill over to white communities.

Along with the accelerating nuclear arms build-up in the 1960s came a massive withdrawal of upper-to-middle-class white folks, including many of the intelligentsia, into small towns beyond the suburban fringe. In the 1970s and 1980s, rural areas continued to grow at a more rapid rate than urban areas. As MacCannell (1984) points out, rather than moving toward a form of Euro-socialism, where minimal standards of living (housing, health care, income) would be created for impoverished ethnic communities, or opting for a renewed commitment to educational and legal justice, the United States began to warehouse its marginalized citizens in large cities. Interestingly, about this time, fiscal policies of public spending to increase investment and employment were replaced with monetary policies that regulated interest rates, moderated investment, and accelerated layoffs. Harvard University president James Bryant Conant, who had been a member of the secret National Defense Research Committee and had helped to target Hiroshima and Nagasaki—in particular, workers and their homes—became an influential educational reformer in the 1950s and early 1960s. In fact, he helped to create the public school system that we have today in the United States.

Conant's national-level involvement in planning the inner-city school curriculum advocated vocational education for Puerto Ricans and African Americans and recommended school counselor–student relationships on the model of the relationship of a probation officer to a parolee that extended four years after completion of high school. MacCannell cites Conant as describing in one of his writings a mixture of Puerto Ricans and blacks found in some New York neighborhoods as "a veritable witches brew" (MacCannell 1984: 43). He also recommended public work projects to provide ghetto-based employment for black male youth. The idea, of course, was to keep them contained in the cities, which were expendable under the "first strike" scenario. He questioned the relevance of having African Americans working on forest projects that would keep them out of the city. In fact, he was opposed to any program that would move black youth out of the city, even temporarily—like those modeled on earlier programs such as the Civilian Conservation Corps during the days of the Great Depression. Conant also argued that the private enterprise that was moving outside the city should not be responsible for the welfare of inner-city inhabitants whom he referred to as "inflammable material." He was against court-ordered busing to desegregate the public schools, even voluntary busing, and argued that ghetto schools must require students to "rise and recite" when spoken to and suggested boys wear ties and jackets to school.

As MacCannell (1984) argues, we see the nuclear unconscious at work in Conant's vision of public schooling and public life. He placed hope for the future of humanity in society's projected survivors (overwhelmingly white) who would live in small cities of populations of 10,000 to 60,000. When you examine the current decay and neglect of urban schools in the United States, some of this can be traced right back to Conant's reform measures for the comprehensive high school. Technology in the form of atomic weaponry could be used to "purify" the cities of people of color while preserving white people in small cities close to agricultural lands.

PJ: How does television fit into this picture?

PM: I figured that you were going to ask me that question sooner or later. We can see the advent of television as an ideological instrument to depress frontal lobe function. This wasn't some conspiracy, to be sure, but it was an outcome of the technology. The frontal lobe organizes plans and sequences our behavior. It is fundamental for making moral judgments, for making discriminating assessments about what we see. We know, for instance, that computer games can cause a decrease in activity in the frontal lobes by overstimulating parts of the brain associated with movement and vision. The work of Marie Winn (2002) has been helpful in addressing the effect on the brain of viewers engaged in the new media landscape. There is the whole question of TV ownership and viewing times of children correlating with a decline in students' SAT tests.

Winn has drawn our attention to extensive television viewing and the effects on young children's verbal development (as distinct from the development of their visual or spatial abilities) and reading scores. Research into the negative effects of TV watching on academic achievement is quite compelling. There is some evidence to suggest that visual and auditory output damages the child's developing brain. According to some brain researchers, when we watch TV, our brain actually shuts off and we are neurologically less able to make judgments about what we see and hear on the screen. I am thinking of Dr. Aric Sigman's work (2007) here on how television creates more separation between thought and emotion and serves to enhance behavior conformity—TV then becomes a great medium of social control and social engineering. It's a perfect instrument for advertisers, it's capitalism's wet-dream machine. As long as you can prevent the fibers connecting the neurons in the frontal lobe from thickening through TV watching, you can create an entire generation of hive dwellers, with little self-control, ready to be manipulated by television gurus—dare we mention Rupert Murdoch?—and the propaganda machines of which they are a part.

One of my professors at the Ontario Institute for Studies in Education, Dr. Fred Rainsberry, who had a special interest in communication theory and curriculum development and was part of the Royal Commission on Violence in the Communications Industry, said that I should be working with Marshall McLuhan as part of my doctoral research, but the year I entered the program, in 1979, McLuhan suffered a stroke. Early on, I suspected McLuhan's work as technologically deterministic but nevertheless chomped at the bit at the idea of working with him. I developed a children's television pilot, called *Kidding Around*, for the fledgling multilingual television station in Toronto at that time. The idea was to visit a different ethnic enclave of the city each week, interview regular folks, and get a sense of their everyday lived experiences. We couldn't find any sponsors and the show never got past the pilot. The programming directors felt that listening to ordinary people would be very boring—yet in a sense we were undertaking a form of visual ethnography, which years later would degenerate into the staged spontaneity known as reality TV. Please don't blame me for the aerosol thoughts on display in the perfumed lives of the Kardashians, and especially don't blame me for Trump's pursed lipped, toe rag rants in *The Apprentice* where he sounds likes he's trying to park the *Schienenzeppelin* in his oral cavity.

PJ: Please link these predigital insights to contemporary information and communication technologies.

PM: I'll give it a try, but forgive me if my answer is circuitous. As David Harvey (1990) and others have pointed out, computerization creates a compression of time/space through an acceleration of capital accumulation where accelerated turnover time in the process of capital accumulation and speedups in exchange and consumption help to produce superficial consumer needs though mass media (i.e., television advertising and the production of spectacles). We see ourselves as agents of change through these superficial commodities, which fester in our neoliberal bowels and are rapidly expelled in an uninterrupted flow to make room for more superficial commodities. Rather than producing durable goods and infrastructure for the public good, we are prone to the production of desire (a mimetic, acquisitive desire for the desire of the other in Girardian (1986) terms), which replaces those very critical systems of intelligibility that could help us to navigate the fault-lines of our subjectivity, to gain some critical purchase on what is happening to the formation of our protagonistic agency as citizens. We are then trapped into becoming activists for types of cultural change that are dependent upon the very corporations that we rail against instead of becoming agents for transforming existing social relations of production so that they will help produce both the systems of intelligibility and the durable, concrete infrastructure necessary to help populations meet their needs. As it stands, we are helping the popular majorities to create digitally and electronically produced subjectivities—bodies without organs—that are nothing but what Alan Watts used to describe in the 1960s as "bags of skin" (1966). Digitally produced skin. We retreat into a politics of immanence while thirsting for a politics of transcendence. But a politics of transcendence would mean we would have to give up the security of our embeddedness in the very corporate commodity culture we supposedly are fighting against.

If everything is compressed into the surface of a decontextualized image, then anything can be substituted for anything else. Using this warped logic, revolutionaries are really just conformists, conforming to the desires of other revolutionaries, and it's better to become a conservative who seeks and finds pleasure in life than a humorless activist who suffers but makes minimal progress in creating a more just and equitable world. You are conditioned to think in false equivalences, that a new cosmetic is as important as the crisis in Ukraine. Both are featured in the media as commensurate. We watch the millions who are addicted to the erotic costumes worn by Miley Cyrus and to her "wardrobe malfunctions" that are done accidentally on purpose, and we can marvel at the power of the media in creating celebrities to distract us from substantive political projects that affect our jobs and livelihoods. Miley is not going to wake up one day as a Marxist and usher in a revolution, as much as that may pique our leftist fantasies. But when the pink slips come their way, Miley's admirers will be searching for another job in retail or as a greeter at Walmart with limited medical benefits. But they can still view themselves as transgressive cultural consumers as they head to the bread lines and soup kitchens. With all of Miley's amazing talent, and her social justice inclinations, we hope she will attend one of the public lectures offered by the International Marxist Humanist Organization.

Technological advances are functionally integrating us to the ideological circuits and global imperatives of the transnational capitalist class, prompting us to perform our identities according to the not-so-hidden transcript of the neoliberal agenda that is hiding in plain sight: to create consumer citizens through a comprador class of cyber-citizenry who serve as sentinels that ensure the promulgation of a state of colonial morbidity. In this way, information technology serves to fire up the cauldron of domestic and political repression, to support the structural violence of capitalism, and to habituate us into the service of empire. No longer do we need to fear being press-ganged into the service of the empire, we have become ideological products of our own manufactured internal restraint, thanks to the technological advances that we all have come to "enjoy." We are all Julian Assange, lecturing from the balcony of the Ecuadorian embassy (or now in London's Belmarsh High Security Prison and Courts, sometimes called "Britain's Guantanamo Bay"). In this case, Elvis has recently left the building after many years in exile. The laces of his blue suede shoes have been tied together.

PJ: In the so-called network society, many occupations have undergone significant transformations—and the mass media have obviously been hit harder than the rest of us (Bird 2009). Please analyze the main developments in mass media during the past few decades. What happens to traditional press in the age of the network?

PM: That's a tough question at a time when Trump has labeled journalists as "enemies of the people." Journalism used to be a way of citizens holding people in power accountable for their actions—and the storied Upton Sinclair is often cited as the prototypical muckraker. But those journalists are few and far between, and their careers in the corporate media rarely last very long. As Sonali Kolhatkar (2014) has noted recently in a conversation with Glenn Greenwald, the mainstream media engage in attack pieces on people like Greenwald and Snowden in ways they would never treat members of Congress. Greenwald and Snowden have become prominent examples of Orwell's "thought criminals" (1949), and the public has been conditioned to view them as traitors to the United States. Yet at the same time I admire the way some mainstream journalists are holding Trump's bone spurred feet to the fire, are taking on the National Rifle Association and exposing the extensive criminal reach of the Trump regime. Witness the remonstrations from today's Republican Party by politicians who have grown more subservient and fawning towards a more demonic and deranged Trump. Their gaslighting of the public and greenwashing of Trump's policies reeks of the type of carnivalesque stunts you might expect at a fraternity house toga party only infinitely more dangerous because Republican politicians have rented asunder any semblance of governing by reason.

I have long been of the opinion that Orwell's *1984* had been upon us long before 1984, this future had always been evident in the present, locked into a reverse form of prefigurative politics. It was evident in the years leading up to the US invasion of Vietnam and became dramatically more pronounced again in 2001, when the press became the echo chamber for the Bush administration in its heinous and successful call for the invasion of Iraq. After World War II, when the United States started to believe its own mythology as the world's eternally invincible superpower, incapable of decline, then the ideological lineaments of 1984 were constructed out of the debris of the dead and fallen corpses of American jihad. When the United States came to believe and act upon the notion that it could reshape the world however it chose through the wrath of the greatest military force in history, then we all became doomed to live permanently in 1984 as the green light was given to the NSA and to corporations to act with the same rights as "religious people," for the government to hasten our extinction through policies that greatly enhance climate change, war, and debt peonage that turns workers into wage slaves of the transnational capitalist class, and ecocide. It is a marker of the sophistication of the US media apparatus that many Americans still believe that they live in a country that exercises the freedom of the press. The press is free, of course, when you consider that the only free cheese is already in the mousetrap. It is free to pursue the objectives and interests of the corporations that own the media outlets. But the outlets are not what determine this situation, it's the sensuous human activity or inactivity of the people.

I agree with Chomsky that the greatest meddling in US elections is not by Russia but by corporate America. Young people today don't read the New York Times or Washington Post—which at least give a narrow range of opinions—they tend to go to social media networks that reinforce their own opinions with more shallow levels of analysis. The big media conglomerates such as Google and Facebook are essentially selling users to advertisers in a manner similar to old media. According to Chomsky, a U.S. media company that works for Trump, Le Pen, and Netanyahu worked with the Facebook office of Berlin to provide them with details on German voters, so that they could microtarget ads to voters in order to influence them to vote for Alternative für Deutschland, the neofascist party (MacLeod 2019).

Even when there is a chance for reporters to investigate a story, other corporations jump into the act using bribery or whatever means available to purchase the silence of potential informants. Recently, for instance, a small town in Ottawa, Canada, received $28,200 from energy company TransCanada Corp. in exchange for keeping silent about the company's proposed Energy East tar sands pipeline project, for five years. TransCanada has agreed to give Mattawa $28,200, so that town can purchase a rescue truck. You now can rescue a body in danger, but you are required to put your moral compass in mortal danger in order to do so. The Energy East pipeline proposal has the potential to generate 30 to 32 million metric tons of greenhouse gas emissions each year that is the equivalent of adding more than seven million cars to the roads (Atkin 2014).

Digital Cultures and Ecopedagogy of Sustainability

PJ: In the age of the Anthropocene, human activities are directly linked to (the present and future of) our planet. On that basis, the recently established movement of ecopedagogy brings ecology in relation to critical pedagogy. In 2007 you chaired the waiver committee for Richard Kahn's doctoral dissertation on the movement. Your book coedited with J. Sandlin, *Critical Pedagogies of Consumption: Living and Learning in the Shadow of the "Shopocalypse"* (2009), is extensively referenced as one of the key readings in the field. You wrote the preface for *Occupy Education* (2012), a book on ecopedagogy by Tina Lynn Evans—and the list of your contributions could go on and on. Can you analyze potentials of ecopedagogy for our explorations of the critical encounter between education and information and communication technologies?

PM: I am not sure that I can give you a satisfactory answer with regard to ecopedagogy in terms of the critical encounter between education and information and communication technologies. After all, ecopedagogy is a relatively new subfield of critical pedagogy—although I should be careful in referring to it as a subfield. While it may be unfair to call it a subfield, it is certainly a trajectory of revolutionary critical pedagogy. Critical pedagogy is becoming more committed to speaking to issues of socioecological sustainability and to sustainability-oriented social change.

With contributions from authors and activists such as Richard Kahn, Tina Evans, David Greenwood, Samuel Fassbinder, Sandy Grande, and Donna Houston (to name just a few), the field of ecopedagogy is now on a potent trajectory. Bringing their contributions into conversation with the efforts of Vandana Shiva, Joan Martinez-Alier, Joel Kovel, Jason W. Moore, and John Bellamy Foster, ecopedagogues have cultivated a landscape of important transnational activism. We are now witnessing a profound demonstration of an efficacious integration of the social, educational, and ecological justice movements. In opposition to capitalist discipline, as it contributes to the ongoing crisis, ecopedagogic practices can be organized into a sort of "ecological discipline" (Fassbinder 2008), which would bind people to the defense of diversities both ecosystemic and social as against capital's manipulation of them as people-commodities.

In this sense, *Occupy Education* (2012), a book by Tina Lynn Evans, is very much a critical pedagogy of convergence and integration bound together by ecological discipline, as the work of European sustainability scholars and activists is brought into dialogue with powerful emergent voices from *las Americas*, both to interrogate the rust-splotched and steampunk metropolises and tumbleweed hinterlands of neoliberal capitalism and to work toward a vision of what a world outside of the menacing disciplines of neoliberal capitalism might look like. Of course, "occupy" means something else to indigenous peoples who have long fought imperial occupation. Nonetheless, the occupy movement was courageous insofar as it put questions of inequality and new "social arcs" for utopia on the map for European/settler populations.

PJ: Indeed—"occupy" can mean different things to different people. What does it mean in the context of Evans' (2012) work and ecopedagogy in general?

PM: What initially strikes the reader as a key theme of Evans' project is the way she establishes the wider context of her point of departure, where place-based sustainability theory and action are applied to multiple contexts of practical lived experience—experience that has been inestimably impacted by neoliberal capitalist globalization and sustained opposition to it. Evans' points of departure emerging from this context are the sufferings of the planetary oppressed, in the process leveraging progressive and radical theories of education, which she employs at risk of losing herself to the very system that she has been trying so valiantly to overcome. Evans rejects a reformist discourse and its hegemonic apparatuses and instead chooses to construct a pedagogy of sustainability that can be used as a strategic instrument for liberation, one that is education-oriented but nonetheless maintains a position of extraordinary political effectivity. Radical indigenous thinkers, like Linda Smith (1999), have, of course, long talked about the tensions between "assimilation" into educational systems and the possibilities for radical pedagogies within formal educational systems.

The upshot of this is the creation of what Richard Kahn calls a "counterhegemonic bloc of ideological alliance" among environmental educators, indigenous scholars, nonacademic knowledge workers, and political activists of various and sundry stripe—or what Kahn in his own pathbreaking work has called "the ecopedagogy movement" (2010). Evans' work is built upon in-depth theories about the nature and purposes of sustainability itself, and Evans is acutely aware that the politics of sustainability is not a pitch-perfect love story and can easily be co-opted by the guardians of the state, who make empty promises to manage the crisis in the interests of the public good (really in the interests of private greed). The discourses of sustainability can be hijacked by the very interests that Evans is out to unmask (see, for example, Josée Johnston's "Who Cares About the Commons?," which argues that "sustainability has come to imply sustainable profits as much as 'saving the earth'" [2003: 1]). Understanding how such hijacking takes place and how the imperial instinct remains alive and well among progressive educators, and comes with a fixed-rate and nonnegotiable commitment to reform over revolution can be brilliantly assisted by engaging with the works of the decolonial school.

PJ: Hijacking progressive movements for one's own purposes is among the oldest and the most successful strategies of capitalist development. What kind of response to this strategy does the contemporary decolonial school offer?

PM: Exponents of this school have charted out the conflictual terrain known as the "coloniality of power" (*patrón de poder colonial*) and "the Eurocentric pattern of colonial/capitalist power" (*el eurocentramiento del patrón colonial/capitalista de poder*) whose scholars and activists working in the areas of decolonizing epistemologies and praxis include Ramón Grosfoguel, Anibal Quijano, Linda Smith, Enrique Dussel, Sandy Grande, and others. In addition to addressing the coloniality of power, a revolutionary critical pedagogy of sustainability is as much about creating what Kahn (2010) calls a "revitalized ecology of body/mind/spirit" and the struggle for "planetarity" as it is a praxiological undertaking to achieve specific, cumulative goals. Thus, for instance, Grosfoguel (2008), as well as Quijano, Dussel, and other decolonial thinkers, suggests new approaches to ecology through viewing the dependent hierarchies of capitalism, spirituality, epistemology, jurisprudence and governance, patriarchy, and imperialism as an entangled, empretzled, and coconstitutive power complex akin to a global ecology.

PJ: What do you make of ecopedagogical politics in the United States today?

PM: One ecopedagogical idea that I support can be illustrated in my admiration of yet at the same time cautious critique of the Green New Deal (GND), drawn up by the wonderful Congresswoman Alexandria Ocasio-Cortez and Ed Markey (Whyte 2019). It's an important document, and I support it, but it doesn't go far enough. Why? Because, to repeat a phrase used by my comrade Peter Hudis (2012), it remains in the precinct of "environmental Keynesianism." The GND's plan for ecological and social reconstruction is premised on substituting renewable energy for fossil fuels while leaving the current global system of expanding capitalist production and consumption intact. It is built on growth-based presuppositions. But we don't need a more expansive capitalism, we need to drastically reduce environmentally destructive sectors of the economy. Sectors that are not environmentally destructive can certainly be encouraged to expand. New growth ultimately means more exploitation, and any environmental benefits of more efficient technological advances made in renewable energy will be canceled out in a spiraling, growth-directed economy. Exponents of ecopedagogy understand that it won't work simply to redistribute the resources from the fossil fuel industry to renewable-energy industries. It won't work. As my friend Peter Hudis (2012) argues, the transition away from a carbon-based productive system toward one driven by renewable energy can be best achieved through freely associated labor among worker-owned and democratically managed cooperatives within civil society that respect the commons.

PJ: Throughout this discussion, I cannot stop thinking of Ivan Illich. From *Deschooling Society* (1971) through *Tools for Conviviality* (1973) to *Medical Nemesis* (1982), Illich offered many innovative insights and strategies for decolonialization of the complex web of relationships between technologies, cultures, education, and ecology. What are the most important lessons we can take from Illich?

PM: Illich offers us so much as does McLuhan, in spite of his technological determinism. While Illich's idea of deschooling is obviously based on a utopian image of human beings (alongside your great work in the field (Jandrić 2014b and 2015), an in-depth critique of Illich's educational ideas in the context of the contemporary Internet can be found in the book called *Wikiworld* (2010) coauthored by my dear friend Juha Suoranta and Tere Vadén), his lasting legacy lies in his profound analyses of the relationships between the human race and its environment. Barry Sanders, coauthor with Illich of *ABC: The Alphabetization of the Popular Mind* (Sanders and Illich 1989), shared the following story about Illich, which has been described as follows by Richard Wall:

> At one point during a talk in Maine, in the midst of Ivan describing his mistrust of electronic technology and in particular his terror of email, a young man leapt to his feet and shouted out, "But, Mr. Illich, don't you want to communicate with us?" Ivan immediately shouted back, "No. I have absolutely no desire to communicate with you. You may not interact with me, nor do I wish to be downloaded by you. I should like very much to talk to you, to stare at the tip of your nose, to embrace you. But to communicate—for that I have no desire." (Sanders and Illich 1989)

Illich taught one to be fearless—on stage or in the audience. I would hate any kind of technophobia or dystopian imagination to destroy the fearlessness we need to move forward toward the future.

PJ: By now we succinctly introduced your critical turn from postmodernism to Marxism, explored the changing modes of production in the network society, and briefly examined critical potentials of ecopedagogy. In order to systematize our thoughts, we approached those issues in neat sequence, one by one—but their real nature is everything but neat and sequential. Scientific discourses do not separate social phenomena because of their nature, but because isolated problems represent small(er) chunks of our reality that are much easier to comprehend for human beings. However, the dialectic nature of our reality always finds its way to the surface. In the field of research methodologies, it is reflected in the need to explore the relationships between technologies and the society using various interdisciplinary, transdisciplinary, and even antidisciplinary approaches (Jandrić 2012 and 2016). In everyday life, it is probably most notable in overarching, elusive yet unavoidable and inevitable concepts such as "digital cultures" (I am deliberately using plural in order to stress multiplicity of backgrounds, narratives, and perspectives). What are the main features of the emerging digital cultures? What are their underlying values and ideologies? Paraphrasing Freire (1972), how do they relate to our reading of the word and our reading of the world?

PM: C. A. Bowers and I have had some spirited if not downright acrimonious debates over the decades, especially in relation to the work of Paulo Freire. At the same time, I want to acknowledge the importance of some of his lucid observations about digital cultures (Bowers 2014). First, it is absolutely essential that we understand the metaphorical nature of language and that intelligence is not limited to what can be explained by the scientific study of the neuro-networks of the human brain. Consciousness, as Gregory Bateson acknowledges, along with Bowers, includes the pathways of all unconscious mentation, which includes those pathways that are automatic and repressed, neural and hormonal. Print-based cultural storage and thinking, which is relied upon by developers of technology, is not rationally based and objective but in fact impedes awareness of what is being communicated through the multiple pathways that differ from culture to culture.

Bowers is right about this, and he worries that computer technology and the digitalized mismeasure of man will offer us a truncated notion of ecological intelligence. Computer technicians and scientists working on artificial intelligence sanctify data and information grounded in print-based cultural storage and thinking. This reinforces surface knowledge, ignores tacit knowledge, presents a false sense of objectivity, and ultimately misrepresents the relational and emergent information-intense pathways of both cultural and natural ecologies. Bowers is very convincing here. Digital communication reproduces the misconceptions encoded in the metaphorically layered language that is often taken for granted by digital technicians.

Computer scientists are using a languaging process based on print literacy that reproduces the myths and deep cultural assumptions that influence thinking and awareness—what is being championed are the myths of individualism and progress and what is being silenced is the need to conserve the cultural commons of non-Western cultures that are able to provide largely nonmonetized systems of mutual support that rely less on exploiting the planet's natural resources. I agree with Bowers' prescient understanding that you can't reduce culture, cultural knowledge systems, and cultural ways of knowing to data and information—especially given the reliance of computer scientists on print and given the fact that there exist 6,000 languages in the world. Words are metaphors whose meanings are framed, as Bowers explains, by the analogues settled upon in previous eras. Craft knowledge and indigenous wisdom traditions have been lost and replaced by Western corporate vocabularies of profits, efficiency, and competition.

There are linguistic and cultural differences that cannot be captured by artificial intelligence. We can't capture what lies beyond the surface of the interplay of individual/cultural/linguistic ecologies. Here we should listen carefully to Bowers' criticism of the root metaphors of Western knowledge systems and the effects they have on colonization of the life worlds of other cultural groups. The digital revolution has encoded dangerous assumptions about endless growth, individualism, and the deepening of the ecological crisis. Ecologically sustainable traditions need to be intergenerationally renewed. The traditions of civil liberties of the complex and nonmonetized traditions of the cultural commons that are still viable within Western cultures must be preserved and the cultural commons of non-Western cultures that do not rely on the exploitation of natural resources need to be intergenerationally renewed. Computer technology is contributing to the ecological crisis as superintelligent computers still rely on print-based cultural storage whose cultural assumptions have been shaped by root metaphors of Western ideas of progress and individualism. We need an earth-centered ecological intelligence. Critical pedagogy can join in such an effort. When my comrade, Sergio Quiroz Miranda, told me he met the few remaining members of an indigenous group who told him that they had chosen not to reproduce because life was too miserable, my heart shattered. This was a group that had chosen to become extinct.

PJ: Digital cultures (I am deliberately using plural in order to stress multiplicity of backgrounds, narratives, and perspectives) have recently acquired a lot of attention from various researchers such as Siân Bayne, Jeremy Knox, Hamish A. Macleod, Jen Ross, Christine Sinclair, and others. During the past several years, they have become an intrinsic part of curricula at various schools and universities (Jandrić et al. 2017). In this mash-up of postmodernist talk about grand narratives, glorifications of technologies, various scepticisms and/or primitivisms, practical inquiry into the ways people use the Internet for this or that purpose, analyses of the relationships between the local and the global, changes in various human activities including but not limited to arts, commerce, government, and education, it is easy to forget that digital cultures are strongly linked to their nondigital background—particularly regarding power relationships. Based on your extensive international experience, particularly in the Americas, please link digital cultures with the distinctions between the global South and the global North, with globalization of capitalism and the archetypes of identity.

PM: That's a challenge I will need to address with a personal story. It's very easy to be distracted by the digital world and culture while you are building a personal identity created in a digital context. It is clear how individuals want to be represented in that world, and some prefer to live in that world than engage in the real world. Recently I returned from teaching a course in popular education and critical pedagogy in Mexico, where we discussed the negative impact of narcocorridos—songs that romanticize the Mexican drug cartels such as the Sinaloa Cartel, the Gulf Cartel, the Juárez Cartel, the Knights Templar Cartel, the Tijuana Cartel, Los Zetas, Jalisco New Generation, Independent Cartel of Acapulco, and La Barredora—on youth. It is part of a movement around music that developed in Culiacán but is now a major commercial business venture in Los Angeles called El Movimiento Alterado.

Here are the words to an outlaw ballad in the Norteño musical style, sung by Alfredo Rios, a song about a notorious drug kingpin.

We take care of El Mayo
Here no one betrays him . . .
We stay tough with AK-47s and bazookas at the neck
Chopping heads off as they come
We're bloody-thirsty crazy men
Who like to kill.

The songs glamorize torture, murder, and decapitations. This particular song glorifies the Sinaloa cartel and its bosses, Ismael "El Mayo" Zambada and Joaquín "El Chapo" Guzmán, and praises Manuel Torres, allegedly a top hit man for Zambada. By the end of 2011, the song had been downloaded 5 million times and the accompanying video had been downloaded 13 million times (USA Today 2011).

Banned on radio stations in parts of Mexico, narcocorridos are everywhere on the Internet. Twin brothers based in Burbank, California, developed the El Alterado culture, which admires the Sinaloa cartel for their violent, murderous lifestyle. They won a Grammy award in 2008 for creating a singer who goes by the name of "El Chapo de Sinaloa." Drug trafficking and torture are being made socially acceptable. There have been roughly 40,000 drug war deaths since former Mexican president Felipe Calderón started to launch a major offensive on cartels as he took office in 2006. One of my doctoral students in Mexico presented on El Movimiento Alterado. He interviewed a number of his twelve-year-old students in Mexicali about why they loved to listen to the narcocorridos. Their answers were very similar:

Because we love violence.
We want to be able to torture people.
We want to grow up so we can kill people.

So there is an entire Internet culture on this. There are video games where you can rape women, you can kill effortlessly, where you can turn yourself into a superhero. So what is the appeal? Are you retreating into your unconscious and connecting with all the frustrations you feel about being just an ordinary bloke in real life? Will you be more prone to act violently to solve problems you might have in real life? To counter this music, we played political protest music, some very contemporary, such as that from Calle 13, a Puerto Rican band formed by two brothers, René Pérez Joglar, who goes by the name "Residente," and Eduardo José Cabra Martínez, who calls himself "Visitante," and their half-sister Ileana Cabra Joglar, aka "PG-13."

Anyway, I returned from Mexico and was walking around the train station and suddenly I was surrounded by superheroes—Batman, Robin, Superman, the Flash, Wonder Woman, Wolverine, Zombies—as the city was hosting a comic book convention and what is called a "nerd prom." So I was thinking, where are the energies of these teens and young adults going? Do they think that by clicking on "Like" in their Facebook exchanges they are participating in a revolution? The contrast between the discussions and work being done in Mexico and the invasion of the nerds in San Diego was striking. In Mexico, Internet culture based in Los Angeles was normalizing drug trafficking and brutal violence, while across the border in Gringolandia, everybody was focused on the world of their superheroes. Capitalist consumer culture hijacks the archetypes of identity—and none of them are fighting capitalism. They might be fighting corrupt capitalists, but not capitalism as wage slavery, as a structure of feeling, as a social sin, as a system of exploitation, as a mode of production based on private ownership of the means of production in which commodities are created for the exchange market, extracting as much labor from the workers as possible at the lowest possible cost.

Critical Technological Consciousness for a New Humanity

PJ: Historically, youth movements have always been important agents of social change. Certain aspects of their struggles can be attributed to a universal clash of generations, while others might have some real potential to bring radical social transformations. In order to make a clear distinction between the eternal and the contemporary, between the basic human need to struggle against authority and the really important argument regarding the future of our society, between the battle to overtake positions of power and the principled struggle against positions of power, between desperate fight against worldwide tyrants such as Saddam Hussein and struggle for a better/more just/ more democratic society, between genuine political change and mere replacement of one political mannequin with another, between real social development and digital Potemkin's villages, can you pinpoint some distinct features of contemporary youth movements that emerge from the context of the network society?

PM: Youth today are learning new ways to refuse the cult of individualism as an antidote to their loss of a sense of self, to their being situated as impersonal agents in a rationalized society that is highly competitive and achievement-oriented and psychotherapeutically oriented. Contemporary youth do not feel themselves embedded in a living reality that will endure within years to come because youth are taught to concentrate on their immediate personal status and well-being. They and their loved ones are not assured of protection from misery and oblivion. The 2011 student mobilization in Chile, the activism of Nigerian youth at the Niger Delta crude oil flow station, the clench-fist protests against the ruling establishments of Tunisia, Egypt, and Libya, the resistance to the austerity measures by the youth in Portugal, Spain, and especially Greece, the South African public students who struggle to secure basic teaching amenities, such as libraries, in their schools, the Occupy Wall Street movement in the United States—all of these are part of a growing culture of contestation with its roots buried in the past, and its arabesque of tendrils arcing toward the future, the result of grafting what is desirable from the past onto new practices of revolt. And look at the recent environmental movement focused on climate change influenced by the activism of sixteen-year-old Greta Thunberg. We should be anything but cynical. This is an important movement.

In the plant-grafting process, when the vascular cambium tissues of the root stock and scion plants have been successfully inosculated, the stem of the stock is pruned just above the newly grafted bud. But the joints formed as a result of the grafting process are not as strong as naturally formed joints. Social movements that have recognized their weak links with the past are not attempting to begin again from the beginning (as this is a constitutive impossibility), but are utilizing technological innovations never before imagined in the history of social movements to refigure the ways in which student protest can be organized to resist the cooptation of the world capitalist aristocracy and to provide new networking potentialities for increasing the pressure on the sentinels of the transnational capitalist class. Some of this they learned from the Situationists, more specifically from the work of Debord. I think it is time to refashion the ways in which we incite people to rebel. At the moment the conditions of possibility for forming a new International that will lead capital to ruin are clearly not present—and that's very likely a bad idea with which to begin. Nor do I think the neo-Dadaist practice of *detournement*—turning capitalist practices against themselves in the form Situationist pranks, punk music, or culture jamming—is sufficient since it is so easily recuperated by the capitalist system. Capitalists augment value from the practices of culture jammers by appropriating their forms of parody and mimicry, turning it into a spray-on, aerosol form of transgression. How about repurposing the general strike? Now that might prove interesting.

PJ: A general strike might indeed prove interesting, but I cannot see it happen. . . . Today's youth, at least in comparison to the generation of 1968, seems increasingly apathetic.

PM: The new youth movements have revealed that a decline in political activism among youth is not an inevitable fact of capitalist life nor is political apathy among youth evidence of a deep normality. However, youth are pulled in sometimes crazed and mostly inconclusive directions. The spectacle of neoliberal capitalism would have us believe that youth protest should be enlivened by constant stimulation of the senses and thus opposed to the course of daily routine of regulation and self-restraint. But protest does not always require youth to shift registers between the everyday and the culture of contestation because contestation can, in fact, be part of everyday praxis, such as in the world of hip-hop culture. Protests can erode our subsequent capacity to endure the strenuous demands of our daily life, which is, of course, a good thing, because they create a space of liminality where youth can cultivate contestation as an art form—ludic resistance against spectacular capitalism (see Barbrook 2014).

Historical necessity does not grant these movements success in advance, nor does divine fiat. This question can only be answered inside the struggles themselves and in terms of the commitment that youth have to the poor, the powerless, the disfavored, and the aggrieved. Of course, much can be learned by engaging in Richard Barbrook's *Class Wargames* (2014), a Situationist politicomilitary simulation analysis of neoliberal capitalist society designed—with Lenin's pamphlet on imperialism as its default setting for understanding geopolitical competition—to create a new generation of cybernetic communist insurgents able to engage strategically in a protracted war against spectacular capitalism. Barbrook's and the Situationists' "accelerationism" certainly is an antidote to postmodern nihilism, and whether it can be an effective challenge to a qualitatively new transnational or global phase of world capitalism characterized by a globally integrated production and financial system that attempts to sustain accumulation in the face of stagnation is worth considering. Especially now when the tech sector is driving the digitalization of the entire global economy and when the global economy is employing what William Robinson (2019) terms "militarized accumulation" or "accumulation by repression" (after all, it was the US military who invented the Internet!).

PJ: What is the role of media in these processes?

PM: The presence of twenty-first-century fascism that involves the fusion of transnational capital with the reactionary and repressive political power of the state—an expression of the dictatorship of transnational capital (Robinson 2019)—needs to be engaged by the left strategically, such as in Barbrook's "two-way media," which he has discussed with you Petar (Jandrić 2017: 77). Here, Barbrook chronicles the dead-end debates between commercial media and state media while the swindlers of hyperbaric entrepreneurialism hold sway. No wonder that this debate was so deeply engrained among intellectuals at the time, a time when technotronics was considered the cell form of capital, when the "fixed media capital" of the machine was thought to have replaced living labor as the motor of history, where the electronic marketplace could regulate itself under the cover of the smoke and mirrors of dot-com culture. Today, for instance, it is not the media that have brainwashed Trump's political base to become supporters of a white nationalist ethno-state. It's because this thinking is so pervasively reflected in what is happening in the United States now, at this sociopolitical conjuncture, at this major historical inflection point, and of course, not just in the United States but in many countries around the world. What a contrast from the 1960s, when the United States was more communist than the Soviet Union, as Barbrook has noted.

I strenuously agree with Barbrook when he argues that "[d]igital technologies should be used to replace markets and bureaucracies with workers' self-management" and that dot-com capitalism in the service of cybernetic communism reflects Engels' objective— that we should work to create a system where people administrate things rather than the other way around (in Jandrić 2017: 89). But will the heirs of do-it-yourself media be able to build the shining city on the hill or be cast into the dung heap of history, having been abandoned altogether by Benjamin's Angel of History? Could network computing for the democratization of the political economy of capitalism, complete with a socialist source code, and carried forward by the collaborative working methods of the Internet, translate into the gravediggers of capitalism and a new stewardship of our communist future if, say, these conditions were able to take over the entire global economy? As long as the working methods are controlled by people and people are not controlled by the methods they initiate—perhaps. As long as people are not tricked into believing that they are shaping the new digital technologies and not the other way around. But this stretches belief. Beware the self-replicating Internet commune! A digitalized cornucopia overflowing with information may on the surface seem to possess a dance floor excitement and soul drenched potential but it can also set the conditions for a dustbowl of the heart, swapping face-to-face human relationality for pixel-to-pixel impersonality. Doesn't it make you wonder why the US military is so interested in artificial intelligence?

PJ: One of the main issues with digital technologies is the staggering lack of privacy— our digital traces are almost impossible to erase and stay with us pretty much forever. This is a pretty big problem for (online) political struggle!

PM: We remain virtually transparent beings, as barriers between the state, the market, and the private realm are being steadily abolished. Anyone who is computer literate can find out more about me than my most intimate friends knew about me in the 1960s and 1970s, before social media databases started compiling information on us, before data mining on a formerly unfathomable scale became normalized in the information age. Individuals and corporations and government agencies know what we like, dislike, they have a direct channel into our shared fantasies—you name it! Harcourt

(2015) writes about how we brush aside being scandalized if it means convenience, exposure, and fame. How technologies that feed our narcissism can help us become the gravediggers of capitalism is much more complex than even the Situationists were prepared to acknowledge. Not even Orwell could predict an "Expository Society" (Harcourt 2015) in which we thrillingly give away secrets about ourselves, knowing we will likely be mocked and ridiculed for doing so! Digital technologies give us the power to crowdfund for worthy causes, but also to join others in attacking individuals in digitalized wolf packs, should they be caught by a cellphone camera doing something we find offensive. But our desire to participate in the Expository Society is, as Harcourt (2015) argues, a desire that is fundamentally at odds with democracy, a desire—or a concentration of desires—designed by corporations to make profits and by unaccountable government agencies to guide our political decisions.

PJ: Governments may indeed have a strong interest in the Internet and artificial intelligence, but the majority of world's digital data is in the hands of private corporations. This brings about a very interesting dynamic between the corporate sector and the state . . .

PM: With the help of tech companies, the state is able to convince the private sector to do some of its dirty work—in the name of fomenting inner compulsions we feel are outwardly justified if we are to be part of a dutiful congregation of consumer citizens. While the state is not monolithic in its politics, it does converge ideologically for the most part on neoliberal imperatives of anti-unionism, procapitalism, etc. Facial biometrics are being sold to us as a way to match our facial image with our passport photos in order to get us seamlessly though the long airport security lines more quickly. Sure, it's all done in the interest of the comfort of the traveler. Did I tell you I have some expensive property in Florida I can sell you dirt cheap? Border guards are doing "suspicionless" digital "strip searches" by requesting that border-crossers hand over their cell phones and passwords. Encryption and strong passwords can help, for the time being. If you have data stored on cloud, you can delete the app before crossing and then download it again after you cross. There are some tricks, but searches are getting worse, not better. The US Border Patrol can now equip all their patrol units with a forward-looking infrared camera, tripod, rangefinder, and battery charger and can spend weeks on end detecting the heat signatures of smugglers from as far away as two miles, use a rangefinder to determine their GPS coordinates, and take it from there. Imagine what technologies can be developed in the future for snatching up critical pedagogues before they can reach large education platforms!

I am only half-kidding. You, Petar, were held up at the US border and interrogated recently. When asked why you were visiting the United States, you mentioned you were visiting a colleague at Chapman University in California to finish this book. The border agent disappeared for a few minutes, returned, and demanded that you explain why you were visiting a known communist and then proceeded to interrogate you for five hours, and then charged you $68 for taking up their extra time! Hey all you Trumpsters, want to become a Virtual Texas Deputy? Just join BlueServo, a Virtual Community Watch and monitor livestreaming cameras of the Texas/Mexico border and catch the "illegals" crossing over. You can do it from your laptop anywhere in the country:

BlueServo[SM] deployed the Virtual Community Watch, an innovative real-time surveillance program designed to empower the public to proactively participate in fighting border crime. The BlueServo[SM] Virtual Community Watch[SM] is a network of cameras and sensors along the Texas–Mexico border that feeds live streaming video to www.BlueServo.net. Users will log in to the BlueServo[SM] website and directly monitor suspicious criminal activity along the border via this virtual fence[SM]. (BlueServo 2019)

Ruling elites who wish to turn greed into an inalienable right are now more fearful than ever that youth-driven democratic social movements might at present spawn a revolutionary upsurge among the popular majorities. So they make undemocratic demands democratically by enforcing brutal austerity measures and ratcheting up a permanent war on terrorism. This constitutes a major challenge for today's cyber-communists.

PJ: How should we go about this challenge?

PM: Imagine a grandmother has lost her grandson to lung disease. Her tears are rolling down the precipice of her sunken eyes like a bucketful of pearls. But when she passes the chemical factory responsible for her grandson's death, her tears shoot out of her eyes in great red molten sparks as if spewed from an ancient volcano buried deep in the sea of her grief. She can do little more at the moment than scream in a high-pitched rage that arcs around the smokestacks that killed her grandson. But can she do more than cry tears of grief and rage?

She can mount a social media campaign against the factory. She can petition the government. She can become an environmental activist. She can enter the digital world of protest. I am not saying that social media is in itself ineffectual. But so many protests these days are by digital petition. It takes less than a minute to sign. They give us the feeling that we are doing something, that we are making a difference, that the world is not hopeless, that we can intervene. My concern is to form a coalition that organizes on the basis of class initiative, that cuts across race and ethnicity and sexuality, that directly confronts the rule of capital. Is this even possible in the digital age? Are we predestined for political fragmentation, for single-issue campaigns that bury struggles that are necessarily universal under a micropolitics of single issues antiseptically cleaved from relations of production?

PJ: Talking about social order, we must revisit contemporary transformations of the concept of the state. Sociologists such as Jan van Dijk (1999) and Manuel Castells (2001) repeatedly assert that global neoliberal capitalism rapidly diminishes the role of the state in everyday affairs. At a phenomenological level, it seems commonly accepted that most traditional functions of the state have been transferred to transnational institutions such as World Trade Organization and International Monetary Fund, corporations richer than many countries, and with increased individual responsibility for issues such as education and health. However, the left side of the political spectrum (Standing 2011 and 2014; Standing and Jandrić 2015; McLaren 2006) constantly emphasizes that the role of the state is as important as ever and seeks to improve its functioning toward increasing social justice. Which concepts of the state are emerging from new social movements? How feasible are they?

PM: Youth resisters who assume the opinion that we live in the information age where we have a knowledge economy of "immaterial labor," where productive capital and the working classes are becoming increasingly irrelevant to social transformation, and that the nation-state is relatively powerless, are likely to adopt a "civil societarian" position (Holst 2002) and put their faith in new social movements—in the "cognitariat" rather than the "proletariat." Many participants in the youth movements of today view the state as the "social state"—here I shall borrow some terms from Tony Smith (2009)— where symbolic and moral philosophy is the systematic expression of the normative principles of the Keynesian welfare state. In other words, it is a version of the state that offers wage labor as the normative principles of modern society.

Some of the more conservative and even liberal-centrist participants in new social movements take a neoliberal state as the norm, which we could call the entrepreneurial state—in which generalized commodity production requires a world market, and they follow Hayek's (1948) principle that capital's law of value in the abstract must be followed. Some of the new social movements look to create a new model of the state, which could be called an "activist state" that is based, in large part, on the work of Polanyi (2001), and includes methods of aggressive state intervention into its industrial policy. International capital still predominates in this model, and there will be an inevitable government and global trade dependence on international capital. Of course, those who govern the activist state desire to place government restrictions on its rules and regulations for attracting global investment capital. So there is a concerted attempt to lessen the worst and most exploitative aspects of the state. Then again, you have some left-liberal social movements who prefer the concept of the "cosmopolitan state." This model is largely derived from the work of Habermas (1970), where forms of global market governance can prevail that are intranational rather than national; here there is a focus on the development of a global civil society (see Holst 2002).

Marxist and anarchist movements don't ascribe to any of these models as it is clear to them that it is impossible to manage democratically wage labor on a global scale by placing severe restrictions on global financial and derivative markets. After all, wage labor only appears to include an equal exchange.

PJ: Being fairly close to anarchist ideas myself, Peter (e.g., Jandrić 2010), I am extremely interested in your last claim. Does that mean that Marxism and anarchism have finally overcome the Bakunin–Marx split from the First International? Can we expect reconciliation of the two political philosophies as the theoretical and practical base for creating a massive anticapitalist front?

PM: As is well known, there are wide variants of anarchism that have been described in the literature under various names, such as individualist anarchism, which rejects all forms of organization; "Black bloc"–style anarchism, which often engages in violent acts; anarcho-syndicalism and libertarian communism, which defend the interests of the working class and become involved in the class struggle; and "primitivist" and green anarchism, which challenge capitalist society or seek to create alternatives to it.

Marxists and anarchists both agree on the goal of a stateless society. Some Marxists stridently maintain that a Leninist-style revolutionary party is necessary to rebuild society from its capitalist ashes, a strong collective, organizing force that goes beyond Bakunin's call during the First International for spontaneous organization of the masses.

I was a member of the Industrial Workers of the World, or "Wobblies," for a short time, and it's an important organization, although not as influential as it once was. I became interested in creating a philosophically driven praxis of liberation, and I soon became drawn to the International Marxist-Humanist Organization (2019), which seeks to conceptualize forms of organization that escape an elitist vanguardism but which offer an organizing force toward developing a socialist alternative to capitalism. The challenge before us is to build such an alternative that can gain hegemonic ascendancy in the minds of the popular majorities worldwide so that we can fight to bring such an alternative into being.

PJ: Please evaluate the social relevance of the new youth movements. Where do they take us, do they have enough power to bring real change?

PM: As they stand, social movements prepare us for the next step, rather than take us to a new space, mainly because we do not know the spatial transformations necessary to prepare us for an alternative to the law of value. They are preparing us to be reborn with a transmuted consciousness, and while they have seen the old vanguard as a hindrance to further social change, they are still wrestling with the forms of organization needed to transform a world stage managed by a transnational capitalist class. These new social movements are the foreconscious of change, whereas what is needed is a change in the subconscious of the historical agent; that is, how do we gain an acceptance in the deep mind for the fact that we need to build a social universe outside of labor's value form? Or is this just some youthful, chiliastic dream-vision? Some aspects of our goal must remain unspecified, our path trackless, our cry soundless, and our destination uncertain, or else we will fall into the trap of imposing a blueprint, or recoding old formulas, but at the very least we have to attune ourselves to history's migratory urge to sublate that which we negate and to move toward a world less populated by human suffering, exploitation, and alienation. That much is known and that much must be accepted before we can build upon the vestiges of past struggles and move into an entirely new terrain of resistance and transformation.

The pent-up force of the unmet shadow that lurks in our consent to the prevailing ideology of the capitalist class has the potential to destroy the very form of our past struggles. New modes of organization are called for. The political imagination must be reconfigured to the challenges of the present. If we view the accumulation of capital and the production of nature as a dialectical unity, we need a new vision of the future that can break free from modernity's mega-strategies of revolution so that we can think of a socialist alternative to capitalism differently, not as some cataclysmic leap by which life advances, but rather as steps—some precarious and some bold—by which life is prepared to evolve. We must recover from our past what the past regarded as utopian and thus was rejected by our predecessors and offer new forms of rebellion that can better ensure that such knowledge will reimpact the present more effectively.

PJ: How can we begin reconfiguring our political imagination to the challenges of the present? And what are the main challenges facing us in this reconfiguration?

PM: We need to know how institutions operate, how people inside of them behave. This is crucial. We can learn, for instance, about war from all the valiant work of Daniel Ellsberg (we made a recording together years ago but it wasn't released because of—yes!—technical problems with the sound). And we can give some credit to Julian Assange and his Wikileaks staff and the efforts of Edward Snowden and Chelsea Manning. And let's not forget the courageous work of Katharine Teresa Gun. We've learned about the deaths of thousands who otherwise would be relegated to the annals of ignominity, to abstractions that we can ignore because we can't picture them in ghastly and gory detail in our minds. There is a lot of information out there—all communication relies on information, but I am concerned here about the providers. Who provides the information, how is it framed or "punctuated," and what are the ideological effects? And how do human beings handle information? How do Americans cope, for instance, with the knowledge that their military has killed millions in its wars of aggression (which are disguised as preconditions for delivering "democracy" by "shock and awe" to those who won't play by our rules) and beaten them through our "humanitarian imperialism" into submission until they become pliable client states? There is no country more than the United States that appreciates quisling nation-states that willingly bend over for whoever is in power in the White House. And no country that has more obsequious politicians who constitute the shame of the nation.

Matt Gaetz, Devin Nunes and Jim Jordan appear right out of central casting for knuckleheaded schemers who would go to any extreme to be able to sniff Trump's plump rump. Given the manner in which they comport themselves to their constituencies, they appear to celebrate with seedy glee the irreducible intimacy between politics and clownishness and rarely miss an opportunity to make common cause with stomach churning buffoonery. They are a cross between Ted Baxter and Michele Bachmann, they are the vomit left at the bottom of the shot glass.

Yes, yes, technology is advancing our capacities for change. But whose labor power services these technological breakthroughs? Yes, Wernher von Braun was lionized for helping US astronauts land on the moon, but the 10,000 enslaved Jews, Roma, Soviet soldiers, and French resistance fighters who died in Mittelbau-Dora concentration camp, those slaves who helped this Nazi Party SS scientist get his V-2 rocket destruction-ready to obliterate London, don't have moon craters named after them! Nor do the epileptic children upon whom Kurt H. Debus, designer of Apollo's pressure suit and onboard life systems, conducted oxygen deprivation experiments (McDonald 2019).

How do young people react to the notion that their country is involved in a "forever war" against terrorism? How do they handle the knowledge that we could be saving millions of people by bringing them medical aid for what are known and treatable diseases—we have the technology to do that – but we don't. Capitalism creates such vast inequalities between groups within states and between states. Pollution from air, water, sanitation, and hygiene is responsible for more deaths than disease in the developing world. The rich countries can afford to export their pollution to the peripheral countries. We know that our fellow human beings, our fellow planetary citizens, are being poisoned by lead, toxic smoke from burning refuse in industrial dumps, from smoking cigarettes, from mercury, hexavalent chromium, and pesticides, which have become obsolete. After a while, the death toll is just too much to bear, but we can fast-forward all the messy details out of our consciousness through digital distractions. Our coping mechanisms involve surfing the television channels or the Internet; we don't have to stay in any one place for too long. Our antiwar efforts are really activated in the arena of cultural protest—through music, dress, plays, Internet sites—that are connected to rebelling against bourgeoisie society—as if war is just another feature of bourgeois society.

PJ: The system cannot be changed from within the system—this is why your shift from postmodernism to Marxism is so important.

PM: What I am concerned with is how war is connected to class structure, to capitalism itself, and I agree here with Garry Leech (2012) that capitalism itself is a type of war, a "structural genocide," and it will take more than transgressions in the arena of culture to combat this genocide. All of us participate in this structural genocide as much by what we choose not to do, as by what actions we deliberately choose to take in our everyday lives. It is the concentration of capital within global corporations, their hegemonic control of the structures of ideological production through media, which largely makes this genocide possible, and, of course, the policies of international regulatory agencies. Even when we choose to resist, we find ourselves regulated in the way in which we are permitted to violate the rules—we are given a certain part of the public square where we can picket, chant slogans, and the like.

Postmodern antirationalism and antiuniversalism from our avant-garde professoriate will not help us here. The struggle is up to us, to make sure we have a historical record that is truthful, and that we have safeguards in place so that corporations and government agencies cannot delete our national history. Because without memory, without collective history, education is impossible. Every educator should be involved in making history by struggling to make the world a better place by connecting their local concerns to larger global concerns—war, industrial pollution, human rights, freedom from constant surveillance. Now there is another issue here about historical records. Who owns our personal historical record? This generation's personal history is recorded in some form—who owns it? Whoever owns it can control us. And I'm not talking here in the language of theosophy or anthroposophy about the Akashic records encoded in the etheric plane. I'm talking about who has the capacity to write or rewrite history via our school curricula, our church sermons, our popular television shows, the hidden transcripts that serve the interests of the ruling class.

Interestingly, as an aside, the surveillance state in which we currently live could be said to have its beginnings in the development of the postal service. During the US Civil War, letters were delivered to soldiers from their loved ones that sometimes contained rumors or incriminating information—that is, about their sex lives—gleaned from the correspondence of their fellows. And letters from soldiers—their acts of "epistolary self-presentation" were frequently recirculated and sometimes published (Henkin 2006). On the positive side, early postal correspondence also allowed people to participate in family life in an intimate way that did not depend upon physical presence.

PJ: Nowadays, various gadgets and services collect enormous amounts of our personal data in exchange for "personalized" services. For instance, my new phone is structurally unable to browse the Internet without knowing my age, occupation, gender, and marital status; in return, I get restaurant recommendations based on my favorite foods and flight discounts based on my typical destinations. However convenient, these developments bring along an elicit in-built ideological baggage, which is painfully absent from our customer contracts. Whenever we subscribe to this or that digital service, a small part of our existence gets a digital life of its own. In the process, it moves out of our control—and returns as a control mechanism for our behavior. What is the real price of our "free" restaurant recommendations, flight discounts, and heart monitors? Are we, like ancient American natives, giving away our best skins and gold in exchange for worthless glass pearls? What is the social role of metadata, and how does it relate to relations of consumption and production?

PM: As Evgeny Morozov wrote in The Observer (2014), our "techno-Kafkaesque" world is being subject to algorithmic regulation through technological innovation, and this will get exponentially worse in the coming years. Our daily activities will be monitored by sensors as part of the "smartification" of everyday life. Google will soon mediate, monitor, and report on everything we do. Procter & Gamble has created a Safeguard Germ Alarm that uses sensors to monitor the doors of toilet stalls in public washrooms. The alarm blares once you leave the stall and can only be stopped by the push of the soap-dispensing button. Morozov mentions that Google plans to expand the use of its Android operation system to include smart watches, smart cars, smart thermostats, and more.

Smart mattresses that track your respiration and heart rates and how much you move at night and smartphones that measure how many steps you take each day, or tools that measure how much you spend as opposed to how much you earn (to fight tax fraud) and "advances" such as remotely controlled cars that can be shut down from a distance if you are being pursued by the police—all of these will increasingly regulate your behavior. When Apple patented technology that deploys sensors in your smartphone that can block your texting feature if it is determined that you are driving and talking on your phone, and when face recognition systems are made public to prevent your car from starting should it fail to recognize the face of the driver (and send the picture to the car's owner), we can rejoice or be wary. I am inclined to feel wary. The age of algorithmic regulation stipulates that we will be hived within a cybernetic feedback society in which the systems regulating our behavior maintain their stability by constantly learning and adapting themselves to changing circumstances. Morozov makes the important point that technologies that will detect credit-card fraud or tax fraud will do nothing to hinder superrich families who write tax exemptions into law or who operate offshore schemes that funnel millions into their bank accounts. These technologies will always be evaded by the rich and powerful.

PJ: Of course! Technologies will always be controlled by their owners—I am much more concerned about their users . . .

PM: Morozov cites the Italian philosopher Giorgio Agamben, who writes about the transformation of the idea of government. We have traditional hierarchical relations between causes and effects. We used to be governed by causes. Now this relationship has been inverted, and we are governed by effects. This is emblematic of modernity, according to Agamben. If the government no longer wants to govern the causes but only manages the effects, then we are in for some difficult times. Don't try to find out the causes of diseases; try to keep yourself out of the health-care system by being healthy. It's the insurance company model of algorithmic regulation, according to Morozov. If our heart rates and our blood pressure can be tracked as a means of proactive protection, will we be considered "deviant" if we choose to refuse these devices? Will we be punished, in other words, with higher insurance premiums? In a cybernetically regulated world powered by the proprivatization agenda of Silicon Valley, if we fail to take adequate responsibility for our health, will we be punished? Will we be seen as failures if we fail to keep healthy?

Well, Morozov makes a good point when he says that this lets the fast food companies off the hook, nor does it address class-based differences and questions of inequality. We all should be monitoring the condition of our feces and if we don't self-track sufficiently, then it is our fault if we get sick. Forget the exploitation by the food and pharmaceutical companies! This is what Morozov calls politics without politics—a politics identified with the "nudging state" that relies on metadata. As correlating aggregate data on individuals becomes more sophisticated, data on individuals goes to the highest bidder, as our personal data become state assets. The algorithmic state is reputation-obsessed and entrepreneurial. One day, everybody will be their own brand, and nearly every key social interaction will be ranked. This leads to the culture of resilience in which it is agreed that we cannot prevent threats to our existence, so we must equip ourselves with the necessary savvy to face these threats individually.

So this world that Morozov describes blithely glances over or studiously avoids serious issues facing humanity such as economic equality and emancipation—all that is important in the cybernetic world of feedback mechanisms in real time is the creation of social homeostasis in a world of polished surfaces, aerosol politics, and epidermal social relations of consumption. What is blurred and discounted are the social relations of production and how these relations are connected to the ongoing centralization of the control of the provenance of information. We are faced with an uncritical rehearsal of *Brave New World* (Huxley 1932), and while the soma might taste good, all life is etherized inside the Internet Box.

PJ: Following recent technological developments in collection, storage, and manipulation of digital information, we have landed into the age of big data—and Huxley's brave new world has indeed graduated from science fiction into the real life. Therefore, it is hardly a surprise that various issues pertaining to big data provoke growing attention in diverse research communities from information science to education (see Ford and Jandrić 2019). Please link big data to manipulation. What is the role of science in the struggle against the digital brave new world?

PM: I am sure you are aware, Petar, that social scientists at Cornell University, the University of California, San Francisco (UCSF), and Facebook have revealed the result of a controversial experiment (controversial because it was covert and relied on proprietary data), in an article entitled "Experimental Evidence of Massive-Scale

Emotional Contagion through Social Networks" published online in Proceedings of the National Academy of Sciences of the United States of America (Kramer, Guillory and Hancock 2014). In their attempt to alter the emotions of 600,000 people, these scientists egregiously breached accepted ethical research standards in discovering, apparently, that emotions can spread among users of online social networks, which can be taken to mean that emotions expressed throughout online social networks (in this case in mood-laden texts) can influence or alter the moods of others (they did this via a Facebook-controlled ranking algorithm that regularly filters posts, stories, and activities shared by friends).

It is still unclear if this experiment was funded by the US Army Research Office or some other branch of the US military. Even if it wasn't, learning how to manipulate how we act and feel in social networks such as Facebook obviously has powerful potential for military attempts to control large populations via the Internet, populations worldwide that are fed up with immiseration capitalism and being forced to comply with government austerity programs that hurt the poor and benefit the transnational capitalist class. Of course, an experiment determining whether 1.28 billion Facebook users could potentially be manipulated through "massive-scale emotional contagion through social networks" (Kramer, Guillory and Hancock 2014) is not simply a means of understanding what advertisements people are likely to respond to but is geared to shed scientific light on how to alter people's emotions so that they can be manipulated collectively.

PJ: Collective manipulation has always been a wet dream of the ruling class, but experiments such as this bring its threat to a completely new level.

PM: When you sign up for Facebook, you give a blanket consent to the company's research group to use you as a potential lab rat, as a condition of using the service, so the university researchers in this case obviously took advantage of the fine print to avoid requiring informed consent from the subjects involved. Apparently, however, in the case of the involvement of Cornell University, approval for the research was only given after the data collection had been completed. Because the responsibility for data collection and analysis was given over by the university researchers to Facebook, the academics involved were said to have "not directly engaged in human research and that no review by the Cornell Human Research Protection Program was required" (Cornell University Media Relations Office 2014). Does this mean academic researchers can also team up with any organization, including the US military, and escape ethical restrictions?

Everywhere you go today, you are forced to consume information that has been tested in order to prompt you to contact certain companies, or purchase certain goods, or remember certain information. At airports, in some supermarkets, at some movie theaters, and on billboards. It's very hard to escape this saturation society. But being the target of deliberate emotional manipulation puts us more squarely into the suffocating world of *1984* (Orwell 1949). We are already there. Have you ever had a dream, Petar, in which you are dreaming inside the dream? And then you awake from the dream in your dream, but when you are awake you are still in the dream. Advances in technology help us awake from the dream in the dream, but they do not help us to live outside of the dream, in the domain of wakefulness. Are the advances in technology worth it, when we no longer have the agency to create ourselves, but are merely flesh-like putty in the hands of the government and corporations? This is why critical pedagogy is so urgent today. Another world is possible and critical pedagogy can play a part in its creation. Yes, I believe in transcendence, and unlike Vattimo or Agamben, I don't believe that transcendence cuts off questions prematurely. We need a philosophy of praxis, a Marxist-humanist pedagogy driven by the desire to live in a world of freely associated labor where value production is no longer the motor of human existence.

PJ: What does it mean to reinvent ourselves in the age of the network? Can you please analyze the role of critical pedagogy in that process?

PM: I'm answering your questions now, Petar, from Ensenada, Mexico. Yesterday at *Instituto McLaren de Pedagogia Critica*, I was speaking to my students about the importance of being attentive to the deep cultural assumptions that provide the deep moral and conceptual frameworks for our pedagogies. I was sharing with them some of the important work of C. A. Bowers (2014), who argues that digital technologies cannot represent the tacit knowledge and cultural norms that represent the daily exchanges in people's everyday lives, knowledges that sustain the natural ecologies of diverse groups of people who inhabit our planet. How, for instance, are face-to-face mentoring relationships that have helped to create the educational commons being superseded by computer programs such as Blackboard and print-based storage systems and thinking that are so prominent in digital technologies? How does corporate-controlled media/digital culture promote a particular form of Western individualism dependent upon consumerism and, for instance, the notion that economic development and growth is automatically a good thing—all of which can lead, of course, to further poverty and the loss of natural resources?

Naturally, it can lead to much more—to structural genocide, ecocide, and epistemicide. As you elaborate in your recent paper (Jandrić 2019a), information and data do not amount to wisdom. Bowers cites the neosocial Darwinian and neoliberal perspectives of Hans Moravec and Ray Kurzweil, who argue that digital technologies are at the point of displacing human beings in the process of evolution by way of self-correcting machine intelligence. Here, in Ensenada, I am thinking of the history of the Cochimies, the Pai-Pai, the Kumiai, the Kiliwa, the Cucapa, the Guayaira, the Pericues—what were the so-called great movements of progress that destroyed their cultural commons generations ago? And how many other *pueblos originales* will be destroyed in the future by the evolution of machine intelligence?

Life Is Jerky

PJ: Let's engage in a wee thought experiment, Peter. Imagine two drawers. The first drawer contains all works of arts, music, and literature—Shakespeare, Hemingway, London, Kerouac . . . /Picasso, da Vinci, Michelangelo . . . /Zappa, Mozart, the Rolling Stones . . . you name it, it's there. The second drawer contains all scientific achievements—physics, chemistry, sociology, anthropology, history . . . Which drawer, in your opinion, contains more knowledge about the world around us?

PM: I would choose the first drawer but would try to steal as much from the second drawer when nobody was looking. Actually, I have an interest in quantum theory.

PJ: What do you think about social networking and websites like Facebook?

PM: Facebook promotes people's narcissism. I prefer email. I have a certain visual aesthetic I enjoy in posting photos. It's mostly a vehicle to promote political causes, that's the best part of it—I am sitting at a coffee shop in LA. People are ignoring their companions. They are obsessed with their phones and iPads. People are redundant.

PJ: You are an avid user of digital gadgets—more than half of this book has been written on your smartphone. How do you feel about the tremendous assimilation of information and communication technologies into our daily lives?

(During our online conversation, Peter provided three different short stories about these developments. They share the same general message, but explore different angles and evoke different feelings. I do not feel that it would be right to publish only one of these stories and restrain readers from the pleasure of engaging with others. Therefore, I will merely list the three responses in reverse chronological order.)

PM: Story 1 (June 30, 2014). Today it was raining heavily in Jinhua, China. Black streaks were running down the cheeks of the buildings like mascara on mothers weeping for their lost children. I stopped by a water-logged restaurant that served countryside-style food, with a yearning for some Jiuqu Hongmei tea. After dinner, while I was admiring posters of Chairman Mao and Chairman Hua Guofeng, I noticed about ten young waitresses in orange uniforms in the upstairs dining area. They were all sitting together in the dark, their faces eerily illuminated by their large Samsung cell phones. They were playing games and watching videos. All of them were silent. There was no dialogue. Occasionally a waitress would leave her chair to attend to a customer, and then it was back to the darkened room to the comfort of her cell phone. Outside the restaurant were unpainted concrete buildings and hydroelectric towers. They also stood silent.

PM: Story 2 (June 27, 2014). Recently I visited a 1000-year-old Buddhist Temple in Hangzhou. Sacred figures from Buddhist history were carved out of stone. Gold painted statues of Buddha loomed over the visitors who were both pious and curious. In one temple, at least a hundred monks were chanting in unison, as great clouds of incense wafted through the open doors. Winding my way down from the highest temple on the hill, I noticed one of the monks on his cell phone. Perhaps he was checking the World Cup results? Or calling his condo in Shanghai?

PM: Story 3 (May 25, 2013). I loathe technology, and yet, like many others, I am addicted to it. I hate cell phones, except for use in emergencies, yet I have an iPhone, which I check regularly. I hate the Internet, yet I spend time on the web each day checking what I have found to be reliable sources and authors. I am irritated when people around me are talking loudly on their cell phones. I greatly dislike the consumer hype around cell phone cases, and the like. There is just too much information available. It is overwhelming. Everybody creates their own Internet worlds, publishes their own journals and blogs, and sometimes you find something of interest.

PJ: Please link these insights to the world of academia.

PM: I remember instances where professors in academic institutions who publish their first few books, suddenly become celebrities among their students. They cultivate their image as social critics, shop carefully for their in-class sunglasses, black attire, and the men sport shadow beards that never seem to grow. Their students have little knowledge about whether their professors' work is good or not but they have published some books, so their students treat them as academic celebrities. I feel it's a little bit like the film *American Psycho* (Harron 2000), when so much fuss is made about business cards, the texture of the paper, the print, the color—it's all just image management. Academics get into their Internet worlds, advertise their work, and all of that.

PJ: 2013 issue of *The International Journal of Critical Pedagogy* entitled "Paulo and Nita: Sharing Life, Love, and Intellect" is dedicated to the concept of revolutionary love and its power to challenge oppressive social relationships. Your paper in that issue, "Reflections on love and revolution" (McLaren 2013), shows that the concept of revolutionary love extends from private sphere into important questions such as re-evaluation of the contemporary role of academics. However, Paulo and Nita Freire lived in the world of one-directional mass media such as television and newspapers. Can you relate the concept of revolutionary love to information and communication technologies?

PM: I believe that love is a social relationship as opposed to an entirely private matter. I believe that love can be productive for the collective emancipation of people. One might think that technological innovations—the social media, for example—have enhanced the possibility of love expanding into the collective arena of social development. But the class interests embedded in the social media—that is, the ideology of individual consumption, the commodification of subjectivities (especially the commodified individualism of neoliberal capital with its exclusive and singular morality), the exploitation of the social labor of others (the bourgeois treatment of people as commodities to be "owned" or possessed, which is increased by economic dependency and the social division of labor dominated by property relations)—have disabled the emancipatory potential of love and collective solidarity. Meeting the material needs of people—rather than treating people as "stranded assets" useful only when they can be maximized for their purchasing power by an embrace of market fundamentalism— creates the necessary conditions of possibility for radical love and the solidarity needed to create a world unburdened by value creation, a world committed to freely associated individuals.

PJ: Joe Kincheloe dubbed you "poet laureate of the educational left" (2000: ix). Your first book *Cries from the Corridor* (reprinted and expanded in *Life in Schools* [McLaren 2016]) is widely considered as a masterpiece of literature. In recent years, you started writing poetry (a few of your poems can be found in *MRZine* [2019]). Overall, your unique expression has made a strong influence on the success of your academic work (more about your relationship to writing can be found in the 2008 interview for the University of Waterloo [McLaren, McMurry, and McGuirk 2008]). I would like to learn about the "mechanics" of your writing. How do you write your poems? Do you use pen and paper, or type them on one of your gadgets? How do you write your articles? Do you do everything on screen, or print your articles and work on them in cafés? Why?

PM: Now as for writing—well, that's an interesting process. People approach me now about my idiosyncratic style, and that's something that they didn't do years ago, so maybe that's a sign that I am getting better. But I think people are starting to appreciate it more and more. My present style has to do with the writing I did in the 1960s, my affinity for the Beat Poets, encouragement I got from meeting Allen Ginsberg, Timothy Leary, and a lot of very creative people. When I write a paper, there are sections that are meant to be read. Then there are just sections that are meant to convey ideas. I am trying to bring a lot more young people into critical pedagogy, and they like the spoken-word sense of some of my paragraphs.

Sometimes I will rip pages out of magazines, shuffle them, and then just look for metaphors and strange combinations of words that have little to do with each other. I'm not sure who did the same, I think perhaps William Burroughs. Some people don't like my work because they find it too self-conscious, as if I am trying too hard to be hip, that kind of thing. But that's how I look at the world, I try to bring a little of a lot of different historical selves into my work—artist, poet, activist, essayist, teacher, student, interlocutor—and writing really does depend on how you feel when you put pen to paper, or finger to keyboard. Sometimes I feel more didactic than at other times. Sometimes more like somebody provoking an idea in the manner of McLuhan's "probes" or "mosaics."

PJ: So that's the "mechanics" of your writing. How does it relate to ideas?

PM: I am always trying to point out that ideas don't leap from some metaphysical springboard in our brainpans into a world unsullied and pristine. Our ideas are always populated by other people's meanings, which is another way of saying that they are always subject to systems of mediation—culture, society, environment, mode of production, etc.—and to swindles of fulfillment. The circumstances in which we engage the world as reflective agents consist, partly, of conditions not of our own making. But the limited choices that we have as social agents can make both an immediate and cumulative imprint upon our present reality. Our ideas are never ideas in themselves since their meanings are always relative to the systems that mediate them. Their meanings are also relative to the ways in which we actively exercise those ideas in our existential engagement with others—in other words, they are praxiological. Critical reflexivity demands a critical language and a language of criticism. For instance, theories of ideology can help us understand the politics of commonsense knowledge, how we come to understand the world as we experience it on a day-to-day basis. The idea of retroactive causation (i.e., an effect that posits in own causes, a contingency that retroactively creates its own necessity) can help us ascertain how our actions are not the results of our intentions, but are retroactively posited after the event—we posit, in other words, the very necessity that determines us (Žižek 2012: 466). We often renarrate or resignify our actions after the event in order to take into account the effects or social impact of our actions, without knowing it. Contingency is therefore embedded in every act of knowing.

This idea helps us understand how our actions are not the result of pure intentionality. We unconsciously reclaim our intentions relative to their social impact, normalizing our actions in the process of recreating "reasonable" reasons for them, reconciling our previous understanding with new knowledge of its effects. In addition, a language of critique helps us grasp the idea that because we are part of reality, we can never be neutral with respect to reality. Our unfinishedness as human beings is the result of the unfinishedness of the world, a world that is always in flux. We cannot separate our ways of knowing reality from reality itself. So I write, and rewrite, with the understanding that my thoughts are never completely satisfying or complete, and that they have been shaped by so many experiences that I am still struggling to understand, even years after they occurred, yes, even decades later. I realize that they are always abandoned thoughts, hung out to dry on history's sagging clothesline. For someone who rips them off the clothesline, they may feel like a hair shirt, or a spiked garter. I am sure that's how members of Opus Dei will feel reading my work on liberation theology. But I am heartened by the knowledge that some of the ideas have been worn in battle, not just at the lecture podium, but in the streets, on the picket line, and on the factory floor—and by inmates who have read my work in prisons. Ideas of Che Guevara, Óscar Romero, Hugo Chávez, Paulo Freire, Leonardo Boff, Jesus Christ, and others whom I have tried to make relevant for building a revolutionary critical pedagogy for these challenging times of resurgent fascism worldwide.

I write mostly on scraps of paper with a pen. Then I put them on the computer. Then back to the pen. And back to the computer, and so on. I just hate reading on the computer. I can't do it, even with a big screen. I have to print out drafts and read them on paper. They only make sense to me on paper. The screen is just part of the work process. And then, I need to read my work in page proofs, in the final typeface. Only then can I judge my work. And I am notorious for making last-minute changes in the page proofs. Always, always there are errors in the book or published essays. I always spot them and they always annoy me. There are few good copyeditors anymore—they have all been phased out by journals and publishers that want to pare down the publishing process . . .

PJ: I'm sure that our publishers will be delighted with your last-minute changes. . . . And what about your public talks? How are they related to your writing?

PM: I always hear my own voice when I read my work. I speak the words to myself. I think a lot of work comes to life when the right person is reading it. I enjoy reading my work at conferences because I wouldn't dream of giving a talk unless I felt I had something to say and the things I have to say I feel passionate about. I am not an academic. I don't care much for academic conventions or academic life. In fact, it's a brutal world. I put a lot of energy into my talks, and few people complain that I "read my paper" instead of being spontaneous because they can see that I am very much emotionally invested in the causes that I write about. On occasion I like to break off from reading my paper and be extemporaneous. Now you might be asking: who cares? You are a revolutionary and you shouldn't really care about all the aesthetic details. Just get the message across. Write like a journalist in the most accessible style possible. I respect that type of journalism but I've never been able to sustain that kind of writing. I have given myself permission to be a stylist with the provision that style can never trump substance, and when it does, put away your pen! Today's politics present challenges. But now everyone can retreat into chat rooms where people share your opinions even if at some level you realize your opinion amounts to stark raving hate-filled madness and your unchecked opinions can become an entire world sealed off from real objective facts, and rational arguments. How do we adjudicate our ideas, proceed with argumentation, assess evidence in order to make decisions? We now inhabit a world of your opinion against my opinion. That's the price we pay for living in a posttruth world of tribal war.

PJ: With Carlos Escaño, you made few videos about possibilities for social change such as *Sí se puede* (Yes it is possible) and a funny yet inspiring blend of technological reality and iconic images of Che Guevara called Life is Jerky. What is that all about? Another vehicle to promote political causes, a new way of expressing your ideas, or a mere creative streak?

PM: I was impressed with Carlos' videos where the image jerks around. I thought to myself: That's what life is like a lot of the time. There has been very little smooth sailing in my life. Life is jerky. It shifts around in fits and starts. It's like driving an old car that shakes and then falls apart. All that is left is you sitting on the seat. The rest of the car is in pieces lying all around you. I feel that the journey we call life is a lot like that. I can deal with the jerks, and being jerked around by people, by circumstances, by the technological changes that speed me up or slow me down, but sometimes I wish the road has less bumps. Of course my life has been filled with much personal trauma so the jerks usually don't seem so bad. But when you are jerking around, your imagination is more difficult to focus. So you need a reprieve. I get that in my writing or my creative work.

PJ: Now that we know what Peter the critical theorist thinks of the Internet, we have arrived at the obvious last question: how do you feel about the Internet?

PM: How do I personally feel about the Internet? I feel it is a tremendous source for cranial addiction. My invitations to contribute essays in journals and books used to arrive in the snail mail; you had around nine months to a year to produce a work. Invitations now come fast and furiously and editors expect you to put something together in less than three months. So it does affect the quality of the work in a negative way, but you are able to get your ideas out there in vaster quantities, which is a good thing if you believe that what you have to say is worthwhile in making the world a better place. But you pay a price. It is more difficult to read books carefully, without being interrupted by the Internet, or rather, allowing the Internet to interrupt you. It is a ferocious distraction from things that need to be done. Cell phones take priority over conversations with family and friends. Once you unplug yourself, you enter a world where everyone else is plugged in. It's become a tool of psychological and image management. It's an alternate reality that entraps you and enables you to feel you are bonding with people in a special way when, in fact, you probably don't mean much to those with whom you are corresponding. For many young people today, it has become a source for bullying, for deception. Just going through hundreds of email messages a day, to see which ones are relevant to your life, takes hours.

Look what Donald Trump has done with tweets. He has sent US democracy reeling, systems of governance have been shattered, the regulatory power of the state has been unmasked as a hideous charade, demagoguery has been normalized and hate speech weaponized into high-grade ideological plutonium, our immortal souls have been algorithmically uploaded in computers ensepulchered in Weber's iron cage set in a global cemetery while our zombified bodies feed on corpses from freshly dug graves, and democracy may not recover. You see, democracy has already been destroyed in a technological apocalypse, and we can only see it in our rearview mirrors as we drive past the wreckage into new oblivions of our own making. I have often fantasized about just getting away from technology, and keeping a ham radio available in case I'm on a boat crossing the Atlantic and a storm is approaching and, say, my companions in the boat are a tiger, an orangutan, a zebra, and a hyena . . .

4

The Critical Challenge of Networked Learning: Using Information Technologies in the Service of Humanity

Critical Learning in Digital Networks

PJ: During the 1970s the relationships between technologies, education, and society attracted a combination of positive curiosity and awe from important critical theorists such as Ivan Illich (1971, 1973) and Everett Reimer (1971). Kahn and Kellner situate economic development through technological modernization processes as the "fourth major platform of the Freirean program"—alongside literacy, radical democracy, and critical consciousness (2007: 434). Back in 2000, you wrote:

> The globalization of capital, the move toward post-Fordist economic arrangements of flexible specialization, and the consolidation of neoliberal educational policies demand not only a vigorous and ongoing engagement with Freire's work, but also a reinvention of Freire in the context of current debates over information technologies and learning, global economic restructuring, and the effort to develop new modes of revolutionary struggle. (McLaren 2000: 15)

Do you think that information and communication technologies are adequately represented in the contemporary discourse of critical education? More generally, what are the basic prerequisites for reinvention of critical education in the context of information and communication technologies?

PM: No, I don't think information and communication technologies are adequately represented in much of the work that falls under the rubric of critical education. As to my previous description of capitalism, I wouldn't describe it today using the same post-Fordist language. As an explanatory principle, I would instead employ the concept by David Harvey of "accumulation by dispossession" and various other Marxist analyses of global capitalism and finance capitalism. I have used analyses of the transnational capitalist class and transnational capitalist state developed by William I. Robinson. Robinson has been accused by critics for maintaining that the nation-state has disappeared or lost its relevance in this era of transnational capital. In my opinion, many of his critics are incorrect on this point. When Robinson asserts the supersession of the nation-state as the organizing principle of capitalism, he still clearly maintains that the nation-state and the interstate system play key roles but that their relationship to capital changes throughout the relations of transnationalization. At no point does Robinson maintain that transnational capitalism is free-floating. The neoliberal state and state power are central to global capitalism, as capitalism cannot exist solely as a market relationship detached from state power, and here Robinson identifies a major political contradiction in that economic globalization takes place within a nation-state-based system that authorizes and legitimizes state power. What is different now is that capitalist development no longer organizes itself primarily into competing national capitals but rather through a "rescaling" of capital so that major spaces of capital are no longer fashioned within a nation-state/interstate system.

This assertion has been repeatedly distorted by Robinson's critics who claim that he views the nation-state and the interstate system as no longer relevant. What he is referring to by asserting the supersession of the nation-state as the organizing principle of capitalism is that as the commanding heights of capital have become integrated transnationally, capital no longer organizes itself into competing national capitals and nation-states that drive capitalist development. Robinson argues that this capitalist development takes place in emergent transnational space and through "rescaling" so that the most significant "spaces of capital" today are no longer organized as a nation-state/interstate system.

Okay, let me bring this conversation back to the concept of schooling. Schooling in most Western countries has been successful to the extent that it has refused to examine itself outside of the hive of capitalist ideology and its cloistered elitism and cold calculus of exploitation—its precepts, its concepts, its epistemicides, and its various literacies of power through which ideas become slurred over time and actions on their behalf are guaranteed to remain as dissipated as a roistering fisherman drunk at sea. It has accepted the fact that answers will remain predesigned before questions can even be formulated. The vision of democracy is inevitably preformed and must be engraved on the minds of its citizens through ideological state apparatuses such as schools (Althusser 2008). As long as the ideas of the ruling class rule us, and they can certainly rule us with the help of new information and communication technologies, what I call state mediaverses for shaping the will without breaking the spirit (to echo Christian fundamentalist James Dobson), we will be hapless apprentices to the anguish of the oppressed.

Teaching can be designed to appear transgressive while at the same time ideas will be guaranteed to remain vacant, hidden in a thicket of "feel-good" bourgeois aesthetics designed to create an intergenerational dependency. The complicity of these ideas with inequality bulks as large as its opposition to it, making it an appropriate ideological form for late capitalist society. Such ideas will be guaranteed not to disturb the comfort zones of those who tenaciously cling to the belief that with hard work and a steel-tempered will, they will reap the rewards of the American Dream—regardless of their race, class, or geographical location. The question for me is, therefore, what role do the new information technologies play in critical education? Do they enhance the mystification and control of dominant Western culture and its ruling factions, or do they enable us to further penetrate such mystification and take action that is both necessary and sufficient to create a different kind of society—a socialist society that is not based on labor's value form?

I don't think that this question has been sufficiently addressed by critical educators. I believe that with a focused imagination, and the courage to suspend at least temporarily our faith in all that we hold dearly as immutable fact, that we can come to see how we see, that we can come to understand how we understand, that we can come to experience how we experience. That we can come to realize that our experiences are not transparent, they are not self-evident, and that they are, in fact, the effects of a constellation of economic, political, and social relationships. We read the world conjuncturally, and relationally, and according to the lexicons that are available to us and which we fight to make available. We need to distinguish pedagogical vernaculars and systems of intelligibility that have been stamped with the imprimatur of sociability and consent and those that have been deemed oppositional and counterhegemonic/ contestatory/revolutionary. But armed with critical lexicons that have been forged in blood-soaked struggles by those who have over centuries fought against the forces of domination and exploitation through poetry, art, philosophy, literature, politics, science, technology, and a search for justice and equality, we can envision and create a new world. And finally, we can see those things that interdict a learner's ability to read the word and the world critically (Freire 1972). The fulcrum of our exigency is cultivating critical consciousness and a categorical obligation to treat others as ends in themselves and not as a means to something else. Can the new information technologies help us to read the word and the world more critically? Can they become one of the new critical lexicons that can assist the current generation in creating a world less infused with the injustices that are evident everywhere that we look?

PJ: Where should we start approaching these questions?

PM: As Zygmunt Bauman (2007, 2012) and others have argued, vulnerability and uncertainty are the foundation of all political power. The protective functions of the state were once directed toward mitigating the extent that citizens were at the mercy of the vulnerability and uncertainty of the market, but in the era of asset capitalism those protections for the unemployable were brutally rescinded by Thatcher and Reagan as the welfare state was systematically dismantled. Government restraints upon market forces and business activities were removed. The market regained its omniscience. Market-generated insecurity that the state could no longer shield its citizens against had to be replaced by something more ominous—the zombies of the underclass—those who were not able to participate in the market. They were pushed into incarceration, the school-to-prison pipeline, or shot on the streets by policemen recruited into highly militarized and fascistic law enforcement agencies. Entrenched and indomitable structures of privilege and power were no longer acknowledged as the poor and powerless were now held responsible for their own immiseration. They were not longer to be protected but instead had to be criminalized for the sake of order-building and full spectrum control of the mind and body. This is a biopolitics beyond biopower. It portends to more than introducing the "zoe" into the sphere of the polis, transforming the relationship between "species being" and man as political subject, but refers to forms of state power that actually usurp the spirit by identifying the spirit as a form of will.

The state acts through what I would call pneumaexitium, the destruction of the spirit without the breaking the will. The will can be broken, but it's bad politics, much like ruling by overt torture. But the spirit cannot be broken, it can only be discovered anew. The grand deception of today's state formations is that they are able to operate through communication technologies that equate the spirit with nothing more than a software platform—the will to produce information. The human will has been reduced to "willingness." A willingness to cooperate, to compete, to produce in the service of the state. The spirit has disappeared entirely, without making a grand exit, so few of us have noticed. The spirit is that subjunctive part of humanity that transcends time and space, the structure of possibility inherent in consciousness itself that enables our energies, efforts, and sufferings to contribute to the arc of liberation, even long after our bodies have been pulverized into dust. We participate in this arc of liberation today in our resistance to the current marketization of the spirit. That history has been cruel.

Those who were unable to participate successfully in the market were held responsible for their own failure instead of being benevolently assisted as personalized solutions were now expected to challenge the systemic contradictions of the capitalist marketplace. The uncomplacent and increasingly belligerent state had to augment the insecurity of the market by intensifying it, transferring its legitimacy to its ability to protect the public from state terrorists through preemptive wars and drone assassinations, etc., and a profligacy of heinous acts justified as protecting its citizenry and its interests. Any state devoted to abolishing terror must itself inspire terror and in fact become more terrifying than the terrorists whom it purports to be fighting. However, this crisis of capitalism has been able to demonstrate to many that egalitarian justice can only be achieved against capitalism, that justice for all cannot be achieved within the framework of a capitalist market economy. For me, the question is—do new information and communication technologies help us or hinder us (or both) in our search for a democratic socialist world outside of the value form of labor?

PJ: For some people, the Internet has brought dematerialization and deterritorialization of labor—for instance, I am writing this text on a beautiful terrace overlooking the Adriatic Sea in ancient Croatian city of Split—while you are, as my Facebook suggests this morning, just about to give keynote talk in Ensenada, Mexico. However, while the Internet provides us—two white male university teachers—with the opportunity to share ideas from restaurants and cafés throughout the world, people who serve our coffees and lunches (who, by the way, also make the majority of contemporary workforce) are still strongly tied to their kitchens and dining halls. Indeed, Peter, it is really hard not to notice strong ties between technology-driven changes in structure of employment and traditional sources of inequality including but not limited to class, race, and gender.

Similarly, the dominating discourse of digital learning does not seem to offer its main promise in increased quality, or personalized content, or creating virtual communities, or whatever information and communication technologies could actually contribute to critical education (in most cases, the contested notion of "quality" is nothing but a smokescreen for marketization of education). Given that the majority of online learners are still white and well-off—at least those enrolled in official accredited programs—it is just as hard not to notice traditional sources of inequality (Jandrić and Boras 2012 and 2015). However, let us take one step at a time. What are the leading ideas behind educational changes driven by contemporary information and communication technologies? Which gospel do they preach?

PM: Excellent points, Petar. The United States is, with good reason, counting on technology to serve as an ideological weapon of death by soft power, death by a thousand cuts across the digitalized brain. For State Department officials and the Pentagon, technology serves as a form of high-tech imperialism, a means to reshape the world's people geopolitically, to transform other populations and nations into likenesses of itself. These Washington warmongers turned imperial geeks who control the world's informational supply chain get themselves into a state of abject bewilderment when some of those peoples (usually those with darker complexions) refuse to take on the values and practices of the world's dominant superpower. The mind-makeover that technology has given us is really death by digital lobotomy because consumer technology has removed the imagination and replaced it with the artificial dreamscape of Google-run-trend analysis—social network profiled—consumer fantasies and heralded it as open democracy. It has firewalled the self, interposing technologies of surveillance between "us" and "them" attempting to turn "them" into "us." It has replaced the struggle for critical citizenship with consumer citizenship and rebranded it as "progress" and, furthermore, labeled any of the world's refuseniks of the American vision of world government as potential terrorists.

Here, I am modifying somewhat Tony Smith's four positions in the globalization debate: the Social-State, Neoliberal, Catalytic-State, Democratic-Cosmopolitan, and Marxist models of globalization (Smith 2009). However, I am not arguing, as Smith does, that a market socialism is the way to go, since I have my doubts about whether the market can be democratized. Those individuals that cannot be integrated into the economy, those who have neither the opportunity nor the means to sell their labor power nor to distribute knowledge, those who are permanently excluded from participation in the market and deemed redundant are criminalized and made productive in the privatized prison system, becoming the guinea pigs for state experiments on spatial and racial apartheid, and technologies of discipline, control, and punishment, preparing the future for totalitarian regimes of which there will be no escape because they will be premised on epistemicide, the destruction of alternative languages of being and becoming the forced disappearance of indigenous ecologies of the mind. There will be no space outside the "what is." There will be no subjunctive mode of consciousness, no "what if?" There will only be the past of the future of the past—that which "will be" will already have come "to pass." We will all be living with an ideological version of the Moebius syndrome.

The key concern for me is the monopoly–oligopoly control of the mass media through the ownership of the means of communication. Those who own the means of communication are obviously associated with other powerful interest groups that are linked to banks and investment firms, hedge funds, etc. Has the mass media ever sided with labor over capital, with the poor over the rich, with the popular majorities over the banks in any major way? The corporate media dominate the flow and access of information and select what is viewed by the public and in what light. Have you ever seen the corporate media critique capitalism or the "free market"? Critical pedagogy provides a countervailing power of ideological critique and class-based organization and struggle. That's what we need for the struggle ahead for a socialist alternative to capitalism. When the term "robot" entered the English language a few years after the release of Czech playwright, Karel Čapek's *R.U.R. (Rosumovi Univerzální Roboti* or *Rossum's Universal Robots)* in 1920 (Čapek 2001), a fear was spawned that humans would become the servants of artificial intelligence. That fear was not unfounded. Not even remotely so.

PJ: As we discussed earlier, what matters most is who owns the technology. However, Peter, ownership can take various forms. For instance, animal lovers know very well that cats and dogs relate with their human "owners" in very different ways—and those differences are built into the very nature of their species. Information and communication technologies are significantly different from their analog predecessors. In one of my favorite descriptions of the dialectical relationships between information and communication technologies and the network society, Manuel Castells asserts that

> [t]he Internet is the fabric of our lives. If information technology is the present-day equivalent of electricity in the industrial era, in our age the Internet could both be linked to the electrical grid and the electric engine because of its ability to distribute the power of information throughout the entire realm of human activity. (Castells 2001: 1)

It seems reasonable to ask: What happens to ownership over technologies during the transition from the mass society to the network society? How does it relate to wider issues such as democracy, global economy, and the concept of the state?

PM: Clearly, Petar, we have entered into a knowledge-based society and are the unwilling servants of a knowledge-based economy. The free flow of information has certainly been hijacked by neoliberal capitalism in its development of informational restructuring of capital. There is a distinct concentration of corporate power and much of this is related, obviously, to the growth of Internet access and informatics. But, as Julian Assange put it recently: "The Internet, our greatest tool of emancipation, has been transformed into the most dangerous facilitator of totalitarianism we have ever seen" (Assange et al. 2012: 1).

In *Cypherpunks: Freedom and the Future of the Internet* (Assange et al. 2012), Assange puts forward an unambiguous—and I dare say poetic—indictment of government and corporate surveillance, anti file-sharing legislation, and the social media phenomenon that has seen users willingly collaborate with sites such as Google, Facebook, and Twitter who wish to collect their personal data. Assange famously described the Internet as similar to "having a tank in your bedroom" (Assange et al. 2012: 33) and wrote that a mobile phone serves merely as a "tracking device that also makes calls" (Assange et al. 2012: 49). To me that sounded like early critics of television who said that television programs are just filler for the advertisements (which is essentially true today, perhaps even more so than in the past). Assange continues with the ominous prediction that "the universality of the Internet will merge global humanity into one giant grid of mass surveillance and mass control" (Assange et al. 2012: 6). Resistance must therefore include encrypting your online activity, so that it will be possible to create an information network that the state will not be able to decipher.

I am in agreement with Assange, essentially, that we are moving very quickly toward a transnational dystopia, in particular, a postmodern surveillance dystopia. Initially Assange was hopeful "that the nature of states, which are defined by how people exchange information, economic value, and force, would also change" (Assange et al. 2012: 2). There certainly was, at the dawn of the information society, the possibility that "the merger between existing state structures and the Internet created an opening to change the nature of states" (Assange et al. 2012: 2). That is, there appeared for a short time the possibility of rebuilding the state from the bottom up through the use of information technologies, which would help to produce more participatory and direct forms of democracy.

PJ: This seems like a very violent way of looking at things!

PM: Assange is clear about the violence brewing just below the surface of the state. He notes: "Most of the time we are not even aware of how close to violence we are, because we all grant concessions to avoid it. Like sailors smelling the breeze, we rarely contemplate how our surface world is propped up from below by darkness" (Assange et al. 2012: 3). He juxtaposes the platonic realm of the Internet to the fascist designs of the state—designs given force by the seizure of the physical infrastructure that makes the global Internet culture possible—fiber optic cables, satellites and their ground stations, computer servers. We are no longer safe within Plato's cave. Everything produced inside the cave has been hijacked, stored in secret warehouses the size of small cities, and freighted by a cornucopia of codes and security firewalls vomited up by computer geeks who watch *Revenge of the Nerds* and *American Pie* in their spare time. Creating a frightening imbalance of power between computer users and those that have the power to sort through and control the information generated in networld. The only force that Assange sees capable of saving democracy is the creation of a "cryptographic veil" to hide the location of our cybernetic platonic caves and to continue to use our knowledge to redefine the state.

So what are the costs of being part of social media networks? We give away our habits, our preferences, our demographics, our purchasing habits, and our cyberhistory. Do we go the route of nanopayments—some kind of democratic remuneration for our intellectual and biometric property, for information we currently give away for free, in our attempt to remuneration create a humanistic and egalitarian information economy as Jaron Lanier suggests in his influential book *You Are Not a Gadget* (2011), or do we take other forms of resistance?

I am certainly convinced that information technologies have facilitated a global reorganization of the market, but to what ends? Markets have been reorganized but they still betray a global division of labor. Are we not still dealing with a relation of exploitation in which workers, separated from the means of production, are compelled to sell their living labor power from which the capitalist extracts surplus value? And is not the laboring subject still the key protagonistic force with the greatest potential to bring down capital?

PJ: Since we already embarked on that path—let's try and provide a more rounded image of the dark side of technology.

PM: Erica Etelson has recently published a wonderful short piece on the perils of technology that I like very much. She describes perils that include economic crisis, war, pandemic disease, and ecological collapse. While clearly technology has helped to sustain seven billion people on our planet, it is unlikely to be able to do so for much longer, even with anticipated innovations. Her point, of course, is that "modern communication technologies may have reached a tipped point where what is authentically created and shared is overshadowed by market-driven, corporate-generated content that is sold or imposed" (Etelson 2014). I think by her definition I might be considered a neo-Luddite—a tradesman or artisan engaged in class protest against "all Machinery hurtful to Commonality"—or what Etelson (2014) describes as "forms of mechanization that damaged people and uprooted communities by forcing skilled workers to become wage slaves in factories."

Firstly, she argues forcefully that technology makes us less resilient, as we are "utterly dependent on the seamless functioning of a fabulously complex global superstructure with millions of impersonal moving parts, none of which most of us have even passing acquaintance with." To illustrate that point, she cites the history of the Arctic Ihalmiut who lost the ability to hunt with bow and arrow after they acquired rifles. Secondly, she also notes that as techno-literacy expands, eco-literacy contracts. The more tech-savvy we become, the more eco-ignorant we become, as we now know more and more about less and less. Etelson also argues that environmental degradation created by technology spawns hubris, as we prefer our techno-nannies to care for us over human community and solidarity. She argues that technology fuels hyperconsumption, as products become cheaper, and it diverts our focus "from natural to human-made wonders."

Thirdly, Etelson argues that "the wicked knot of inertia, corruption and hubris" in which we are inextricably trapped, which is part and parcel of our "techno-topian delusion" accelerates environmental ruin, resource depletion, and resource wars. We are at the cusp of the sixth mass extinction. Our nonrenewable resources are being depleted, atmospheric carbon is at the tipping point, and renewable resources such as forests, aquifers, and fisheries are being stripped faster than they are being regenerated. World conflicts now center around natural gas, water, oil, minerals, metals, and food. Fourthly, she argues that technology carries very frightening risks. We can't presume products are safe until proven harmful. Etelson uses the example of cell phones and Wi-Fi, widely adopted despite 75 percent of nonindustry sponsored studies that claim that cell phones damage our DNA. Brain cancer in children has increased 1 percent a year for the past twenty years. If the cleaning up of Fukushima goes amiss (this kind of cleanup has never occurred before), the entire West Coast of the United States might have to be evacuated, not to mention what will happen in Japan itself. And then there is hydrofracking and the endless contamination of our water sources.

Fifthly, Etelson argues that technology often diminishes rather than enriches our quality of life. We turn to machines rather than to people. Etelson's sixth point is that technology erodes our privacy—do we need to go further here than the revelations of Julian Assange and Edward Snowden? Seventh, technology deepens inequality. The US manufacturing worker productivity has increased more than eightfold since 1947, thanks to robotics, etc. But we haven't seen higher wages for workers. Or shorter working hours. Corporations own 46 percent of global wealth. Even if we had a democratic socialist utopia, Etelson argues that too much productivity—even if the profits were shared more equitably—would lead to more pollution. Technology-induced unemployment is a serious problem. It would take five planet earths to enable everyone to have the same standard of living that we have in North America.

We already have most of the technologies we need to live comfortably and we don't need more unnecessary technologies. Etelson offers some strategies such as stripping corporations of constitutional personhood, replacing the Gross Domestic Product indicator with the Genuine Progress Indicator (which takes stock of the risk factors of technology), and she has some other suggestions, of course. But Petar, the situation is dire, our world is shattering, imploding, and crying out to us to stop!

PJ: The question concerning technology inevitably brings us to the classic Marxist theme—the dichotomy between capital and labor—thus fully supporting your critique of postmodernism. Having said that, let us not forget that traditional Marxism is also strongly based on substantive critique of technologies. Marx's attitudes toward technology are often generally outlined by the famous quote from *The Poverty of Philosophy—Answer to the Philosophy of Poverty by M. Proudhon*: "The windmill gives you society with the feudal lord; the steam mill, society with the industrial capitalist" (Marx 1955). What do information and communication technologies give us regarding the contemporary relationship between capital and labor?

PM: That's the key relationship driving our entire social universe, our entire world! Capital's political command over labor power is the central antagonism facing capitalist societies worldwide. I agree with some of the autonomist Marxists that capitalism does use technological renovation as a weapon to defeat the working class and that this certainly helps to explain capital's tendency to expand the proportion of dead or "constant" capital as against living or "variable" capital involved in the production process. The proliferation of information and communication technologies has to be understood in the context of the struggle between capital and labor. But capital still remains dependent on collective labor as the source of surplus value. So capitalism has constantly to reorganize itself through a recomposition of the state—today we find this as an inexorable push toward social fascism—and to recompose the workforce—whether under the umbrella of lifelong learning strategies, telecommunications, flexible labor policies, a growth of the service economy, and the criminalization of those who cannot compete in the workforce and then privatizing the prisons and turning them into sites of surplus value production.

While it is true that in *The Grundrisse*, Marx anticipated that one day knowledge as a form of the objectified general intellect (general social knowledge) will become a direct force of production, not subjected to existing industrial regimes, new concepts designed to capture labor–capital antagonisms such as "cognitive capitalism" (understood as the most recent phase of capitalism) or "immaterial or digital labor processes" can have some explanatory power here. For instance, new Web 2.0 technologies that have impacted the mode of production and have refashioned our conception of labor to a certain extent. The works of autonomous Marxists have clearly provided us with some important insights into workers' self-organization and have assisted our understanding of how intellectual property rights, copyright laws, the circulation and distribution of proprietary information, and corporate sponsorships within various knowledge sector industries can create artificial conditions of relative scarcity. Where I depart from some of the theories of immaterial labor is that I view the growing technological potential of the knowledge industry as a productive force in advanced capitalist countries as linked to the physical infrastructure—a privately owned infrastructure—in which the digital commons are dependent. Hence it is material production processes—the ownership of data by corporations and the selling of user information to advertisers—that anchor the digital economy. The cultural commons created by various digital architectures and platforms—no matter how community-based they are—remain ripe for exploitation as long as there exists private ownership of the means of production.

Clearly, the world could be headed toward the type of informatics dystopia dominated by the guardians of the security state, as Assange notes. But that of course does not rule out entirely the use of information and communication technology to create sites of resistance and transformation. As technological innovation becomes a permanent feature of capitalist relations of production within the new network society, production becomes intensified around cultivating new consumers by producing "transhumans" with new needs, as countries in the global periphery are turned into a giant factory and others are turned into giant fortresses of consumption. Network society is trapped within structured inequalities, and there is strong evidence that information and communication technology is further entrenching such structured inequality rather than abating it.

As long as capital governs technology (and not the other way around) in its attempts to commodify every niche of the lifeworld, technology will perilously serve as an instrument of converting all aspects of nature into commodity form, rupturing and turning into raw materials whatever planetary metabolism remains life-sustaining. The technoscientific agenda of capital is ominous and has resulted in epistemicide and the destruction of many indigenous approaches to the relationship between humans and planetary ecosystems. While there are efforts to create counter knowledge that take into account self-reflexivity and recursive interactions between nature and technology, how can they be delinked from capitalist appropriation of social knowledge in all of its forms? Marx talked about the possibility of machines becoming organs of participation in nature. But capital will always hijack this process, which is why we need to create a social universe that is not ruled by the sovereignty of labor's value form.

The violently wielded dominative power of machine technology cannot be contested through the creation of a noncapitalist commonwealth based on democratic principles. We can't turn our intellectual activity into intellectual capital so that it becomes an appropriated commodity form by universities or other corporatized entities. The same with online teaching in virtual learning factories where what cannot be digitalized loses value and significance.

PJ: What happens to human beings in the contemporary struggle between capital and labor?

PM: Petar, we have a responsibility for our personal role in history, and we need to know how it contributes, wittingly or unwittingly, to the oppression of the poor and the powerless. In our work we cannot romanticize the proletariat, and divide the world into some kind of brute, simplified Manichean divide—on the one side, we have the good socialists and revolutionaries and on the other side, we have the evil capitalists most of whom reside in the Western democracies. Why? Because socialists and revolutionaries have woven into the tapestry of their subjectivity, their agency, capitalist desires. We are as contaminated by capitalism and imbued with the spirit of the bourgeoisie as much as the waters bathing the fuel rods from the storage pool at the Fukushima Daiichi nuclear power plant are saturated by radiation.

We need to recognize that critical educators are cultural workers from various constituencies that continue to build upon a global, class-conscious, anti-racist, feminist movement, and whose participants can be found at the forefront of the important struggles of our day, fighting as nonbinary abolitionists, as queer activists rupturing the seemingly seamless hegemony of cisheteronormativity, as public intellectuals, as feminists, as persons of religious faith, as atheists, as freedom fighters opposing the school-to-prison pipeline, as trans activists, prounion organizers, antiracists, democratic socialists, antifascists, Marxist humanists, as environmental activists, as land rights warriors, as anarchists and antiwar activists. Critical educators are themselves willing to be educated—we certainly hope!—and are struggling to overcome the violence of our white supremacist capitalist patriarchy through the radical transformation of our social, cultural, and economic universe.

Revolutionaries can win by means of a seizure of power through protest—look what happened in Egypt, for example—but this is not enough since what often happens is that such an assault on power reproduces in greater proportions the logic of fascism and militarism that the revolution was intended to eliminate. Nor do I subscribe to the notion that before we engage in revolutionary struggle, we must undergo some kind of quasi-religious conversion to socialism, for that is merely a recipe for the indefinite postponement of the revolution. We are all accomplices to capitalism; we are bathed in the fetid and putrid waters of commercialism and imbibe the vapors of consumerism. Even if we are able to expropriate from the expropriators, what good will this do if we still are subjectively capital as Glenn Rikowski and others have noted? We have become capital! We are the enfleshment of capital!

We don't want to re-establish the bourgeois oppression we carry within ourselves, as both victim and victimizer. We must root out our desire for personal gain—founded on the illusion that we are guided by "self-interest" or personal gain—but that is not easy. What distinguishes us from self-interested animals is our obligation to serve others less fortunate, to treat all human beings as ends and not as a means for something else, to treat everyone with dignity. (Now of course I don't treat fascists with dignity, but I would hope that I could convince them to treat others with dignity and thus be themselves transformed in the process.) Witness so many revolutions that have turned into their opposite. This requires the development of a philosophy of praxis. Right now in the United States, we are experiencing the slaying in cold blood of black men with impunity by the police. This to me cannot be resolved by simply examining our values or attitudes and trying to understand how racism is constructed by the media and throughout our everyday lives—although this is certainly an important task.

PJ: Please say more about racism—by and large, this important theme is absent from discussions about technology.

PM: I want here to share some ideas summarized by the eminent sociologist William I. Robinson (2014). Robinson identifies three distinct types of racist structures—structures that scaffold relations between dominant and minority groups. He refers to the first structure as "middle men minorities," the second as "super-exploitation/disorganization of the working class," and the third as "appropriation of natural resources." He is writing about these in relation to the current global war economy we are living amidst, what he refers to as "militarized accumulation to control and contain the downtrodden and marginalized and to sustain accumulation in the face of crisis," which Robinson believes are giving rise to fascist political tendencies and to a pregenocidal politics. In the first racist structure,

> the minority group has a relationship of mediation between the dominant and the subordinate groups. This was historically the experience of Chinese overseas traders in Asia, Lebanese and Syrians in West Africa, Indians in East Africa, Coloureds in South Africa, and Jews in Europe. When "middle men minorities" lose their function as structures change they can be absorbed into the new order or can become subject to scapegoating and even genocide. (Robinson 2014)

With respect to the second type of racist structure—"super-exploitation/disorganization of the working class"—we see the racially subordinate and oppressed sector within the exploited class occupying the lowest rungs of the particular economy and society within a racially or ethnically stratified working class. Robinson expands on this idea as follows:

> What is key here is that the labor of the subordinate group—that is, their bodies, their existence—is needed by the dominant system even if the group experiences cultural and social marginalization and political disenfranchisement. This was the historical post-slavery experience of African-Americans in the United States, as well as that of the Irish in Britain, Latinos/as currently in the United States, Mayan Indians in Guatemala, Africans in South Africa under apartheid, and so on. These groups are often subordinated socially, culturally and politically, either de facto or de jure. They represent the super-exploited and discriminated sector of racially and ethnically divided working and popular classes. (Robinson 2014)

The third racist structure summarized by Robinson is exclusion and appropriation of natural resources. Here, the dominant system needs the resources of the subordinate group but not their labor—that is, their physical existence is not useful or needed. Robinson identifies this structure as the one most likely to lead to genocide. He writes:

> It was the experience of Native Americans in North America. Dominant groups needed their land, but not their labor or their bodies—since African slaves and European immigrants provided the labor needed for the new system—and so they experienced genocide. It has been the experience of the indigenous groups in Amazonia—vast new mineral and energy resources have been discovered on their lands, yet their bodies stand in the way of access to these resources by transnational capital, literally, and are not needed, hence there are today genocidal pressures in Amazonia.
>
> This is the more recent condition that African-Americans face in the United States. Many African-Americans went from being the super-exploited sector of the working class to being marginalized as employers switched from drawing on black labor to Latino/an immigrant labor as a super-exploited workforce. As African-Americans have become structurally marginalized in significant number, they are subject to heightened disenfranchisement, criminalization, a bogus "war on drugs," mass incarceration and police and state terror, seen by the system as necessary to control a superfluous and potentially rebellious population. (Robinson 2014)

So here, you see, the African Americans are no longer needed for their labor. They have been replaced. They are now considered to be superfluous and expendable. They are put in the school-to-prison pipeline. They serve as cheap labor in the prisons, that's all. The Palestinians are now superfluous populations in Israel, their labor has been replaced by African, Asian, and other migrants. Here in the United States, when you have an expendable population, it doesn't resort to genocide as we normally think of it, because the political and ideological conditions are not fully present, but perhaps we are in a kind of pregenocidal state. In order to challenge this situation, I am calling for a philosophy of praxis grounded in the concrete and historical and its contemporary applicability. Julian Assange recently called Google the privatized arm of the NSA. So I would ask: How can we marshal a philosophy of praxis in the service of twenty-first-century socialism in the face of twenty-first-century fascism?

We Need to Stop Being Academics and Start Becoming Activists

PJ: *The First International Conference on Critical Education* was held in Athens at the beginning of July 2011—during the short period of peace between two violent antigovernment demonstrations. You, Dave Hill, Kostas Skordoulis, me, and few other comrades sat at a small terrace on Exarcheia square in Athens. The night was hot, and the square was full of broken glass. While we slowly sipped our drinks and discussed the political situation in the Western Balkans, I remember looking down at my comfy flip-flops, then to your robust Doc Martens boots, then again at my flip-flops, and feeling embarrassed: if the police arrive, how am I gonna run in those shoes?

During the past years, we have seen an upsurge in usage of information and communication technologies for social change in movements from Latin America to Arab Spring. Considering that the majority of physical Internet infrastructure lies in firm grasp of the establishment, how do you see the potentials of information and communication technologies for contemporary social struggles? Can they be compared to open flip-flops, comfy but too gentle for revolutionary activities, or to robust military boots, heavy but always ready for action?

PM: I like your use of metaphor! You capture the situation well. I have to say that since Athens my Doc Martens have given way to sneakers, the result of a knee replacement. But all the better to run from the riot police, assuming I am even able to run with this artificial knee. As to your question, I would say that, in the main, we need to strive for cooperative, freely associated labor that is not value-producing. We need to look to the new social movements and uprisings throughout the world for new organizational forms, including those of non-Western peoples. New forms of organization that reflect our new ways of thinking. But no matter how we are thinking about a subject, it will be of little use if our imagination in out of focus. Blueprints are only temporary— and sometimes necessary—artifices in a world of imaginative thinking. Socialism is not an inevitability, despite what teleologically driven Marxists might tell you. Right now capitalism is reorganizing itself and attempting to reconstitute the working class by criminalizing it and disaggregating its revolutionary potential through new information and communication technologies. Can democracy survive this historical self-immolation? I would say, no, not without the rise of social fascism. And then what kind of democracy would that be? A democracy in name only—which is not far from what we already have in the United States at the moment. We are not assisted in our struggle by academicians, whether they are technical utilitarians, naturalist skeptics, ill-tempered empiricists, or postmodern antifoundationalists unless they are prepared to argue that ethical judgments comprise the fundamental condition of possibility for scientific reasoning of all sorts.

Let me rehearse a bit of what I said earlier on before I get into the potential of information and communication technologies to usher in some kind of meaningful alternative to capitalism. Clearly, immaterial labor—crowdsourcing, digital labor, free access, communally generated production, cognitive activities, and affective and embodied performances—does not escape circuits of capitalist exploitation and control. Reorganization of our lives through better self-management is not the answer because we need transnational movements of resistance. We can all now shop at thrift stores, wear woolen Tibetan hats, drink kale smoothies, be Coney Island-of-the-Mind-bohemians, look cool in our Cuban shades, and create "affirm my coolness please!" blogs. But so what? Working-class resistance is continually being undermined through information and communication technology. Immaterial production is not the production of ideas that float through space like a papier-mâché asteroid affixed on a blue screen with wallpaper paste, spinning through the galaxy of our remastered universe but the production of a class relation, the reproduction of a specific division of labor, and despite what affective or emotion labor we might produce through our user-generated content platforms, what cognitive spectacles and identity performances we might contribute to the mediaverse through our art house communties, we know who is winning the class war and it is not the working class.

Digitalized globalization has redivided labor on a transnational scale. We cannot make history through our own volition, that is, without the cooperation of the social world, which is the crucible in which our human will is forged and enjoined with spirit. We are produced, let's face it, as market relations, objectified social relations, as commodity formations, and thus are *de facto* proletariats; we exist as human capital, as formations of bourgeois subjectivity, even if we prefer to (mistakenly) think of ourselves as cognitariats who work in realms autonomous or partially autonomous from capital. This notion that because we operate in collective decision-making networks that are supposedly free from the snares of capital, that we actually are free from the snares, is keenly wrong-headed. We have already consented to the rule of capital, even as we supposedly make "free" democratic choices in our exchanges and activities. We are not really free to make free exchanges (even if we carry paper or metal straws) although we mistake them as free exchanges because we do not see the objectified and impersonal forces that underlie such exchanges—we can resist capital only because we are constituted by it even as we caterwaul against it.

PJ: Living in a capitalist society, we lose our freedom to make free choices. How can we regain this freedom?

PM: Glenn Rikowski notes that labor power has a reality only within the person and "is generally under the sway of a potentially hostile will" (McLaren 2006; McLaren and Rikowski 2001). Here we are talking about socially average labor power that uniquely constitutes value—this is the foundation of the abstract labor that forms value. Human labor power at the socially average constitutes value; concrete labor does not constitute value. No matter what the level of technological development, without human labor power there is no value and no capital. However, as we undergo the process of schooling, we are being transformed into a new life form: capital. But our social existence as labor places limits on our existence as capital, making us a living contradiction in the social universe of capital—these are the contingencies of consciousness and protagonistic action. We are in a process of becoming, and we have the capacity to struggle against that which society has made of us that we no longer want to be. That capacity is available to us because of our unfinishedness, because of spirit which enables us to engage the untested feasibility of our world not as a limit situation but as an orthopraxis contributing to our greater humanity, as Paulo Freire might put it. We do this, Rikowski reminds us, by abolishing the social relations and forces that nurture and sustain capital and capitalist society. Rikowski makes the important point that technologies are concrete expressions of the social production of labor power and the generation of value and the increase of relative surplus value in the labor process. We can fight for free expression of our productive capacities and free association with other workers in productive works. We need to use our labor capacity outside and beyond capitalist production relations. This is what critical pedagogy is all about—that is why it is often called revolutionary.

Of course capital has colonized spheres of circulation and reproduction as the social conditions for generating corporate profit have proliferated and intensified with the advent of the information society. I think much of the discussion of issues such as the economic wage versus the social wage, productive versus reproductive labor, and the factory versus the knowledge industry is useful, especially in the context of discussions of sexism and racism and how they are reconfigured within the new social factory and knowledge economy. And of course, we know that in order to fight back, social movements need to fight in global, regional, national, and transnational struggles— and the challenge is how to articulate them in our struggles against the global economy, multilateral financial institutions such as the World Trade Organization and the International Monetary Fund, nonstate actors such as corporations, and the transnational capitalist class.

PJ: Contemporary media are packed with examples of various social movements powered by information and communication technologies. . . . Perhaps that is the way to go?

PM: Yes, I know that the popular Korean boy band Dong Ban Shin Ki sparked a nationwide protest over the purchase of meat produced in the United States during fears of a mad cow disease epidemic and almost destroyed the presidency of South Korea's Lee Myung-bak. That is true. And there are many other examples of Internet protests carrying tremendous power and force, but the truth is that just as in the case of analog media you need a break to get access to public attention in the digital media. Sure, you can publish all the time, and there are plenty of people out there who are worth listening to (we have what Clay Shirky (2011) calls "cognitive surplus"), but who is going to listen to you unless you are already a celebrity or somebody that has some credibility? Or somebody who is a celebrity but has lost political credibility. So do we get sports figures explaining the relationship between inequality and racism or Miley Cyrus showing us the path to socialism? We already have Kayne West in a Make America Great Again (MAGA) hat explaining the history of slavery to African Americans. And look how that has worked out. We know that you need leverage to get a wide audience and not everybody will be able to affect such leverage, as Mathew Battles (2011) points out, because the transmedia conglomerates are more successful leveraging their power in the world media of scarcity. Basically, they dominate the traffic, as Battles puts it.

PJ: Your example hits the nail on the head. Obviously, the problem is much deeper than simple instrumental inquiry into the possible ways of using technology in order to produce this or that social outcome. In this place, it is worthwhile to revisit a famous passage from Martin Heidegger's *The Question Concerning Technology*:

> Likewise, the essence of technology is by no means anything technological. Thus we shall never experience our relationship to the essence of technology so long as we merely conceive and push forward the technological, put up with it, or evade it. Everywhere we remain unfree and chained to technology, whether we passionately affirm or deny it. But we are delivered over to it in the worst possible way when we regard it as something neutral; for this conception of it, to which today we particularly like to do homage, makes us utterly blind to the essence of technology. (Heidegger 1977: 4)

Information and communication technologies are dialectically chained to our reality and cannot be either dismissed or idealized. Therefore, the only remaining option is to try and position them appropriately in the wider fabric of our everyday praxis. What happens next with revolutionary critical pedagogy in the context of the network society?

PM: Speaking only about my own contribution, my goal is to participate in transnational interactions from below—from the exploited and the excluded—and this may be called a counterhegemonic globalization process if you want. These are local struggles that need to be globalized—and we know what they are. Boaventura de Sousa Santos has listed some of these as transnational solidarity networks, new labor internationalism, international networks of alternative legal aid, transnational human rights organizations, feminist movements, indigenous movements, ecological movements, alternative development movements and associations, literary, artistic, and scientific movements on the periphery of the world system in search of nonimperialist, antihegemonic cultural and educational values (Dalea and Robertson 2004). As to the issue of how to struggle and how information technologies could help, let me repeat some comments I made with respect to my trip to Turkey in 2013 (McLaren and Fassbinder 2013).

For one thing, all of the movements that I have witnessed of late—the Occupy Movement, the uprising in Greece, protests of university students in Mexico, the Indignados, etc.—are making more than minor demands. They are struggling for an entirely different kind of future, and the originality and creativity of their protests speak to that future. They are not just about negating the present but about reclaiming large-scale space—parks, public squares, university buildings, and other spaces—where they can enact a new, more horizontal form of governance and decision-making. They are moving beyond narrow sectarian interests and seeking to put participatory democracy into practice as an alternative to vertical forms of organization favored by liberal, representative democracy. And, of course, they are fighting state authoritarianism. They are seeking to challenge consumer citizens to become critical citizens again, as many citizens strove to become before the era of asset capitalism or neoliberal capitalism.

But the movement goes beyond nostalgia for the past—since most of the youth have only known neoliberal capitalism all of their lives. The youth have also figured out that parliamentary forms of representation can no longer suffice in creating democracy in a social universe of asset or finance capitalism, which requires a neofascist reorganization of the state in order to preserve massive profits for the transnational capitalist class. Youth protesters today are struggling for participatory forms of association using new social media and new convergent media production as digital tools, as technological literacies to educate themselves and their comrades to link their experiences of struggle to goal-directed actions. They are struggling for different forms of social life through their protests against neoextractivism, unequal ecological exchange rates, high tuition fees in education, and the chaos the capitalist class has decreed into law by treating rabid corporations as people.

PJ: You said that most of the youth have only known neoliberal capitalism all of their lives—and I would add that most of the youth have only known information and communication technologies all of their lives. Those observations deeply resonate with the shared experience of my generation in Croatia—we had the "privilege" to live in communism and capitalism, in the world of analog television and in the world of broadband Internet, in the world sharply divided between two major blocs and in the globalized world of today, in the mass society and in the network society. However, not everyone has had the opportunity to experience various political systems and technologies. Most countries such as the United States, Cuba, France, or China have only experienced one political system; a large part of world's population is still on the nonprivileged side of the digital divide and has never seen a computer.

Based on biological age at which information and communication technologies have been introduced into people's lives, in the seminal article *Digital Natives, Digital Immigrants*, Marc Prensky (2001) divides our contemporary population in two distinct categories. Digital natives are people who were born into the world of information and communication technologies—for them, using computers and touchscreens comes as naturally as acquisition of mother tongue. Digital immigrants are people who encountered information and communication technologies later in their lives and had to put conscious effort into learning how to use them—therefore, their command of digital artifacts will always bear traces of predigital ways of thinking. Certainly, this is a principled rather than analytic distinction, which has recently provoked a lot of critique (e.g., Bayne and Ross 2011)—the global South is populated by hundreds of millions of underage digital immigrants, while the global North sports a smaller but equally impressive number of digital natives in their twenties and thirties. Despite theoretical imprecisions, however, Prensky's distinction opens several interesting questions. What are the main strategies of using information and communication technologies in contemporary social movements? Are they digitally native or digitally immigrant?

PM: Those are important questions, Petar. In contemporary youth social movements, the digital media do not become ends in themselves but augment or supplement real-world experiences of struggle for popular sovereignty—and in the case of the Zapatistas in Chiapas, the Idle No More struggles of First Nations peoples in Canada or the Purépecha nation in Cherán, Mexico, an autonomous community within the state. As a result of these struggles, these tools become more integrated as part of an effort to creative a collective intelligence with multiple visions of a socially just or at least fairer and more equitable world. As Greek scholar and activist, Panagiotis Sotiris, wrote,

> contrary to the supposedly post-modern tendency towards virtual communities digitally connecting fragmented individuals, as expressed in various cyberspace trends, but also in the whole concept of a potential online "democracy" and "consultation," nothing can beat the appeal and the power of people meeting in the street, joining forces, creating communities of struggle and resistance. (Sotiris 2013)

According to the semiofficial Anadolu Agency news service, during a recent protest in Izmir, police have arrested twenty-five people on accusations of using social media networks such as Twitter to spread false details about the antigovernment protests and police reaction to them. Many youth can see that the survival of neoliberal capitalism requires the state to reorganize itself in more fascist formations—and this is no less true of the youth in Turkey, where many young people in support of a secular state are fearful of the intolerance towards diverse lifestyles by the Islamist-rooted government. Again, as Panagiotis Sotiris lucidly proclaims:

> The importance of youth in all these movements should not lead us to treat them as student or youth movements. Rather, youth who are at the epicentre of the current capitalist attempt to change the balance of forces in favor of capital, and are being treated in some cases as a "lost generation," and almost always as the generation that will receive the full blow of capitalist restructuring, act like the vanguard of more generalized and deeper forms of discontent. This has to do with the particular quality of youth as potential labor power. Contemporary youth are more educated, more skilled and at the same time face precarization and the consequences of the economic crisis. However, they have the communication skills to make their discontent more evident than ever and are in a position to create networks of struggle and solidarity, thus making themselves more than instrumental for the creation of new public spaces, both real and virtual. (Sotiris 2013)

I strongly agree with this observation of Sotiris and with his conviction that these movements are also productive sites of knowledge and potentially counterhegemonic projects. He makes profound sense when he argues, additionally, that the left needs to be more proactive in helping to transform such movements from spontaneous uprisings to historical blocs in the Gramscian sense that involve

> combinations between social forces, new forms of political organization and new social configurations as alternative narratives that do not simply repeat historical left-wing projects, but actually attempt to think how to move beyond neoliberal capitalism . . . from the current "age of insurrections" to a new "age of revolutions." (Sotiris 2013)

That said, I do believe there is an ongoing danger of communitarian popular fronts. Think of Poland and Iran in 1979–1981. Mass movements in these countries were taken over by Catholic reactionaries in the former and Islamic fundamentalists in the latter, and both movements had progressive elements such as women's movements and workers' councils. Political parties have a history of taking over various forms of spontaneous movements. Think of the Hobbit Camps in 1970s Italy that combined fascism, neo-traditionalism, and anti-capitalism. I think popular-frontism could become reified as the "lost generation" versus the bankers and hedge fund profiteers (Sotiris 2013). We have to be wary of the struggle becoming the "good capitalists" who are against monopolies, etc., versus the unproductive parasites in the finance sector who accumulate their fortunes on the shoulders of others who are forced to sell their labor power for a wage. We must begin to wage a struggle for an alternative to capitalism based on the creation of real wealth rather than the value form of labor. For me, social justice is more than a plastic Jesus sitting on the dashboard of my mind. It is the grit and fiber of class and cultural struggle in a world that too often watches with indifference.

Who Wants to Be Downloaded?

PJ: A bit earlier, you briefly mentioned that education is opposed to schooling—and I simply could not let this passing remark unnoticed. Radical thinkers have always heavily despised schools. Schools have been accused—and rightfully so—for many evils such as social reproduction, indoctrination, failing to respect individual needs of their patrons, stupefying. . . . In order to fight against those evils, radical educators have developed an impressive body of educational alternatives, which have replaced institutionalized schools by less formal approaches. However, only the rare and the few have dared to challenge the very essence of the concept of schooling.

Far on the fringes of educational praxis, much further than "regular" radicals who oppose traditional schools because they inculcate the wrong ideas or fail to respect pupils' personality, there is a small stream of educators that wants to completely abandon the concept of schooling. Those people agree that education is an intrinsic part of human nature: we all learn and unlearn from cradle to grave. However, they point out that schooling is an institutionalized process of meeting certain educational outcomes. They are not against education: they merely claim that the process of education is completely detached from the process of schooling, and that schools should be replaced in favor of more efficient educational processes. In the recent study, Joséph Todd describes the project of deschooling as follows: "Anarchists and deschoolers, as well as educational theorists, argue for the creation of networks, as opposed to institutions, that are temporary, autonomous, and nonhierarchical, and facilitate a variety of diverse models of learning and community interaction" (Todd 2012: 78).

The genesis of argument against schooling can be traced in several major works such as Everett Reimer's *School is Dead* (1971), Paul Goodman's *Compulsory Miseducation* (1973), and Matt Hern's *Deschooling Our Lives* (1998). Back in 1971, however, the small book called *Deschooling Society* has provoked worldwide debates about the future of schooling and has placed Ivan Illich on the unofficial throne of the project of deschooling. Such positioning of Illich's work has not arrived from thin air. According to Atasay, "what distinguishes Illich's work from other critiques of industrial everyday life (. . .) is that Illich offers us alternatives, tools that can influence power and offer individuals and communal settings the potential for alternative vernacular practices to emerge in culture" (2013: 58). In order to replace traditional schools, Illich proposes creating a large-scale noninstitutional educational infrastructure, which consists of a set of four interlocking educational networks: reference services to educational objects, skill exchanges, peer-matching, and reference services to educators-at-large (Illich 1971).

Based on that proposition, Hart concludes that "it is not too far-fetched to assert that Illich predicted the World Wide Web" (2001: 72). In my recent work, I have thoroughly analyzed various features of contemporary information and communication technologies and concluded that they provide adequate technical infrastructure for Illich's educational networks (Jandrić 2011; Jandrić and Boras 2012: 72–74; Jandrić 2014b, 2015). During a recent conversation, your former student Tyson Marsh told me that you extensively used Illich's work during doctoral seminars. Can you evaluate contemporary potentials of deschooling for critical revolutionary pedagogy?

PM: Here perhaps I have more questions for you than answers. I have been blessed with former students like Tyson Marsh and Richard Kahn. We obviously are all invested pedagogically in the following question: How can we help students teetering on the precipice of despair? A well-tempered chorus of answers has been forthcoming from a variety of perspectives, as we all know. But my questions are as follows: Can the technological infrastructure of which you speak realize the goal of Illich's deschooling society such that the youth of today are not simply left to generate individual solutions to problems produced by and enmeshed within the structural inequalities wrought by capitalism? How can you avoid such infrastructure remaining tethered to capitalism without first creating spaces in which capitalist relations of production and consumption are not reproduced? Can the Internet help produce such spaces? Do they exist, and where? If the subjectivities produced in your Illich-inspired infrastructure remain trapped in the thrall of the value form of labor, then the pedagogical imperative guiding the construction of such an infrastructure cannot remain consistent with its own principles since it will remain hospitable with the view that social justice is possible within a capitalist society; so how can your infrastructure remain autonomous from capital? There is no solution on the horizon that commands uncontested authority, I admit, so that we must continue to experiment. We cannot prevent the future by banning *a priori* the admissibility that another form of education is possible, perhaps a new digital humanism can be created through forms of postsymbolic communication, which breach the prescribed boundaries between bodies and minds, but are such forms possible only within infuriatingly rare niche "online" communities? And what would the environmental costs be of the manufacturing of your infrastructure? Would it perhaps prolong adolescence, as Jaron Lanier (2011) warns?

Illich wrote in *Deschooling Society* (1971) that "Man now defines himself as the furnace which burns up the values produced by his tools. And there is no limit to his capacity. His is the act of Prometheus carried to an extreme." Is network society another Promethean fallacy? Near the end of *Deschooling Society*, he again writes:

> The Pythia of Delphi has now been replaced by a computer which hovers above the panels and punch cards. The hexameters of the oracle have given way to 16-bit codes of instructions. Man the helmsman has turned the rudder over to the cybernetic machine. The ultimate machine emerges to direct our destinies. (Illich 1971)

If humankind is the helmsman, then who builds the ship? And in *Tools for Conviviality*, Illich writes:

> Honesty requires that we each recognize the need to limit procreation, consumption and waste, but equally we must radically reduce our expectations that machines will do our work for us or that therapists can make us learned or healthy. The only solution to the environmental crisis is the shared insight of people that they would be happier if they could work together and care for each other. Such an inversion of the current world view requires intellectual courage, for it exposes us to the unenlightened yet painful criticism of being not only anti-people and

against economic progress, but equally against liberal education and scientific and technological advance. We must face the fact that the imbalance between man and the environment is just one of several mutually reinforcing stresses, each distorting the balance of life in a different dimension. In this view, overpopulation is the result of a distortion in the balance of learning, dependence on affluence is the result of a radical monopoly of institutional over personal values, and faulty technology is inexorably consequent upon a transformation of means into ends. (Illich 1973)

PJ: You touched upon a very interesting and urgent matter: the relationships between online and offline public spheres, between online and offline participation in the society.

PM: Yes, okay, here is the problem as I see it. The Internet and social media provide a kind of limbic cave, a space of refuge for us to vent our emotions, reactivate our most torpid memories, and quiet our most primal fears, and eventually to focus our rage on everything and everyone we hate—and love. We find people who share our beliefs and who resent the same people and situations and we communicate with them on a daily basis, and given that the Internet is so vast, we can tap into a considerable number of like-minded people who can validate and animate our obsessions, whether those have to do with Kim Kardashian's buttocks or Birkenstock sandals, or whether Shakespeare wrote his own plays or whether it was Edward de Vere, 17th Earl of Oxford. We can shut out opposing groups, and not be called upon to debate and defend our ideas. We isolate ourselves in a fiber optic cocoon; we form our own hive, where we protect ourselves from being accountable for our opinions. We are uncomfortable going out into the real world because suddenly we are being asked uncomfortable questions that we really don't know how to answer. We feel threatened by the real world of public participation because we have just been living this rage through our self-confirming, self-affirming group of Internet companions.

This has a polarizing effect on the national culture. People are drawn into camps and barricade themselves from participating in the public sphere. Young white men in the United States who are fearful of the impending demographic winter (when white people fail to reproduce in sufficient numbers to prevent people of color from overtaking them demographically) seeth in university classrooms when some "snowflake" professor like me raises the topic of white privilege. They might secretly be having wet dreams about becoming the next Richard Spencer. People think they are participating, but they are merely communicating in an echo chamber with people who reflect their own ideas. This goes for the left as much as the right, although those terms have often become toxified into meaningless designations today. Even when people do debate real issues, they do so in formats where their ideas are reduced to soundbytes. I was once on a TV talk show in Hollywood, where during the commercial break the producer asked me to overturn a table in anger. I refused to do it. And I refused to let the host set the terms of the discussion. The show was never aired. So what does this tell us about public participation in reinvigorating the public sphere?

PJ: During the hippie revolution, computers had been developed and used primarily in isolated basements of scientific institutes—with a strong military presence dating at least from World War II and Alan Touring's hacking of Enigma. During the 1970s and 1980s, computers had slowly gained commercial applications in large-scale industry and service sector institutions such as banks and insurance companies. Finally, sometime during the 1990s, the marriage between the personal computer and broadband Internet inspired numerous applications in the broadest field of education from informal language courses to accredited university degrees. At the brink of the millennia, the next big thing in education was called numerous names such as "multimedia learning, technology-enhanced learning (TEL), computer-based instruction (CBI), computer-based training (CBT), computer-assisted instruction or computer-aided instruction (CAI), Internet-based training (IBT), web-based training (WBT), online education, virtual education, virtual learning environments (VLE) (which are also called learning platforms), m-learning, and digital educational collaboration" (this list is from Wikipedia (2019b), which seems to reflect the latest changes in the field).

The "new" approaches to education have seemed to offer a lot of promise regarding the optimization of educational processes. However, the past few decades have brought a growing body of research which points toward the dark side of the marriage between education and information and communication technologies. In their Foucauldian analysis of education, Fejes and Nicoll have succinctly summarized its main problems in the conclusion that "discourses of e-learning have tended largely to construct the area of study as about the mechanics of its implementation (the appropriate use of technology in education, the effective delivery of educational messages, the efficient systems for materials production and so on)" (2008: 174). What is your take on the promise of online education?

PM: Well, that's a complicated question, Petar. Many of my colleagues in various universities who have fallen prey to digital settlers are out there creating new learning management systems for all of us, professors, to jump on board and become part of the new techno-utopia of online learning. I don't think cybernetic systems of information are the best way to apprehend reality and I don't buy into the cyber-armageddon-catacylsm eschatology that humans will become obsolete when machines get more sophisticated and we are run by nonhuman or meta-human nanorobots. Call me "old school" if you wish.

Developments in information and communication technologies and the creation of cyberinfrastructures certainly effect the production and dissemination of knowledge—knowledge flows, and new modalities of teaching and learning. Open Learning and Open Innovation, E-learning and Cyberlearning, user-generated and user-created media, networked learning, etc., provide opportunities for more customized and individualized learning. This is all good and exciting as far as our imagination is concerned. Social networks such as Facebook, LinkedIn, Flickr, Second Life, World of Warcraft, Wikipedia, Ning, and YouTube and Peer-to-Peer (P2P) networks are part of the new wave of knowledge production and consumption. Some would herald this as the new communism in the sense that the rhizomatic network has replaced the isolated individual as the unit of analysis and has the potential to bring about new ecologies of participation and meaning-making and perhaps a new digital socialism for the twenty-first century. My concern is that it will bring about new formations of ideological production in which each process of our identity formation will be reterritorialized and rewired to the initiatives and interests of the state.

I like what Brian McKenna says in his recent wide-ranging article on this topic. In *The Predatory Pedagogy of Online Education*, McKenna (2013) quotes the author of *Digital Diploma Mills*, David Noble, who writes:

> Once faculty and courses go online, administrators gain much greater direct control over faculty performance and course content than ever before and the potential for administrative scrutiny, supervision, regimentation, discipline and even censorship increase dramatically. At the same time, the use of the technology entails an inevitable extension of working time and an intensification of work as faculty struggle at all hours of the day and night to stay on top of the technology and respond, via chat rooms, virtual office hours, and e-mail, to both students and administrators to whom they have now become instantly and continuously accessible. The technology also allows for much more careful administrative monitoring of faculty availability, activities, and responsiveness. (Noble 2001)

In support of Noble's comment, McKenna (2013) makes the following lucid observation: "With the introduction of advanced corporate learning platforms many teachers will watch what they say in class. There are topics and dialogic digressions that many will not want recorded and made available for administrators to scrutinize." McKenna also cites Richard Sennett (2012), who makes a case for face-to-face interaction, drawing from the work of Saul Alinsky and Jane Addams. Sennett writes that "modern society is 'deskilling' people in practicing cooperation" (2012: 8). In other words, "people are losing skills to deal with intractable differences as material inequality isolates them, short-term labor makes their social contacts more superficial and activates anxiety about the Other" (Sennett 2012: 9). For McKenna, online education offers capital another avenue for appropriating the process of knowledge production. He is worth quoting at length:

> A rereading of Harry Braverman's classic, Labor and Monopoly Capital (1974: 1998) is necessary. Braverman conducted an ethnographic analysis of the labor process and revealed how capital (1) appropriates all historical knowledge from the craftsmen, (2) separate conception from execution and (3) employs the new found monopoly of knowledge to control every step of the labor process and hire unskilled workers who are interchangeable and cheap. It's called Taylorization, or scientific management. The new technology makes this amazingly simple. Joanne Bujes points out one aspect of this invasion: "they will pick 100 teachers and get them on tape for e-learning. And then professors will be reduced to grad students leading a discussion section once a week. Are people going to go into debt half their lives for this?" (McKenna 2013)

PJ: This dark note resonates with many important topics such as literacy, morality, and self-realization (see Jandrić 2019b) . . .

PM: It does indeed. I agree with Barry Sanders in his book, *A Is for Ox* (1995), that oralicy, the precursor to literacy and abstract thinking, demands human interaction, and was often nurtured by storytelling mothers, and this helped develop the imagination so necessary to reading readiness. Now, however, the development of vernacular language is being replaced by video games and Internet culture and Silicon Valley dreams, and youth today are less likely to engage in print literacy through books—which contributes mightily to violence in today's society. Sanders, a student of Ivan Illich, is, of course, onto something important when he argues that we are seeing among our youth the disappearance of self-literacy through an engagement with reading books and the creation of the inner space of morality. Reading books provides the foundation for self-reflexive moral choices and that foundation has been eroded through Internet culture. I have always supported critical media literacy in schools, and of course, teacher education programs. Of course, we can argue that students acquire multiple literacies today via Internet culture and social networking—in their formation as transhumans within the metaverse of the Internet—but we have to keep examining how these multiple literacies fare in creating the foundations of moral reasoning, as distinct from the forms of moral reasoning that readers acquire by engaging in print literacy—all of which takes me back to my days in Canada reading Marshall McLuhan.

My own take is quite similar to Sanders' in many respects, however, as I do feel what makes us human through our social interactions—creating a "haptic" sense of life—is slowly dying. Sanders links the rise of humanity's disembodiment to the industrial revolution, and he draws our attention, for instance, to the technology-enabled slaughter of the American Civil War and World War I. Sanders makes the claim that modernity and the enlightenment confronted the disappearance of human beings and their commodification. Postmodernity only produced a more tragic state. What began to connect us—the telephone, the telegraph, fax machines, and the Internet—can now be seen in hindsight as the formation of a world, where we became more connected but in ways that actually produced more isolation from our humanity—something Sherry Turkle has noted in her book *Alone Together* (2012). As we fall prey to the all-pervasive influence of corporations and their attempts to re-create us into a desiring machine (desiring what the corporations have to sell us), we have become a less mindful, less vigilant citizenry, watching passively as civil life becomes swallowed up by the logic of capital, consumption, and corporatism. People no longer seem to want to become actors—they want to become celebrities.

PJ: And "influencers"—whatever that means.

PM: Our rhizomatic culture has become corralled by capital, so that it appears as if we are autonomous and in a constant state of self-actualization, but in reality we are making ourselves more vulnerable to the crippling control of Big Brother. Of course, it is easy to sink into a dystopian malaise and to be so fearful of the future that we end up in the thrall of paralysis. For me, technologies are not something to be feared for the electric age has brought us wonderful treasures. The problem is how they have been harnessed by capital, and how we have been harnessed along with them, how we have been capitalized, how we have become capital, and how these technologies have helped in that process. For some, however, technology is a direct instrument of demonic forces!

Let's hear from a Catholic priest, Father Kevin Cusick of the Archdiocese of Washington, D.C., who claimed on Twitter that God supports his ban on women's bare shoulders. He wants women to cover their shoulders to protect men's purity. He was attacked on Twitter, and his response was to compare his struggle to that of Jesus on the cross. He also went on an anti-LGBTQ harangue. Here is Father Cusick's opinion of Twitter:

> Twitter has a dark, demonic side, raging against God and the Church . . .
>
> That brood of vipers and braying, bloodthirsty hounds lurking in readiness was visited upon me with nearly unrelenting fury and incredible magnitude last week. . . . Wave after wave of calumnious, blasphemous, and obscene memes, gifs, and messages were posted with comments, likes, and retweets ranging up to the tens of thousands. Those who styled themselves my enemies crowed with pleasure that I had been "ratioed"—when negative comments outnumber likes and retweets. Many called for me to delete my account when they weren't wishing a more horrible fate upon me. Blue check mark accounts with nearly 200k followers piled on. (Badash 2019)

Father Cusick's solution was to delete his Twitter account. But now we know that demons command the stone-cold hearts of Twitter users. Thank you for alerting us, Father.

PJ: So we have extreme observations from clearly crazed religious autocrats, Peter, but let's return to some sobriety. What about real problems pertaining to technology, such as automation of work and potential technological unemployment?

PM: Your recent book *Education and Technological Unemployment* (Peters, Jandrić, and Means 2019) speaks about the rise of the robot work force. Authors in the book mention how so-called experts maintain the view that technology has made human beings more productive—that is, making office workers more productive through word processing, or making surgeons more productive through robotics in the operating room; and the argument is always that new jobs unheard of today will be made possible by the technology of tomorrow. Other experts are not so sure. Your book highlights how machines today are beginning to be able to learn rather than follow instructions— for instance, some of them are now able to respond to human language and movement. We have self-driving vehicles that could eventually put truck drivers and taxi drivers out of work. Sales agents and pilots will decline as flying is more automated and as software does most of the flying and placing search ads. Telemarketers are also at risk. Even physical therapists are at risk by machines that recognize and correct a person's movements. Machines are learning children's expressions and estimating their pain levels. The Thai government has a robot that tastes Thai food and estimates whether it tastes sufficiently "authentic." The computer system called Watson advises military veterans on where to live and which insurance to buy. It also creates new recipes for chefs. A third of a panel of leading economists admitted that technology is centrally implicated in the stagnation of median wages. And all of this weak wage growth is occurring amidst surging corporate profits. The US government continually weakens what few safeguards there are left to help regulate the market and prevent the kind of savage inequality we are experiencing from getting exponentially worse. Are we entering the age of *Blade Runner*, among perhaps the most famous of the dystopian films? I think that is the trajectory we are on. How far we will go depends upon the nature, purpose, and function of the social movements we create to intervene into and replace transnational capitalism with a socialist alternative.

PJ: What is the role of critical pedagogy in these processes?

PM: The idea always is to make the political more pedagogical and the pedagogical more political. It has, I believe, a number of important implications, Petar, for critical pedagogy. As I have written elsewhere, capitalism as a discourse is self-validating and self-perpetuating and as a social relation works as a self-fueling engine whose capacity to travel around the globe and devour everything in its path is expanding exponentially. As a discourse and social practice that in its current neoliberal incarnation shatters collective experience into monadic bits and pieces, bifurcating students' relationship to their bodies, brutally taxonomizing human behavior into mind and body, into manual and mental labor, capitalism is a colossus that bestrides the world, wreaking havoc. It possesses a terrible power of psychologizing entrenched and dependent hierarchies of power and privilege and reformulating them into homogeneous and private individual experiences. So that 99 percent of the world are made to feel responsible for their plight.

Let me repeat what I have said before on many occasions—even using the same metaphors. To fight this juggernaut of cruelty that would profit from the tears of the poor if it knew how to market them effectively, critical pedagogy flouts the frontier between scholarship and activism and, as such, works to create a counterpublic sphere. We are askew to traditional academia and are not enmortgaged to its status and do not represent the ivory tower. Many of us loathe academia as it stands and are flailing away inside the system trying to make changes. Yes, we work in the academy but are not traditional academics. And yes, we are complicit in its contradictions. Sure, we sometimes use a rarefied language but we want to mediate human needs and social relations in publicly discussable form, so as to create a commonality of purpose, a species of solidarity able to withstand the plutocracies arrayed against us, a transnational social movement of aggressively oppositional power.

However, critical pedagogy is not yet in a position to play a substantial role in the struggle for a socialist future. Not in North America, in my view. At least not yet. We need to find ways of helping teachers to become agents of revolutionary transformation. As I wrote in my book *Pedagogy of Insurrection* (McLaren 2015b) we need to transition, to pivot, from a pedagogy of insurrection to a pedagogy of revolution. But this is becoming more difficult in an academy that is moving on a path to intellectual oblivion, political complacency, and civic ineptitude. Today academia is becoming more about negotiating prestige than furthering knowledge; about inflicting revenge for insignificant injuries and personal slights; about ratifying the paralysis of theory over the importance—no, the necessity—of praxis; about replacing the historical grasp of theory with impious sloganeering and empty rhetorical formulations; about replacing debate with debacle; about enforcing opinion and flavor-of-the-day ideas over argumentation; about fostering the promotional worth of stardom and the quivering thrall of fandom over the collective worth of the community; about throwing in one's lot with the board of governors rather than governing in the service of the common good, of the commonweal; about turning critiques of commodity culture into commodity criticism; about encouraging us to long for more than the system permits us to achieve while electrifying the barriers of that same system; about glorifying our serfdom to our ambitions yet enforcing our own dissatisfaction with our achievements; about preaching social justice and laying claim to political authenticity while spending weekends at luxury item outlets and bourgeois health spas; about accepting positions in the hierarchy of power and privilege yet appointing the most corrupt and ruthless members to the top of that hierarchy.

The history of technology is that of a lost horizon, a forgotten future. Today, where we have seen our humanity collapsing like scorched lungs in a wildfire, we know that we—as humans—will reemerge again. We will reappear on the horizon again, one that is being reclaimed today in the smouldering haze of tear gas and struggle. A new revolutionary consciousness is being born that seeks to use technology in the service of humanity—to fight disease, to feed the poor, to eliminate poverty, to save the biosphere, to reclaim dignity for all of us. If you can silence your mind for a moment, take your eyes off your computer screen, and turn off your cell phone, you will hear it. In the darkness of an eclipsed moon, in the unfamiliar air of things-to-come, you will hear the sweltering gasp of a new humanity. Let us not dull our senses so much by extending them digitally such that we do not hear it. Let us listen with our imagination, remembering always that thought is spirit.

Revolutionary Critical Pedagogy
Meets Liberation Theology

5

From Liberation to Salvation: Revolutionary Critical Pedagogy Meets Liberation Theology

PJ: Please describe your journey to liberation theology, Peter. Did you experience some kind of transcendental experience; did you arrive at liberation pedagogy by the way of intellectual development; or perhaps both?

PM: The short answer: both. But there's even more to it. I am aware that many of our readers might be unfamiliar with the political history of South America, so please permit me to provide some context for my discussion of the theology of liberation. Before I begin, I need to tell you that I have not had any formal training in theology but as a Catholic convert and a Marxist educator, I have for a long time followed the work of a number of theologians associated with this tradition. In my teenage years, I contemplated going into the priesthood but became swept away by the indulgences of every kind and stripe that were available in the 1960s and my life has been anything but priestly. I converted to Catholicism later in my life, in my thirties, having been raised an Anglican. But my mother, Frances Teresa Bernadette McLaren, was, as you might guess from her name, Catholic and my father, Lawrence Omand McLaren, was brought up Presbyterian. They wanted to raise me in a religious tradition separate from theirs. And St. Luke's Anglican parish wasn't too far from where I lived in Winnipeg, Manitoba, during my formative years.

I became serious about revolutionary politics about the time of my conversion to Catholicism, while I was studying for my PhD in Toronto, and at the same time I was drawn to numerous spiritual traditions. Not long after I moved to the United States and took up a position at Miami University of Ohio, I began receiving invitations to speak in Latin America and the Caribbean, eventually over the years working with educators and activist groups in Argentina, Mexico, Peru, Brazil, Colombia, Venezuela, Cuba, Puerto Rico, and Costa Rica. Well, the late 1960s, 1970s, and 1980s were especially brutal years for campesinos, workers, activists, teachers, and revolutionaries throughout Latin America, especially in the Southern Cone. After the government assassination of six Jesuit scholars, their housekeeper, and her daughter on November 16, 1989, on the campus of Universidad Centroamericana in San Salvador, El Salvador, the world finally started to take serious notice, especially since the archbishop of San Salvador, Óscar Romero, had been assassinated in 1980 while offering mass in the chapel of the Hospital of Divine Providence after famously speaking out against poverty, social injustice, and torture. Romero has recently been made a saint—not an event that I would think has conservative Catholics rejoicing.

PJ: During recent years, you often visited Venezuela and conversed with the late president Hugo Chávez. Were you involved with the Catholic Church during your visits to Venezuela?

PM: No, I did not make any connections with Catholic organizations during my visits. I wish I had. The limited but highly influential times that I spent in Venezuela were important in my formation as a critical educator mostly by learning—despite my limited Spanish—from the local people. And while I remain a supporter of the Bolivarian revolution, I acknowledge that there have been mistakes. But unlike those conservative Catholics who work for USAID, the Council on Foreign Relations or other CIA-friendly organizations, and who like to write articles for Catholic publications, Catholics whose political imaginations have become febrile in their moral indignation and condemnation of Venezuela's revolutionaries (and who ridiculously proclaim that Chávez died as a result of the incompetence of Cuban doctors), I refuse to glorify the church in Venezuela as a place of sanctuary during the Bolivarian revolution but rather condemn it for not committing itself more fervently to the struggle of the poor. Critics of the Bolivarian revolution who with steadfast vile heap condemnations upon Venezuela's revolutionary government rarely criticize the opposition, and the attempts, both overt and covert, to destroy the revolution with the assistance of the United States and the transnational corporations. Yes, revolutions sometimes turn into their opposite, look at the case of Nicaragua under Ortega. Yes, I get it. But critics of Venezuela cannot overlook their own political myopia, and that's mostly what I see in their fetid commentaries.

PJ: Please situate your personal path toward liberation theology in a broader historical perspective.

PM: I just finished an autobiographical work with artist Miles Wilson on that very topic (McLaren 2019b) as a comic book—yes a comic book!—to reach an undergraduate university audience who are likely unfamiliar with liberation theology and Marx. But let me give your question a try. Much had been happening in Latin America and the Caribbean long before the abovementioned atrocities were reported in the international press—if we want to be historically expansive, we could say that the problems began with the European colonization of Las Americas, beginning in 1492 when the indigenous populations were enslaved or exterminated—a classic case of genocide and epistemicide. But in more recent times, we need only to look at Cuba. When Cuba moved to a people-centered economy in 1959, the United States organized the Bay of Pigs invasion, and in the ensuing years throughout Latin America, the United States has been behind the establishment of military regimes that included Chile, Guatemala, Nicaragua, Uruguay, Brazil, and Argentina. As early as 1969, The Rockefeller Report (The Rockefeller Foundation 1969) identified liberation theology as a threat to the corporate interests and the security of the United States.

Then there was the clandestine Operation Condor (*Operación Cóndor* or *Plan Cóndor*) (McSherry 2005) that was a major plan of interservice and regional cooperation and a sharing of joint intelligence among the United States and the right-wing dictatorships of the Southern Cone of South America, including Argentina, Chile, Uruguay, Paraguay, Bolivia, and Brazil, in order to maintain a program of state terror and political repression. The program began in 1968 but was fully implemented by 1975 and was responsible for as many or more than 60,000 deaths up until 1989. (Imagine what operations are like in this digital age, with revelations about USAID's creation of ZunZuneo, a social network in Cuba, or the NSA's PRISM program, exposed by Edward Snowden!) In Argentina alone, over 150 priests and nuns were killed, along with peasants, workers, intellectuals, and anyone associated with being part of or sympathetic toward leftist guerilla movements. Put that in your pipe and smoke it, all you conservative Catholics calling for regime changes in Latin America. The program—which can be traced to the infamous US School of the Americas (renamed the Western Hemisphere Institute for Security Cooperation because of its historical association with the training of Latin American death squads)—was created to advance joint counterinsurgency operations designed to eradicate communist subversives and ideas and to suppress the influence of liberation theology and other oppositional political or ideological movements.

Through the Central Intelligence Agency (CIA), the US military, and the State Department, the US government helped to bring military dictatorships to power and secure their stability by imposing sanctions designed to destabilize the economies of socialist-leaning regimes and by supporting and training black-op and execution squads. While the United States was not an official member of the Condor consortium, documents that were later uncovered revealed that during this time the United States provided major organizational, financial, and technical assistance to the repressive regimes involved. The secret papers of the Seventeenth Conference of American Armies in Mar del Plata in 1987 revealed that the US military initiated numerous discussions about how to wage sociopsychological warfare against liberation theology, ecclesial, and base communities through LIC (Low Intensity Conflict) strategies using misinformation and ideological subversion (Duchrow 1999). Nice work, Elliott Abrams! It's entirely clear now why you were selected by the Trump administration to become the special envoy of Venezuela. You did enough damage in Nicaragua with your friends, the Contras, and ran cover for genocidal campaigns against Mayan communities throughout Ecuador.

Of course, when the assassinations of the Jesuits broke into the news, there was international pressure to shut down the death squads. As a young man, I followed many of these events in the alternative media and they disturbed me greatly! I have been reading works by liberation theologians since the 1980s, after I had become interested in radical politics beginning with my trip to the United States in 1968, and my protesting against the US invasion of Vietnam during that time—in my hippie years, hitchhiking from Toronto to San Francisco and Los Angeles California, and beyond. Dropping acid with Timothy Leary and meeting Allen Ginsberg may have been great fun at the moment, but there was also a serious side to my political formation at that time, and much of it was influenced by liberation theologians.

PJ: What caused so much resistance toward liberation theology? Why was it so threatening?

PM: Why was liberation theology so threatening? That's a key question. To answer that question we need to consider the Conference of Latin American Bishops that was held in 1968 in Medellín, Colombia. It was here that bishops from all over Latin America agreed that the church should take "preferential option for the poor." The bishops decided to form Christian base communities where they would create literacy programs, and this captured the attention of Paulo Freire. The goal of the bishops was to support conditions so that the poor could liberate themselves from the "institutionalized violence" of poverty. The year that marked the beginning of Operation Condor was the same year—1968—that this conference in Medellín, Colombia, took place—and, interestingly, the year I left Toronto to explore the Californian counterculture. What emerged from the Medellín conference was to become known as liberation theology.

However, John Paul II was very much opposed to communism, having grown up in communist Poland, and he considered liberation theology a dangerous development within the Catholic Church. In the late 1970s, shortly after he was elected Pope, he began to oppose liberation theology directly and the church hierarchy moved decidedly to the right, in lockstep with John Paul's own political disposition. He put Joseph Cardinal Ratzinger (later Pope Benedict XVI) in charge of countering the theological interpretations and actions of liberation theologians. It was no accident that Pope John Paul II made numerous trips to Latin America. In 1983, the pope visited Nicaragua to scold Father Ernesto Cardenal and to oppose liberation theology. I had the good fortune of meeting Ernesto on a television show hosted by President Hugo Chávez in 2006. John Paul II defrocked Cardenal because of his participation in liberation theology and his work in the Sandinista government. Fortunately, Pope Francis overturned this decision in 2014. What drives home the heinous actions of US attempts to destroy liberation theology is that the School of the Americas actually bragged that it helped foster liberation theology's demise! (Isacson and Olson 1999).

How can you boast about facilitating torture and murder? How can you advertise your complicity in the execution of men, women, schoolteachers, and priests? Well, I suppose that if you serve in the US military you can always find a way. Just label them communists or communist sympathizers. The gospels have a radical pacifist message. But that doesn't mean Christians need to remain silent in the face of exploitation and government terror. Quite the opposite. I am against the ecclesiastical guardianship of our lives—economic, social, political. Liberation theologians found the work of Karl Marx and some Marxist writers to have an explanatory potency in understanding the role that capitalism plays in structuring the life chances of millions of impoverished campesinos in Latin America. The US government and conservative Catholics worried that liberation theology was sympathetic to communism and the fight was on to stop this dangerously subversive implications of what was to become known as the social gospel of Jesus Christ.

PJ: Let's jump into the moment here and now. Immediately after its publication, your book *Pedagogy of Insurrection: From Resurrection to Revolution* (McLaren 2015b) provoked widespread attention. For instance, it came under heavy attack from a radical leftist anarchist educator, who claims that your work in the field of liberation theology is well below the standards for social science research. Can you please respond to this argument? What makes liberation theology real, alive, and relevant for social science and beyond?

PM: Well, one response would be: Are we talking about the Hegelian conception of science—dialectical reasoning—or the vulgar empiricist conception of science? Marx's concept of "value," for instance, has nothing to do with corporeal existence. Value is not a thing but a relationship. Dialectical reasoning brings capitalism's "internal relations" to the forefront, which cannot be reduced to their "thing-ness"—this mandates that we assume an ethical standpoint in our social science deliberations and take into consideration the standpoint epistemology of the dispossessed and understand the workings of the capitalist system from the perspective of the oppressed, and also, most assuredly, from the standpoint of the oppressor. Our analysis cannot remain neutral. To assume a position of neutrality is to assume a God's eye view of the workings of the world and is in my opinion a form of sociological idolatry and there is a certain hubris that goes along with assuming a God's eye view of the universe and all of its workings.

Liberation theology displays a praxiological dimension where thought and action come together as orthopraxis to transform the world in the interests of a greater justice that can be gauged by the extent to which it eliminates needless pain and suffering linked to scarcity, to the cruel machinations of political repression, to the exploitation of human labor. It is my belief that God becomes uniquely visible when people put their lives on the line for others, especially when they sacrifice themselves for those who are most vulnerable to exploitation and alienation and the ravages of capitalism. Vulgar empiricism and materialist dogmatism cannot help us grasp the idea behind the transaction between the capitalist and the laborer. What is sold in this exchange, Marx tells us, is not labor—but labor power. There is plenty of pseudoMarxist theory out there, as well as anarchist theory that claims that theology is a flabby discipline. Of course, there *is* flabby theology, but it would be impertinent and glib to claim this for all theological traditions.

I think social science is very relevant for theology, and vice versa. Just as Marx's work revolutionized the science of history in his discovery of the workings of the mode of production by means of scientific dialectics, so Christian theology, including liberation theology, has revolutionized our understanding of faith. Theology challenges positivistic science and empiricism, but that does not render it unscientific. Liberation theologians may challenge the materialism of the anti-Hegelians, or they may take a different approach. Certainly, the principles of natural science are not the only principles by which to verify truth. But liberation theology needs social science as much as social science needs theology. We need to understand the world in order to change it—after all, this was a major imperative for Marx as it was for Jesus. Jesus taught us not through social science theories but through parables.

PJ: Theology and (social) science are written using radically different languages—therefore, we need to read them in radically different ways. Most of our readers will be familiar with reading one or another language of science. How should we go about reading the gospels?

PM: That's a question that has exercised theologians for centuries. Remember it was in 2004, a year before Cardinal Joseph Aloisius Ratzinger became Pope Benedict XVI, that Ratzinger engaged in his famous dialogue with Jurgen Habermas! How to read the gospels as part of humanity's transformation into a postsecular age was one of the themes. I don't believe humanity fell from some state of sublime benevolence in the Garden of Eden. Each generation that feels alienated from their humanity retroactively creates the ideal/mythic state of being from which they feel alienated. But there are objective forms of alienation. For instance, Marx sees this alienated state as the result of capitalist relations of production wherein the worker's species being—or living labor— becomes reduced, reified as abstract labor. To overcome such alienation, we should seek to transcend the value form of labor in a society of freely associated producers. I quite agree.

We are also alienated by the instrumental rationality of our age, by our enthrallment or entrainment to the society of the spectacle. Opposing the unpurged residue of alienation brought by value production does not necessitate that human beings corral their ideas within strategically secular precincts, or forever abide in the political sanctuary of the Paris Commune or the golden age of Latin America when Cristina Kirchner, Ricardo Lagos, Lula (Luiz Inácio Lula da Silva), Evo Morales, Hugo Chávez, Rafael Correa, and Fidel Castro simultaneously held power. My God that was a sublime moment in history! We can indeed attempt to integrate the secular and the religious, as Habermas and Ratzinger did in their famous dialogue in 2004 hosted by the Bavarian Catholic Academy in Munich as a discussion under the title "Vorpolitische moralische Grundlagen eines freiheitlichen Staates" ("Pre-political moral foundations in the construction of a free civil society") (Habermas and Ratzinger 2005). Hopefully our fumbling attempts in following Habermas won't lead to some theological paleo-orthodoxy or neoorthodoxy, or confine religion to the latest mysteries confronting quantum mechanics.

PJ: How should we proceed in formulating moral foundations within which we can abide as human beings?

PM: While I am not a strong follower of the work of Habermas, I nevertheless agree that we can try to adopt Habermas's notion of "saving translation." By translating the contents of prepolitical religious symbols into secular-rational ones, and vice versa, we can create epistemic/moral foundations for shared, solidaristic postsecular cognitive dispositions. Translating Christian moral principles such that they can be assimilated into European philosophy—through inviting a reciprocal exchange/cooperative learning between Christian and secular traditions—is certainly a worthwhile and ambitious endeavor. And if anyone is up to the task, it most certainly would be Habermas—but any struggle to create a normative collective insight that will help establish the moral foundation of a new postsecular society is certainly fraught with challenges, not in the least being the preservation of the separation of the church and state. Can we really use religious rituals to functionally integrate postsecular societies and regulate behavior therein? Well, it's something that Durkheim would likely support. But I'm not convinced. Would such rituals lead to new habits in the Deweyean sense? Possibly. But attempting this type of reciprocal/dialogical pedagogy in the

United States in the age of Trump would be especially difficult at a time of Christian ethno-nationalist fascism. And especially since Trump has been crowned by Christian evangelicals—mostly of the prosperity gospel persuasion—as the "chosen one" of God. (Should we start speaking in tongues now, Petar?) How would you attempt to integrate the cognitive and epistemic dispositions of religious and nonreligious citizens when you are faced with the likes of a Matt Shea, a Washington state Republican representative and right-wing dominionist who published recently a "Biblical Basis for War" manifesto (Shea 2018) outlining a step-by-step strategy based largely on Old Testament readings (and ideologically consistent with the Christian Identity/Aryan Nations movement) for right-wing Christians to seize power and kill their political enemies should they refuse to yield to orders to stop all abortions, same-sex marriages, and the support of communism?

Another challenge: How do you create this normative consciousness, this shared religious and secular epistemology through Habermas's type of a reciprocal/complementary learning process (which I regard as resembling some aspects of critical pedagogy since it requires critical hermeneutical reflexivity and shared multicultural, doctrinal, and secular understandings) in the age of postdigital and genetic technology, artificial intelligence, and cyborg citizenship? How can political neutrality be maintained in integrating religion into a constitutionally legitimate postsecular moral economy? Does our answer to these questions require that we forge a new language combining secular and religious symbols? How do we prevent our attempts from mutating into societies that nurtured ideologies such as Nazism, or Zen Buddhist support for Japanese militarism and their murderous colonial conquest during World War II (Victoria 2006), to name just two examples? My early work on ritual and schooling (McLaren 1999) suggests that secular and religious rituals are already hybridizing and working to reinforce syncretically the ruling ideology required for the reproduction of capitalist social relations and obedience to official Catholic dogma. To engage in Habermas's project would require a deep understanding of the role of ritual as performative of social relations of production. And it would require nonreligious capitalists to be open to postmetaphysical Christian understandings and assumptions.

PJ: And how do we teach the gospels?

PM: Both Jesus and Marx maintained a commitment to the poor and the powerless. In the case of Jesus, his story is the embodiment of the word of God. Theology helps us to gain a deeper understanding of the meaning of Jesus' life. Jesus comes to the encounter with the divine as a new form of praxis, an incarnation that radiates love through a concretization of prophetic justice. Of course, when we attempt to fathom the paschal mystery, we are guided by our own history, our own formation, what German theorists of self-cultivation such as Heinz-Joachim Heydorn refer to as *Bildung* (I recommend the work of Heinz Sünker on this topic). Here we adhere to historicocritical exegesis with an understanding that a purely scientific exegesis does not eliminate divergent interpretations, since it is impossible to rid ourselves of all of our theologiodogmatic presuppositions. When we read the scriptures, we have to acknowledge that our interpretations are guided by our own biographies and by suffering Christian communities throughout the ages who read the gospels through contextually specific eschatological, soteriological, and Christological themes—mainly with a kerygmatic intention. As Leonardo Boff (1987) would put it, reading the gospels is not the same as reading facts of history, because in such a reading you are dealing with history, the interpretation of history, and a profession of faith working together to understand the totality of Christianity from an apologetical viewpoint. Christ destroys all of our previous images of God, as Christ suffers for all the crucified of history. As Boff (1987) notes, this is a mystery inaccessible to discursive reason but capable of being understood through human praxis. We are resurrected through our refusal to cooperate with the social sin of this world.

Remember, Petar, that Paulo Freire wrote that the prophetic position of the church "demands a critical analysis of the social structures in which . . . conflict takes place. This means it demands of its followers a knowledge of socio-political science, since this science cannot be neutral; this demands an ideological choice" (1973: 14). Here Freire admits to the notion that all science is a form of ideology and that there is an ideological choice in choosing particular types of science with which to clarify and deepen our understanding of the struggle for liberation. Part of the prophetic vision of the church demands an engagement with social science that can help unpeel the veneer of mystification that keeps us from knowing reality. Freire writes that a prophetic perspective "does not represent an escape into a world of unattainable dreams. It demands a scientific knowledge of the world as it really is" (1973: 14). But note that for Freire—and I cannot underscore this enough—this scientific understanding of the world is found through praxis, through revolutionary praxis. Freire warns that "to denounce the present reality and announce its radical transformation into another reality capable of giving birth to new men and women, implies gaining through praxis a new knowledge of reality" (1973: 14). Freire criticizes the petit bourgeois dimension of the church today and urges theologians to consider in their work the so-called Third World that exists within their own so-called First World—in the outskirts of their cities. And I would add—within our segregated inner cities throughout North America. I have tried to develop some of these ideas in *Pedagogy of Insurrection*.

PJ: After *Pedagogy of Insurrection* (McLaren 2015b) you have been attacked by a former admirer of your work as no better than historical tyrants who use God as a cover for their crimes. This is because you came out as a devout Catholic and very likely many of your leftist admirers assume you are an atheist. This kind of *argumentum ad hominem* is obviously wrong. Yet, I completely agree with Derek Ford's review, which says that publishing *Pedagogy of Insurrection* "is certainly a risky move for McLaren, for he risks both the condemnation of the Christian right as well as contemporary atheists. Interestingly, these two groups have quite a bit in common" (Ford 2016).

What is the connection between left-wing and right-wing critiques of your work? Here, I am especially interested in critiques arriving from the left: the closer they are, the more they hurt. Some left-wing theorists, especially those arriving from anarchist circles, say that religion and capitalism are mutually foundational—in this view, religion simply does not work together with socialism. What do you make of this critique? How, and under which condition, can we divorce religion from capitalism and build a theist socialist future?

PM: I regard the particular attack to which you refer as an example of what Lenin would call an infantilism of the left. Which is not to say I regard all atheists in this way, far from it. But let us get to the bigger picture here. Of course I agree with Herbert Marcuse (2011) when he wrote in "The role of religion in a changing society" that no evaluation of that role can be made without meeting Marx's criticism of religion. I have never veered from this position. But Christianity, as Miranda notes (1974, 1980, 2004), is not something that should be absorbed into a religion. Marx attacks Christianity to the extent that it has been calcified into a religion, and a crusty one at that. Marx was certainly anticlerical but both Marx and Engels, I believe, saw their work as a continuation of the authentic message of Jesus. Marx applied the term "Christian" to himself in a letter to Ludwig Kugelmann in 1870, constantly made biblical references throughout his works, and compared the persecutions against the international as the persecutions of primitive Christians by the Romans.

As a Marxist humanist who works in the tradition of revolutionary critical pedagogy—and as a Catholic—I have been greatly influenced by the work of the great Jesuit theologian and educator José Porfirio Miranda. So much of what I am offering as a response to your question is indebted to his work, especially his classic work, *Marx against the Marxists* (Miranda 1980), that readers will need to seriously engage this work in order to get the details. In his world-shaking critique of capitalism, Marx regards people as endowed with the capacity to make history. Marx affirms "the cunning of reason" as the means by which human actors shape history. This type of reason is neither an abstraction, nor is it attached to the notion of history as some kind of abstract entity of its own that floats above the messy web of human strife and turmoil. Reason in this larger sense has, according to Marx, created the conditions of possibility for a truly humane society to emerge out of the ruins of capital. But the foundational issue here is: Why must a new society emerge from the extraction of surplus value from alienated labor?

The destruction of capital becomes, for Marx, the immanent form for a higher principle that makes possible capitalism's ability to cede its place to a communist society. Marx's entire corpus of works is oriented toward this historical eschatology in his denunciation of the worship of the God of Money. The cunning or subtlety of reason creates the conditions of possibility for results that are contrary to those that the capitalists were pursuing. Miranda is very convincing here when he affirms that Marx appeals to this eschatological aspect of history—this affirming of the eschaton or Kingdom of God of which Jesus preached. This eschaton is occurring in history itself and not in some other world, some cosmic hinterland where people float around as disembodied ectoplasmic spirits. Churches and Christians everywhere tragically refuse to hear this message. Marx has this eschatological awareness, his writings are full of it, and I do not have space here to recite all the instances in his writings where this is evident—they can be found in the works of Miranda.

PJ: Please say a bit more about the eschatological aspect of history. How can it be confirmed; how does it link to liberation?

PM: After reading Marx, we cannot easily clap our eyes on reality since our reading strategies have been taken from the smoke and mirror catechism of capitalist catachresis and sealed inside indoctrination factories built to siphon away creativity. Faith in those who brandish the evidence for our understanding of the world sacralizes all of our knowledge, despite our appeals to scientific objectivity that yolk us to work of liberal rationality. Yet the scientific principles to which we allegedly claim allegiance invest our ideas with a type of divine power that such scientific rationality was initially set up to eliminate. In capitalist society we are able to ineluctably advocate for our most cherished and beloved illusions that, *prima facie*, have been afloat throughout the centers of bourgeois ideology, carefully administered and monitored by those who speak with portentously self-aggrandizing authority, and protected by those who are able to trace their royalist lines of descent, and who can be counted on for their patronage for older and more established political dispensations.

Let me delve into your question further by maintaining that we cannot affirm the existence of an eschaton unless we affirm the existence of a God guiding history. The eschaton for Christ meant that injustice and exploitation will disappear once and for all. Atheists reject the eschaton, clearly. I hold that both Jesus and Marx maintained the reality of the eschaton. Engels and Marx's work reveals this both implicitly and explicitly. The reason that is wholly immanent in history is God. This I believe is reflected in the notion of hope that can be seen in the writings of both Marx and Engels. Clearly Marx understood Kant's categorical imperative as "bad infinity," that is, the eternal return of the same in which an imperative is reiterated but is never fully realized. Marx rejected Kant's antieschatological and antimessianic attitudes of eternal deferment and postponement. And what about Hegel? Marx had a profound critique of Hegel's work, but he did not dismiss Hegel's affirmation of the final end of history through an intervening Absolute that can bring the endless return of the same to a halt.

PJ: Why cannot we affirm the existence of an eschaton unless we affirm the existence of a God guiding history?

PM: There are basically two ways of doing Christology. One starts with the life and ministry of Jesus, his crucifixion and resurrection as the Christ, and has an upward arc. This is Christology from below; it deals with the historical narrative of Jesus, his life, death, and resurrection. The other type of Christology begins with God as Word, the Word becoming Flesh in Jesus and dwelling among the human family, and has a downward arc. How did the Word descend into the world? How was the world created by the Word, and how was it crystalized in the person of Jesus on earth? This is known as doing Christology from above. The Gospel of Mark is a good example of the former, the Gospel of John is a good example of the latter. Most people are more comfortable with a Christology from below, as you might imagine, the historical narrative. Both approaches to Christology are dialectically related (see Johnson 2018). Johnson refers to Christology from above as "an inspired interpretation" (2018: 150) which requires you to accept the authority of the church, to accept the doctrines, and to know something about Hellenistic and Jewish culture, philosophical categories, and the like.

It's not easy to engage in hermeneutics of this sort. You need to challenge yourself with questions such as: How, for instance, did the early disciples of Jesus come to believe that "Jesus Christ is not only *with* and *for* human beings but is present *as* a human being" (Johnson 2018: 161)? How is it possible that through Jesus, "God joined earthly life as a participant, possessing a history, a time, and a death that constitute a profoundly personal, novel divine relationship to the world that hadn't existed before" (Johnson 2018: 161)? At times you will catch me speaking a Christology from below, but in my more speculative metaphysical moments I will be engaging in a Christology analysis from above. Over the years through advances in technology, science, and in doing theology, interpretations of how God could become Flesh have become much richer. How can we talk about salvation today, for instance, from a theology from above? The field of interpretation is more open today, and in some ways perhaps more perilous. So in my discussion of liberation theology, I am engaging and challenging ideas from both a Christology from below and a Christology from above, and I hope that doesn't add to any confusion.

In my view, Petar, speaking from within a Christology from above emphasis, God is the intervening Absolute who relativizes the eternal return of the same and delinks us from it so that we have enough space—enough liminal space—such that we are able to seize the torch of liberation. Jesus came to revolutionize the social structure of religion, not to occupy a throne reserved for him by "religious" functionaries of the state who have been made illustrious in the capitalist world by their unslakable thirst for power and class privilege. Do we recognize these Philistines? There are plenty of them in Trump's inner circle. As Miranda argues, rebellion against religion is mandatory for anyone who wants to bring justice to the world. Charles Reitz, who has adumbrated a Marxist atheist position, is correct here in arguing for a communal politics of justice and commonwealth by means of a dialectical sublation of religion, surpassing its inadequacies yet preserving its worthwhile historical contributions. Here, Reitz (2015) starts with humanity's oldest philosophical and religious sources in Africa that reflects that "communally laboring humanity can be seen as the source of ethics." This ethics of caring, reciprocity, and the "golden rule" includes emancipatory religious practice, as in the civil rights movement. Here the struggle for justice includes the struggle against racism, sexism, patriarchy, and capitalism. Can we not hear the words of Jesus: "Woe to you rich, for your consolation is now" (Luke 6:24) or "Blessed are you poor; the reign of God is yours" (Luke 6:20)?

Jesus Was a Communist

PJ: The understanding of money as a god that rules human beings fascinates me! Can we say that it is one of the central points of connection between Christianity and Marxism?

PM: We absolutely can, Petar. Jesus talked so much about economic sin that it is unfathomable why this is not a central part of the teachings of Christianity. The Lucan part of the Bible explicitly teaches communism (Acts 4:32; 4:34; 2:44; Luke 14:33).

Miranda argues that the origin of the communist idea in the history of the West is not to be found in Plato or Marx but rather in the New Testament. The Bible clearly condemns acquired wealth and established wealth and also the means by which this wealth came to be—including various kinds of profit, such as interest on loans, and the expropriation of the produce of the workers' labor by agricultural entrepreneurs (James 5:1–6). Jesus is not against generalized wealth *per se*, such as the wealth of a people, but against relative or differentiating wealth. Someone cannot be rich while another remains poor. Mark 10:25 and Luke 6:20, 6:24, 16:19–31, 1:53 are interpreted by Miranda as arguing that there is no legitimately moral means of acquiring differentiating wealth and that Jesus maintains (Luke 16:29, 16:31) that the same condemnation of wealth can be found in the Old Testament.

Actually, three types of profit are attacked in the scriptures. (Apologies to Joel Osteen and Paula White.) The Bible itemizes its reproof of profit-taking as occurring through commerce (Ecclus 27:1–2), loans on interest (Exodus 22:24; Leviticus 25:36, 25:37; Deuteronomy 23:19; Ezekiel 18:8, 18:13, 18:17, 22:12; Psalms 15:5; Proverbs 28:8.), and productive activity or the process of production (James 5:1–6). There is something about the process itself of being able to grow rich that is wicked and unjust (Isaiah 53:9). The acquisition of wealth itself is possible only by exploiting the poor (Job 20:19; Psalm 37). Micha 2-1-2 and Isaiah 5:8 focus on how the rich keep acquiring property. Miranda (1974, 1980) makes a convincing case that the Bible condemns the exploitation suffered by the poor at the hands of the rich and creates an identity between the rich and the unjust (Isaiah 53:9). Jesus' teachings that enabled the first Christians to base their community on communism can be found in Mark 10:25, Luke 6:20, 24, Matthew 6:24, and Luke 16:19–31.

In fact, Miranda (1980) makes the claim that Jesus was a communist, which can be seen in John 12:6, 13:29, and Luke 8:1–3. Oh can't you hear the evangelical Christians and conservative Catholics howling now, Petar. Let them howl! Did not Jesus make the renunciation of property a condition for entering into the Kingdom of God? How can God make it possible for a rich person to enter the Kingdom of God? The answer is clearly provided by the Bible. According to Miranda, this answer is: By ceasing to be rich (Mark 10:21, 25, 27) and giving away one's wealth to the poor. (Well, Donald Trump is supposed to be the "chosen one" of God. Won't he at least sell his Trump Towers in Şişli, Istanbul, to pay for the funerals of the Kurds he abandoned in Syria?) The scriptural exegesis undertaken by Miranda is, to me, thoroughly persuasive. As a revolutionary Marxist, I am certainly drawn to a number of Miranda's works, *Marx and the Bible* (1974) and *Marx against the Marxists* (1980).

PJ: Poverty is a central point of departure for Jesus, Marx, and Paulo Freire. Yet, their answers to the question of poverty seem to collide. For Jesus, the poor will inherit the Kingdom of God; for Marx and Freire, the poor should take matters in own hands here and now . . .

PM: Those are important observations, Petar. Jesus did not sacralize poverty or preach resignation to it because there will be some extraterrestrial compensation for it in the afterlife. That would be a glib and cynical assessment, and it erases the prophetic nature of such a pronouncement. To say the poor are blessed is not an involuntary justification of the relations and structures of exploitation. The poor are blessed because the coming of the Kingdom in the fullness of history will put an end—in the concrete sociological sense—to their poverty and suffering. Poverty is a form of structural sin that is incompatible with the Kingdom of God. I am not trying to reduce the gospel to a manual for attaining political consciousness but maintaining that the gospel has an inherent political dimension. As Gustavo Gutiérrez notes,

> This conscienticizing of the preaching of the Gospel, which rejects any aseptic presentation of the message, should lead to a profound revision of the pastoral activity of the Church . . . the oppressed themselves should be the agents of their own pastoral activity. (Gutiérrez 1988: 154–55)

PJ: Christianity seems to have a fairly straightforward attitude to authority: "Let everyone be subject to the governing authorities, for there is no authority except that which God has established. The authorities that exist have been established by God" (Romans 13:1). How does liberation theology deal with this apparent contradiction between biblical messages and critical pedagogy? How can we subject ourselves to the governing authorities and at the same time engage in revolutionary struggle?

PM: Those are the key questions facing critical educators and those of us who have been influenced by liberation theology. Saint Paul, who was once a Pharisee, campaigned heavily against the legalism that perverted Christianity. Are we not justified by faith and not our adherence to the law? We need to seek to embody our own insight from our own age and not look to entrenched conceptions of the law established in very different historical epochs. We need to constantly renew our understanding of the gospels given the lessons of our own age. People wrestle with many statements made in the Bible that were historically and geopolitically specific to the times.

Liberation theologians focus on the sociohistorical captivity of people in the grip of the pretentions of absolute authority and who are the gravest victims of the alienation brought about by capitalism. They seek a reciprocal salvation in their universal and ontological solidarity with the poor and with all of humanity, which is the possibility of our redemption and liberation. This is what critical pedagogy is about. Beginning with biographical experiences of the people, their lived, hermeneutical engagement with others, and interrogating those experiences in the context of those experiences being situated on a larger locus of the capitalist mode of production and what Jesus refers to as "the money of iniquity" (Luke 16:9, 11). A subversive praxis of faith challenges the systemization of governing authorities and their closed systems of authority and reprobates all measures of accumulating profit under the vice grip of their authority. Established authority that protects freedom and establishes the conditions of possibility of freedom from necessity and from senseless suffering can certainly be conserved, but in other instances when it works to despoil society, it should be challenged by seeking a qualitative transformation of society in the interests of justice and solidarity.

PJ: In Latin America, liberation theology is far from a theory—instead, it is true emancipatory revolutionary praxis. In many cases, actually, practice has clearly pre-dated theory, so our conversation stands on the shoulders of a long radical tradition. What can we learn from the practical examples of liberation theology in Latin America?

PM: I am not sure, Petar, how many of our readers are old enough to remember two earth-trembling and maleficent incidents in El Salvador that occurred in the 1980s during the civil war that broke out during the military dictatorship from 1979 to 1992. I am referring to the five priests and two women who were murdered outside the Jesuit residence of the Universidad Centroamericana (UCA; founded in 1965), San Salvador, in November 1989. Those murdered were the university rector Ignacio Ellacuría, an internationally recognized liberation theologian; Segundo Montes, dean of the sociology department and director of the University Institute of Human Rights; Ignacio Martín Baró, head of the psychology department; theology professors Juan Ramón Moreno and Amando López; and Joaquin López y López, who headed the Fe y Alegría network of schools for the poor. Julia Elba Ramos, wife of the caretaker at the UCA and her daughter Celina were also killed (Ellacuría and Sobrino 1993).

Prior to this horrendous event, in 1980, (the now beatified) Archbishop Óscar Arnulfo Romero was gunned down saying mass in a small hospital chapel. Before the military regime came to power in 1970s' El Salvador, a number of Jesuits there had begun rethinking and repivoting their work in a concerted attempt to embrace fully the preferential option for the poor that emerged from the conference in Medellín, Colombia, and to stand shoulder to shoulder and heart to heart with the poor and powerless campesinos. They understood this to mean actively supporting the rights of campesinos and civilian movements promoting social, economic, and political reform.

During the years of the military regime, it was Father Ignacio Ellacuría, rector at the UCA, who played an influential role in reframing the university's mission that involved standing in solidarity with the country's impoverished majorities. Ensepulchred in a cemetery of silence and fear, the campesinos were in dire need of government reforms as well as protection from the church, which often stood silent in the face of large-scale torture and mass killings carried out by the heavily armed military regime. Echoing the language of Medellín, the university's 1979 mission was inextricably linked to the service of the people and, in fact, the mission of the university was in a large sense oriented by the oppressed campesinos themselves (Ellacuría and Sobrino 1993).

Evidently, the Salvadoran government viewed Father Ignacio Ellacuría and the UCA as a serious threat to the United States' continued financial and political backing. The US-backed military dictatorship was well aware that if Salvadorean liberation theologians flagged the US Congress about human rights abuses by the government, it might withdraw its crucial financial support, weapons sales, and military training (including methods of torture) in the School of the Americas operated by the United States. The US-trained Atlacatl Battalion (who trained as well as served in the Salvadorean death squads) massacred thousands of unarmed peasants during the dirty war and hundreds were slain in the village of El Mozote alone in 1981. They did not want the Catholic Church interfering in their practices of slaughtering innocent peasants whom they suspected of supporting guerilla fighters. The government saw this reign of terror as a necessary step in ridding the country of a communist menace that, if not stamped out, they felt would eviscerate the established Salvadorean ruling class.

PJ: Can we say that it was their Christian faith, and the backup of the institution of the Catholic Church, that made resistance so powerful?

PM: Certainly . . . but there was another factor at play among the Jesuits that made them so fearless. There was an influence on the Jesuits' work more immediate than Medellín's teaching of social justice: the example of the martyr Archbishop Óscar Romero. Shortly after the murders, Major Eric Warren Buckland, a senior US military adviser in El Salvador, testified that his Salvadoran counterpart, Colonel Carlos Armando Avilés Butrago, chief of psychological operations for the Salvadoran Joint Command, informed him in advance of the planned killing. He later retracted his statement under pressure. Is it so incredible to think that at least one US official had knowledge of the plot to kill the Jesuits weeks before the event? And did nothing?

In *Pedagogy of Insurrection* (McLaren 2015b), I wrote a last chapter that I named "critical rage pedagogy." Here I unleashed a critical rage—using a combination of spoken word and other literary tropes—at the history of human atrocity. To me, the Kingdom of God is not removed from, say, a Beethoven symphony, Gregorian chants, the ecstasy of contemplating a mathematical formula, or from a painting by one of the great masters (although I certainly love art and music—not so much mathematics, I will confess). For me, the Kingdom of God is found more tangibly on the picket line, in solidarity with the suffering of those who are being brutalized everyday by capitalism, by governments, by death squads, and by religious edicts that marginalize them and exclude them from their full humanity. The Kingdom of God is found in the act of struggling and sacrificing for the other. Not speaking out for the other, since groups can very often speak for themselves, but speaking alongside and with others, as allies, as friends, as comrades, and as brothers and sisters in Christ.

PJ: Christians in Latin America went through some terrible experiences . . .

PM: Without a doubt, Petar, experiences that I can barely fathom, they were so mind-numbing and horrific. It is difficult for some people outside of Latin America to comprehend the horrific suffering endured by Catholic priests and nuns in that part of the world during the dirty wars in the 1970s and 1980s, wars involving military dictatorships supported by the United States and death squads trained by the US military. In 1980, four US women, two Maryknoll nuns, an Ursuline nun, and a lay volunteer were stopped by the military in El Salvador as they traveled from the airport on their way to work with impoverished campesino communities. With encouragement from their commander, a group of National Guardsmen took the women to a cow pasture where they were tortured, raped, and murdered. The rapes and assassinations of Maryknoll nuns, Sister Maura Clarke and Sister Ita Ford, Ursuline Sister Dorothy Kazel, and lay missionary Jean Donovan shocked the world. Sister Ita Ford was targeted specifically by US-backed Salvadoran death squads because she was an outspoken critic in defense of the poor. She wrote the following in a letter to her sister:

> You say you don't want anything to happen to me. . . . I'd prefer it that way myself—but I don't see that we have control over the forces of madness, and if you could choose to enter into other people's suffering, or to love others, you at least have to consent in some way to the possible consequences. Actually what I've learned here

is that death is not the worst evil. We look death in the face every day. But the cause of the death is evil. That's what we have to wrestle and fight against. (Dear 2006)

Many priests and nuns had committed themselves to those who had been victimized by military regimes; they had placed themselves squarely in solidarity with the crucified of history, those whose lives had been devastated by what Leonardo Boff calls the "international sin" of poverty (Boff 1987: 118) and those who were brutally tortured and "disappeared" by the military regimes. Boff draws our attention to the case of Franciscan Father Ivan Bettencourt, a Colombian diocesan missionary who worked in the Olancho province of Honduras. In 1976, Bettencourt was tortured and killed along with US citizen Father Michael Cypher and 10 campesino organizers after speaking out and organizing against a local land grab in Honduras. This event became known as the "Horcones Massacre." Boff writes that Bettencourt was seized and interrogated to force him to confess that he was a "Marxist subversive." They cut off his ears and interrogated him. They cut off his nose and interrogated him some more. They cut out his tongue and declared the interrogation at an end. They sliced his body to ribbons. He was still twitching so they machine-gunned him. Finally, they threw him into a well and hid the well under earth and rubble. Father Ivan died defending his brothers and sisters (Boff 1987: 120).

PJ: These priests and nuns have exhibited remarkable stamina and courage. What can we learn from their stories and experiences?

PM: Yes, as well as the campesinos who witnessed their newborn infants being thrown into the air and impaled on the bayonets of the soldiers, campesinos who were forced to wear rubber hoods filled with insecticide. Some compare the courage and bravery of some of the renegade priests and nuns to that of Che Guevara. Che's motto was *Hay que endurecerse sin perder jamas la ternura* (One must endure [become hard, toughen oneself] without losing tenderness). Some see Che as a secular saint, who gave his life for the poor and the suffering in America Latina. Risking death for the cause of the crucified and impoverished of this world gives life meaning, and Che's legacy inspired millions throughout Latin America and the Caribbean. Priests informed by liberation theology saw their mission in light of the social gospel of Jesus Christ, that is, in terms of the political import of the message of Jesus, and bringing about the reign of the Kingdom of God, which included finding collective transcendence in the Suffering Servant through forgiveness, and through trust and faith in God. We cannot focus on the Christ of personal salvation alone, which is what many evangelicals would have us do. Our individual sins must be reflectively engaged and confronted in light of the gospel message, of course, but we cannot forget the social sins, such as austerity capitalism, which we know is dependent for its survival on surplus value and the exploitation of human labor. Part of what we need to do is to evaluate the events in Jesus' life in light of their sociohistorical context. This demands a social-scientific approach to the gospel message as well as historical-critical approaches. But the social justice aspect of the gospel of Jesus Christ cannot be denied.

I look at the US social order today in terms of the popularity at the moment of Donald Trump; in this cult of personality there appears to be a blend of social Darwinism and the racial superiority of white Europeans, nationalism in the form of American exceptionalism, and of course, a religious triumphalism in terms of a God that has given the United States a providential role to play in history. Against this White Jesus of the diseased colonial imagination that secured the privilege of whites is the Black Jesus, who grasps the perils of racism and imperialism and financial prosperity that has grown out of the prosperity gospel of US capitalism. Reggie Williams has written an interesting book, *Bonhoeffer's Black Jesus: Harlem Renaissance Theology and an Ethic of Resistance* (Williams 2014), that illustrates the impact that the preaching of Adam Clayton Powell Sr, pastor of Harlem's Abyssinian Baptist Church, had on Dietrich Bonhoeffer when he was a Sloane Fellow at Union Theological Seminary in New York for the 1930–1931 academic year. His understanding of the black experience of suffering, resistance, and transcendence helped him to understand what the Nazis were trying to do to the oppressed peoples of his homeland and also helped him understand the perils of developments within European Christianity. For his efforts, Bonhoeffer was imprisoned and eventually forced to walk naked to the gallows prepared for him by his Nazi captors.

PJ: What about armed revolutionary violence?

PM: Some scholars and activists cite Frantz Fanon to support acts of violence on the part of revolutionaries, in that Fanon believed violence helps colonized peoples overcome their inferiority complex and gives colonized subjects the necessary courage to continue their struggle. However, Peter Hudis offers a different perspective. In his magisterial book on Fanon, he cites recent studies by Marnia Lazreg and others, based on interviews with Front de Libération Nationale (FLN) militants, which maintain "that violence has, at best, an ephemeral 'cleansing' role. More often it dehumanizes and produces long-term distress in its participants" (Hudis 2015: 121). This, I am sure, was not lost on Fanon. Throughout the conflicts in Latin America throughout the 1970s and 1980s, priests certainly put their lives on the line to protect and serve the oppressed. Some even joined revolutionary battalions to work as chaplains.

The First Religious War of the Twenty-First Century

PJ: By standing on the side of the poor, liberation theology has entered the highest spheres of international politics. . . . How does this politics work in practice?

PM: That's been part of the problem, Petar, it was too effective on an international scale and had to be confronted and crushed. I agree with Noam Chomsky who says that "the U.S. has often been bitterly opposed to Christianity" (in Chaudary 2007) and describes the attacks on liberation theology by the US administration as "the first religious war of the 21st century" (in Rivage-Seul 2016). Petar, to back up some of my claims, just read some of the following cables that were released by Wikileaks. In 2013, Daniel Kovalik examined very revealing cables released by Wikileaks that were sent by the US Embassy to the Vatican. For example, in one cable headed "The 'Threat' of Liberation Theology" dated May 6, 2007, the Embassy reveals its unvarnished ideological stance against liberation theology in a message related to the visit of Pope Benedict XVI to Brazil:

> Another major contextual issue for the visit is the challenge to the traditional Church played by liberation theology. Pope John Paul (aided by the current pope when he was Cardinal Ratzinger) made major efforts to stamp out this Marxist analysis of class struggle. It had come to be promoted by a significant number of Catholic clergy and lay people, who in a political compromise sometimes sanctioned violence "on behalf of the people." The more orthodox form of liberation theology that sided with the poor and oppressed had undergone a reductionist reading that the Vatican sought to correct. To a large extent, Pope John Paul II beat down "liberation theology," but in the past few years, it has seen a resurgence in various parts of Latin America. (Kovalik 2013)

Another cable from the US Embassy to the Vatican, on January 14, 2008, included a summary of Pope Benedict's current views on Liberation Theology:

> Also important—and disturbing—to the Holy See is the resilience of Latin American liberation theology. During his time as the powerful Prefect of the Congregation for the Doctrine of the Faith in the 1980s and 1990s, the then Cardinal Joséph Ratzinger opposed liberation theology for its overt sympathy for revolutionary movements. Some of the supporters of this theology—including former clerics—now occupy prominent political positions in countries like Bolivia and Paraguay, a phenomenon that one commentator has described as the secular reincarnation of liberation theology. For the Holy See, the Church Magisterium (the teachings of the Catholic Church) on social issues already advocates strongly for the rights of the underprivileged. This advocacy, often described as the Church's "preferential option for the poor," should not include clerics assuming high level governmental positions or running for office. In calling for a reduction of domestic tensions in Latin America, the Holy See hopes to prevent a climate fertile for activist, progressive clerics to coalesce with populist, authoritarian governments. (Kovalik 2013)

What follows is an excerpt from a cable from September 27, 2005 released by the US Embassy in San Salvador entitled, "El Salvador: The Declining Influence of The Roman Catholic Church." This cable states that

> In 1977, former Archbishop Oscar Arnulfo Romero adopted an outspoken stance in favor of "liberation theology" that alienated many of the church's most influential members. Archbishop Arturo Rivera y Damas followed Romero's example during his 1983–1994 tenure. Much changed in the years following the 1992 Peace Accords, which ended repression and violence on the part of government forces and guerillas. With the selection of Fernando Saenz Lacalle as Archbishop of San Salvador in 1995, the Catholic Church entered a new era during which it withdrew its support for "liberation theology"; Saenz Lacalle has placed a renewed emphasis

on individual salvation and morality. However, an underlying division still exists within the Salvadoran Catholic Church vis–vis such political issues. (Kovalik 2013)

The Embassy later explains that "[t]he Salvadoran Catholic Church has in effect been 'reRomanized' . . ." (Kovalik 2013). Kovalik comments on this cable as follows:

> what is left unspoken is that it was the murder of good people like Archbishop Romero that led to the Church "re-Romanizing"—a term with a double meaning, for it can properly mean that the Church is again in line with the Vatican in Rome (the intended meaning), but also that it has returned to the pro-Empire stance the Church has maintained (with limited interruption after the second Vatican Council in 1962) since 324 A.D. In other words, mission accomplished for both the Vatican and the U.S. (Kovalik 2013)

Another cable from San Salvador, dated June 24, 2008, attempts its own historical overview of the FMLN (Frente Farabundo Martí para la Liberación Nacional or Farabundo Martí National Liberation). The Embassy offers a highly distorted picture when it writes:

> During the 12 year Salvadoran civil war (1980-92), the FMLN attempted to overthrow the government utilizing a strategy that included armed struggle, terrorism, socialist/communist political indoctrination. The liberation theology movement within the Catholic Church and labor unions largely supported these efforts. The group received monetary support and arms from the Soviet Bloc and Cuba. (Kovalik 2013)

Here the liberation theology movement is unjustly painted as supporting terrorism with the clandestine support from the Soviet Union and Cuba. Absent from these overblown claims is the fact that the US-backed military and paramilitary death squads in El Salvador committed horrendous acts of terrorism against the civilian population that has been clearly documented. Furthermore, the leading proponents of the liberation theology movement, such as Archbishop Romero, condemned violence from both sides of the conflict. The release of these confidential cables from the US Embassy by Wikileaks, as reported by Daniel Kovalik, reveals the staggering extent of the current war against liberation theology by the US State Department. Given the history of coordinated US attacks on liberation theology, it is difficult to disagree with Noam Chomsky when he states that

> the U.S. Army helped defeat liberation theology, which was a dominant force, and it was an enemy for the same reason that secular nationalism in the Arab world was an enemy—it was working for the poor. This is the same reason why Hamas and Hezbollah are enemies: they are working for the poor. It doesn't matter if they are Catholic or Muslim or anything else; that is intolerable. The Church of Latin America had undertaken "the preferential option for the poor." They committed the crime of going back to the Gospels. The contents of the Gospels are mostly

suppressed (in the U.S.); they are a radical pacifist collection of documents. It was turned into the religion of the rich by the Emperor Constantine, who eviscerated its content. If anyone dares to go back to the Gospels, they become the enemy, which is what liberation theology was doing. (in Chaudary 2007)

PJ: Speaking with and speaking together with the poor is one of the central messages of both liberation theology and revolutionary critical pedagogy. In the capitalist world, however, the very act of speaking is privileged—so many people are excluded from full participation in economic, political, and other spheres.

PM: Yes, in the capitalist world we really do have a social universe of the excluded, the immiserated, the powerless, the "wretched of the Earth" as Frantz Fanon (2001) put it. William Robinson (2004, 2014, 2016a, b) has reported that approximately one-third of humanity is locked out of productive participation in the capitalist economy. We can find a larger number of this group in Latin America. There has been a dramatic shift in the United States and other countries since the end of World War II from an admirable concern with social welfare to a preoccupation with social control and creating a national security state. There is a pronounced fear now among the ruling elite that outraged workers will rise up and protest living in what is fast becoming planet slum. Robinson notes that the role of the state in creating social cohesion through the accumulation of capital is fracturing as a result of the crisis of capitalist overaccumulation. Consequently, the state is fast losing its "legitimatizing" function, and we can see this now in the election cycle here in the United States when outsiders to the government—such as Trump—are rising up and urging people to demonize the surplus population through a logic overlain with hate and violence and punctuated by ethno-nationalism and white supremacy.

PJ: More often than not, the concept of surplus population (which is a terrible phrase in its own right) is linked to changes in the structure of employment caused by new technologies (see Peters, Jandrić, and Means 2019). What is the role of technology in this context?

PM: I think it plays an important role, Petar. Not only is capitalism retooling itself, but also hiring practices for college graduates are likely to shift in an ominous direction. Very likely it will not be too long before human resource professionals hired by your potential employer will determine your fitness for employment, extensions of credit, or admission to certain schools, based on computerized personality screening and data collection. For example, personality tests designed by computer programs that capture and evaluate your "Likes" on Facebook and other digital markers could follow you throughout your career or perhaps even "haunt" you. Wu Youyou, Michael Kosinski, Thore Graepel, and David Stillwell of Cambridge University's Department of Psychology and the Stanford University Department of Computer Science are developing a computer model of psychological assessment and personality profiling that assesses their subjects' personalities based on their "generic digital footprint" and employs what they call a "five-factor model" consisting of a standardized set of personality traits that measure Extraversion, Agreeableness, Conscientiousness, Neuroticism (sometimes named by its polar opposite, Emotional Stability), and Openness to Experience (Kosinski, Stillwell, and Graepel 2013; Youyou, Kosinski, and Stillwell 2015).

Computerized programs like this one—which the researchers argue are better equipped to assess personality traits than living and breathing human beings—are very likely to be utilized by future employers. This type of research goes much further than the "predictive analytics" used by Facebook and other social media sites. Certain algorithms or websites that you visit will determine that you are unsuited for jobs that you want. How has technology turned into such a companion of the security state? Freire maintained that "education for liberation does not merely free students from blackboards just to offer them projectors" (1973: 4). Computer science programs have become completely domesticating. They are the result of the contradictions within their own power structures, serving capital by instrumentalizing our personalities and subjective agency.

Is this so surprising today, when public education is being turned into a series of investment opportunities? We see it in the retooling of colleges in order to serve better financial and military-industrial interests, in the overuse and exploitation of contingent faculty, in the growth of for-profit degree-granting institutions, in rising tuition and, not to mention, the assault on critical citizenship in favor of consumer citizenship. There are many struggles to take up in the making of the Kingdom of God.

Toward a Global Ethics of Solidarity

PJ: I am fascinated by your stories and examples from South America, and I deeply sympathize with the message of liberation theology. Yet, Peter, I come from a radically different context—Eastern Europe—where various Christian denominations are traditionally on the side of the right.

PM: When I look at the Catholic Church in Canada (my native country) and the United States (my adopted country), and North and South America as a whole, I acknowledge and condemn the church's complicity in the genocide of the indigenous peoples. Canadian prime minister Justin Trudeau invited Pope Francis to visit Canada to apologize to indigenous peoples for what amounted to "cultural genocide" as a result of the Catholic Church's treatment of aboriginal children in Canada's residential schools. Needless to say, I can't imagine a gesture like this from Trump. This doesn't mean we ignore Trudeau's past history of wearing blackface. But his gesture of apology was a step forward. Of course we can also examine the slaughtering of native Americans in the United States and the extermination of indigenous peoples in America Latina by the Spaniards—this is well known on this continent.

Looking back to Croatian history (of which I am certainly no expert), Roman Catholic Croatian activities at the Jasenovac concentration camp, and throughout Croatia during World War II, have left a tragic mark on Croatia's Catholic Church. In the case of Croatia, where the often troglodytic Vatican has been accused of complicity in the genocide committed in the Independent State of Croatia during World War II,

I am wondering how this history has played out among contemporary Croat Catholics. During World War II, Croatia was a Roman Catholic state sponsored by the Vatican. Considering the context of the political and ideological developments of the time, this sponsorship occurred at a historical conjuncture of severe anti-Judaism and anti-Semitism worldwide (the question of whether Christian anti-Judaism can be seen as significantly different from racial anti-Semitism is still open for debate today). We know that during this time, anti-Jewish legislation was written with Catholic support in Poland, Italy, Hungary, and Slovakia. The history of World War II is complex, and the historical legacy of the church's participation in that war is still being rewritten. Yes, I am aware that Catholics in Rome sheltered Jews, I'm aware of the many Jews saved in Budapest as a result of the heroism of Raoul Wallenberg and papal nuncio, Angelo Rotta.

PJ: Why did the Catholic Church not do something about it?

PM: That's the key question! The reasons why no explicit message emerged from the Holy See about the extermination of the Jews by the Nazis are admittedly complex, and diplomacy between the Vatican and the Axis alliance and its victims is a many-layered story burdened by rebuke and obfuscation. True, in the 1939 encyclical, *Summi Pontificatus*, Pius XII emphasized the unity of the human race, but the statement was vague and did not deal sufficiently with "the Jewish question." The encyclical *Mit Brennender Sorge* (March 14, 1937) was critical of Hitler for violating the terms of the *Reichskonkordat* (Concordat) of 1933. But this was mainly out of a concern for the fact that pagan rites and beliefs were part of Nazi ideology—something the Vatican could not tolerate. Madame Blavatsky be warned! According to the Vatican's recent release of documents during the war years, Pius XII did make some attempts to challenge Hitler, but the Pontiff's public statements were vague and suggestive, not propositional, refusing to commit to an unvarnished condemnation of the Holocaust.

Defenders of Pius XXII argue that an explicit statement condemning the Nazi treatment of the Jews would have put the lives of Jews and Catholics of Jewish descent in greater danger from a retaliatory German leadership. Clearly, it's been reported that some Nazis did see the Pope's Christmas message of 1942 as an attack on National Socialism, but again, the wording of the Pope's message was purposefully vague. And it is legitimate to ask: Was the concern of Pius XXII about *ad maiora mala vitanda* (to avoid making the situation worse) mainly in regard to Jews in general, or in regard to Jews who had converted to Catholicism?

Throughout World War II, the Vatican took an official position of neutrality in the social and political sphere, and Pius XXII was understandably fearful that a concerted attack on Hitler would result in the German Catholic Church being expelled from Germany. Still it is difficult to ignore the fact that Germany's Catholic Center Party enabled Hitler's rise to power. No doubt the Concordat signed in Vatican City in 1933 during the pontificate of Pius XI was interpreted by some Nazis as a commitment by the Vatican not to interfere with the Nazis' "Final Solution" to the "Jewish Question" so long as this excluded baptized Jewish converts. Here again, the church's civil autonomy was diminished by requiring the bishops' oath of loyalty to the Reich. But while we need to acknowledge documented attempts by the Vatican and individual priests to hide Jews from the Nazis—attempts that were not publicized at the time—we can certainly agree that the Vatican's actions throughout World War II remain worthy of serious scrutiny. Not only does the Vatican need to be challenged for its appeasement with the Nazis during the war but also for its role in helping Nazi war criminals escape to Latin America after the war—which was not just a matter of isolated cases undertaken by a small handful of priests.

PJ: Can you say a bit more about the relationships between the Catholic Church and fascism?

PM: I can try. In *History vs. Apologetics: The Holocaust, the Third Reich, and the Catholic Church*, David Cymet (2011) argues that Vatican officials frequently assisted the escape of genocide perpetrators during the postwar years of Pius XII's pontificate. Did the Vatican know the war crimes of these perpetrators? If they did, was it because they were supporters of National Socialism? Was it because they wanted to bolster Catholicism in Latin America against the threat of communism? Other reasons? While the answers to those questions remain unclear, what is certain is that what mattered most to the Vatican was the preservation of their ecclesiastic structures. But at what price? What exactly was the relationship between the Vatican and clerofascist regimes like the Slovak People's Party? The Yugoslav National Movement? Portugal's Salazar regime? Vichy France? Franco's Spain? Italy's Partido Popolare Italiano? Belgium's Rexist Party? Romania's Iron Guard?

More specific to my question, how has the history of the Ustaše under the leadership of Ante Pavelić, the Croat *Führer* that exterminated 487,000 Serb Orthodox Christians and also 30,000 Jews and 27,000 Gypsies, affected the Croatian Catholic Church? Surely contemporary Croats know the history of Glina and Otočac. The very next month after Otočac, Pavelić was greeted warmly by the Vatican. Maybe that massacre was not known by the Vatican at the time but they most likely were known to the Croatian Catholic clergy and to the episcopate. But the atrocities carried out by the Ustaša NDH regime were certainly well known by the Vatican as early as 1941. That the Ustaša NDH desired to exterminate the Serbian, Jewish, and Roma populations of Croatia and Bosnia-Hercegovina was no secret. Yet nothing was said by the Vatican about the continuing slaughter throughout the rest of the war. It was openly announced, I think, by the education minister, that the official NDH policy was to kill a third, deport a third, and forcefully convert a third of the Serbian population of Croatia and Bosnia. Why did Pius XXII send Papal Nuncio Giuseppe Ramiro Marcone (1882–1952) to Ante Pavelić to serve as his personal envoy, even if the Vatican did not legally recognize the NDH but still had unofficial diplomatic relations?

Of course, later in the 1990s, you have Croats massacred at Tenja, Tordinci, Lovas, and many other places, as history again reclaims its legacy of blood and bone through the founding event of all cultures that began in murder—traced back to the Biblical Cain (see the work of René Girard). But here I am emphasizing World War II. These are tough questions for all Catholics. Do the neo-Nazis in the United States who are chanting "Jews will not replace us" and "blood and soil" and fighting for a white ethno-state know this history? And are they getting support from right-wing Catholics or their white Christian evangelical churches? Here, again, the development of liberation theology is crucial.

PJ: History is never black or white; while publicly serving Ante Pavelić's fascist regime, the Croatian Catholic Church has also exhibited some resistance. However, even with the wisdom of seventy-year hindsight, it is very hard to assess this dynamic between support and resistance. A typical case in the point is Cardinal Alojzije Stepinac, who served as archbishop of Zagreb during NDH and publicly opposed racial laws, deportations, concentration camps, forced conversions, and other atrocities of the regime throughout World War II. Stepinac is also said to have clandestinely helped many individual victims of the NDH regime. Yet "there are serious shortcomings in Stepinac's statements and actions toward the Ustashe regime and its genocidal actions against the Serbs and the Serbian Orthodox Church" (Tomasevich 2001: 564). After the war, the Yugoslav communist regime sentenced Stepinac for treason and collaboration with Ustaše. These days, Croatian Catholic Church works hard on the beatification of Stepinac, while some other voices (including, but far from limited to, victims of the NDH regime) strongly oppose these efforts. What do you make of this complex dialectic between support and resistance, which, I believe, can be generalized to all churches and all societies?

PM: Yes, it can certainly be generalized, I agree. Certainly Croatia's archbishop of Zagreb, Alojzije Stepinac, saw the role of the Catholic Church in creation of the Independent State of Croatia as a bulwark against what he considered the ruthless atheism of communism. In Vatican City, Stepinac defended Catholic priests who spread propaganda in support of Pavelić's call to "Free Croatia!" Pavelić had been condemned in France, as the mastermind of the 1934 double assassination of Yugoslavian King Alexander I and French foreign minister Louis Barthou. But this was before the atrocities began. Stepinac blessed the Ustaše leader and regime at a banquet held in Pavelić's honor perhaps unaware at the time of Pavelić's complicity in atrocities at Glina four days earlier—atrocities that included locking hundreds of Serbian Orthodox believers inside their church and setting it ablaze. Stepinac repeatedly appeared in public with Pavelić—"the Poglavnik"—while the official Croatian Catholic newspaper *Nedelja* supported both Pavelić and Hitler (lots of people supported Hitler). Fueled by a hatred of Protestantism, Freemasonry, and Neo-Paganism, upset with the Serbs for converting to the Eastern Orthodox Church (conversions likely done for political rather than religious reasons), Stepinac continually sided with the Vatican, which, after all, had supported the Catholic dictator Franco during the Spanish Civil War (Franco always traveled with the mummified right arm of Saint Teresa of Avila, which was on his bedside table when he died).

The official Croatian Catholic newspaper *Nedelja* praised both Pavelić and Hitler. Stepinac even accepted an Order of Merit medal from Pavelić! While certainly Stepinac would have been horrified to learn that the Orthodox archbishop of Zagreb was jailed and tortured by the Ustaše, who also killed 157 Orthodox priests, among them 3 Serb Orthodox bishops, it is a little more than curious that by the time Stepinac began to decry in public the atrocities of the Ustaše, the genocides had already been committed, and it was becoming increasingly clear by 1943 that the Germans were going to lose the war. In an article published in the *Jerusalem Post*, Julia Gorin (2010) writes:

... Germany entrusted Croatia with running its own concentration camps, without oversight. Shamefully, clergy members took a voracious dive into the bloodbath, serving as guards, commanders and executioners at the 40 camps, most famously Jasenovac, the Holocaust's third-largest yet least spoken-of camp. There, they killed Serbs, Jews, Gypsies and anti-fascist Croats. On August 29, 1942, a friar from the monastery of Siroki Brijeg, named Petar Brzica, won first place for killing the most Serbs in the shortest time, boasting 1,350 throats slit in one night.

Historian Carl Savich quotes an AP report stating that "a priest from Petricevac led Croat fascists, armed with hatchets and knives, to a nearby village. In the 1942 attack, they butchered 2,300 Serbs." Testimony from a survivor of that February 7 massacre, Selo Drakulic, reads: Prior to killing the adults, unborn children were violently cut from their mothers' womb[s] and slaughtered. Of the remaining children in the village, all under the age of 12, the Ustashas brutally removed arms, legs, noses, ears and genitals. Young girls were raped and killed, while their families were forced to witness the violation and carnage. The most grotesque torture of all was the decapitation of children, their heads thrown into the laps of their mothers, who were themselves then killed. (Gorin 2010)

Archive photos of sadism that would make horror filmmakers blush survive today: Ustašas displaying an Orthodox priest's head; an eyeless peasant woman; Serbs and Jews being pushed off a cliff; a Serb with a saw to his neck; and a smiling Ustaša holding the still-beating heart of prominent industrialist Miloš Teslić, who had been castrated, disemboweled, and his ears and lips cut off. Italian writer Curzio Malaparte in his 1944 book *Kaputt* offers this detail: "While [Pavelic] spoke, I gazed at a wicker basket on the Poglavnik's desk [which] seemed to be filled with mussels, or shelled oysters. . . . 'Are they Dalmatian oysters?' I asked. [Pavelic] said smiling, 'It is a present from my loyal Ustashas. . . . Forty pounds of human eyes" (Malaparte 1944 [2005]). In their book *Unholy Trinity: The Vatican, the Nazis and the Swiss Banks*, reporter Mark Aarons and former Justice Department attorney John Loftus (Aarons and Loftus 1998) corroborate the grisly Croatian crimes, as does *Genocide in Satellite Croatia, 1941–1945: A Record of Racial and Religious Persecutions and Massacres* by Edmond Paris: "The Italians photographed an Ustaša wearing two chains of human tongues and ears around his neck" (Paris 2011).

I certainly can accept that Stepinac stood against all forms of totalitarianism and cruelty, but, understandably for a Catholic archbishop, he held communism as the greatest of all evils that threatened the survival and sanctity of the Catholic Church. This opposition to communism perhaps diminished possible actions he could—and should—have taken in condemning the horrors of the Ustaše, which certainly deserved as much condemnation as the actions of Stalin. I wonder what the administration and students at Archbishop Stepinac High School in White Plains, New York, feel about this. In the face of peasants being slaughtered by the death squads of the fascist

Salvadorean Armed Forces, Saint Óscar Romero courageously spoke out against such injustices. I wonder what a conversation between these two saints—who admittedly lived in different geographical and historical contexts, would look like.

You are a Croat, Peter, and I would like to hear what happens to Croatian Catholic Church today. Are ethnoreligious divisions still strong in the region in which you live, among predominantly Orthodox Christian Serbs, Muslim Bosniaks, and Catholic Croats? Is the Croatian Catholic Church a political force in Croatian politics?

PJ: I'm simultaneously glad you asked this question and horrified of my own answer, Peter. The Croatian Catholic Church is indeed a big political force in Croatia. Its influence is particularly strong in public services such as education, health care, army, and juridical system. Unfortunately, instead of using its privileged social position for the benefit of the community, Croatian Catholic Church uses its power to exacerbate own fortune and influence. Let me give you an example from Croatian schools. In 1990s the newly minted Croatian state and the Vatican have signed a set of international agreements. According to these agreements, Catechism is an elective course in Croatian primary and secondary public schools. The state has almost no power over instruction of Catechism—the church independently decides about the curriculum, selection and employment of teachers (usually priests or nuns), etc. And what does the Catholic Church do? More often than not, for six-, seven-, eight-, or nine-year-olds, they schedule the "elective" course in the middle of the school day. Schoolmasters, many of whom are either on the side of the church or too afraid to resist, often do not organize any supervised activity for these children—so you effectively have these little kids sitting unsupervised in school corridors for 45 minutes, just because their parents did not enroll them to Catechism. Under such pressure, many parents enroll their kids to Catechism just to avoid making them stand out from the crowd. Those who decide to swim against the stream often end up bullied—implicitly, by being forced to sit alone in an empty corridor, and/or explicitly, by other teachers and kids. And can you try and guess the most cynical thing about this? The state pays Catechism textbooks, the state pays Catechism teachers . . . I, taxpayer, am paying the Catholic Church to bully my kid and other kids.

Such examples can be found in all walks of life, but you asked about ethnoreligious divisions—and that is another wonderful example of the Croatian Catholic Church *modus operandi*. In communist Yugoslavia, it was not wise to express too much national identity. Since the majority of Croats are Catholic, the majority of Serbs are Orthodox, and the majority of Bosniaks are Muslim, apparently an easier way to express your national identity without being called a nationalist was through religion. (I carefully wrote apparently, because during communist times, many people have been quite open about their nationality and without consequences—as it happens in the Balkans, everyone has their own interpretation of recent history.) Anyway, I don't think that Mexican Catholic Church would see itself as a "keeper of Mexican national identity" in relation to, for instance, Guatemalan Catholic Church. But that's exactly what happened in the Balkans during recent wars, where each respective church has developed strong relationships to national identity. In this way, the notion of Croatian Catholic has become a badge of identity, regardless of one's true religious beliefs.

However, Peter, this is just a tip of a much larger iceberg. During the 1991–1995 wars, for instance, you could see prominent Croatian priests blessing canons and other deadly weapons that were about to be thrown at the enemy. (Admittedly, Serbian side did exactly the same, and this fact is often used by the Croatian Catholic Church to justify such actions.) So during 1990s, you would turn on the telly, and you would see someone from the piece-loving, love-thy-neighbor Christian religion blessing devices used to kill, injure, and destroy. And then, a few years after, you would hear the same person on the same telly speaking of love and respect to thy neighbor. . . . But their deeds speak stronger than their words, and it is very hard to imagine their love and respect for thy *Serbian* neighbor. Slowly but surely, the Croatian Catholic Church has sided with some of the most extreme right-wing parts of Croatian society. For instance, every year the church openly serves masses for anniversary of Ante Pavelić's death. Given all atrocities you just described, how crazy is that? Obviously, celebrating Ante Pavelić in Croatia is like celebrating Adolf Hitler in Germany—you cannot really do it in public. But the Church seems to be above Croatian laws, and they regularly use their freedom of religious profession for profession of fascism.

In short, Peter, the Croatian Catholic Church has a huge social influence in Croatia. While the church does help the poor in free kitchens and shelters, the majority of its wealth and influence is used to amass even more wealth and influence. In the process, the Croatian Catholic Church has sided with the right wing and some of the meanest fascists to boot. While some simpletons, priests, and laypeople might be honestly deluded by nationalism, I am deeply convinced that Croatian Catholic Church primarily uses nationalism as a tool for promoting its own material and ideological interests. After years of bloody wars, nationalist discourse resonates with many disadvantaged people—and the Croatian Catholic Church uses this fact to own advantage. I could tell you much more about the Croatian Catholic Church, Peter, but the more I write, the dirtier I feel. So let me ask: How do you go about such contradictions between the talk and walk of the Catholic Church?

PM: I am not surprised, Petar, about the church in Croatia. We have a strong right-wing Catholic movement here in the United States that is decidedly against Pope Francis and liberation theology. Francis is not a proponent of liberation theology but of what developed in his native Argentina as *teologia del pueblo*, or theology of the people. It begins with the experiences of the oppression of people in the face of neoliberal capitalism and corporate globalization. The Catholic Church is not monolithic. There are fundamental ideological differences within the church. I think that Pope Francis's experiences with the military dictatorship and his contact with fellow Jesuits who did support liberation theology made a powerful impact on him and helped him to adopt certain perspectives from liberation theology, such as a critique of global capitalism.

Liberation theologians openly contest certain positions taken by the established Church, just as Pope Francis does. Francis is more moderate in many of his views than many of the prominent exponents of liberation theology. Nevertheless, he has taken strong positions against global capitalism and environmental destruction that I welcome and applaud. Do we obscure the spiritual nature of the gospel by calling for more than just an identification with the poor but rather a robust confrontation with the rich and powerful? Do we administer to the poor without asking why they are poor? Here we need to recall the words of Brazil's Dom Hélder Câmara, whom Paulo Freire very much admired: "When I give food to the poor, they call me a saint; when I ask why the poor have no food, they call me a communist" (Câmara 2009).

In 1965, as the famous Vatican II Council was coming to a close, Hélder Câmara led forty bishops late at night into the Catacombs of Domitilla outside of Rome. After celebrating the Eucharist, they signed a document under the title of the Pact of the Catacombs, challenging themselves and others to live lives of evangelical poverty and to dedicate themselves to serving the two-thirds of humanity who live in poverty and deprivation. There are certainly ideological differences within the church and in some countries—such as Croatia and Poland—the right-wing factions of the church hold sway.

PJ: Your answer reflects political tensions between the left-wing and the right-wing political factions within the church. However, I am conflicted about much more "mundane" things, and the ones that the whole Catholic Church seems to agree about. Examples include the explicit position of the global Catholic Church against using condoms, against abortion, and against LGBTQ rights. In some areas of Africa, for instance, AIDS kills significant parts of the population, while the official church position—articulated, among others, by Pope Benedict XVI—claims that the HIV epidemic is "a tragedy that cannot be overcome by money alone, that cannot be overcome through the distribution of condoms, which even aggravates the problems" (in Butt 2009). How do you go about such teachings and their consequences? More generally, how do you reconcile them with the message of liberation and emancipation?

PM: Yes, there are positions taken by the church hierarchy that are firmly established and to which I remain in trenchant disagreement. And yes, they involve many of the same "mundane" issues to which you allude, but I do not think they are so much mundane as pervasive and impacting everyday life. I remember a Paulist father once telling me that I should never lose my critical approach to questions of dogma and faith. We want you to be a thinking Catholic, he told me. I do not believe the guardians of the faith would be very pleased with revolutionary priests accompanying guerilla armies as chaplains, such as Camilo Torres of Colombia or Gaspar García Laviana of Spain. Yet I see their actions as heroic. We must act according to our conscience, in deep reflection and contemplation.

Going back to the powerful analysis by Noam Chomsky, we should also consider the conditions in which these positions are being developed. Speaking about the US context, Chomsky says:

> There is a correlation, common in other parts of the world as well. When life is not offering expected benefits, people commonly turn to some means of support from religion. Furthermore, there is a lot of cynicism. It was recognized by party managers of both parties (Republicans and Democrats) that if they can throw some red meat to religious fundamentalist constituencies, like say we are against gay rights, they can pick up votes. In fact, maybe a third of the electorate—if you

cater to elements of the religious right in ways that the business world, the real constituency, doesn't care that much about. (in Chaudary 2007)

These messages of the church hierarchy are being heavily instrumentalized by politicians, who gain cheap votes over issues such as abortion or gay rights.

PJ: And what about spiritual aspects of these messages?

PM: I very much appreciate indigenous traditions and what they bring to discussions of spirituality. My approach is broadly ecumenical and includes Buddha, Mohammed, Krishna, and the Great Spirit of the Native American traditions. Here I stand with Meister Eckhart, Thomas Merton and Matthew Fox and their creation spirituality and emphasis on God born within each of us, Apophatic Divinity, and the ground of being. Human welfare and well-being should be placed above the law. Condemnation of homosexuality in the Bible is very different from the way progressive individuals view homosexuality today, which is grounded in post-Enlightenment science (Rivage-Seul 2008). It seems to some exegetes that what was forbidden was not homosexuality itself but heterosexuals engaged in homosexual acts (Rivage-Seul 2008). Jesus himself was silent on the question of homosexuality. I agree with Boff when he writes that "The paradox of the cross is incomprehensible both to formal and to dialectical reason" (1987: 135), but this should not be used as a pretext for blind obedience to law. What is concealed in this mystery will be revealed through struggle—that is, through praxis— and not simply reflection or adherence to laws with which we disagree. Boff writes that "the incarnation is already present at the beginning of the universe" (1997: 178) and "the universe culminates in each individual in the form of consciousness" (1997: 121). He writes that "all energies and morphogenetic fields have acted synergistically so that each one might be born and be that singular and unique person that he or she is" and so it seems to me that we each have something very worthwhile to contribute to the debate through a cultivation of critical consciousness.

We have, all of us, been here since the beginning of the universe and are made out of stardust. And it is the guiding principles of the universe that brought us here, and that has resulted in the potential for our self-actualization, and that has taken 15 billion years of evolutionary processes. We had better start to listen to indigenous sages who have understood this far better in their ayahuasca huts in the Amazon basin than we Euro-Americans here in beer halls of Babylon. We need to abandon our anthropocentric and mimetic desires and subject ourselves to a global ethics of solidarity, compassion, and fellowship so that our outer ecologies can be brought into cosmogenetic harmony with our inner ecology of the mind and spirit. And here we bring our maieutic processes of pedagogy into dialogue with a Freirean approach to conscientization. In other words, we bring together history, mind, and spirit. I reject a turgid monotheism that would cleave us from spiritual traditions that predate Christianity. In short, I would say that we must act in accordance with our own conscience.

The Bible is a document written by those inspired to understand the relationship of human beings to divine power and such divine power was often conceptualized by its all-too-human authors as viciously inhuman—the punishing of children for the crimes of their father, for example, the treatment of women as chattel, and other "un-American" examples that we find in the Bible. The teachings of Jesus were far more humane than the pronouncements and actions of the God of the Old Testament. Nevertheless, I would still want to protect the United States from ever becoming officially a Christian state simply because our Constitution protects the separation of church and state for what I believe to be good reasons, religious freedom being one of them. I am not a supporter of Christian nationalism, since I mistrust those Christian demagogues who use literal translations of the Bible to do terrible things in the name of divine providence—the mistreatment of LGBTQ communities as one example, support for the death penalty being another. The Declaration of Independence and the Constitution should protect us from the repressive theocratic designs of the Christian nationalists—and only time will tell if this will remain the case. The creation of the anti-Kingdom by Trump and his quisling henchmen has just raised the stakes considerably on whether democracy will perish in the United States in our lifetime or that of our children.

Between the Material and the Spiritual

PJ: Are there any theoretical and/or practical dissonances between Marxism and Christianity in your theory? If there are, how do you go about them?

PM: While some might argue that traditional nonreligious Marxism is not as equipped as theological traditions to engage fundamental questions pertaining to the hermeneutics of spirituality, there are numerous Marxist theorists who have written profoundly about issues of the spirit—here, I am thinking of Ernst Bloch, Walter Benjamin, and Erich Fromm, just to name a few. I think Marxism does address issues of the human spirit, but what interests me, in particular, is an engagement with a tradition that deals with a triune god. Of course, liberation theology comes in many forms: Chicano liberation theology; Latinx liberation theology; Native American liberation theology; African American liberation theology. Therefore, I do not want to limit liberation theology to the political theology that comes out of Europe, or to the Latin American liberation theology that is primarily Catholic and pastoral.

I work as a Marxist materialist but I believe there is a world beyond physicalism. That world constitutes for me a world of hope. Hope is conjugated in opposition to injustice and gestated in the struggle of humanity against inhumanity. Rubem Alves writes of hope as follows:

> Hope is the presentiment that the imagination is more real, and reality less real, than we had thought. It is the sensation that the last word does not belong to the brutality of facts with their oppression and repression. It is the suspicion that reality is far more complex than realism would have us believe, that the frontiers of the possible are not determined by the limits of the present, and that, miraculously and surprisingly, life is readying the creative event that will open the way to freedom and resurrection. (Alves in Boff 1987: 124)

Hope does not deliver us from suffering. But hope, I believe, can deliver us from the fear of suffering. It does this by giving us the courage to believe that we are not fated to live in misery, that light does shine through the cracks of the day-to-day sepulcher in which we find ourselves, in this cold and damp undercroft, in this darkness of inevitability.

PJ: What are the more general challenges that you encountered on the path of reconciliation between the spiritual and the scientific?

PM: First of all, Petar, we need to examine the gospels scientifically, that is hermeneutically, and one way that we can do this is to examine the metaphors used to describe the paschal mystery, the mystery of Jesus's lifework, death, and resurrection. We have in the West a persistent medieval theory about Christian salvation that should be put to rest—what Johnson (2018) refers to as "satisfaction theology." We can move beyond this theology if we understand that it represents but one of many interpretations that arose from the metaphors used by early Christians to describe the paschal mystery. These metaphors reveal a much more variegated and pluriform understanding of salvation than the still-dominant theory first developed by Anselm—that God required a debt to be "satisfied" before humanity could be saved, that debt being the sacrifice of God's son, Jesus, who was required to die in order to pay off the sins of humanity. As Johnson writes: "A rainbow of metaphors can refract the same religious reality" (2018: 119). But not all metaphors used in the New Testament—"medical, military, diplomatic, financial, legal, liberative, sacrificial, and familial"—would be appealing to people today since they arose from first-century Jewish and Hellenitic circles (Johnson 2018: 153). These vibrant metaphors, however, helped Christians identify, understand, and explain the salvation brought by the death and resurrection of Jesus.

Winning in conflicts was the generalized salvific theme during the first millennium of Christianity, and reconciliation was the other. God's victory in Christ and God's redeeming grace reconciling us to the Godself. Justification is another theme. You are acquitted of your wrongdoings. The juridical metaphor is applied here to the paschal mystery. Everyone is divinely acquitted. Everyone, regardless of their wrongdoings! These metaphors resonated during the first century with all those suffering under the brutal lash of the Roman empire, who endured great pain "actively inflicted by unjust structures" (Johnson 2018: 107). God's justice was perceived as far more just than that of the empire. There were also sacrificial metaphors according to ancient Jewish theology and ritual, such as Jesus the Lamb of God. And there was the servant metaphor associated with Jesus, the Suffering Servant.

PJ: What happens with these metaphors today?

PM: More recently, liberation theologians have used and are continuing to use the metaphor of becoming free, which was also a metaphor used by early Christians. Which is why I chose the title, *Breaking Free*, for my comic book (McLaren 2019). Liberation theologians have used the metaphor of liberation but interpreted the gospel in contemporary contexts of oppression—such as US imperialist attacks on the people of underdeveloped countries, and in the context of war criminals and capitalism as a structure of exploitation. According to Johnson (2018: 131), "liberation theologians have lifted up what we might call this submerged metaphor and given it a powerful new lease on life." Liberation from bondage of all kinds! The metaphor of salvation through suffering can be misused, obviously, since it is not a call for people to suffer—it is incomparably more complex than that. This refers to suffering freely endured by others out of love for the people, as in the case of Archbishop Romero, who was assassinated while saying mass, assassinated while acting in the role of a servant, called by God.

The sheer variety of metaphors used to understand salvation through Christ should put to rest the prevailing "satisfaction theory" in Christian theology—that God required a debt to be satisfied, that debt being the sacrifice of his son, Jesus, before humanity could be saved from eternal damnation. The core assumption of this "satisfactory theory" is flawed. Yet it still persists—in fact, remains dominant—today! We can't read New Testament metaphors simply in light of the theory that God's own son became human in order to die and pay the debt for our sins since Christ came into the world as a free gift, not to pay some otherworldly debt. God does not need payment for the forgiveness of sins. Johnson (2018: 155) reminds us that the notion of satisfaction of a debt as a condition of forgiveness "contradicts the mercy of God as revealed in the scriptures." We should interpret the root metaphors of such theories in the framework of the original experience of salvation felt by the earl Christians, and, as Johnson (2018: 156) recommends, not according to an early medieval explanatory theory that attempted to explain salvation as some kind of tit-for-tat mechanism.

The idea here argued by Johnson is that our understanding of God's liberating mercy has developed over time, and Johnson counterposes to the "satisfaction theory of salvation" what she calls the "narrative theology of God's accompaniment that brings salvation" (2018: 158). What I really appreciate about Johnson's "accompaniment theology" is that it is grounded in a double solidarity—a solidarity between Jesus and humanity and a solidarity between God and Jesus. But this solidarity extends to the entire planet and all of creation, since human beings are genetically related in kinship to all other species on our planet. She writes that the living community we call Earth is composed of chemicals that have been condensed from debris left by a previous generation of stars. It is a theology of relationality—of the goodness of creation—and not a just a theology "from above" where spirit is held to be more important than the material world. All of creation is worthy of salvation, and the material world, including our own bodies, is worthy of God's grace. Jesus, after all, was accused of being a drunk and a glutton!

PJ: So what about the relationships between science and religion?

PM: Writing *Pedagogy of Insurrection* (McLaren 2015b) brought me face-to-face with questions that by no means have I worked out to my satisfaction. What I can say is that I certainly do not believe that knowledge is simply produced by the rational permutations of the brain. I do believe that it is possible to posit a divine consciousness that pervades our existence. But I have been inundated with books and articles by colleagues and feel the specter of New Age thought crawling up my spine. Some of it is interesting but maybe in the way pornography is interesting to an adolescent. What do you make of any of this? I will note parenthetically or in passing only that there are some interesting speculative developments in theology centered around some ideas in quantum mechanics where field-based waves are seen as producing the hardware of the universe and the entities of the space–time domain, while the scalar or nonvectorial waves produce information without carrying energy and act like the software of the universe. The information that interconnects entities throughout space–time includes upward and downward causation, which helps to explain why the past is always present. Here, a definition of God might include the potentials of the universe for its self-creation, which might involve, for instance, tuning the universe to the evolution of complexity. But this is hardly satisfying and for all I know is little more than scribbling on a cosmic iPad.

Here, Teilhard de Chardin's work (1959, 1964, 1965, 1966a, b, 1968) becomes even more interesting and more relevant to me. In this view, God can influence the course of evolution without interfering with the laws of nature. Some physicists argue that the original presence of this information can be ascribed to a transcendental creative act where the growth and development of this information are considered immanent. I am not well-versed enough in physics to evaluate this speculative argument.

However, there are several practice-oriented codes of moral behavior that have been generated out of this work by Ervin László (2014), who has come up with a minimum moral code (live so that others can live) and a maximum moral code (act so as to further the evolution of a humanly favorable dynamic equilibrium in the biosphere). I would modify this, however, to include nonhuman animals. To me, holistic and local domains of consciousness are interdependent and material and mental domains are bidirectional so that when unconscious contents become conscious, this transition could possibly alter the unconscious memories left behind. But this takes us into some strange terrain and it comes too close to magical thinking for me. When it comes to quantum physics, I do not have a sufficient background to understand what its implications might be for theology.

PJ: What are the ontological implications of this? Are you saying that something can exist beyond matter?

PM: Let us just say that I remain open-minded about the transphysical. The idea of a nonemergent irreducible mind within a psychophysical world is worth considering in my estimation and this, of course, would take us to the Renaissance Neoplatonists and also to Bergson, Emerson, Schopenhauer, and Kant. Here I would need a broader theological framework that many Marxist traditions are not equipped to handle. An expanded view of mind is not, in my view, antithetical to Marxism. Consciousness is not a mere epiphenomenon of the material brain. We need new visionary taxonomies to help us understand anomalous experiences that cannot be explained by a physicalist interpretation. Does that mean that I believe the cosmos was created by an upwelling of the mind of God? Does that mean that Joséph of Copertino could actually fly? I do not spend a lot of time pondering these questions. I am more concerned with living with clarity and in preferential solidarity with those who are victims of the scandal of poverty and who belong to despised racial and ethnic groups and exploited social classes.

I am not here trying to push a Neoplatonist line of reasoning—yet, I remain open to various explanations of how the cosmos came into being. In my political work, I remain very much a historical materialist. I think this is the best approach for understanding the dialectical relationship between capitalism and labor (and materialism and idealism, for that matter) in the larger struggle for a socialist future. While I do not deny the material world, I am very interested in the nature of consciousness, and I would not in the least be surprised if consciousness exists independently of the brain, with the brain serving as a type of filtering device to gain access to the deep layers of the psyche. The brain here is conceived as a system that constrains the supraliminal conscious expression of normally inaccessible subliminal contents. And here I am echoing the work of F. W. H. Myers and William James and the work of contemporary researcher Edward Kelly (Kelly et al. 2007; Kelly, Crabtree, and Marshall 2015) and the notions of the subliminal self and the supraliminal self.

Now all of this interest I have in religious experiences, the nature of consciousness, etc., is mostly just engaging in thought games. One day perhaps I will be able to make more nuanced reflections about the nature of the cosmos, our role on this earth, and the place that faith plays in our lives. Yes, I do return over and over again to certain questions, figures, and memories. I return to questions "on the ground," questions that involve what Michelle Alexander (2010) calls "the new Jim Crow." The massive discrimination policies directed toward people of color in the areas of education, employment, public benefits; the mass incarceration of African Americans and Latinos through the war on drugs and anticrime policies; a criminal justice system responsible for creating and reproducing the racial hierarchy in the United States; or what could be called the American Caste System—the privatization of prisons ensuring large incarceration rates of prisoners of color.

PJ: I am interested in this dialectic between the material and the spiritual, the real and the mystical, the human and the divine . . . and I guess that, in order to remain living in this world and with this world, one needs to find a certain balance between those radically different views to our earthly existence. How do you go about obvious and inherent differences and contradictions contained in these dichotomies? What keeps your materialist critique from plunging into pure mystics; what keeps your spiritual worldview attached to the material world?

PM: As a dissident educator whose resistance has been forged on picket lines, on marches, amidst military sweeps of unruly neighborhoods, in libraries, churches, seminar rooms, museums, revolutionary institutes, classrooms, clandestine meeting places, and public squares, I have always felt that I live in the interstices of internal contradictions, in the hinterlands of the unexcluded third, in the fructifying poetry of chaos and the absurdity of being, in the pluriverse of values in which we are pushed to make choices, where being and nonbeing interpenetrate amidst the explosion of metaphors and magical incantations, where everything transforms into something else, where whispers from primeval groves of evergreens turn into thunderclaps, where an infant's sigh turns into the oratory of a politician, where journeys begin at their destinations, where coherence mingles amicably with ambiguity.

As a teenager I was very interested in Theosophy, eastern religions, the Christian mystics, the desert fathers, and the lives of saints. I do not pay much attention in my recent work to Bruno Giordano, Marcion, Valentinus, Simon Magus, Appelles, or the Christological or ecclesial Gnosticism or Docetism that is associated with their teachings, which is not to say they do not offer some interesting points of debate. In this respect, however, I follow Jon Sobrino in defending the living, breathing, bleeding, and pulsating flesh of the man we call the Christ, the *ecce homo*. Of course I am inspired by the life of the saints and martyrs such as Saint Maximilian Kolbe, patron saint of drug addicts and political prisoners, whose prison cell I visited last year in Auschwitz. In my own work I have found it important to uphold the humanity of Christ without de-emphasizing Christ's divinity, and for me the humanity of Christ is best embodied historically in Jesus' birth, death, and resurrection, and all that occurred during his dispensation among us. Here I am emphasizing Christ walking among us, among the victims of the brutality of structural sin, among the sick, the homeless, the diseased, the despised, those who despair of life, those whose pilloried flesh stands as a testament to the injustice meted out by the powerful to the most vulnerable. In other words, I try to concern myself with the story or narrative of Christ, his narrative being that in no way denies Christ's divinity.

But we can very easily become lost in the unreality, the mystical body of Christ, or the church, for that matter. Our humanness, our soft flesh, and breakable bones are what Sobrino (2001: 276) refers to as "the condition of possibility of salvation" through the "homo verus" (Sobrino 2001: 278), that is, through Christ's constitutive relationship with God and history, and history and transcendence. We need, as Sobrino argues, a truly humanized Christ, not simply a demythified Christ produced in the libraries and sanctuaries of Rome by theologians of various ecclesiastical stripes. Let us not get too tangled up in what is real in Christ and what is divine, for what is truly human is that which can bring us victory over inhumanity, over the anti-Kingdom, through speaking truth to the demonic power ensepulchred in the vaults of alienation wrought by capitalism and its attendant antagonisms. So, for me, developing a philosophy of praxis means learning how to walk in history, as both the subject and the object of our human story, lacing up our thirsty boots and refreshing our parched spirit as we journey alongside the victims of social sin, moving from the historical to the transcendent through faith. It is said that faith is a gift from God. In this regard, I consider myself to be ungifted, unfaithed. Or perhaps I have discovered the limits of my faith. All that I can do is accept with sincerity those limits and with whatever time I have left kick up the empirical dirt a bit like a good social scientist while at the same time scratch the rocks of unexplored caves of the soul. Because I notice that a lot has been happening on those damp and clammy walls.

6

Karl Marx and Liberation Theology: Dialectical Materialism and Christian Spirituality in, against and beyond Contemporary Capitalism

Early Thoughts about Karl Marx

PJ: This book bursts with references to Marxian and Marxist thought. Now that we are about to discuss relationships between Marxism and liberation theology, it is about time to provide our readers with a whole-rounded overview of our views on Karl Marx and his theories.

PM: Much of what is said about Marx, especially by bourgeois academics—for instance, that his ideas have been fossilized over time—is utter highbrow bilge. I found that out by returning to Marx's own works, and then by reading interpretations of Marx side-by-side with Marx's writings. I turned to interpreters of Marx who included, among others, Karel Kosik, István Mészáros, Robert Brenner, Leo Panitch, Adorno, Althusser, Bloch, Adorno, Benjamin, Marcuse, Eagleton, Callinicos, Holloway, John Bellamy Foster, David Harvey, Paula Allman, Jameson, Moishe Postone, Castoriadis, Lefebvre, Trotsky, Poulantzas, Lukács, Mariátegui, Williams, Lebowitz, Negri and the usual suspects. More recently I have relied on the interpretations of trusted comrades such as Peter Hudis and Kevin Anderson. What I found to be most helpful in my engagement with Marx was, first of all, trying to get a grasp of Hegel's dialectic of negativity (it is nearly impossible to appreciate Marx absent a familiarity with Hegel's works), and attempting to grasp Marx's labor theory of value. I published some work on this topic nearly twenty years ago in a dialogue with Glenn Rikowski (McLaren and Rikowski 2001) and in some other publications, and my understanding of what I consider to be Marx's breakthrough insight remains essentially the same. It would be a good idea, Petar, for me to summarize this again. Especially when our discussion leads to postdigital technology and the formation of consciousness, it's important that I make my Marxist credentials clear in case I might be mistaken for a woolly headed transcendentalist. So I am going to summarize, and pretty much reproduce, word for word, some of my comments from that interview.

PJ: Please go ahead, Peter!

PM: I'm certainly no expert when it comes to having a granular grasp of the full corpus of Marx's work as revealed in the Marx-Engels *Gesaumtausgabe*. I'm still very much engaged in studying Marx's works and I fervently believe that some essential understanding of Marx is necessary if we are going to pursue liberation theology and revolutionary critical pedagogy. In a nutshell, I follow Marx in arguing that capital grounds all social mediation as a form of value, and that the substance of labor itself must be interrogated because doing so brings us closer to understanding the nature of capital's social universe out of which our subjectivities are created. There are only a few places in the world—perhaps among tribes in the Brazilian rainforest, for example—where the logic of capitalist work has not infused all forms of human sociability. Thus, we can describe capitalist society as a totality of different types of labor. But what are the particular forms that labor takes within capitalism? To answer this cardinal question, we need to examine value as a social relation, not as some kind of accounting device—a computer program or a Chinese abacus—to quantify rates of exploitation or domination. This is really the *pont d'appui* of Marx's approach. We can't simply take labor as a *given* category; we need to examine the concept of labor critically, interrogate it as an *object of critique*, and examine this term as Marx would have us do, as an abstract social structure. What stands out as crucially important when you examine Marx's value theory of labor is that Marx does not attempt to reduce labor to an economic category alone, but he analyses the internal relations of capital to illustrate how labor as value form constitutes our very social universe, one that has been underwritten by the logic of capital. What Marx is concerned with here is comprehending the transformation of *human* relations at the point of production and in society as a whole.

As I have repeated numerous times in my work, and I believe it bears repeating again, value is not some hollow formality, neutral precinct, or barren hinterland emptied of power and politics but the "very matter and anti-matter of Marx's social universe" (Neary and Rikowski 2000). Something to keep in mind is that the production of value is not the same as the production of wealth. The production of value is historically specific and emerges whenever labor assumes its dual character. This is most clearly explicated in Marx's discussion of the contradictory nature of the commodity form and the expansive capacity of the commodity known as labor power. Labor power is the key term here, because Marx reveals how and why labor power becomes the supreme commodity, the source of all value. For Marx, the commodity is highly unstable, and nonidentical. Its concrete particularity (use value) is subsumed by its existence as value-in-motion or by what we have come to know as "capital" (value is always in motion because of the increase in capital's productivity that is required to maintain expansion).

I have quoted Raya Dunayevskaya's (1978) insight here that "the commodity in embryo contains all the contradictions of capitalism precisely because of the contradictory nature of labor." What kind of labor creates value? Abstract universal labor linked to a certain organization of society, under capitalism. The dual aspect of labor within the commodity (use value and exchange value) enables one single commodity—money—to act as the value measure of the commodity. Money becomes, as Dunayevskaya notes, the representative of labor in its abstract form.

This insight makes clear that the commodity must not be considered a thing, but a social relationship. Dunayevskaya identified the "soul" of capitalist production as the extraction from living labor of all the unpaid hours of labor that amounts to surplus value or profit. When you look at neo-Marxist educationalists or left progressives, they are always talking about the market and they are not examining in granular detail the process of production itself. What is lacking in much leftist work today—and this cuts across many disciplines—is an analysis of the fetishism of the commodity form.

PJ: What do you mean by the fetishism of the commodity form?

PM: We know, for instance, that workers are exploited for their surplus value, that is a commonplace observation by Marxists, but it is also clear that all forms of human sociability are constituted by the logic of capitalist work. We can't simply view labor as the negation of capital or the antithesis of capital. But, as Neary and Rikowski (2000) and Allman (1999 and 2001) have argued, capitalist relations of production become hegemonic precisely when the process of the production of abstraction conquers the concrete processes of production, resulting in the expansion of the logic of capitalist work. Remember, concrete labor is dominated by labor conforming to an abstract average, by the socially necessary labor time on a global level. Workers have no control over this impersonal force that is at work behind the backs of the producers. A focus on abstract labor and socially necessary labor time ignores the real, sensuous needs of workers. Technological innovations that are designed to increase the productivity of labor are responsible for a fluctuation in this social average. This insight compels us to consider that we have to move beyond the fetishized form of labor (as organizational forms of labor such as labor movements or new forms of work organization) and concentrate instead upon new forms of human sociability (Neary and Rikowski 2000; Allman 1999 and 2001). When we pay close attention to how is labor constituted as a social relation within capitalism, we are getting to the root of the inner dynamics of capitalism. It is not abstract or dead labor but rather living labor that creates the value form of wealth that is historically specific to capitalism. We live in a world in which labor must be compatible with valorization, with value augmentation. If it is to be worth something, labor must accumulate profit and capital. It is capital's self-expanding value that is at issue here.

Capitalists are frenetically driven to augment value. That is the name of the game. To understand capitalism in a more robust fashion, we need to examine the processes by which capitalism raises social productivity to a level of mind-numbing enormity. At the same time, we have to understand that capitalism does nothing to limit scarcity. Paula Allman (1999 and 2001) makes clear how capitalism's relations of distribution are simply the results of the relations of production, placing a limit on consumption by limiting the "effective" demand of the vast majority of the world's population. She reveals, in turn, how material use values are only available in the commodity form, and how use value is internally related and thus inseparable from the exchange value of the commodity, which is determined by labor time. She writes that the wealth that is constituted by capitalist societies is not just a vast array of use values (it appears as this), but value itself.

Wealth in capitalist society takes a perverted form. We see this everyday as some people are forced to sell their souls for a wage, and others who own the means of production have a much better chance at living a financially secure life. Capitalism leads capitalists on a *global quest to produce value*. Its totalizing and universalizing tendencies are frightening. Its forms of global social domination are, of course, historically specific. Allman (1999 and 2001) uses some of the insights of Moishe Postone (1996) to argue some very important points. One is that while capitalist exploitation through the production of value is abstract, it is also quasi-objective and concrete. Allman writes that people *experience* abstract labor in concrete or objective formations that are constituted subjectively in human actions and in human feelings, compulsions, and emotions. This is a powerful insight and makes us feel that there is no alternative to the reality in which one is situated—it helps to normalize and legitimate capitalism. Value produced by abstract labor is fundamentally objective *but it is also personal*. Abstract labor has a personal "hold" on each and every one of us, it structures our feelings in specific and deleterious ways.

PJ: In this way the economic becomes personal, and the personal becomes economic. What are the main consequences of these processes for education?

PM: Allman (1999 and 2001) reveals the manner in which the value form helps to habituate capitalist social relations into an interlocking network whose social structure works as a type of dependent hierarchy. In my critical work in the field of education, I have tried to lay bare the contradictions that lay at the heart of the social relations of production. The value form of labor is what gives a specific shape to the internal relations and contradictions produced by capitalism, and this has a powerful impact on the objective conditions within which people labor, but also on the domain of subjectivity or human agency itself. The value form of labor mediates our lives in fundamental ways and turns us into human capital that flows outside, inside, and alongside us at every moment in every day that we spend living and laboring in capitalist society.

I have great respect for progressive educators who advocate for a fairer distribution of wealth, and who become vocal critics of the inequitable distribution that characterizes contemporary capitalist societies, which, as we all recognize, are grounded in property relations, in the private ownership of the means of production. For Paula Allman, Glenn Rikowski, and others, including myself, this doesn't go nearly far enough. The more fundamental issue here is the internal or dialectical relation that exists between capital and labor within the capitalist production process itself—a social relation in which capitalism is intransigently rooted. This social relation—essential or fundamental to the production of abstract labor—deals with how already existing value is preserved and new value (surplus value) is created. It is this internal dialectical relationship that is mainly responsible for the inequitable and unjust distribution of use values and the accumulation of capital that ensures that the rich get richer and the poor get poorer. It is this relation between capital and labor that sets in perilous motion the conditions that make possible today's dictatorship by the transnational capitalist class through practices such as designating production for the market, fostering market relations and competitiveness, and producing the historically specific laws and tendencies of capital.

PJ: What, if anything, can we do about that?

PM: A point to remember is that human subjectivity is never completely absorbed by its objectification and commodification, and we, as workers, are never completely sealed away in a totalizing prison house without any means of escape. If this were not the case we would be compelled to exist in a black box without the possibility of resistance, of transforming our conditions of exploitation, of alienation, by effecting a radical break from capital. The long-range plan is the abolition of the labor–capital relationship as the means for laying the groundwork for liberation from scarcity. Peter Hudis (2000a, b) poses a crucial question that faces all people who strain under the weight of the capitalist system: What kind of labor should a human being do? It seems to me that strategizing against capital means working with those in the technologically underdeveloped world, and part of the challenge stipulates that we go beyond empirical treatments of categories developed by Marx and engaging them dialectically. Capital, as Marx has pointed out, is a social relation of labor; it constitutes objectified, abstract, undifferentiated—and hence alienated—labor. Capital cannot be controlled or abolished through external means without dispensing with value production and creating new forms of nonalienated labor. Creating these new forms of nonalienated labor is the hope and promise of the future.

We are faced with the horrific prospect of living in a world of neoliberal terror, with its harsh reality of permanent mass unemployment, contingent workforces, financial insecurity. As harsh as this reality is, we can still strategically participate in resistance movements with some hope of success since capitalism in no way subsumes class struggle or the subjectivity of the workers. Peter Hudis (2000a, b) looks for a solution in the works of Hegel and Marx. For Hegel, the solution is Absolute knowledge (the realm of realized transcendence), which Marx referred to as the new society. While Hegel's self-referential, all-embracing, totalizing Absolute is greatly admired by Marx, it is nevertheless greatly modified by him. For Marx, Absolute knowledge (or the self-movement of pure thought) did not absorb objective reality or objects of thought but provided a ground from which alienation could be transcended. By reinserting the human subject into the dialectic, and by defining the subject as corporal being (rather than pure thought or abstract self-consciousness), Marx appropriates Hegel's self-movement of subjectivity as an act of transcendence and transforms it into a critical humanism.

The value form of labor (abstract labor) that has been transmogrified into the autonomous moment of dead labor, eating up everything that it is not, can be challenged by freely associated labor and concrete, human sensuousness. The answer is in envisioning a noncapitalist future that can be achieved, as Hudis (2000b) notes, after Dunayevskaya, by means of subjective self-movement through absolute negativity so that a new relation between theory and practice can connect us to the idea of freedom. Hudis (2000b) argues that the abolition of private property does not necessarily lead to the abolition of capital. We need, therefore, to examine the direct relation between the worker and production. Here, our sole emphasis should not be on the abolition of private property, which is the product of alienated labor; it must be on the abolition of alienated labor itself. Marx gave us some clues as to how transcend alienation, ideas that he developed from Hegel's concept of second or absolute negativity or "the negation of the negation." Marx engaged in a materialist rereading of Hegel. In his work, the abolition of private property constitutes the first negation. The second is the negation of the negation of private property. This double negation refers to a self-reflected negativity, and what Hudis (2000b) refers to as the basis for a positive humanism. It was insights such as this, and reading works by Peter Hudis, Dave Hill, Paula Allman, Mike Cole, and Glenn Rikowski, that shifted me from a critical postmodernism to a Marxist humanism.

PJ: We already explored your shift from a critical postmodernism to a Marxist humanism in earlier chapters—yet, it would be good to hear more about your motivations behind the shift.

PM: What also helped me to transition from critical postmodernism to a Marxist-humanist position was the work of David McNally. McNally published an illuminating critique of Saussure, Derrida, and the poststructuralists—as well as a celebration of Voloshinov/Bakhtin and especially Benjamin—in his book *Bodies of Meaning* (McNally 2001). His basic argument is that economic concepts figure centrally in their approaches to linguistic science. I recall that he argued the following points. Postmodern theorists model language on their specific understanding of the capitalist marketplace. McNally makes a good case that, in the process of such modeling, formal linguistics turns language into the dead labor of fetishistic commodities. It does this by decapitating signifiers and their meaning-making process from their fundamental connection to living labor. For example, Saussure and Derrida equate the general phenomenon of linguistic value with the role of "money" as a general equivalent of exchange. McNally calls Derrida the philosopher of fictitious capital. Derrida criticizes Saussure for positing an invariant or transcendental signified, or what McNally calls a "gold standard" against which signs can be measured or interpreted.

Derrida, as you will recall, argues that there is only *differance*, that unknowable form prior to language, that condition of undecidability and the very condition of possibility of that undecidability that permits the endless play of reference that Derrida famously discusses in his large corpus of work (Derrida seems enraptured by difference and enraged by sameness, norms, standards). When Derrida makes the claim that *differance* is the most general structure of the economy, he denies the praxis and labor that ground economic relations. That's because money lacks a referent, according to Derrida. It has no material foundation; money circulates without any referents. You can, for instance, have bad checks, fraudulent credit cards—and these function as money. Credit and speculation become a form of "fictitious" capital. McNally's most trenchant critique is reserved for Baudrillard, and how in his system sign values are independent of external referents, they refer, in other words, only to *themselves*. Baudrillard's is an economy of internal relations, following its own code. Baudrillard lives in a techno-crazed universe of techno-mediatic power where labor is always already dead, where political economy is dead, where everything is virtual, the economy is virtual, and where use values have disappeared. But use values do not transcend the codes that encapsulate them and give them life. That is worth remembering.

The Socialist Kingdom of God

PJ: What are the main points of convergence between liberation theology and the works of Karl Marx?

PM: In his 1980 masterwork, *Marx against the Marxists: The Christian Humanism of Karl Marx,* José Porfirio Miranda, who was educated at the Pontifical Biblical Institute in Rome and who had previously studied sociology in the Frankfurt School, argues that Marx was a Christian humanist who understood the extortionate and unscrupulous characteristics of Christianity and how it was turned into a fraudulent and profiteering caricature of the gospels when Christianity became the God of Empire. Post-Vatican era liberation theologians such as Miranda have recognized and attempted to provide a more transcendent role for the church which at present serves as reproductive of structural sin (the social relations of capitalist exploitation). They would like to see the church be instrumental in the development of forms of liberating praxis, creating the conditions of possibility to find justice in history. According to Boff, in the first post-Vatican II era (1965–70)

> there arose an extraordinary effort on the part of the clergy to divest itself of the signs of power, to enter more deeply among the people, living their ministry not as someone above and beyond the faithful (priest), but as a principle of encouragement, unity, and service (ordained minister). (Boff 1982: 96)

In the second post-Vatican age (1970–80), campesinos and lay people began to organize themselves into base communities, "where there is an experience of a true ecclesiogenesis" (Boff 1982: 96).

Boff (1982: 98) contends that the poor serve as the sacrament of Christ, who, "as eschatological judge . . . judges each one according to the love that either liberates from poverty or rejects its plea." The idea of God as eschatological judge permeates Miranda's magisterial works of liberation theology and I assume this position as foundational in my own work, Petar. Rather than antiseptically cleaving liberation theology from Marx's historical dialectics, as one often discovers in the congeries of opinions of liberation theologians, Miranda sees their intimate connection as a leavening of social justice. Neil Hinnem (2013) is correct in locating the convergence between Miranda's understanding of the biblical perspective on history and Marx's historical dialectics in Miranda's articulation of orthopraxis and his concept of historical events, the most important event for Miranda being the intervention of Yahweh into human history. As Hinnem writes:

> History is not an evolutionary process: rather, it is punctuated by revolutionary events. For Miranda, these events are the interventions of God in history for the sake of human justice, culminating in the Christ event, ushering all believers in the Kingdom of God. This event leads, consequently, to the Kingdom's underlying hope, its absolute command, that justice be achieved. "In the historical event of Jesus Christ," writes Miranda, "the messianic kingdom has arrived." (Hinnem 2013)

For Miranda, the Bible is a subversive document that preached communism long before the time of Karl Marx. Miranda sees much in common between history as liberation from alienation as described by Marx, and the eschaton, or the divine plan for the realization of the Kingdom of God.

PJ: An important aspect of Christian mysticism—and the one you earlier identified as one of the main intersections between Christianity and Marxism—is the eschatological aspect of history. For Christians, this eschaton is the (arrival of) the Kingdom of God; for Marx and Engels, it is utopian socialism predicted as early as in the Communist Manifesto (Marx and Engels 1848). Can you elaborate upon this eschaton a little deeper? What, for you, is the Kingdom of God?

PM: We talk about the eschaton, we are compelled to honor the victims, speak to their lives of suffering in their theological reality. As Sobrino notes, the crucified peoples of this earth must not be remembered as some historical add-ons to our Sunday sermons but as those who were victims of the anti-Kingdom. After all, the anti-Kingdom is the Kingdom of Capital, of Wall Street and the world of value production (i.e., monetized wealth), of profit, of the exploitation and alienation of human labor, of private ownership of the means of production, of the market mechanism that forces capitalists (regardless of whether or not they are intrinsically good people) to exploit workers, of emergent transnational capital consolidated in a global capitalist historic bloc and the pillage zones of América Latina, and of the deregulated, informalized, and deunionized capital-labor relation and the worldwide subordination of labor. It's not only the anti-Kingdom of Trump, but the anti-Kingdom that incorporates all nations that are dependent on the augmentation of value to survive, all nations where people are forced to sell their labor power to the owners of the means of production.

But here I need to emphasize something Sobrino (2001) has discussed at length in his many important writings. While we focus on the divine in Christ, we often forget the Kingdom of God of which Christ speaks. So when we identify as Catholics, why have we forgotten the primacy of creating the Kingdom of God and bringing it forth as Christ exhorted us to do? In my view, it is because our entire system operates as the anti-Kingdom. Christianity itself is undergirded by the imperatives of the anti-Kingdom in that it has attached itself to the imperatives of capitalism. To create the Kingdom of God means seeking the creation of a social universe outside of value production, or the production of profit for the rich. Creating the Kingdom of God means liberating the poor, and this means ending the brutal war against the poor unleashed by the deregulation of the market. It means challenging the anti-Kingdom that stands against immigrants seeking a better life, against migrant workers, against refugees, and the intergenerationally reproduced barrios of planet slum. Instead of joining the workers in the union halls and creating dialogue circles, we focus instead on eternal life, on gnostic mysteries, or, perhaps more perversely, distance ourselves from the Kingdom of God by rejoicing in the wonky world of reality TV and the hundreds of TV channels we have at our disposal. We confuse the drive to increase material wealth with the drive to produce value or create endless profits that can be expanded indefinitely.

In our forays into the hinterlands of mysticism, we cannot forget that the Kingdom of God is, in Sobrino's terms, a "type of historical-social-collective reality" (2001: 334) and not, as the old union song has it, a "pie in the sky when you die." The Kingdom of God is not some metaphor for an unearthly paradise, some ecclesiastical makeover of the earth in terms of the divine Christ or such that the holy and apostolic church becomes the prime sign or marker of the Kingdom. Clearly, for me, the Kingdom of

God is not some place where well-heeled and aristocratic-looking souls lounge about in togas, sandals, and golden wreaths. For me, the Kingdom of God is more likely found on the picket lines, in the temple cleared of the moneylenders, in a world where the rich no longer dominate, a village where death squads do not murder peasants with impunity, and where poor tenants do not confront racist landlords and developers do not build themselves towers in glorious homage to their wealth and power while others are forced to sleep under bridges.

PJ: Let's explore some practical aspects of the eschaton. What are the main obstacles to its arrival?

PM: We have failed to reason dialectically and to construct in our daily lives a philosophy of praxis grounded in a Christian Marxist humanism. Consequently, we are suffocating—here in the United States—in the furious winds of this Armageddon culture filled with doomsday pronouncements and with extreme right-wing conspiracy theories about a cabal of international bankers taking over the world and leaving the United States in the wake of the corporate globalist elite. This so-called cabal of corporate globalists has left poor whites barricaded in their crumbling towns and inner cities to be monitored by black helicopters from the United Nations and devoured by groups such as Black Lives Matter activists, immigrants of all stripes, Muslims, feminists, West Coast climate activists, and those who run the entertainment industry in the heart of Sodom. The Avenging Angel of the God of Money is a transnational capitalist billionaire and media personality who judges the entire world through the eyes of a circus ringmaster and a beauty pageant judge. Unbeknown to the working classes, this is exactly the type of savior who will hurt their ranks the most. What has hurt them the most is not the elite political class who run the government, but the economic system that the government has been set up to defend.

PJ: Where should we seek novel patterns of revolution for social justice?

PM: The Kingdom of God is not suddenly going to appear after the apocalypse that is haunting us retroactively from the future that has eliminated evil once and for all. The Kingdom of God is not designed to save capitalism but to replace it with a more just and humane system that is not driven by the profit motive. The eschaton is now, and it is the struggle for social justice that makes it immanent. We are not talking about the struggle shouldered by liberals singing their sundry progressive platitudes all the way to the offices of their investment bankers. The struggle for social justice stipulates that we come together and figure out how to create a social universe outside of capitalist value production, where the profit motive is eliminated. Education should play a significant role in this struggle, but it does not. This is why I have been trying to advance critical pedagogy as a transnational social movement to bring progressive educators together to face the problems of contemporary capitalism and to seek alternatives, because we are facing a capitalism that has continuously played a role in genocide, ecocide, and epistemicide, the latter referring to the disappearance and destruction of ecologies of knowing of indigenous peoples, knowledge that cannot be conserved digitally in computer storage platforms without losing its authenticity.

The international law introduced by the 1948 United Nations Convention on Genocide makes it abundantly clear that the United States systematically sought the complete expiration of native Americans amounting to genocide against first nations peoples. Have we not recently destroyed the nation of Iraq? Have we not tortured and traumatized its population? Have we not soaked its gene pool in depleted uranium and ensured birth defects for generations to come? Has not the United States intervened militarily in approximately fifty countries since World War II? We have a long revolution ahead of us to stop such a global system of war and aggression and to replace capitalism with a socialist alternative.

For many Americans who have been in an ongoing dispute with complex thought, whose brains have been addled from decades of submersion in the ensanguined brine of historical amnesia, or who simply wish to avoid the terrifying vituperations of colleagues, socialism remains tantamount to anti-Americanism. This attitude is emblematic of a pattern that runs through the history of US political life. For those drip-fed over decades the idea that socialism is evil and who remain untethered from historical reality, they would no doubt find incredulous the following sentiments from one the greatest American politicians, Eugene Debs, who ran for president of the United States as a candidate for the Socialist Party of America in the early 1900s. Debs vociferously maintained "that Jesus came to destroy class rule and set up the common people as the sole and rightful inheritors of the earth" (Hedges 2018a: 104) and when asked to describe socialism, answered: "Merely Christianity in action" (Hedges 2018a: 104). In fact, Debs helped to found the Industrial Workers of the World, who came to be known as the Wobblies, of which I was a member for a short period of time. Clearly, the problem with such narrowmindedness in the United States is the lack of dialectical reasoning. A dialectical understanding of meaning helps us to consider truth as historically specific—a truth might be true now but not hold in the future—and has different levels. This has to do with understanding the internally related unity of opposites.

Paula Allman (2001: 236) rightly asserts that there are different levels of truth: meta-transhistorical truths, which appear to hold across the history of humanity but about which we must always remain skeptical; transhistorical truths, yet which are susceptible to future revision; truths that are specific to a particular social formation; and conjuncturally specific truths, which are transient but attain validity in the contextual specificity of the developmental processes of which they are a part and which may endure beyond that specific conjuncture. While I agree that epistemological viewpoints about the world are value-laden and theory-laden, unlike postmodernists, I do not believe that we can alter the world simply by changing our beliefs about it.

PJ: So let's speculate how the pattern of revolution for social justice might look like!

PM: The pattern of revolution for social justice—for socialism—will not be a straight line but will always be up and down, a path of walking through darkness and light, fighting inside the belly of the beast until, like Jonah, we are spit out onto the shore of hope. Is Jonah inside the belly of the whale not a story of entering the darkness, of being betrayed, of being the scapegoat, of being victimized by power, in order, finally, to land on the shore where we can regain our breath, where we can be bathed in the light of truth? Is not the story of Jonah inside the whale, really an antisign, another way of rendering the doctrine of the cross? Is this not what is called "the paschal mystery"? As Rohr (2016) reminds us, mystery is not something that is impossible to understand, it is "something that you can endlessly understand," since at no point can you say, "I've got it!" Sometimes the descent is so great, so steep, that there seems no hope, just a vortex of horror and turmoil. It seems impossible at times to fathom how humanity can survive the horror of existence, especially during times of war, of economic catastrophe, of existential desperation and despair. How can God be found in this darkness? This truly is the paschal mystery.

PJ: Can you link this paschal mystery, the Christian eschaton described as the Kingdom of God, to Marx's prophecy of the future socialist society?

PM: I do see socialism as fitting in with the Kingdom of God announced by Jesus. Socialists in the past have sometimes made such a connection. Take the case of Helen Macfarlane. In 1850, Scottish governess, Helen Macfarlane, wrote polemical treatises supporting the Chartist movement. She was the first person to translate Hegel's philosophical writings into English and the first person to translate "The Communist Manifesto" into English. The Chartists were the first working-class movement to fight the British establishment in order to secure rights for the working class. For a time, Macfarlane supported Chartist leader Julian Harney in rebuilding the movement from a socialist and international perspective and refused to moderate the movement to win over the radical liberals. She allied herself with Marx and Engels and took on literary giants such as Thomas Carlyle and Charles Dickens. She interpreted Hegel as a humanist pantheist, and she defined pantheism in humanistic terms. Her work reflects the Hegelian pantheism of David Strauss, and her engagement with the writings of Marx and Engels helped her to radicalize Strauss's critical Hegelianism. For Hegel, the importance of the gospels was their symbolic content. For David Strauss, what was important about the gospels was their historicity—as myths that contained the Messianic desires of the early Christian communities (Black 2014: xvii).

Feuerbach believed that theological knowledge was subjective and that the final criterion for the truth was to be found in the senses. Here the ego remains passive and determined by objective reality. For Marx, truth was found through historical praxis, through the negation of the negation. What is interesting about Macfarlane was her ability to merge the ideas of socialism, left Hegelianism, and Marxism with the teachings of Jesus and in doing so spiritualize the struggle for social justice. In 1850 she wrote:

> We Socialist-democrats are the soldiers of a holy cause; we are the exponents of a sublime idea; we are the apostles of the sacred religion of universal humanity. We have sworn by the God who "made of one blood all nations of the Earth," that we will not pause till we have finished the great work—begun by the Nazarean— of man's redemption from the social miseries which destroy body and soul. (Macfarlane in Black 2014: 22)

PJ: If the Kingdom of God is a "type of historical-social-collective reality" (Sobrino 2001: 334), why should we not just stick to Marx and Engels' utopian socialism? Why, in this context, do we need a God?

PM: As a species on the verge of extinction, we have an ongoing obligation today to commit ourselves to build a network among the working class, the peasantry, and the urban cognitariat and precariat in order to break down the immutable hierarchies of power and privilege concomitant with the workings of capitalist society. In our struggle to achieve this, God will be revealed. As Miranda writes: "Only in a world of justice will God be" (1977: 45). The revolution therefore depends not on the man himself or the woman herself or on the collectivity (which would be merely expanded egoism), but on the Other. Providing for each according to his or her needs presupposes caring for people simply because they exist and are God's children. The social relations of capitalist exploitation can force us to yield, but they cannot oblige us to obey. At times I personally feel too strong to yield but too weak to overcome the obstacles we face in building a revolution. It appears to me that God is the moral imperative itself, the imperative to struggle against injustice and innocent suffering. God's presence in history, the true revelatory intervention of the God of the Bible in human history, occurs when we take up the struggle for social justice.

It is interesting to note that Marx and Engels entered an organization in 1872 that was founded by Wilhelm Weitling, the founder of German communism. Weitling's organization was based on a communism grounded entirely in the gospel, as can be seen in his 1845 book, *The Gospel of a Poor Sinner* (Miranda 1980). Marx was a great admirer of the Peasants' War organized and directed by Thomas Munzer in the sixteenth century. This was, in effect, the first anticapitalist revolution. Munzer argued that the Kingdom of God is a condition of society without class differences, without private property, and without state powers opposed to the members of society.

The God of the Rich and the God of the Poor

PJ: Your work is a masterpiece of dialectics! Where issues pertaining to ontology and epistemology pour into issues pertaining to politics and emancipation, there still is—even if only historically constructed—some sort of division of work between the different approaches and disciplines. What is the main strength of Marxism in the context of liberation theology?

PM: I return to the basic issues of the violence of capitalism, colonization (in particular, the coloniality of power as articulated by Anibal Quijano), genocide, ecocide, and the underlying epistemicide that has cost us so dearly in our ontological vocation of becoming more fully human, which can be best understood as the destruction of epistemologies, ways of knowing, and ecologies of the mind of indigenous peoples throughout the world. Now for some proponents of liberation theology communism as Marx envisioned is normative in the message of Jesus. And I have faith that the Kingdom of God will overcome the world of suffering precisely because I have faith in the people, the workers, the masses to defeat capital and bring about a more loving and human system for providing for the material needs of humanity. Terry Eagleton writes:

> I have argued already that reason alone can face down a barbarous irrationalism,
> but that to do so it must draw upon forces and sources of faith which run deeper

than itself, and which can therefore bear an unsettling resemblance to the very irrationalism one is seeking to repel. (Eagleton 2009: 161)

It is worth remembering, as Eagleton notes, "The Christian way of indicating that faith is not in the end a question of choice is the notion of grace. Like the world itself from a Christian viewpoint, faith is a gift" (2009: 138). Of course, this does not mean we cease examining our faith with evidence from the phenomenal world. Eagleton sees the great struggle today as one in which culture is pitted against civilization. He notes that "culture . . . is too much a matter of affirming what you are or have been, rather than what you might become" (2009: 165). And as for religion? Eagleton writes:

What we know as Christendom saw itself as a unity of culture and civilization. If religion has proved far and away the most powerful, tenacious, universal symbolic form humanity has yet to come up with, it is partly on this account. What other symbolic form has managed to forge such direct links between the most absolute and universal of truths and the everyday practices of countless millions of men and women? What other way of life has brought the most rarefied of ideas and the most palpable of human realities into such intimate relationship? Religious faith has established a hotline from personal interiority to transcendent authority—an achievement upon which the advocates of culture can only gaze with envy. Yet religion is as powerless as culture to emancipate the dispossessed. For the most part, it has not the slightest interest in doing so. (2009: 165–66)

But what of Marxism's potential in reconciling culture and civilization? Eagleton responds as follows:

If Marxism holds out a promise of reconciling culture and civilization, it is among other things because its founder was both a Romantic humanist and an heir of Enlightenment rationalism. Marxism is about culture and civilization together— sensuous particularity and universality, worker and citizen of the world, local allegiances and international solidarity, the free selfrealization of flesh-and-blood individuals and a global cooperative commonwealth of them. But Marxism has suffered in our time a staggering political rebuff; and one of the places to which those radical impulses have migrated is—of all things—theology. It is in some sectors of theology nowadays that one can find some of the most informed and animated discussions of Deleuze and Badiou, Foucault and feminism, Marx and Heidegger. (2009: 167)

What I find most important in Marxism is its eschatological view of history, embedded in its long explanatory arc of making sense of how capitalism works to necessarily exploit workers and the environment, provoking workers to rise up and replace capitalism with socialism, and eventually forcing the state to wither under communism. Both Jesus and Marx have an eschatological view of history, and as Michael Rivage-Seul (2008) notes, Jesus challenges us to reject the worship of a divinized violence that feeds the "satanic military industrial complex" and practice a nonviolent form of resistance against differentiating wealth.

PJ: How does this eschatological view of history shared between Marxism and Christianity relate to the crucial mission of critical pedagogy: the development of critical consciousness?

PM: A commitment to the oppressed leads to action in and on the world on behalf of the aggrieved of this world. Critical reflection on that action leads to what I refer to as protagonistic agency, a praxis of liberation. Protagonistic agency pulls out of the darkness of probability and potentiality the reality of social change, bringing it into the realm of actuality. Through a concentration of will—a type of hyperintentionality—critical educators can submerge their ideas in their unconscious where they can confront their fears and traumas surrounding the risks and reprisals that they may face in their struggle for social justice. Such a struggle in the Golgotha of their hearts can direct their ideas into the light of reflective awareness without overidentifying with their feelings because these ideas have now been conditioned to ratify a new reality rather than remaining trapped by the old. This is fundamentally a dialectical process, an embrace of absolute negativity that leads to new beginnings.

PJ: There are many different religions in the contemporary world. Can we generalize emancipatory and educational potentials of Christianity to all religious systems of belief, or should we be more careful about such generalizations?

PM: The realm of religion is the realm of myth, symbol, art, mystery, legend, theater, and poetry—realms where we can delve deeply into the meaning of life. I am an ecumenist and do not believe God is revealed only through Christianity. I have helped marry a couple during an Umbanda ceremony in Brazil, presided over by a *pai-de-santo* (*babalorishá*) who had incorporated the Orisha Exú, have received an award for defending African-Brazilian religion in Brazil from attacks by Christian evangelists, have met with Santeria priests and practitioners in Cuba and Puerto Rico, have visited Buddhist temples in mainland China, Taiwan, and Malaysia, prayed at the Vatican and at the tomb of Enrique Ángel Angelelli in the Cathedral in La Rioja, Argentina, prayed before the cell of Maximilian Kolbe in Auschwitz, knelt in prayer at indigenous churches throughout Mexico, including the Church of St. Juan Bautista in Chiapas that mixes Mayan shamanic and Catholic rituals, visited Shinto shrines and Zen monasteries in Japan, prayed at mosques in Turkey, explored questions of faith in Pakistan with both Sunni and Shia Muslims, and in Israel with Israelis and Palestinians and had my carved whalebone *hei-tiki* blessed by a Maori priest. I traveled to Culiacán to the shrine of the narco-saint, Jesús Malverde, so that I could pay my respects to this Robin Hood figure. I have yet to visit the Church of Saint John Will-I-Am Coltrane, founded in 1982, where followers and aficionados of this jazz great can come closer to God through weekly "sound baptisms" focusing on their patron saint's later albums, including "A Love Supreme."

So it is safe to say that while I practice my Catholic faith, I am a full-blooded ecumenist, open to various ways on engaging ourselves in the world of flesh and spirit. Yes, I do agree with Girard that Judeo-Christian religion is unique, and yes it provides, in my view, one of the keys to the Kingdom. But I cannot simply dismiss neo-Druids or practitioners of Wicca, or pantheists searching the skies for signs that our alien ancestors are returning as pagans destined for the fiery pits.

PJ: This goes directly against the Christian idea of one and only God, probably best summarized in the opening phrase of the Ten Commandments: I am the Lord your God.

PM: Do we really believe that the Christian God.

Do we believe that the Christian God is monolithic? In the Christian Bible, there is a plethora of gods—the God of Empire that Christianity has supported since the fourth century, the God of Eve, the God of Abraham and Moses, the God of Cain, the God of Satan, and the God of Jesus. According to Rivage-Seul (2008), Jesus is the prophet whose revelation ultimately decided that the God of Moses and Abraham (the God of the poor and the suffering) was the true God of Israel. Should we believe that the rich and the poor worship the same God? Take Hitler, for example. Hitler claimed to be Christian, but he only used "religious" language as a propaganda tool and he stated in Goebbels' diaries that "as soon as the war is over" the Nazis will go after "the real enemy"—the Catholics. Pius XII referred to Hitler as "an indispensable bulwark against the Russians" (Johnson 1977: 490 cited in Rivage-Seul 2008: 109). According to Rivage-Seul, the God of the Bible is not neutral and could not have been the God of both Hitler and Yahweh. Was the God of Ronald Reagan the same God as the God of Reagan's "Godless communists"—the Sandinistas? Is not the God of Christian fundamentalism and the prosperity gospel arrayed against Jesus who stands on the side of the poor and the oppressed?

Rivage-Seul (2008: 114) believes that liberation theology is closer theologically to the idea that God is experienced not just in nature but in history; is revealed primarily in Exodus; is concerned with justice as true worship; is class-biased in favor of the poor; endorses an ethic of love and self-sacrifice; protects freedom from exploitation; permits violence to defend the poor from exploiters; is anti-imperialist; considers the ultimate revelation of Jesus to be that God stands with the poor, and that an accumulation of riches presumes an engagement with forms of exploitation. We should always be careful about what we generalize to other religious systems of belief. If I were to generalize, however, it would be from the perspective of a theology of liberation. I would never want to generalize precepts and principles from any organization that serves mainly to strengthen and reproduce systems of power and privilege that serve the rich at the expense of the poor. To support the reproduction of the power and privilege of the rich would be counter to the teachings of Jesus, who was against any system that produced differentiating wealth or what some call today "economic inequality." Such a term is too weak for me. I would call it, plain and simple, capitalist exploitation.

PJ: Your response seems to more or less explicitly refer to Catholicism. Yet, almost 40 percent of Christians are Protestants, and then there are also many smaller movements such as Pentecostalism (Pew Research Center 2011). Obviously, Catholic and Protestant traditions will have a different relationship to capitalism (just think of the proverbial

Protestant work ethic), and movements such as Pentecostalism are gaining members much faster than mainstream Catholicism and Protestantism. What do you make of these differences and developments?

PM: According to a recent paper by Allan Anderson (2019), American Pentecostal denominations like the Assemblies of God now have a vast international membership (around 80 percent) in Latin America, Africa, and Asia. The expansion of Pentecostalism in the last half-century has been staggering. Pentecostals are not widely known for being involved in social issues such as race, class, or gender equality; in fact, they have generally been supportive of white supremacist capitalist society. Anderson (2019) is correct when he says about Pentecostals that "[t] hey have been accused of an otherworldly spirituality that avoids involvement in 'worldly' issues like politics and the struggle for liberation and justice." He rightly acknowledges that "[t]hey have sometimes been justifiably charged with proclaiming a gospel that either spiritualizes or individualizes social problems" and that this has resulted in "a tendency either to accept present oppressive social conditions or to promote a 'prosperity gospel' that makes material gain a spiritual virtue." Anderson speaks about the "potential of Pentecostalism for a politically and socially relevant engagement, particularly because of its tendency to attract marginalized and working-class people." While this is certainly true, the politically and socially relevant engagement that Anderson speaks about has to do with the logic of charitable giving. And while this is certainly admirable, it does not confront the structure and logic of capitalism and thus can only serve as supporting it. To do otherwise means that Pentecostals would need to refrain from separating the spiritual from the physical, and "integrat[ing] them in a holistic whole, leading to involvement in social issues and politics" (Anderson 2019).

Anderson (2019) notes that for many Pentecostals "political structures are often seen as part of the 'evil world' that Pentecostals are exhorted to have nothing to do with." Anderson (2019) reports that this "eschatological dimension" takes the position that "current political events are taken as negative signs of the times, proof that the Lord is coming back soon." Anderson is worth quoting further:

> Harvey Cox lists several characteristics of what he calls "very unattractive political and theological currents" running through American Pentecostalism. He discusses their participation in right-wing politics, by which Pentecostalism might "lose touch completely with its humble origins and become the righteous spiritual ideology of an affluent middle class." Most American Pentecostals supported the "religious right" during the Reagan years. Pat Robertson, a Charismatic Baptist and founder of CBN and Regent University in Virginia Beach, was a leading contender for the right-wing Republican presidential nomination in 1988. He has made many public statements to articulate his extreme views. He called for the assassination of Venezuelan President Hugo Chavez by American operatives in August 2005. For this he later apologized, while at the same time likening his call to that of Bonhoeffer supporting the assassination of Hitler. Robertson and the vast majority of white American evangelicals have been conspicuous in their support of Donald Trump since the 2016 presidential elections. In Guatemala,

Rios Montt, president of the country from 1982-83 and leader of an oppressive military dictatorship, was a member of an independent Charismatic church and leader of a conservative political party.

There have also been serious criticisms of the "prosperity gospel" propagated by certain sections of Pentecostalism and the so-called "Americanization" of global Christianity, where it is claimed that the Bible was being used to further the USA's economic and political ends. (Anderson 2019)

While there might be some self-criticism among Pentecostals about their lack of progressive political engagement, Anderson notes that

Pentecostals sometimes cloud the differences between moral issues like abortion and sexuality, and political ones. The result is that right-wing politicians who promote these issues as a political agenda to win votes are seen as having "Christian values"—without regard to other policies and practices which are antithetical to Christian ethics. A connected reason for this about-turn may be wily politicians who court the Pentecostal vote being conscious of their significance. There can be no doubt that this was the strategy of Donald Trump, and he successfully gained a huge portion of white American Pentecostal support. Pentecostals have also been influenced by a premillennial eschatology that saw Communism (and now, radical Islam) as anti-Christian; so they believed that support for the state of Israel (and opposition for Palestine) was a biblical duty. Unfortunately, these views have tended to be shared mostly by figures like Trump representing the wealthy middle class and political right, which has sat uncomfortably with those Pentecostals of more humble status. Pentecostals have also been accused of being representatives of colonialism and obstacles to liberation. In general, they are seen as "apolitical" and otherworldly. These examples might certainly give support to these views. (Anderson 2019)

As Anderson rightly points out, the Pentecostals were often ardent supporters of violent Latin American military dictatorships. Leaders of the Iglesia Metodista had a friendly relationship with the Pinochet government and Pinochet even showed up at Pentecostal functions. While some Pentecostals "who resisted Pinochet's regime . . . were harassed, tortured and even killed" (Anderson 2019), the truth is that Pentecostalism was largely implicated in the horrors of repressive regimes throughout Latin America through its shameful silence. In fact, liberation theology that came out of the pastoral tradition of the Catholic Church was seen as a threat to these tyrannical regimes, often being accused of harboring communist sympathies, and the US government supported Pentecostalism as a buffer against liberation theology.

While I agree with Anderson that Pentecostalism has potential for a more robust form of social engagement, such engagement rarely goes beyond giving solace to the poor—that they will get their reward in heaven—or giving them inspiration to people for the purpose of social uplift, such as laying out antidrug programs or providing services and humanitarian assistance such as welfare assistance, medical facilities all done under the theme of self-help. Pentecostals need to engage with the work of

Marx, Malcolm X, Martin Luther King. "Let freedom ring from Stone Mountain of Georgia!"—that was the cry of Martin Luther King (1963) [2003]. Will freedom ever reign in Stone Mountain, where the children of slaves and slave owners would all sit down together at the banquet of freedom? That was part of Martin Luther King's dream. How many Pentecostals attended the annual Ku Klux Klan cross burnings that went on for forty years at Stone Mountain from 1915 to 1955? Or Catholics? How many still flock to Trump rallies? How many believe in supporting charities yet fail to challenge the fundamental structures of racism, sexism, homophobia, and class exploitation?

PJ: Glad you mentioned Trump—his relationship with religion is interesting in its own right.

PM: What do we make of Trump's personal pastor, televangelist, and prosperity gospel preacher, Paula White, who owns multimillion-dollar homes in Trump Tower and Florida? Some have credited White with Donald Trump's conversion to Christianity. Can Trump's conversion even be plausible? White provided the invocation prayer during Trump's inauguration ceremony. She recently announced that everywhere she stands should be considered holy ground. Burris (2019) writes:

> President Donald Trump's favorite pastor believes that she is such a powerful figure that wherever she stands should be sanctioned as holy ground. "The church is Christ's body in which he speaks and acts and by which he fills everything, including the White House, including government halls," White told the crowd.
>
> "How does he do that?" she asked. "He does that through you. He does that through me. Wherever I go, God rules. When I walk on White House grounds, God walks on White House grounds. When I walked in The River, God walked in The River. When I go in the dry cleaners, that dry cleaning place becomes holy. I have every right and authority to declare the White House as holy ground because I was standing there and where I stand is holy." (Burris 2019)

White has promised that donations to her organization would secure for the donors everlasting life. Burris (2016) writes that White offers her followers a "resurrection seed" for $1,144 that would guarantee them eternal life since the seeds were "set by God." Quoting White, Burris (2016) reports:

> "There's someone that God is speaking to, to click on that donation button by minimizing the screen. And when you do to sow $1,144," she [White] told the crowd. "It's not often I ask very specifically but God has instructed me and I want you to hear. This isn't for everyone but this is for someone. When you sow that $1,144 based on John 11:44 I believe for resurrection life. You say, Paula, I just don't have that, then sow $144. I don't have that. Sow $44 but stand on John Chapter 11:44."
>
> Then like an infomercial proclaiming "but wait! There's more!" White promised those buying the "resurrection seed" that they would also get some special prayer cloths that might cause "miracles, signs and wonders."

"There have been times that I have taken prayer cloths that have been anointed as a point of contact. I put them in my loved one's sneakers, I put them under their bed. I put them on parts of my body that I believe God for healing," said White.

But if someone purchases the "resurrection seed" and finds that it has failed to resurrect anyone, White explained that it's probably user error. "Cause there are things I've prayed out of ignorance or asked out of my own desire and I said God, but your will be done." "Cause I knew, His word is His will. See His will is for whatever is dead in your life to come back to life. How do I know? John 10:10. Jesus came to give you life and give you life more abundantly," she explained. "So click on and minimize that screen and right now sow your miracle resurrection seed as we stand in faith together and I believe God for your miracle." (Burris 2016)

White uses her Christian credentials to support Trump's egregious immigration policy. Stephen Johnson (2019) quotes Paula White as follows:

I think so many people have taken biblical scriptures out of context on this, to say stuff like, "Well, Jesus was a refugee. . . . And yes, he did live in Egypt for three and a half years. But it was not illegal. If he had broke the law, then he would have been sinful and he would not have been our Messiah."

Yes, thank you Paula. You are a true tractor beam for pulling gullible fools into the heart of Las Vegas-style Christianity.

PJ: In *Pedagogy of Insurrection*, you write:

Critical pedagogy is the lucubration of a whole philosophy of praxis that predates Marx and can be found in biblical texts. If we wish to break from alienated labor, then we must break completely with the logic of capitalist accumulation and profit, and this is something to which Marx and Jesus would agree. (McLaren 2015b: 54–55)

If Marx and Jesus would agree with the break from alienated labor, why does contemporary revolutionary pedagogy need an additional layer of rituals and beliefs offered by Christianity? More generally, what are the unique emancipatory and educational potentials of Christianity, which cannot be found in traditional nonreligious Marxism?

PM: My early work was on the topic of ritual—*Schooling as a Ritual Performance: Towards a Political Economy of Educational Symbols and Gestures* (McLaren 1999). Here I followed the work of contemporary symbolic anthropologists—especially Victor Turner—in examining rituals as embodied metaphors and in relation to the construction of liminality. I applied these theories in a critical ethnography I undertook at a Catholic middle school in the Azorean community of Toronto. I was able to discern rituals of instruction, of accommodation, and how an antistructure of resistance was possible under certain conditions. I also identified micro and macro rituals in school settings and how they can be both emancipatory and contribute to the reproduction of hierarchies of power and privilege. I articulated a theory of the teacher as a liminal servant and how the construction of liminality in the classroom can be the seedbed of true creativity, but at the same time a flashpoint for violence. Much of the important work in applied theater, in drama, and in performance studies builds on conceptions of ritual. This can be seen in the writings of my late thesis adviser and mentor, Richard Courtney, and is paramount in the work of Augusto Boal—especially in his magisterial volume *Theatre of the Oppressed* (2008), which was very much influenced by the work of his fellow Brazilian Paulo Freire.

I was fortunate to participate in a public dialogue with Freire and Boal at the Rose Theater in Omaha, Nebraska, in the early 1990s. It was the first time Freire and Boal had appeared together in such a venue and I was honored to have been a part of this historic event. From their work, and the work of Victor Turner, I came to see that symbols have a fecundity that becomes animated in rituals. Symbols are brought to life and live inside of us through play, through rituals, and their elaboration can be seen in the evolution of drama and thought. Symbols are enacted and work synergistically with other symbols; I have termed this process "enfleshment." Here religious and secular symbols can, under specific historical and existential circumstances, hemorrhage into each other and can work in very liberating and also in very dangerous ways. Just think of Francoist Spain and the rituals that linked Catholic symbols to fascism.

PJ: Arguably, the notion of ritual in theater, in drama, and in performance studies is very different from the notion of ritual in religion. What can we get from religious ritual in relation to the break from alienated labor?

PM: According to Miranda (1980) Jesus was the first human being in history to denounce money as the object of idolatry, which centuries later Marx referred to variously as the biblical idols of Baal, Mammon, and Moloch. In fact, when discussing the commodity form of production, he used these terms as much as he did the word "fetish." When Saint Paul talks about the "lust which is idolatry," he is referring to money. Book Three of *Capital* (Marx 1981) makes clear that the capitalist mode of production is not the origin of class violence in capitalist society. As Miranda (1980) notes, the class division is created outside the sphere of production, when money becomes god, and it was this god that created the conditions of possibility for the capitalist mode of production. Money as exchange value stands outside production and circulation and yet dominates both. Money represents the autonomous existence of value as the concretization of human labor. It is when money no longer represents commodities, but when commodities represent money, that money becomes a god. Money is the god of all people living under the commodity mode of production, and money had already become a god during the time of Jesus. In other words, the accumulation of capital is not enough to automatically create the mode of production we know today as capitalism, because it takes a certain type of historically produced civilization. The transformation of money into capital requires a certain kind of historical circumstance. Today, capitalism still functions as the institutionalization of the worship of Mammon.

Marx does a brilliant job of explaining how money was transformed into a god ruling human beings. Marx reveals how money is both the object and fountainhead of greed, of *auri sacra fames*, the product of a historically conditioned environment. According to Miranda (1980), Marx perceived the switching of the subject into an object and the transformation of the ends into the means as the centerpiece of the making of a false religion. Marx then applied this "conversion" to economics, to the production of value. Capital finds a way to exchange itself for a commodity that produces more value than the commodity itself—labor power. Capital moves into production through an exchange with labor power, via wage labor, which brings about the separation of the direct producers from the owners of the means of production. Interest-bearing capital is a fetish, a self-expanding value, and it expands its value independently of reproduction, which is a reversal of the relationship between persons and things—all pointing to Marx's anathematization of the worship of money as god. Miranda (2004) points out that at the very central point of his analysis of capital, at the very point where he uncovers the birth of money as a commodity, Marx cites two entire verses from the Apocalypse (17:13; 13:17). Marx offers a scientific elaboration of Christ's teaching about the god Mammon.

PJ: Socialist society may indeed be very close to the Kingdom of God, yet Marxist and Christian methods for achieving the eschaton seem quite different. In the *Communist Manifesto*, Marx and Engels write: "Workers of the World, Unite. You have nothing to lose but your chains!"[1] Yet, Matthew 5:5 says: "Blessed are the meek: for they shall inherit the earth." We already discussed some of these differences in relation to human agency. What is their relationship to labor?

PM: For Marx, human beings clearly are subjects, subjects of history. The subject of history is related to Marx's concept of living labor, of labor power, the potential for laboring, the capacity for labor, its possibility and potency. It is living labor that is present in time and throughout human history as possibility, whereas objectified labor serves the means and instruments of production and has no role in liberation from oppression. Marx describes how the capitalist production process makes relationships between persons seem as relationships between things. For Marx, capital grounds all social mediation as a form of value, and the substance of labor itself must be interrogated because doing so brings us closer to understanding the nature of capital's social universe out of which our subjectivities are created. Because the logic of capitalist work has invaded all forms of human sociability, society can be considered to be a totality of different types of labor. What is important here is to examine the particular forms that labor takes within capitalism. In other words, we need to examine value as a social relation, not as some kind of accounting device to measure rates of exploitation or domination. Consequently, labor should not be taken simply as a "given" category, but interrogated as an *object of critique*, and examined as an abstract social structure.

For Marx, the commodity is highly unstable and nonidentical. Its concrete particularity (use value) is subsumed by its existence as value-in-motion or by what we have come to know as "capital." Value is always in motion because of the increase in capital's productivity that is required to maintain expansion. The dual aspect of labor within the commodity (use value and exchange value) enables one single commodity—

---

[1] I am well aware that this phrase is a popularization, which does not exist in the *Communist Manifesto*—yet, it does adequately describe the dichotomy between Marxist and Christian views to human agency.

money—to act as the value measure of the commodity. Thus, the commodity must not be considered a thing, but a social relationship. You could describe the "soul" of capitalist production as the extraction from living labor of all the unpaid hours of labor that amounts to surplus value or profit. Marx's analysis of the fetishism of the commodity form bears a strong kinship to the New Testament's references to "false gods." But, as Lebacqz argues,

> [. . .] in spite of its affinity with Marx's analytic methods and social goals, the view of justice provided in liberation theology is not simply a new version of "to each according to need." Justice is not a simple formula for distribution. Justice would not be accomplished merely by offering programs that meet basic needs of the poor. Justice requires the kind of liberating activity that characterizes God's behaviour toward the poor and oppressed [. . .] there is no separation of "love" and "justice." God's justice is God's love or compassion on those who suffer. God's love is God's justice or liberation of the oppressed. (Lebacqz 1986: 107)

Marx was a humanist, and this is clear in both his private letters and his published works, but whether he was a Christian humanist as Miranda maintains remains very much an open question.

PJ: Marxism aims at social change through collective action, while Christianity is much more focused on individual development. Obviously, this is not an either-or relationship—as Paulo Freire (1972) would say, collective acts of emancipation are necessarily preconfigured by individual consciousness. What is your take on this tension between (Christian) individualism and (Marxist) collectivism?

PM: The emphasis in Christianity on otherworldliness (don't worry if the bad people are not caught and punished, they will be punished in the afterlife) has often been used as a moral justification for the consecration of deception, either by encouraging passive resistance to exploitation or labeling the unmasking of deeper truths about empire as too subversive, too "anti-American"—a posture that tends to make people unworldly or uncaring about others. Yet, as De La Torre (2015: 162) warns: "History demonstrates the futility of simply denouncing unjust social structures for those whom the structures privilege will never willingly abdicate what they consider to be their birthright." The mere moral exercise of political power through passive protest is not a convincing answer since

> the idea of the moral exercise of political power ignores what political power is: the state is (not as an abuse but by definition) "the monopoly of legitimate violence." While parts of the state machine may be "very peaceful," the threat of violence, backed up by armed forces, is always presupposed. And the practice of politics, whether in office or in opposition, is always war (mainly class war) carried on by other means. Non-violent politics is a contradiction in terms. (Collier 2001: 104)

So instead of fighting to change the structures of oppression, people either focus on remaking themselves as individuals into better persons (there are plenty of self-help books out there) or they become indelibly indifferent to politics or political change.

Marxism rejects this Cartesian sense of "liberty of indifference" (changing oneself rather than changing the world) and "the preference for autoplastic solutions which underlies it" (Collier 2001: 100). While one is necessarily changed by changing the world (what we call praxis), that does not mean that all attempts to change ourselves are unnecessary or futile—since resistance to oppression requires us to adapt to changing circumstances, and adaptation requires all kinds of strategies of self-change. After all, in *Theses on Feuerbach* Marx (1976) writes that: "The coincidence of the changing of circumstances and of human activity or self-changing can be conceived and rationally understood only as *revolutionary practice.*" If we act as if the eschaton has already arrived, and we are preparing for the reign of God, then is this not necessarily a quixotic predicament, but a form of prefigurative politics.

In letting the reign of God be prefigured in our present lives, whether we image that reign to be a communist society or the Kingdom of God, there is no guarantee that our good actions will bring about its completion—but if we postdate our best ethics to the future communist society or Kingdom of God, then our good actions will, at least, have intrinsic values in themselves. I believe that our organization and actions should prefigure the socialist revolution or the coming of the Kingdom of God. While it may be true that means do not always resemble ends, Collier argues that "[s]o long as human authority exists, it should as far as possible be organized so that the greatest power serves the least powerful with all its might," which in its contemporary form is called "the dictatorship of the proletariat" (Collier 2001: 122).

PJ: Both the Bible and the works of Marx can be read in many different ways—I surely don't need to remind you of historical atrocities, which resulted from certain readings of both doctrines. . . . While it is tempting to seek concordances between seminal Christian and Marxist texts, I would like to ask a more fundamental philosophical question: How commensurable are the philosophies of Marxism and Christianity?

PM: Denys Turner (1983) has contributed some important insights with respect to the compatibility of Marxism and Christianity that are worth repeating here. Both Marxism and Christianity are compatible with a materialist theory of history yet hold to a denial of ontological materialism. We are talking here not about a formal or Cartesian logical consistency between Marxism and Christianity but a dialectical consistency. It is true that there exists no coherent synthesis between Christian doctrines and Marxist theory, but that all the more makes it imperative that we abandon the rhetorical homologies often found in liberation theology—"the *anawim* [the poor and the oppressed referred to in the Old Testament] become the proletariat, liberation becomes redemption politicised, alienation is original sin [. . .] the priesthood metamorphosized into Lenin's revolutionary leadership" (Turner 1983: 211–12). These homologies are useful, politically, to inspire the struggle of impoverished communities against well-armed death squads, but they must not be viewed as strict equivalences, since this could lead to uncritical forms of triumphalism.

PJ: I'm glad we're on the same page!

PM: While Marxism and Christianity seem to be incommensurable languages, both are constitutively necessary to explain reality and to understand what forces and relations shape the human condition. Both are part of the praxis of history and can be viewed as historically conditioned action systems, defined by their relationship to historical contingencies. As Turner (1983) reminds us, Marxism requires abolishing the conditions which require it—capitalist exploitation. Similarly, according to Turner, Christianity will realize itself only at the cost of its abolition *as Christianity* since its realization will become a fully human reality rather than a sacred reality—a fully socialized humanity and a fully humanized society consisting of love.

However, as Turner (1983) cogently argues, because God is nonidentical with the contingencies of any particular form of history, our full humanity can only be known through aspirations for liberation, which cannot be realized in practice. We need to secure the conditions of that absence of a presence, which we can only symbolize and understand heuristically. We cannot love, we cannot be free, we cannot know God, we cannot know how we can live without oppression, because the Kingdom of God has not been realized; we can only work as Christians and Marxists *to secure the conditions of the possibility of loving and living freely*. Under capitalism, under the prevailing institutional structures of exploitation, love and freedom can only ever be ideological. We can only anticipate love in its absence, we can never truly see love fulfilled under the conditions of capitalism. In the conditions of bourgeois society, any further claims about love are only ideological. In a world of dehumanized, alienated social relationships, we can only symbolize love through its absence, and so we can say that love, and generosity, and goodness, and Christ are present in this world *but present only in the form of their absence*.

The Morality of Dialectical Materialism

PJ: Speaking of the conditions of freedom, and of anticipation, we enter directly into the area of morality. Christian morality is quite theoretically robust, yet, as Rosen (2000: 21) says, "the question whether Marx's theory has a moral or ethical dimension is one of the most controversial of all issues of Marx interpretation." What is your take on that question?

PM: Marxism is, in this sense, morality itself, because, as Turner (1983: 215) argues, "it consists in the knowledge of what to do given the 'facts.'" Marxism is the fundamental science of capitalism and reveals morality in capitalist society to be ideologically bourgeois. Marxism is thus all that morality can be—it represents the outer limits of morality—given today's existing conditions of capitalist exploitation and oppression. Marxism is "the theory and the practice of realizing the conditions of the possibility of morality" (Turner 1983: 215), while at the same time, it is not possible for Christianity to be regarded as coterminous with Marxism even when Marxism "is demonstrably the scientifically warranted response" to "the conditions of any particular historical epoch" (Turner 1983: 213). And this is true "even if it follows from the fact that Christianity can know itself and the nature of its praxis only through the Marxist criticism of it" (Turner 1983: 213). So while Marxism argues about "the impossibility of moral knowledge in capitalist conditions," it exists as a revolutionary form of praxis in that it points out how it is impossible for capitalism to conform to its own truth in practice "since conformity is structurally impossible for capitalism" (Turner 1983: 213).

Christianity attempts to "symbolize the depths of what is to be human in the form of a sacredness, in the form of the refusal to admit what is most fully human could be compatible with the conditions of alienation and exploitation which historically obtain" (Turner 1983: 213). Thus, Christianity recognizes love as the point of its praxis, but it is a love that, under capitalism, can only be anticipated. Turner makes a prescient point when he argues that the absence of morality in Marxism is not in any sense a "*mere* amoralism" because it reveals that it is capitalism, not Marxism, which is amoralistic. In other words, Marxism reveals the "platitudinous imperatives, so forthcoming from Christians, to 'love' within conditions of gross and systematic exploitation" (Turner 1983: 216) and Christianity's "transhistorical pretentiousness" in believing that Christ's presence in history is not historically contingent, that is, not dependent on any particular historical or economic conditions.

Adopting a transcendent morality among Christians is what Turner rejects as Christian "fidelism," which focuses on the Kingdom of God being "within you." This is not to deny the presence of God, but that such presence is not in the form of some supernatural text that has already been written; rather, "the unwritten text *is* present in the struggle to write it" (Turner 1983: 219). This is very much like the popular proverb by Antonio Machado that one makes the road by walking (*Caminante, no hay camino, se have camino al andar*). Both Marxism and Christianity have the resources within their own traditions for rejecting immorality—for instance, for rejecting meta-moral principles where, for example, communist society is made into a moral absolute or Christianity is presented as an already written moral text to which only Christians or particularly enlightened Christians have access.

According to Turner, Marx rejected theism as false, because it "supposes an opposition between God and man" (Turner 1983: 165), and he criticizes atheism "because it accepts the terms which theism lays down and can speak of man only indirectly, that is, via the negation of theism" (Turner 1983: 165). Marx rejected the theologically and politically conservative Christianity of his day, as well as the radical Christianity that made its appearances throughout his lifetime. Marx claims that questions pertaining to the existence of God arise only among those who fail to understand their own natural human origins. Turner recognized that Marx rejected contemporary immanentist theologies because he viewed them as a partial regression to negative atheism itself. While Marx rejected negative atheism, Turner does not take that to mean Marx was not an atheist.

PJ: I could somehow swallow that Marx was not a (complete) atheist, but it cannot be disputed that he was very anticlerical. How does liberation theology, with its close relationships to the church, absorb Marx's negativity toward its own being?

PM: Marx was anticlerical, and so would any rational person be during the time of Marx who recognized that Jesus was the antithesis of clericalism, a clericalism whose world-denying conciliar prohibitions infected by monarchism and paternalism, disallowed justice for all. It was a temporal power that germinated autocracy and was leavened by obedience to a hierarchy that almost always sided with the imperial and structural intentionality of the state. It was clear to Marx and like-minded others that the ecclesiology that developed from the law, especially canon law, gave the papacy unrestricted power over the laity, resulting in a religious hubris of unrelenting fidelity to empire. It had ripped away from early Christianity sanctioned disobedience to imperial law. Now it demanded compliance to the dictatorship of the ruling class and its despotic commands often leading to brutishness, cruelty, and unvarnished terror, to prioritizing sacred laws over human welfare and making the Law of Christ coextensive with the Law of Empire and its imperial covenant directed at capital accumulation by dispossession.

In liberation theology, however, there must be a principled intransigence toward authoritarian power rather than a creative adaptation to it, an ecclesiogenesis[2] that lives in dialectical tension between the pneumatological[3] and doctrinal aspect of the church and the base of the Church of the Poor. The church proclaims a Kingdom of God that it can never put into practice, similar to capitalism that installs the very conditions (wage labor, value augmentation, social relations of production) under which wealth and prosperity are available onto to a few. Yet both cannot abandon the teachings they cannot follow.

PJ: Marx was a scientist, and his worldview is based on dialectical materialism. Liberation theology is built on religion, and its worldview is based on faith. How do you reconcile these radically different approaches to reality?

PM: Today in our efforts to create a society constructed upon principles of social justice, we have approached our projects as scientifically distilled data—big data serves both as our compass and as our destination. But allegiance to data removes the consensus-generating process that is part of collective reflection and systematic rationality, as Miranda explains so well. Interpersonal dialogue has to be part of the object of study and rational reflection—since relations between people are the basis of the relations between things. We can't forget this. As Miranda (1980: 306) notes, the "communitarian process leading to consensus can evade the arbitrariness or naivete of extrascientific motives only if we, in all frankness, realize that dialogic discussion does exist, that it is moral in character, and that it is thus a matter of conscience." Without this consideration articulated by Miranda, and reflected in Paulo Freire's (1972) *Pedagogy of the Oppressed*, we will etherize the role that our conscience must play and fall prey to corruption and self-interest.

We can't separate norms and facts, facts and value, for this expunges meaning from history, and both Marx and the teachings of the gospels recognize this. As Miranda (1980: 307) notes, "[t]he eschaton of Marx, which is the same as that of the gospel, is what gives meaning to history." The project of immanentizing the eschaton is one that has historically struck fear in the hearts of conservatives who use the term pejoratively

---

[2] The term "ecclesiogenesis" is used by liberation theologian Leonardo Boff to describe the new ecclesiological experience within the Basic Christian Communities created in Latin America in which attempts are made by popular constituencies to create authentic Christian communities. Participants see this as creating a new form of church outside of the institutional structures of the traditional Catholic hierarchy (see Boff 1986).

[3] In Christianity, the term "pneumatology" refers to the study of the Holy Spirit.

because it refers to attempts to bring about the Kingdom of God in the immanent world. The conservatives equate this with socialism, communism, antiracism, and even Nazism. But reading the gospel from below mandates that such a project is already in the making, with the intervention of Christ into human history. It is rejected by conservatives for fear of the rise of totalitarianism. But at the root of such fear is that panic in the hearts of those who stand to lose their wealth and status should a state of egalitarianism and equality be achieved.

PJ: What is the main message of Marx's work for liberation theology positioned in, against, and beyond contemporary capitalism (see Holloway 2016)?

PM: All of us can become blinded by virtue of our own interests, whether we are atheists, agnostics, Christians, Christian communists, or members of other religious faiths. For example, the capitalist does not realize that what is sold in the transaction between the capitalists is labor power, not labor—sold at its exchange value, and so the capitalist is willfully blinded to the fact that labor power produces much more than it is worth simply as exchange value (the laborer works much more than it takes to reproduce his or her own necessities for survival) and operates out of a motivated amnesia that the capitalist has been stealing surplus value from his workers. The Christian and the capitalist rarely think deeply about Marx's notion of value, and both adhere to the empiricist expression "price of labor," which hides the fact that the wage system is, in reality, a form of slavery. This, according to Marx, is an epistemological issue as much as a moral issue. As Miranda points out, Marx did not adhere to a materialist dogmatism that limited epistemology to social class. He recognized that the very mechanism of cognition itself is ideological, and that there are moral values embedded in the process of cognition—that within the apologetics and empiricist ideologies of economists there exist hidden interests, which he viewed as ideological.

It is worth remembering Miranda's (1980: 303) insight: "Empiricism sticks to things. Marx dissolves things into relations between persons because conscience is not troubled by any moral obligation whatsoever when it confronts things." Hence, it is important for both Christians and Marxists to remember that exploitation and oppression can only be overcome by a sincere willingness to know the truth. Yes, truth is always partial, contingent, and contextual, but it can be known. Which is why I believe the work of Marx is so essential to Christianity and why liberation theology needs to be continually reinvented for the current times, especially after such brutal efforts by the Reagan administration and Pope John Paul II to silence it, and efforts by right-wing dictatorships throughout Latin America to crush it by murdering priests and exponents of the Church of the Poor in the 1970s and 1980s. Today, especially today, the world needs liberation theology, which, by the way, is not restricted to Christianity or Christians but to all those who seek justice in these exceedingly brutal times. In the United States, Trump has given Christianity over to a pack of vipers and it is time to raise our voices in a heavenly choir of protest. And that is just the beginning.

7

Paulo Freire and Liberation Theology: The Christian Consciousness of Critical Pedagogy

The Life and Work of Paulo Freire

PJ: Please say a few words about the life and work of Paulo Freire.

PM: I'm going to draw on a description I have used in other works, since it covers some of the very basic facts of Paulo's life (see McLaren 1997b). Paulo Reglus Neves Freire was born on September 19, 1921, in Recife, in the Northeast of Brazil. He was a profoundly courageous and humble scholar, social activist, philosopher of praxis, and cultural worker. Freire was able to develop an anti-imperialist and anticapitalist literacy praxis that served as the foundation for a more broadly based struggle for liberation. In his first experiment in 1963, Freire taught 300 adults to read and write in forty-five days. This method was adopted by Pernambuco, a sugar-cane-growing state 1,160 miles northeast of Rio. This success marked the beginning of what was to become a legendary approach in education.

In 1964 a right-wing military coup overthrew the democratically elected government of President João Goulart. Freire became a target of the military junta who accused him of preaching communism and so they arrested him and put him in prison for seventy days. He went into self-exile when he was released. His activities in the national literacy campaign, of which he had served as director, had been just too much for the junta to accept. The Brazilian military considered Freire "an international subversive," "a traitor to Christ and the Brazilian people," and accused him of developing a teaching method "similar to that of Stalin, Hitler, Peron, and Mussolini." He was furthermore accused of trying to turn Brazil into a "Bolshevik country" (Gadotti 1994).

Freire spent sixteen years in exile. During this time his life was punctuated by a five-year stay in Chile as a UNESCO consultant with the Research and Training Institute for Agrarian Reform; an appointment in 1969 to Harvard University's Center for Studies in Development and Social Change; a move to Geneva, Switzerland, in 1970 as consultant to the Office of Education of the World Council of Churches, where he developed literacy programs for Tanzania and Guinea-Bissau that focused on the re-Africanization of their countries; the development of literacy programs in some postrevolutionary former Portuguese colonies such as Angola and Mozambique; assisting the governments of Peru and Nicaragua with their literacy campaigns; the establishment of the Institute of Cultural Action in Geneva in 1971; a brief return to

Chile after Salvador Allende was assassinated in 1973, provoking General Pinochet to declare Freire a subversive; his brief visit to Brazil under a political amnesty in 1979; and his final return to Brazil in 1980 to teach at the Pontifícia Universidade Católica in São Paulo and the Universidade de Campinas in São Paulo. These events were accompanied by numerous works, most notably *Pedagogy of the Oppressed* (Freire 1972), *Cultural Action for Freedom* (Freire 1970), and *Pedagogy in Process: Letters to Guinea-Bissau* (Freire 1978). In more recent years, Freire worked briefly as Secretary of Education of São Paulo, continuing his radical agenda of literacy reform for the people of that city.

Freire's literacy programs were designed for exploited peasant populations and are now employed in countries all over the world. Freire was able to employ categories in his pedagogy such as history, politics, economics, and class, and relate these to the concepts of culture and power. The result was the development of both a language of critique and a language of hope. These two discourses work conjointly and dialectically and have not only proven successful in helping generations of disenfranchised peoples to liberate themselves in Brazil but are used in teacher education programs worldwide.

PJ: Please say more about Freire's famous approach to literacy. Back in the day, why was it considered so dangerous?

PM: Freire's literacy method grew out of the Movement for Popular Culture in Recife that had set up "cultural circles" (discussion groups with nonliterates) by the end of the 1950s. Freire believed that the oppressed could learn to read provided that reading was not imposed upon them in an authoritarian manner and that the process of reading validated their own lived experiences. After all, adults could speak an extraordinarily rich and complex language but lacked the graphical skills to write their ideas down. Freire understood that the popular majorities that constituted the oppressed are rarely heard by the dominant members of their society, creating what Paulo referred to as a "culture of silence." That did not mean that the oppressed could not respond to their own reality but that such a response often lacked a critical dimension. In the cultural circle (*circulo de cultura*), educators and learners were able to respond to their own existential realities by employing codifications to engage in dialogue about the social, cultural, and material conditions that impacted their lives on a daily basis. The peer group had an important role to play in providing the theoretical context for critical reflection. The result was that Freire's students were both equipped and emboldened to transform their interpretations of reality from the production of "everyday commonsense" knowledges to a more critical knowledge, what we might call "critical consciousness."

Freire and his colleagues formed these cultural circle settings mostly in rural contexts, making a list of the words used, the expressions, the informal jargon, and the characteristic mannerisms that accompanied certain phrases in order to gain an understanding of the "cultural capital" of the people. There were many topics that proved important to the peasants' road to literacy—to reading the word with, against, and alongside the world which included nationalism, development, democracy, and illiteracy. These were introduced through the use of slides or pictures, followed by a dialogue. The words identified by Freire's students and chosen by Freire and his team "codified" the ways of life and the lived experiences of the local community members. But words were not the only means of codifying lived experiences. Other codifications included photographs and drawings. All of these together served as representations that permitted extended dialogue and an analysis of the concrete reality of the adult learners. Codifications mediated between the everyday lived experiences of the people and the theorizing that took place related to the context of everyday life. Codifications not created in a top-down fashion. They were co-constructed between Freire's team and the learners.

This was very different than learning to read from a primer. To learn to read from a primer meant that learners must accept the experiences inscribed in the primer as more important than their own. The key for Freire was his ability to work with learners in identifying generative themes that permeated the lives of the learners. These consisted of the experiences of learners who had internalized very negative images of themselves that disbarred them from challenging the current conditions of their existence—such as poverty and illiteracy. They was because they believed that all of their misgivings were due to fate, or to chance, or to their own constitutive inferiority which made them feel incapable of taking active participation in reshaping the lineaments of their lives with a greater sense of critical agency.

PJ: How did Freire's approach to literacy work in practice?

PM: Let me repeat what I have written elsewhere. The generative themes that grew out of the time that Freire spent with the oppressed amounted to a collection of codifications of complex experiences that had a great deal of social meaning and political significance for the group. These were precisely the themes that were likely to generate considerable discussion and analysis because they were generated out of the lived history and circumstances of the learners. They were also chosen for their syllabic length and with the goal of presenting all the phonemes of the Portuguese language. So there was, first of all, an investigative stage of finding the words and generative themes of a group in terms of their social class relevance and meaning for that group. Generative themes were often codified into generative words—more specifically, trisyllabic words that could be broken down into syllabic parts and used to generate other words (Brown 1987). Freire and his culture circles practiced a form of decodification that broke up a codification into its constituent elements so that the learners began to perceive relationships between elements of the codification and other experiences in their day-to-day lives. Such decodification took place through dialogue, in which familiar, everyday experiences were made strange and the strange or unknown process of generating critical knowledge was made familiar.

Freire followed the creation of generative themes with the process of thematization, where generative themes were codified and decodified and replaced by a critical social vision. New generative themes were then discovered and instructors were able to breakdown and identify phonetic groups at this stage. This was followed by problematization (the antithesis of problem-solving) that consisted of codifying reality into symbols that could generate critical consciousness. During the problematization stage, the group within the cultural circle examined the limits and possibilities of the existential situations that emerged from the previous stage. Critical consciousness demanded a rejection of passivity and the practice of dialogue. Critical consciousness was brought about not through an individual or intellectual effort, but through conscientization or identifying contradictions in one's lived experience, and understanding and overcoming dominant myths, traditions, and ideologies in order to reach new levels of awareness of being an "object" in a world where only "subjects" have the means to determine the direction of their lives. The process of conscientization involved becoming a "subject" with other oppressed subjects and taking part in humanizing the world through collective struggle and praxis. Conscientization involved experiencing oppressive reality as a process that can be overcome through transformative praxis. Such a praxis (a cycle of action–reflection–action) involved overcoming through concrete actions and group effort those obstacles to the process of becoming human (Gadotti 1994). Freire's approach to literacy created the conditions for the oppressed to liberate themselves and, in the process, liberate their oppressors. All of what I have said is summarized by Cynthia Brown (1987).

PJ: You are too humble, Peter—your own books, such as *Che Guevara, Paulo Freire, and the Pedagogy of Revolution* (McLaren 2000), are among the richest sources on Paulo Freire! But let's move on: Please link Freire's approach to literacy with his understanding of knowledge.

PM: Freire was one of the first educational philosophers to underscore repeatedly the concept of "knowing" as a political act. One way of examining knowledge that is highly indebted to the ideas of Freire is to see educators as working within the intersection of temporality and narrative as a dialectical event. Here, experience, temporality, reflection, and social action come together in what is commonly referred to in Freirean discourse as praxis. In the field of anthropology, the profane or historical time of contemporary social groups (involving the concreteness, linearity, and irreversibility of time) is often juxtaposed with the mythical time of so-called archaic societies (time that repeats paradigmatic or archetypal gestures that are filled with deep meaning for the participants who use such recurrent mythical forms as a prism for personhood). Freire's notion of praxis, however, brings both conceptions of time into the narrative fabric of the emergent self.

The act of knowing is grounded in a type of mythopoetic desire (a desire to raise our own existence to a level of greater meaningfulness) (see Freeman 1998) linked to community, to a new level of sacred authenticity, to organizing life in imaginatively new ways that refuse to reproduce the alienation and objectification necessarily found in the world of abstract labor. Here, revolutionary praxis folds historical and mythical time into an act of negating what is, in anticipation of what could be. Schematically put, the line (the perpetual reappearance of the present in historical time) is folded into the circle (the primordial horizon of the irredeemably configured past).

One of Freire's goals is becoming conscious of and transcending the limits in which we can make ourselves. We achieve this through externalizing, historicizing, and objectifying our vision of liberation, in treating theory as a form of practice and practice as a form of theory as we contest the psychopathology of everyday life incarnate in capitalism's social division of labor. We do this with the intention of never separating the production of knowledge from praxis, from reading the word and the world dialectically (Stetsenko 2002). In so doing we maintain that practice serves as the ultimate ground for advancing and verifying theories as well as for providing warrants for knowledge claims. These warrants are not connected to some fixed principles that exist outside of the knowledge claims themselves but are derived by identifying and laying bare the ideological and ethical potentialities of a given theory as a form of practice (Stetsenko 2002). Critical educators seek to uncover what at first blush may appear as the ordinary, transparent relations and practices that make up our quotidian existence—what we might even call mundane social realities. We take these relationships and practices and try to examine their contractions when seen in relation to the totality of social relations in which those particular relations and practices unfold. Such an examination takes place against a transdisciplinary backdrop that reads the word and the world historically.

PJ: Back in the day, Freire's work profoundly shaped the landscape of education. What about its contemporary legacy?

PM: Freire's work has had a strikingly significant impact on the genesis and ongoing development of the field of critical pedagogy. Critical pedagogy is constituted by a body of theory associated with Freire's work and critical social theory more generally that emphasize praxis. The field of critical pedagogy has recently expanded its purview to include revolutionary critical pedagogy, an attempt to reclaim Freire's Marxist epistemological roots through the development of a philosophy of praxis driven primarily by the work of Marx and Hegel. Freire's research has been felt in the fields of theology, literacy, composition studies, literary studies, applied linguistics, sociology, anthropology, and political philosophy. That his work has cross-fertilized so many areas of research is a testament to its transdisciplinary reach.

PJ: One of the main strengths of Freire's work is its versatility. His legacy constantly (re) appears in radically different contexts and situations, and *Pedagogy of the Oppressed* (Freire 1972) is the third most cited book in the history of the social sciences (Green 2016). Comprehending such diversity is beyond human means, so it's worth asking: What, for you, is the essence of Freire's work?

PM: The grand mysterium of Freire's work was his ability to cultivate an armed love, a critical approach to reading the word and the world animated by love and compassion. He achieved this through a deeply philosophical and spiritual understanding of how the co-construction of knowledge among teachers and learners partakes of both transgressive and transformative dimensions that can be cultivated for the purpose of creating new freedoms from the prison house of suffering.

Paulo Freire and Liberation Theology

PJ: After the publication of *Pedagogy of Insurrection* (McLaren 2015b), liberation theology has slowly but surely resurfaced in the discourse of (revolutionary) critical pedagogy. What is the main point of convergence between Freire and liberation theology?

PM: Freire was a Christian and sympathetic to Marx, and while I never had a chance to discuss with Paulo the topic of liberation theology, I believe that it would have been a fascinating dialogue. For me, critical consciousness is something that is central to the movement of liberation theology. In the sense that Christians come to recognize not only their preferential option for the poor but, as I would put it, their preferential obligation and commitment to the poor. Critically conscious Christians do not only come to recognize their political formation as subjects—their standpoint epistemology—in relation to others, but also gain ontological and ethical clarity on their role as Christians.

PJ: It's a shame that you and Freire never discussed liberation theology, yet we can still discuss liberation theology in relation to Freire's work. For starters, liberation theology and Freire's works have developed roughly at the same time and in the same place—the second half of twentieth century in Latin America.

PM: I was often overwhelmed by the gentle force of this man of God. I was surprised that he knew my work, and even more surprised that he described us as intellectual cousins in a preface that he did for one of my books (Freire 1995: x). His comments gave me the confidence that I was sorely lacking at the time to continue my work in critical pedagogy. I came to liberation theology out of my own spiritual yearning, my fear that religion was created by those whose denial of death led them to project a fantasy of salvation into the world that resulted in the development of a religious faith in a supreme being. And I was depressed at the thought that death terminates consciousness for eternity. I was ready to accept being an atheist. But some of the titles in the catalog of Orbis Books caught my attention. Orbis Books was the publishing house for liberation theology in the United States beginning as far back in the 1970s. Orbis Books, is an American imprint of the Maryknoll order founded by Nicaraguan Maryknoll priest Miguel D'Escoto with Philip J. Scharper in 1970 and what a blessing this publishing house was to me during periods that reflected my dark night of the soul.

Liberation theology was born out of the self-theologizing of radical Catholic Action communities in America Latina. There were Protestant variants as well; since the 1970s, many variants of liberation theology have emerged such as Jewish Liberation theology, Black Liberation Theology, Feminist Liberation Theology, and Latino/a Liberation Theology. Liberation theology is systematically opposed to the trenchant conservative politics of white evangelical America in the United States who encourage individual charity over a distributive social justice that mandates the economic restructuring of society—a dilemma so familiar to many living in the richest country in the world. There arose among both lay persons and clergy within the Catholic Church grievous concern surrounding the economic consequences following the rise of Latin American populist governments of the 1950s and 1960s—especially those of Perón in Argentina, Vargas in Brazil, and Cárdenas in Mexico. In failing to eradicate dependency, poverty, and injustice, and carrying the burden of helping both to legitimate and reproduce the power and authority of the capitalist state for over five centuries, liberation theologians considered the church an egregious failure in its mission to create the Kingdom of God, which they understood in the context of creating a just society on earth, not some misty paradise beyond the pale of distant clouds, but a world in the here and now—what we could call in Blochian language a concrete utopia. Liberation theology, which coalesced into a movement throughout the 1960s and 1970s, attempted to establish the potential for a return of the role of the church to the people (similar to the conditions that existed in earliest Christian communities) by nurturing critical-autonomous "protagonistic agency" among the popular sectors, creating the conditions of possibility for consciousness-raising among peasants and proletarianized multitudes. (I recently coined the term protagonistic agency, to emphasize Freire's (1972) idea of being the subject of history rather than the object of history.)

PJ: Please outline Freire's influence on liberation pedagogy in more detail.

PM: Theologian William Herzog II is roundly critical of literary-critical readings of the parables of Jesus, especially their focus on narrativity and metaphoricity, their literary forms and parabolic and paradoxical aspects, which often results in "forcing the reader to reinterpret the meaning of interpretation itself" (1994: 13). In such readings, the parable "was being moved from the world . . . [and] . . . being situated most comfortably in the world of the interpreter" (1994: 13). In contrast to literary-critical readings, Herzog approves of comparing the parables of Jesus with the quest for the historical Jesus, and he approaches the understanding of Jesus' parables through the work of Paulo Freire—especially Freire's approach to critical consciousness. Herzog writes:

> In addition to their obvious differences, Jesus and Paulo have some things in common. Both figures worked with poor and oppressed peoples, and both worked with peasants. Although Freire's work with urban laborers has no counterpart in Jesus' public activity, their peasant audiences are similar. . . . Both figures labored in societies that had been deformed by colonial exploitation whose presence continued to shape the life of its inhabitants. (Herzog 1994: 25)

Herzog examines the similarities faced by the peasants to whom Jesus' parables spoke and Freire's own students. He writes:

> Freire was clearly focused on the twin tasks of teaching literacy and social analysis. But what about Jesus? Taking a cue from Freire, one may propose that Jesus' parables dealt with issues of interest to his "students." Their social scenes are therefore important for what they tell us of the world in which the peasants and rural underclass lived. To use Freire's language, they encode generative themes and objectify conditions of oppression so that they can be examined. All of this implies that some of the parables function in a manner similar to what Freire calls "codifications." They re-present a familiar or typified scene for the purpose of generating conversation about it and stimulating the kind of reflection that expose contradictions in popularly held beliefs or traditional thinking. (Herzog 1994: 26)

There was another point of similarity between Jesus and Freire. According to Herzog, "[b]oth men were considered politically subversive, and both suffered political consequences because of their work" (Herzog 1994: 27). Freire was imprisoned in Brazil and later was forced into self-exile. Jesus "was crucified between two 'social bandits' ... on the charge of subversion because he claimed to be 'king of the Jews'" (Herzog 1994: 27).

According to Herzog, "[w]ithout invoking the entire program developed by Freire, it is possible to propose that Jesus used parables to present situations familiar to the rural poor, to encode the systems of oppression that controlled their lives and held them in bondage" (Herzog 1994: 27). Jesus, who lived in an oral culture, used storytelling; living in a visual culture, Freire used pictures as codifications. Herzog has appropriated Freire's methods of creating generative words, leading to codifications, then to decoding, problematizing, and recodifying, using vocabulary and phonetic cards right up to the postliteracy phase to analyze the parables that appear in the Bible. In the final phase of Freire's literacy campaign, generative words were gathered "in an effort to identify the thematic universe they revealed" (Herzog 1994: 23). According to Herzog,

> [E]very historical epoch is marked by large themes, and people participate in their historical eras to the degree that they identify, shape, create, and recreate those themes. Passive spectators of history live by the themes determined by others, who in turn define their lives and limits. The failure to perceive and participate in the naming of epoch-making themes leads to a withdrawal from history as well as an abdication of the responsibility to remake history. Every such retreat ends in hopelessness. The generative themes of any era define its aspirations and the impediments that would repress their fulfillment and name the tasks that must be undertaken to realize those aspirations. Every exploration of a generative theme, then, involves interpreters more deeply in their new role as subjects capable of comprehending their world and translating their newly constituted knowledge into programs of action. The mystified illiterates became critical-thinking readers of their world. (Herzog 1994: 23–24)

PJ: A similar focus on the poor is also present in the works of Karl Marx. However, Freire was a Christian believer while Marx was, as we discussed earlier, more or less an atheist. Your liberation theology is deeply situated in both traditions, and *Pedagogy of Insurrection* (McLaren 2015b) clearly leans toward the Latin American approach that sees Christianity as compatible with, and even beneficial to, revolutionary critical pedagogy. What are the reasons behind such direction of development of your thought?

PM: Freire has addressed the role of theologians and the church—its formalism, supposed neutrality, and captivity in a complex web of bureaucratic rites that pretends to serve the oppressed but actually supports the power elite—from the perspective of the philosophy of praxis that he developed throughout his life. For Freire, critical consciousness (conscientization) cannot be divorced from Christian consciousness. Freire's attack on bourgeois subjective idealism as "naïve consciousness" approaches the transformation of consciousness as a political act: to speak a true word, according to Freire, is to transform the world. The ruling class, from Freire's perspective, views consciousness as something that can be transformed by "lessons, lectures and eloquent sermons" (Freire 1973: 2). In this instance, consciousness is essentially static, necrophilic (deathloving) as distinct from biophilic (life-loving), constitutes "an uncritical adherence to the ruling class" (Freire 1973: 2), and serves as a means of "emptying conscientization of its dialectical content" (Freire 1973: 3).

Freire calls for a type of class suicide in which the bourgeoisie takes on a new apprenticeship of dying to their own class interests and experiencing their own Easter moment through a form of mutual understanding and transcendence. Freire argues that the theologians of Latin America must move forward and transform the dominant class interests in the interests of the suffering poor "if they are to experience 'death' as an oppressed class and be born again to liberation" (Freire 1973: 6). Or else, they will be implicated within a church "which forbids itself the Easter which it preaches" (Freire 1973: 5–6). Freire borrowed the concept of class suicide from Amilcar Cabral, the Guinea-Bissauan and Cape Verdean revolutionary and political leader who was assassinated in 1973. For Freire, insight into the conditions of social injustice of this world stipulates that the privileged must commit a type of class suicide where they self-consciously attempt to divest themselves of their power and privilege and willingly commit themselves to unlearning their attachment to their own self-interest. Essentially, this was a type of Easter experience in which a person willingly sacrifices his or her middle or ruling class interests in order to be reborn through a personal commitment to suffering alongside the poor.

Of course, this class suicide takes place in the context of a larger mission to end the social sin of poverty itself. It is a transformational process in which a person identifies with the poor and the oppressed and commits oneself to taking down all victims from the cross. Here we find an echo of the teachings of St Francis. Both Freire and St Francis understood that a transcendence of oppression—a striving upward—in the struggle for liberation was not enough. As Leonardo Boff notes in his majesterial study of St Francis (1982), a striving "upwards" away from the travails of the world through the attainment of a mystical consciousness is not enough. What is also needed, and even more so, is a "trans-descendence"—a kenotic act of self-emptying, an openness to the lives of those below—the poor, the stigmatized, the despised—and a willingness to integrate them into a community of love, kindness, and solidarity—a fraternal solidarity with those suffering from the scourge of life's deprivations. Christ encountered such trans-descendence in the wretched of the earth, in the crucified of history.

PJ: In theory, the concept of class suicide somehow seems much more viable than in practice. . . . How can we move on from theory to praxis?

PM: Let us examine some of Freire's positions here. Freire writes that the praxis by which consciousness is changed "is not only action but action and reflection" (Freire 1973: 3). He argues that theoretic praxis is only authentic when it maintains the dialectical movement between itself and the contextual specificity of the praxis one wishes to carry out, that is, when it is cognizant of the unity between practice and theory in which both are constructed, shaped, and reshaped. Authentic praxis, in other words, is a "dialectical movement which relates critical reflection on past action to the continuing struggle" (Freire 1973: 3). For Freire, a pedagogy of liberation involves "social praxis" that is all about "helping to free human beings from the oppression which strangles them in their objective reality" (Freire 1973: 4). Social praxis, as explained by Freire, is what drew me to the Latin American tradition of liberation theology, precisely because it's a theology that encourages the oppressed to create and recreate themselves in history in a concrete fashion rather than participate in what Freire calls "a reformed repetition of the present" (Freire 1973: 4). Freire writes:

> I cannot permit myself to be a mere spectator. On the contrary, I must demand my place in the process of change. So the dramatic tension between the past and the future, death and life, being and non-being, is not longer a kind of dead-end for me; I can see it for what it really is: a permanent challenge to which I must respond. And my response can be none other than my historical praxis—in other words, revolutionary praxis. (Freire 1973: 7)

The Prophetic Church of Paulo Freire

PJ: In the article "Education, Liberation and The Church" (Freire 1973), Freire analyses the three main types of church: the traditionalist, the modernizing, and the prophetic church. These days, when Pope Francis fights a battle of epic proportions against conservative fractions in the Catholic Church, Freire's analysis seems particularly interesting. What kind of church would provide the best fit for liberation theology as you see it?

PM: Nita Freire, Paulo's widow, can be quoted to help illuminate an answer to your question. In an interview with James Kirylo, Nita writes that

> Paulo was a man of authentic faith that believed in God. And while he was Catholic, he was not caught up in the "religiosity" of the faith. He believed in Jesus Christ, and in His kindness, wisdom, and goodness. He did, however, have grave concerns with the Church, particularly the contradictions of its actions, and the actions of the priests. For example, he observed, since his childhood, how so many priests ate well and gained weight, yet the poor remained poor and hungry, only to hear the priests say to them, "Don't worry, God is with you, and your reward is great in heaven." For Paulo, many priests, with their belly full, did not have authentic compassion and empathy for the poor, and were not consistent with what they had said and what they did. (Kirylo 2011: 278)

Nita also mentions Paulo's work on the distinctions among the church. She notes that

> When Gustavo Gutiérrez invited Paulo to work on some components related to liberation theology, Paulo began to analyze the distinct differences among what he called the traditional church, modern church, and the prophetic church. The

prophetic church is one that gives witness and is a liberated church, one that "feels" with you; one that is in solidarity with you, with all the oppressed in the world, the exploited ones, and ones that are victimized by a capitalist society. (Kirylo 2011: 278)

Given Nita's insights, the most significant aspect of Freire's work on the different roles of the church, at least as it pertains to the context of the revolutionary critical pedagogy developed in my own work, would be what Paulo refers to as the prophetic church. This captures much of the spirit of José Porfirio Miranda's work in liberation theology and the work of Jon Sobrino, Leonardo Boff, Gustavo Gutiérrez, James Cone, and many others. It certainly captures the spirit of the Reverend Martin Luther King. There is a 1989 American biopic depicting the story of Salvadoran Archbishop Óscar Romero (played by actor Raúl Juliá), who was assassinated while saying mass in 1980, having begun to organize nonviolent resistance to the brutal Salvadorian military dictatorship. I show *Romero* (Duigan 1989) to my students on a regular basis because it depicts priests who represent the traditional, modern, and prophetic church. The focus of the film is on the transformation undergone by Romero from being a supporter of the traditional church, with an acceptance of its modernizing aspects, to affirming the importance of the prophetic church, as he confronts the violence of El Salvador's civil war and the *conscientização* or consciousness-raising of some of his priests. One of his priests ends up carrying an automatic rifle, and Romero is quick to respond to this revolutionary violence by warning that it can only provoke further reactionary violence on the part of the more powerful state. Jesus refused to engage in organized revolutionary violence, although he most certainly could be considered a revolutionary, but an apocalyptist rather than a guerilla fighter. It was unlikely that Jesus was a Zealot but surely he was sympathetic to resistance against the Roman occupation of Judea and the collaborationist Sadducees. Jesus was not a Judas Maccabaeus figure.

Romero (Duigan 1989) shows how the prophetic church grew out of the contradictions embedded with social relations of production, relations supported by government corruption, the exploitation of the poor, and class war that exploded within a brutal comprador capitalist system (a system where local elites work on behalf of foreign governments in return for a share of the profits). It was the members of the prophetic church that risked their lives for the sake of the well-being of the poor, the exploited, those who were the targets of a brutal military regime. But the prophetic church is at work in every community where faith, solidarity, and struggle are conjugated with hope for a better world. Here we need to remember the words of Dom Hélder Câmara, a Brazilian Roman Catholic archbishop of Olinda and Recife, who had a profound influence on Freire: "When I give food to the poor, they call me a saint. When I ask why the poor have no food, they call me a communist" (Câmara 2009).

PJ: The prophetic church is about the dialectic between being and becoming that Freire understood so well . . . as Antonio Machado would say, we make the road by walking. Can you say a bit more about Freire's insights into this dialectic?

PM: It is not difficult to become depressed and drowned in cynicism given the state of the current historical conjuncture. Freire always reminded us to take stock of possibilities for liberation enfolded in current historical conditions. The bones of hope can often be seen jutting out from the carcass of despair if we are not too overwhelmed by the apotheosis of failure seemingly engrained in the current *Weltanschauung* of authoritarianism and brutality. Bones last longer than flesh, they are the reminders that we once lived in and through others. Today, in the anti-Kingdom of Trump, following the spiritual and moral imperatives of liberation theology poses a special challenge, especially for those trying to follow Freire's example of rectitude. Not the least of these is the persistence of capitalism. The revolting infection of capitalism and its implacable steel cast culture of unbridled viciousness that we know as austerity capitalism has devastated the soil of humanity, creating armies of weary and dispirited victims oscillating between hopelessness, futile gestures of defiance, and unfounded acts of optimism.

Arguments claiming the indisputable equivalence between capitalism and democracy have become all but superfluous today, revealed as a bitterly vehement propaganda ruse, as waves of immigrants lucky to survive the vortex of terror in their own war-torn native countries arrive via some miracle of discipline and focused desperation, at the gates of their vastly more prosperous neighbors. Many of them are sent back to face again the merciless torrents of war or conditions of austerity sure to increase their privations at a colossal scale. Hamstrung by the dogged defenders of white supremacy, remorseless outbreaks of nationalism, as well as scathing spectacles of indifference, those seeking refuge headed back into the abyss, victims of appalling attrition, casualties of the ghastly struggle for capitalist accumulation at a time when capitalism, inflated by its own success, has already passed its high-water mark. Alternatives to capitalism might as well be forbidden, as socialism and communism have become so unremittingly condemned for decades, that any thought of rehabilitation is now considered unthinkable.

As Marxist-humanist social justice educators, it is imperative that we work toward the creation of a social universe absent of the value form of labor. What I admire so much about Freire is that he had always been a staunch opponent of capitalism, aggravating the hegemony of this unstoppable colossus. He has picked apart the fallacious reasoning of the dung masters of colonialism. He refuses to disfigure what we have arrived at through our imagination, yet at the same time is at pains to engage in a dialectics of the concrete. He has brought down the curtain on the hypocrisy of bourgeois progressivists whose advocacy for the poor remains but as an advertisement for themselves. Paulo's generosity in response to my work gave me confidence. As a young scholar and activist in the mid-1980s, I admired how he was able to live an exemplary life. He displayed an independence of mind that did not fit easily into prevailing orthodoxies surrounding pedagogy. Freire understood that building a new society required not only material conditions but a utopian imagination, a living theory that mediated possibilities buried in actualities.

PJ: In a recent book chapter I wrote: "Revolutionary critical pedagogy respects its teachers, but does not create idols—as a live struggle, it constantly questions and reinvents its main figures and their works" (Jandrić 2018b: 199). Which aspect of Freire's work should we reinvent in and for the moment here and now? How should we go about it?

PM: There is no unimpeachable justification for regarding certain individuals as iconic figures—since there is a danger in being susceptible to the thrall of charismatic figures through the cult of personality. Yet there was something profoundly and earnestly iconic in the way that Paulo practiced the path that he exhorted others to follow, and a generosity of spirit that animated his relationships with others. Paulo's own unslakable thirst for learning and deepening his understanding of social life was guided by a humility born out of his own early experiences of hardship and a commitment to create the conditions of possibility for justice through dialogue—a dialogue that actively illuminated the internal contradictions of society, contradictions that, sadly, induce many of us through the sheer force of despair to underestimate the importance of struggle at every level of society. Such struggle stands under the scrutiny of its valiant history of political activism, of which Paulo played an important role. He was a materialist and a Catholic, but he did not have an ideological belief in materialism, and this helped to open the door to a form of utopianism, one that often bore the brunt of derision from some of his fellow philosophers, very often economistic Marxists. I saw his utopianism as critical to his work—which displayed a union of objectivity and subjectivity. What we need to recognize when we are looking to liberation theology is a connection to feminist liberation theology.

PJ: Freire was not exactly a feminist, especially in his early works. . . . Please say more about recent developments in feminist liberation theology.

PM: As Elizabeth Johnson lucidly notes in her powerful book, *She Who Is: The Mystery of God in Feminist Theological Discourse* (2002), we can only attempt to know an unknowable God—a God beyond the human imagination—through our lived—and very human—experiences. If you examine Judaic and Christian history, you can't miss the influence of patriarchy in the way God has been described. God is hypermasculine, a type of king wielding a sword. God the Father, the Lord of the Universe, is described using masculine images and even when we use abstractions that are not gender specific, we often carry with us the idea of God as a male being, which of course denies women their gender identity. The possibilities of God having more relational characteristics more commonly associated with women are smothered by the image of the theistic monarch who demands obedience and seeks revenge. Johnson provides an important feminist rethinking of the image and attributes of our normative conception of God in Western societies and provides an important female symbology grounded in the way women interpret their own experiences.

The way we think about God mediates the way we think about and shape our everyday life—how we become more fully human. It's part of our ontological vocation. Johnson argues that we must move beyond self-containment, ensepulchuring ourselves in a patriarchal worldview that undervalues the importance of bonding, nurturing, and relationship-building, which in the end can only capsize our theological endeavors. Instead we need to emphasize a Trinitarian union of relationality and love. But there are so many important strands of liberation theology, and not all of them come from the pastoral tradition in the Latin American church. There is, for example, James Cone's *A Black Theology of Liberation* (2010), which examines theological issues from a "contextual theology" perspective, focusing on the history of African Americans and their struggle for freedom. Powerful work has been done by black and Latina theologians such as feminist theologian Maria Pilar Aquino, womanist theologian Stacey Floyd-Thomas, and *mujerista* theologian Ada Maria Isasi-Diaz. The field of liberation theology is growing steadily and in powerful new ways.

PJ: Such as?

PM: Don't let me forget jazz theology! Let me say a bit on this. I like the way K. Shackelford (2014) puts it, when he perceptively notes:

> Through jazz, we find the evocation of diverse emotions of the human spirit—depression, happiness, pain and love—sonically conjured through its dissonant chords and jagged rhythmic constructions. Indeed, the deepest and most hidden emotions are provoked and dealt with, sensitizing a greater awareness about ourselves which can elicit self-reflection and divine peace. In this way, a jazz piece can have a spiritually anodynic or healing power. (Shackelford 2014)

Jeremy Begbie, a preeminent jazz theologian, maintains that the miracle of jazz is that "it can take up dissonance into a dynamic of hope" (Schakelford 2014). He goes on to say:

> A great deal of jazz has a streak of pathos, a kind of dark color to it, however joyful or celebratory the piece as a whole may be. A part of that is the pervasiveness of the blues, the blues scale, which brings a tinge of lament and restlessness to the music. Moreover, the blues brings to us the awareness of the fragility and sometimes the injustice of life. Jazz at its best faces up to these things, and actually incorporates those darker tones into a "bigger picture." That's the real miracle of this music: the way it can take up dissonance into a dynamic of hope. I think that's what the best kinds of jazz are doing. (Shackelford 2014)

Begbie also makes the connection between jazz, God, order, and nonorder. So, Petar, when somebody asks me about how I approach God, I often ask them to go and listen to a recording of John Coltrane's *A Love Supreme* (1965). I've been listening to this amazing piece since 1965. Some folks find the aggressive dissonance difficult to listen to. His variations on a four-note motif are raw and rare genius! I particularly like the fourth movement that ends with the exhilarating words, "Elation. Elegance. Exaltation. All from God. Thank you God. Amen." I bought my LP at Sam the Record Man on Yonge Street in Toronto—what a place that was for music in the 60s!

PM: Let's go back to Freire, Peter. How do these developments fit with his work?

PM: Right, I was about to get caught up in more '60s nostalgia. Thanks for keeping me on task. Were Freire alive today, I am sure he would be inspired by these developments in liberation theology. And while I don't know if Paulo liked jazz (I do know he liked Villa-Lobos), I remember the time when Donaldo Macedo and Paulo brought me to a Portuguese restaurant in Boston that featured a band playing. As a joke, Donaldo asked the band to play the happy birthday theme for me, again, as a joke, since it wasn't my birthday. Donaldo had them do it about a half-dozen times. Luckily there weren't many patrons in the restaurant at the time. Paulo was in stitches. Whenever I walk into a restaurant with live music, I momentarily relive this moment.

Paulo's understanding of the future was one that refused to ignore the difficulties of living everyday life in the capitalist present. Paulo's utopianism did not pull a veil over the challenges offered by the present. His was a concrete utopianism grounded in the struggle of everyday life, in a manner similar to the way Ernst Bloch treated the topic—that we can get glimpses of the future by examining the contradictions of the present. Of course, there is also a danger of utopianism being appropriated by fascism, of which Bloch was acutely aware. Today, there are currents of this appropriation in Trump's mission to "Make America Great Again," which prefigures a mythical past of an ideal society where white men were in control of all aspects of their lives. Marx's work was important in the way that it brought together a critique of political economy in the world dominated by capitalism and visions that were popular among utopian socialist movements who based their understanding of everyday life on what was lacking—triggering ideas for addressing the injustice in such a lack in the material conditions that mediated everyday life—making utopia context-specific to the contradictions in which people were living, yet at the same time providing the conditions for a universal vision for what a just society could look like.

Revolutionary Critical Pedagogy in, against and beyond Transnational Capitalism

8

We Must Save Ourselves: Revolutionary Critical Pedagogy in, against and beyond Global Neoliberal Fascism

Transnational Capitalism, Authoritarianism and Fascism

PJ: These days we are witnessing a global surge of economic inequality. This gives rise to new social arrangements, new forms of public discourse, and new forms of politics. Being good Marxists, let us start discussing these issues from the standpoint of political economy. What happens to neoliberalism in year 2020?

PM: The vaunted promises of neoliberalism have been a tragic failure, as anyone who survived the economic crisis of 2007–8 can attest. We are surrounded by a garish display of concentrated (and consecrated) wealth among today's transnational capitalist class that would surely elicit a collective gag reflex among 99 percent of the population. I say "consecrated" because capitalists have surely given their sacred imprimatur to the accumulation of wealth in the service of a system of production and exchange that will ensure such accumulation continues, and, if possible, expands exponentially. Chris Hedges notes that

> Concentrating wealth in the hands of a global oligarchic elite—eight families now hold as much wealth as 50 percent of the world's population—while demolishing government controls and regulations always creates massive income inequality and monopoly power, fuels political extremism and destroys democracy. (Hedges 2018b)

Hedges goes on to point out that, as early as the 1970s, Keynesian economics was purged from economics departments in universities, institutions such as the International Monetary Fund and the World Bank, and the media. At that time capitalism was in trouble. Blessed by the Chicago boys like Milton Friedman and controlled by institutions such as the World Bank and the World Trade Organization, the prevailing ideas such as market liberalization, privatization, entrepreneurialism, and possessive individualism have become known as the neoliberal agenda. This was well-orchestrated class warfare, and slowly but surely the working class were singled out and demonized as welfare cheaters while organizations designed to protect workers—such as labor unions—were dismantled. This was predicted of course, by Marx. The capitalist class went transnational, and in the process became more unified.

PJ: What are the main consequences of this transnationalization?

PM: The "transnational capitalist class" is a term used by William Robinson, Jerry Harris, Leslie Sklair, and others. According to these scholars, the transnational capitalist class refers to the segment of the bourgeoisie that controls supranational instruments of the global economy such as transnational corporations. It is a multipronged organization with two main structural features—corporations and the state. It is essentially a global ruling class. The transnational capitalist class collaborates across national borders to achieve their objectives of increasing value production. The state often serves the corporations through organizations such as Business Roundtable and the Chamber of Commerce rather than being served by corporations. This is not to say that corporations don't benefit states, and it is certainly true that the states help to serve corporate interests through offering tax breaks and other incentives to make manufacturing more profitable, or for attracting corporate head offices to locate in their state. But what is new is the shift toward transnational capitalist arrangements.

Robinson points out that the very first transnational oil company to be assisted by the US State Department in the wake of the US invasion and occupation of Iraq "was the 'French' oil company Total, followed by Chinese oil companies who were able to enter the Iraqi oil market thanks to the US occupation" (2017a: 173). Robinson asks:

> If the US intervention was about US rivalry with other states and "their" national capitals, then why would the US proconsul in Iraq, Paul Brenner, have declared just weeks into the occupation that Iraq was "open to business" to investors from anywhere in the world under the protective canopy of the US occupation? (Robinson 2017a: 173)

What we are witnessing is the rise of truly transnational capital and a transnational capitalist class, which, Robinson notes, operates as part of a dialectical struggle with global labor. It's all about global accumulation and production rather than national accumulation and production.

PJ: Who runs the transnational capitalist class?

PM: Not the Illuminati or the Deep State, and I'm sorry if this will disappoint followers of David Icke, QAnon, and those readers who like to glom onto the latest conspiracy theories about rigged elections or fake news. Conspiracism is certainly a reflection of the times, and I'm not saying all conspiracy theories are wrong simply because they are conspiracy theories. But the transnational capitalist class, in my view, can be described as a new global ruling class that controls a global power bloc consisting of allied groups and strata that together form alliances and long-term strategies. This group doesn't meet in secret chambers where arcane rituals are practiced involving the skull of Geronimo. It is really an attempt to create a global hegemonic bloc, where the transnational capitalist class is able to manipulate the consent of all of those who attempt to join the bloc while at the same time keeping those outside of the bloc contained or excluded entirely. Included in the transnational capitalist class are the supranational agencies such as the International Monetary Fund, the World Bank, and the World Trade Organization, dominant political parties, media conglomerates, and technocratic elites and state managers in both North and South, as well as public intellectuals on the right and in the center or center-left who provide ideological legitimacy, moral ballast, and technical solutions.

I believe that it's worthwhile to examine how the modern national state has fused with national markets and rising capitalist groups to form the modern nation-states that today define the international system. Robinson notes: "State forms evolve in consonance with the evolution of world capitalism and the particular forms of the capitalist state are historical. To the extent that they posit the nation state system as an *ontological* feature of world capitalism, extant approaches reify the nation state" (2017a: 174). In other words, "the state does not have a form independent of the constellations of class and social forces that configure the state" (2017a: 174). Robinson provides us with an important historical perspective when he writes:

> If capital was born out of the violent creation of a world market through colonial conquest and primitive accumulation, capitalist classes did incubate and develop in the cocoon of the nation state. As national capitalist classes from the cores of world capitalism conquered domestic markets they utilized their national states to protect these markets from the competition of capitalist classes of other nation states and to expand outward in conquest of new markets, sources of labor and raw materials. The classical theories of imperialism put forth by Lenin, Luxembourg, and others were not "wrong" but grounded in a set of historical conditions that have since evolved. As the mercantile era gave way to industrial capitalism, national capitalist classes internationalized through the expansion of exports and market competition and also through the nineteenth century wave of capital exports identified by Hobson, Lenin, and others. The dramatic expansion of world trade in the late nineteenth and early twentieth century along with the fierce competition for markets and control among national capitalist classes is what some social scientists refer to as the "first wave" of globalization. The appearance of the multinational corporation (MNC), which paved the way in the ensuing decades for the rise of a globally integrated production and financial system. This does not mean that such a system is harmonious. Far from it; it is wracked by fierce contradictions and conflicts, within the emerging TCC, between the TCC and more nationally and regionally oriented capitalists and elites, and between the global ruling class and the global working class. Nonetheless, what characterizes this new period is the globalization of production itself through the rise of a globally integrated production and financial system. (Robinson 2017a: 174)

PJ: How does the transnational capitalist class exert its influence?

PM: The key to constructing fascist social relations and structures to support them is to have in your service an effective group of demagogues—what I call "channel masters" or media-savvy right-wing pundits who specialize in "othering"; that is, channeling the rage and frustration of the exploited and immiserated away from the elites and toward racialized and sexualized others who could be immigrants, people of color, members of transgender groups, etc. These demagogues disguise themselves as friends of the working class, yet they serve as predators whose own fortunes rely on moving wealth from labor to capital and accomplish their objectives by supporting the most obscene reductions of taxes for America's most succulently rich. Government revenue for keeping America's infrastructure from collapsing will, as usual, come from the working classes, redistributing wealth upward from the working classes to the elite few. What were once public goods and services become open to seizure by the lords of capital who use it to extract value for themselves, and they can use it to build more commodity markets that they can dominate. And all of this is done under the banner of patriotism and free market democracy. If this has an analogue in theology, it would be the prosperity gospel.

Chris Hedges offers a succinct summation: "Housing for the lower-income population was often seen as a social obligation. Now everything has to go through the market. You impose a market logic on areas that shouldn't be open to market" (2018b). When you take the brakes off the financial system, you end up with financialization where you end up with inflation, mergers, acquisitions, credit and stock manipulation, and other truly nefarious schemes. Chris Hedges puts it bluntly: "Neoliberalism, wielding tremendous financial power, is able to manufacture economic crises to depress the value of assets and then seize them" (2018b). Quoting David Harvey, Hedges notes:

> "One of the ways in which you can engineer a crisis is to cut off the flow of credit," he said. "This was done in Eastern, Southeast Asia in 1997 and 1998. Suddenly, liquidity dried up. Major institutions would not lend money. There had been a big flow of foreign capital into Indonesia. They turned off the tap. Foreign capital flowed out. They turned it off in part because once all the firms went bankrupt, they could be bought up and put back to work again. We saw the same thing during the housing crisis here [in the United States]. The foreclosures of the housing left lots of housing out there, which could be picked up very cheaply. Blackstone comes in, buys up all of the housing, and is now the biggest landlord in all of the United States. It has 200,000 properties or something like that. It's waiting for the market to turn. When the market turns, which it did do briefly, then you can sell off or rent out and make a killing out of it. Blackstone has made a killing off of the foreclosure crisis where everyone lost. It was a massive transfer of wealth." (Hedges 2018b)

PJ: The nefarious logic is clear—first manufacture a crisis, and then profit from misery of people affected by the crisis. Nothing new under the sun; as you said earlier, the Bible has condemned this logic as early as the Old Testament. However, this logic seems to be an inherent feature of the free market. How do you go about fighting against the manufacture of crises without ending up with a leftist version of *Manufacturing Consent* (Herman and Chomsky 1988)?

PM: Before I answer your question, I just wanted to say that this predatory logic is part of war and war economies. Blow civilizations back to the Stone Age and then employ your corporations to rebuild, and retain as much ownership as you can. Now to your question. We have all heard the difference between freedom to and freedom from. Freedom to pursue our own interests, and freedom from being persecuted from pursuing our own interests, for example. Hedges refers to Polanyi when he describes the freedom that operates within a capitalist system, this time referring to "good freedoms" and "bad freedoms":

> There are the bad freedoms to exploit those around us and extract huge profits without regard to the common good, including what is done to the ecosystem and democratic institutions. These bad freedoms see corporations monopolize technologies and scientific advances to make huge profits, even when, as with the pharmaceutical industry, a monopoly means lives of those who cannot pay exorbitant prices are put in jeopardy. The good freedoms—freedom of conscience, freedom of speech, freedom of meeting, freedom of association, freedom to choose one's job—are eventually snuffed out by the primacy of the bad freedoms. (Hedges 2018b)

In other words, everyone is free to sleep under a bridge or highway overpass, but you don't see many rich folks inclined to make that choice.

So, for Hedges, the tributaries of neofascism percolate out of the cesspools of neoliberalism, abolishing civil liberties under the cover of the national security state, activating the mimetic scapegoat mechanism by branding critics, including the media, as enemies of the state. He also describes it as "the militarized instrument used by the ruling elites to maintain control, divide and tear apart the society and further accelerate pillage and social inequality. The ruling ideology, no longer credible, is replaced with the jackboot" (Hedges 2018b). The takeaway from all of this is to recognize and appreciate the shifts in the forces and relations of production from industrial capitalism, to global capitalism to transnational capitalism. And to take these shifts into account when trying to formulate a transition to socialism.

PJ: Your jackboot metaphor invokes some dark overtones of authoritarianism and fascism . . .

PM: The term "authoritarianism" has become a hot topic for op-eds in journals and magazines since the ascendancy of Trump to the presidency of the United States. Of course, this was a topic that also interested members of the Frankfurt School. Readers of *The Authoritarian Personality*, authored by Theodor Adorno and University of California-Berkeley psychologists Else Frenkel-Brunswik, Daniel Levinson, and Nevitt Sanford (Adorno et al. 1950), cannot forget the famous Fascism Scale developed by the authors who were trying to quantify the dimensions of the prepolitical personality traits that led individuals and groups to support fascist policies and practices. The study was based on depth interviews conducted between 1944 and 1946 in California and Washington D.C. with college students, prisoners, veterans, and men and women from the working class as well as the middle class. Of course, the authors, along with many leftists of the day, believed that fascism was latent in all Western societies. The authors came up with the famous "F scale" or Fascism Scale that was correlated with other quantified indexes, interlocking the "AS Scale"; for anti-Semitism; the "PEC Scale" for Politico-Economic Conservatism (largely based on the subjects' class attitudes); and the "E Scale" for ethnocentrism, which had a number of subscales: the "N Scale" for attitudes toward "Negroes," an "M Scale" for minorities in general, and a "P Scale" for patriotism (by which they meant a kind of blind, exclusionary nationalism). (Vials 2017)

PJ: This is really interesting! Can you briefly summarize the "F scale"?

PM: Christopher Vials recently summarized the "F scale" as follows:

According to Adorno et al, if you strongly agreed with the following statements, you might not be a fascist right now, but you would be the kind of person who would probably fall for a fascist demagogue when one came calling:

- There is too much emphasis in college on intellectual and theoretical topics, not enough emphasis on practical matters and on the homely virtues of living.
- Homosexuality is a particularly rotten form of delinquency and ought to be severely punished.
- Human nature being what it is, there will always be war and conflict.
- There are some things too intimate or personal to talk about even with one's closest friends.
- There are some activities so flagrantly un-American that, when responsible officials won't take the proper steps, the wide-awake citizen should take the law into his own hands.
- No insult to our honor should ever go unpunished.
- Every person should have a deep faith in some supernatural force higher than himself to which he gives total allegiance and whose decisions he does not question.
- Too many people today are living in an unnatural, soft way; we should return to the fundamentals, to a more red-blooded, active way of life. (Vials 2017)

The main features of the authoritarian personality were, Vials notes,

conventionalism ("rigid adherence to middle class values"); authoritarian submission ("uncritical attitude toward idealized moral authorities of the ingroup"); authoritarian aggression (a desire to punish those who transgress conventional values); anti-intraception (a rejection of imaginative, reflective, or empathetic people); superstition and stereotypy ("the belief in mystical determinates of the individual's fate; the disposition to think in rigid categories"); power and toughness ("preoccupation with the dominance-submission, strong-weak, leader-follower dimension"); projectivity ("the disposition to believe that wild and dangerous things go on in the world"), and sex ("exaggerated concern with sexual 'goings-on'"). (Vials 2017)

PJ: I cannot help but ask you to apply the "F scale" to Donald Trump!

PM: That's not a problem. Vials has already done a good job with evaluating Trump. Vials notes that while Donald Trump adheres to an essentially fascist rhetoric, he doesn't necessarily need a fascist state to achieve his goals, since his rhetoric largely appeals to those with a similar personality structure. These individuals constitute his fan base. If he were to command a fascist regime, then the world would face unprecedented danger. That hasn't happened yet, at least at the time of this writing. Ideological repression in the United States during the McCarthy era was viewed

> in the context of a larger, postwar social transformation that bore uncanny similarities to the very regimes they fought against in World War II: the permanent militarization of society necessitated by the Cold War; a growing anti-intellectualism, cultural homogenization and conformity; a violent, racial reaction against the nascent civil rights movement; and perhaps most dramatically, the rehabilitation of Germany, Spain and Japan as "bulwarks against communism" coupled with a disturbing silence about their recent victims (notably the millions murdered in the Nazi holocaust). (Vials 2017)

So there are similarities and differences among the fascist regimes that wreaked global havoc during World War II, postwar fascist regimes in Europe, Asia and Latin America, and the McCarthy era in the United States. We need to examine these similarities and differences—economic, geopolitical, cultural, religious—and offer an explanatory account of their historical specificity prior to undertaking our own assessments of the extent to which the United States is prone to turning full-throated fascist. As in the case of the authors of *The Authoritarian Personality* (Adorno et al. 1950), I similarly hold that fascism presents the gravest danger facing the United States.

PJ: In which phase of human life does the authoritarian personality develop? And what do you make of its links with brain structure?

PM: Vials notes that Adorno and his coauthors viewed personality as a structure initially formed in childhood and impacted by the larger social environment throughout a person's life. This personality is mediated by larger social forces but not necessarily rigidly determined by them, since the personality can also shape those larger social forces. Let's not forget our dialectics here! The personality and those social forces could be said to be mutually constitutive. Ideology and social forces mediate each other, are mutually constitutive, and constitute over time a culturally, historically, and economically integrated worldview. In the history of fascism, personality and political traits have been linked to brain structure. There is something in this that reeks of eugenics, of Nazis measuring skulls with calipers. Are government authorities going to institute mandatory brain scans to weed out the liberals and lock them up? Will government jobs be assigned according to brain scans? Will we only reward military generals with five stars who possess the largest anterior cingulate gyrus? So how do we imagine Trump's brain? I'm sure someone is already writing that book.

PJ: My thoughts exactly! While I find your and Vials' (2017) overview of *The Authoritarian Personality* (Adorno et al. 1950) extremely useful, I am frightened by these attempts at biological explanations of political differences.

PM: I am as well! Adorno makes a fascinating description of who he refers to as the "pseudoconservative." Vials is worth quoting at length in this instance:

> Unlike conservatives who understand how capitalism functions and defend its class structures accordingly, the pseudoconservative suffers from a failed identification with established structures and would destroy the very institutions he sought to defend. The pseudoconservative type—which Adorno found to be a very common phenomenon on the American right—is characterized by a rebelliousness that is ultimately subservient to authority.
>
> The authors of *The Authoritarian Personality* argued that this quality arose from a veiled resentment toward the patriarch of the family. His or her total inability to critique the patriarch (that develops into an inability to critique any ingroup authorities) leads to a projection of rebellious, resentful impulses onto some outgroup.
>
> All repressed and unutterable animosities toward the overbearing father, for example, could be projected onto the Jews—or onto the people of another nation—who become an all-powerful, all-controlling force that must be stopped. (Vials 2017)

Pseudoconservatives want private sector employers to be in control of the country because they are perceived as the most powerful group. When the government tries to intervene to help the employees, the government is viewed as traitorous. That the left is now examining the roots of fascism is a good sign for the country but not a good sign for Trump's fan base.

The Frankfurt School theorists are criticized by the pseudointellectuals of the alt-right as being responsible for the crimes and evils of feminism, political correctness, LGBTQ rights, and multiculturalism. Yet clearly it is the present-day fascists who view the Frankfurt School theorists as such a threat to America the Great because these German Jewish intellectuals were among the first to peel away the layers of the authoritarian personality, which are the building blocks of present-day American fascism as acted out every day by Trump supporters following Trump's ideologically weaponized tweets. Critical pedagogy is one possible antidote to the creation of the authoritarian populism and fascism, and this has been the motivation for my work over the years for developing pedagogies that can influence young people before their personality structures become too encysted in complex psychological processes that favor the development of young fascists.

PJ: While I clearly see the links between right-wing nationalism, misogyny, and capitalism, I do want to point out that these relationships are far from straightforward. A typical case in the point is "the Californian ideology" (Barbrook and Cameron 1996) of Silicon Valley entrepreneurs and tech companies. In their "hippie version of neoliberal capitalism" (Jandrić 2017: 80), these people combine radical free market capitalism with cultural openness to issues such as LGBTQ rights, same-sex marriage, religion, etc. How do you go about dealing with this tension?

PM: I can answer you with reference to some recent reading. In a recent news posting on *RawStory*, Greta Christina (2019) does a very simple takedown of the archetypal Republican who says

> Well, I'm conservative, but I'm not one of those racist, homophobic, dripping-with-hate Tea Party bigots! I'm pro-choice! I'm pro-same-sex-marriage! I'm not a racist! I just want lower taxes, and smaller government, and less government regulation of business. I'm fiscally conservative, and socially liberal. (Christina 2019)

Her argument doesn't go far enough, but she makes strong enough points that you can put them to the test with conservative friends and acquaintances without too much embarrassment. She sums up her argument as follows:

> You can't separate fiscal issues from social issues. They're deeply intertwined. They affect each other. Economic issues often *are* social issues. And conservative fiscal policies do enormous social harm. That's true even for the mildest, most generous version of "fiscal conservatism"—low taxes, small government, reduced regulation, a free market. These policies perpetuate human rights abuses. They make life harder for people who already have hard lives. Even if the people supporting these policies don't intend this, the policies are racist, sexist, classist (obviously), ableist, homophobic, transphobic, and otherwise socially retrograde. In many ways, they do more harm than so-called "social policies" that are supposedly separate from economic ones. (Christina 2019)

She continues by offering a litany of reasons that make the assertion, "fiscally conservative, socially liberal" highly problematic—even ludicrous.

First, she argues that poverty is a cycle that can trap generations, making it difficult to escape, since education and job training are less available to those who have to hold down numerous jobs in order to survive. She rightly observes that the struggle to keep a job

> means you can't afford to unionize, or otherwise push back against your wages and working conditions. It means that a temporary crisis—sickness or injury, job loss, death in the family—can destroy your life: you have no cushion, nobody you know has a cushion, a month or two without income and you're totally screwed. If you do lose your job, or if you're disabled, the labyrinthine bureaucracy of unemployment and disability benefits is exhausting: if you do manage to navigate it, it can deplete your ability to do much of anything else to improve your life—and if you can't navigate it, that's very likely going to tank your life. (Christina 2019)

She argues that being poor means you cannot purchase in bulk, afford medical insurance, repair or replace your car. You can't afford a house, you are severely limited in what jobs are available to you, and you may have to frequently move to find work. People born into poverty are likely to stay poor and their children are likely to remain poor—so we can talk about intergenerational poverty. Poor children are less likely to be well nourished and to enjoy safe environments. And, of course, it needs to be recognized that poverty disproportionately affects Latino/s, African Americans, other people of color, people who are disabled, women, trans people, and many other groups who are marginalized in US society.

PJ: So "fiscally conservative, socially liberal" (Christina 2019) is another myth that serves to perpetuate social differences—rich people's ideology for maintaining and enhancing their own privilege.

PM: Fiscal policy advantages the rich, and here we can refer to minimum wages, resources for public education, tax policy, banking and lending laws, public transportation, medical insurance, unemployment benefits, childcare, neoliberal economic deregulation—all of these fall within the purview of fiscal policy. Poverty contributes to domestic violence, which disproportionately affects women of color and also exacerbates racism, homophobia, transphobia, and misogyny. Christina (2019) also mentions political disenfranchisement too often accompanying poverty—such as the current voter identification laws, gerrymandering, voter suppression, etc. Then there is racist policing, which could be reduced with a fiscal policy that helps to monitor police encounters with civilians. And then there are the drug laws and prison policies, which create a permanent black and brown underclass. The private prisons need to be filled to the brim to make profits. It doesn't take rocket science to ascertain which racial and ethnic groups are targeted the most by corporations that actually benefit from high crime rates. And of course, free trade is a policy that helps keep people in poverty by hiring labor in countries that can best exploit their workforce, where children can be forced out of necessity to work for less than a dollar a day. So much for claiming you are fiscally conservative. The above reveals that by adopting such a position you are opening a Pandora's Box filled with unimaginable horrors.

The Curious Case of Donald Trump

PJ: These days, probably the best example of problems with popular political choices is the election of Donald Trump. Who votes for Trump, and why?

PM: Bobby Azarian (2018) has attempted to understand the psychological and neural factors of the Trump phenomenon—the people who will support Trump for any and all circumstances. He writes that many business owners will view a practical financial gain through Trump's tax cuts as more important than Trump's sexual transgressions and other odious behavior. Working-class men and women support Trump's assertions that he will bring jobs back to the United States from China, Mexico, and other countries. Trump's uniquely staged showman/circus persona engages the brain more than most politicians, arousing the emotions and fascinating many who disagree with him. Azarian writes that the brain's attention system resonates well with Trump's histrionics. We forgive Trump for his many faults because he already had become a celebrity. He entertains us, even if we don't like him.

PJ: In my recent book, Paul Levinson applies Marshall McLuhan's distinction between hot and cool media to conclude that "the combination of Trump's hotness on the surface and coolness in terms of the empty essence of his message tends to get people more physically angry" (in Jandrić 2017: 279). What do you think of this analysis?

PM: You are making me nostalgic for McLuhan's coach house lectures in downtown Toronto. Nostalgia is a real trap, especially for someone my age who grew up bohemian in the '50s and '60s; that's a rabbit hole in which I can go down too easily and get lost. Okay, I think that Levinson is correct. Also, some people are thrilled by the chaos Trump has created and enjoy the fact that he is destructing the political system that many people feel has failed them. It's a particularly despicable type of *Schadenfreude*. Brain studies—I hope you don't think my comments on the brain reveal a fascist tendency on my part, Petar—have revealed that conservatives have a more exaggerated response to fear when compared to people who demonstrate more progressive political attributes. Conservatives are, Azarian notes, more sensitive to existential threats to their safety and security. They "have a stronger physiological reaction to startling noises and graphic images compared to liberals." Azarian cites the well-known Terror Management Theory that maintains that fear mongering as practiced by Trump has a powerful effect on human beings who have a "unique awareness of their own mortality" (Azarian 2018).

Humans constantly live with the realization of the inevitably of their own death. The existential terror and anxiety are managed by cultural worldviews such as religion, national, ethnic, political identities, etc. These worldviews give life meaning and serve as a buffer to this constant fear of mortality. Trump reminds people of their own mortality through his practices of fearmongering. Constantly emphasizing existential threats to mortality motivates people to affirm with others their cultural, religious and racial identities, and leads people—even those who are inclined to think progressively—to shift their opinions toward the right. It also encourages defensive, aggressive behavior as well as increased nationalism and voting behavior. In fact, Azarian warns that

> in a study with American students, scientists found that making mortality salient increased support for extreme military interventions by American forces that could kill thousands of civilians overseas. Interestingly, the effect was present only in conservatives, which can likely be attributed to their heightened fear response. (Azarian 2018)

The Dunning–Kruger effect helps to explain why Trump supporters take Trump's words at face value, affording Trump's statements unconditional truth value. The problem is that these people are not aware that they are misinformed by Trump since their cognitive bias "prevents them from realizing that they lack expertise" (Azarian 2018). Such people are likely to believe that other people need to be educated about the truth, not themselves. Also, many Trump's supporters have, Azarian notes, a misguided sense of entitlement—they feel that they are superior to many of those who have had less financial success than they have. This is what Azarian calls "relative deprivation." He further notes that they lack exposure to dissimilar others, that is, they stay within the confines of their own ethnic, religious, or political groups. He points to the relative racial and ethnic isolation of whites. Azarian reports that Trump's supporters can be predicted by their zip-code and notes that "researchers found that support for Trump increased with the voters' physical distance from the Mexican border" (Azarian 2018). Okay, I do have reservations about this type of research, but at the very least it can be a starting point for discussing the Trump effect, the cult of personality, and the extreme polarization between Trump supporters and those who revile the man.

PJ: I get your point about mortality and fear. Yet, we are speaking of twenty-first-century United States of America—arguably one of the world's most technologically advanced countries, which has not had wars on its territory for centuries. One large terrorist attack that happened eighteen years ago surely cannot justify such intensity of collective fear. . . . Looking from a European tradition of the social state, I could understand the fear of dying from curable illness, which people cannot afford to treat—but then, judging from Trump's attitude toward Obamacare, I don't think that is what his voters have in mind. What is it that Trump's supporters are exactly afraid of, Peter?

PM: Azarian notes that many Trump supporters hold extreme conspiracy theories and "many of them suffer from psychological illnesses that involve paranoia and delusions, such as schizophrenia, or are at least vulnerable to them, like those with schizotypy personalities." This, of course, is an easy generalization to make. He writes that researchers have discovered that "those who were more likely to believe in outlandish conspiracy theories, such as the idea that the U.S. government created the AIDS epidemic, consistently scored high on measures of 'odd beliefs and magical thinking'" (Azarian 2018). I agree that some of this can be confirmed by visiting alt-right websites and discussion boards. And, of course, the United States suffers from what Azarian calls "collective narcissism." Americans believe they belong to the greatest country in the world. White Americans are fearful that they will become, demographically, a minority population over the next few decades. To me, it is this racial animus toward people of color that is most responsible for the fear factor among Trump supporters. According to Azarian, research supports "a direct link between national collective narcissism and support for Donald Trump" (Azarian 2018). He further reports that "[w]here individual narcissism causes aggressiveness toward other individuals, collective narcissism involves negative attitudes and aggression toward 'outsider' groups (outgroups), who are perceived as threats" (Azarian 2018). Azarian is worth quoting further on this:

> Donald Trump exacerbates collective narcissism with his anti-immigrant, anti-elitist, and strongly nationalistic rhetoric. By referring to his supporters, an overwhelmingly white group, as being "true patriots" or "real Americans," he promotes a brand of populism that is the epitome of "identity politics," a term that is usually associated with the political left. Left-wing identity politics, as misguided as they may sometimes be, are generally aimed at achieving equality, while the right-wing brand is based on a belief that one nationality and race is superior or entitled to success and wealth for no other reason than identity. (Azarian 2018)

Finally, Azarian points to "social dominance orientation which is related to authoritarian personality syndrome. This refers to people who believe that they should have the right to exert power over those they perceive as having lesser status. Trump distinguishes between white groups and inferior 'others'" (Azarian 2018).

Azarian provides research that reveals that those who scored high on both social dominance orientation and authoritarianism were those who were most interested in voting for Trump. This observation reflects some of the arguments put forward by Adorno and the Frankfurt School theorists. The authoritarian personality syndrome helps explain much of the support for Trump. Azarian notes that "authoritarianism refers to the advocacy or enforcement of strict obedience to authority at the expense of personal freedom, and is commonly associated with a lack of concern for the opinions or needs of others" (Azarian 2018). This helps to explain why Trump supporters display such aggression toward outgroup members. They are resistant to new experiences, display aggression toward outgroup members, submissiveness to authority, resistance to new experiences, and have a very static and unyielding need to a strict, hierarchical society. The syndrome, worldwide, is more common among the right. And we need not go into racism and bigotry, as contemporary racism is a practice that is highly correlated with Trump's supporters. So we are getting interesting findings from neuroscientists such as Azarian and others about what creates political motivation and agency. I'm not altogether sure how this information will help us elect more progressive candidates to which socialism will have a greater appeal. But it could help us become more strategic in the way we build our revolutionary solidarity for social justice.

Again, I wouldn't put that much stock in neuroscience providing us with an adequate explanatory framework for US politics. We need to take into consideration the decline of symbolic efficiency in today's late capitalist society, and the shift from the use to the circulation value of communicative utterances—something that Jodi Dean talks about in her important work (see Dean, Medak, and Jandrić 2019). What are the belief structures that foreclose political efficacy when it comes to social movements? The exchange value of messages are taking over their use values, we are ontologizing the political in our obsession with identity politics while at the same time foreclosing revolutionary action, we are fetishizing technology and thus foreclosing its potential for social transformation by giving the green light to corporations to use technology to consolidate their political power. In our obsession with the deep state, we have given up the idea of taking state power for building socialism.

PJ: Let us focus a bit more on American "collective narcissism," and more generally to relationships between (American) nationalism and capitalism—which have the potential to develop into new forms of fascism.

PM: Following from Lowy's early work on the relationship between nationalism and capitalism (Lowy 1993), we can appreciate William Robinson's (2017a, b, 2018a, b) work on the transnational capitalist class and its relationship to current fascist trends worldwide. At this point in time, it is imperative that we see the relationship between fascism and transnational capital. Today's transnational capitalism is facing an unprecedented crisis of social polarization, political legitimacy (hegemony), sustainability, and overaccumulation. According to Robinson (2017a, b, 2018a, b), it is fundamentally important that we distinguish former fascist regimes that were the result of an infusion of national capital with reactionary political power with today's infusion of transnational capital with reactionary and repressive political power. Robinson distinguishes the difference when he writes:

> Trumpism's veiled and at times openly racist and neo-fascist discourse has legitimized and unleashed ultra-racist and fascist movements in US civil society. I have been writing about the danger of "21st century fascism" as a response to the escalating crisis of global capitalism. The response to this crisis was the rise a neo-fascist Right in both Western and Eastern Europe, the vengeful resurgence of a neo-fascist Right in Latin America, and the turn towards neo-fascism in Turkey, Israel, the Philippines, India, and elsewhere. One key difference between 20th-century fascism and 21st-century fascism is that the former involved the fusion of *national capital* with reactionary and repressive political power, whereas the latter involves the fusion of *transnational capital* with reactionary political power. It is crucial to stress that Trumpism does not represent a break with capitalist globalization, but rather a recomposition of political forces as the crisis deepens. If we want to understand political phenomena we must not confuse surface appearance (or discourse) with underlying essence (or structure). (Robinson 2017b)

An intensification of neoliberalism in the United States that assigns a major role to the state in subsidizing transnational capital accumulation in the face of stagnation and overaccumulation is, in Robinson's view, bound to open the floodgates of authoritarian populism that could well instantiate fascism within the very structures of the American state. Robinson writes:

> For example, Trump's heralded proposal to invest one trillion dollars in infrastructure, when we examine it closely, is in reality a proposal to privatize public infrastructure and to transfer wealth from labor to capital by way of corporate tax breaks and subsidies for the construction of privatized infrastructural works. We can expect under the Trump regime an effort to further privatize what remains of the public sector, including schools, veterans affairs, and possibly social security, along with deregulation and a further transfer of wealth from labor to capital through corporate tax cuts and austerity. (Robinson 2017b)

Trumpism is part of the normal progression of global capitalism, not some feckless aberration. And the same can be said, in my view, about the rise of fascism worldwide. Not only has the transnational capitalist class "turned to mind-boggling levels of financial speculation, to the raiding and sacking of public budgets," it has also resorted to what Robinson calls "militarized accumulation" or what Robinson (2017b) describes as "endless cycles of war, destruction, and reconstruction." It has also resorted to what Robinson (2017b) calls "accumulation by repression" by which Robinson refers to the "building of private prisons and immigrant detention centers, border walls, homeland security technologies, etc." And finally, the transnational capitalist class is partaking in "the construction of a global police state to defend the global war economy from rebellions from below" (Robinson 2017b).

We are not only facing a crossroads of political will, but we are facing the precipice of ecological catastrophe. Unless we overthrow the capitalist state, we will be facing a relentless, merciless worldwide transnational elite who will not abate their machinations that only intensify "the predation and rapaciousness of global capital" (Robinson 2017b) and who will unhesitatingly make alliances with the bourgeoisie and together they will literally wage war against the struggling popular majorities. Meanwhile the ecosystems of the planet will be in an unrepairable state. The surveillance state is already being constructed such that there will be little room to maneuver, to engage our strategies and tactics against this transnational terrorist regime.

PJ: This is scary! I find it much easier to think of Donald Trump as an anomaly within the system than as an inherent feature of the system.

PM: For those readers who are unfamiliar with the terms *Sturmabteilung* or *Braunhemden*,[1] I suggest you become familiar with their meaning and the history behind them. Because it is a similar future we are sure to face, and the paramilitary forces here in the United States are already preparing, but the militia movement here is not an immediate threat. If it were a threat, then we had better fare better than the *Rotfrontkämpferbund* (Red Front Fighters) did against Hitler's Brownshirts or we will be in for some major physical and existential misery. Now, of course, this is a worst-case scenario, and it is always problematic to compare the United States under Trump to Nazi Germany. We have to be careful not to downplay the horrors that Nazi Germany imposed upon Jews, and there has been criticism of those critics of the Trump regime calling the detention centers for immigrant refugees "concentration camps" even as we acknowledge how such refugees and their children are dehumanized and treated with contempt by border agents. While the children languish in cages, their parents are forced to drink their water from toilets.

While a comparison of conditions in the United States under Trump with Nazi Germany may be inappropriate, many of my friends and colleagues find it more plausible than at any other time in their memory that American citizens could, under certain conditions, come to embrace a fascist regime. They see the 40 percent support for Trump as proof of this. Just read the comments to some stories that have come out in a major Orange County media outlet about my political work (Pignataro 2019)— it's seems that a lot of people are actually thirsting for fascism. The infrastructure for a new American-style *Schutzstaffelhas* has already been established via the National Security System. Thanks to Trump's rallies and tweets, the working classes are ripe for consolidating their own form of white nationalist identity formation, and you can bet your shirt that the US armed services will heed the call "blood and soil!" It's all about fascist tendencies, rather than full-blown fascism, seeding the conditions for

---

[1] The *Sturmabteilung* or SA (literally translated from German as Storm Detachment) was a paramilitary organization associated with Hitler's Nazi Party. Based on the color of their shirts, the *Sturmabteilung* were sometimes also called the *Braunhemden* (literally translated from German as Brown Shirts).

white nationalism. This, of course, insulates US citizens from critical and democratic discussions in the public sphere surrounding decision-making about the ownership of the means of production and creating alternative models of value production. Resistance to this right-wing authoritarian populism must entail building a counterpublic sphere and a political party that can carry the socialist revolution forward into the future. The transnational capitalist class—especially since 2008—have been readying themselves for a fierce engagement and a pitched battle against antifascists and all forms of popular grassroots and popular organizations. But are *we* ready?

PJ: Reading your analysis, I just cannot avoid the question of immigration and Trump's infamous wall. Living quite close to the Mexican border, in Orange, California, how does this rhetoric reflect on your daily experience?

PM: I've been in Mexico numerous times each year since 1987, years before Instituto McLaren was established in 2006. One of the most criminal aspects of living in the United States today is how the country profits from the war on immigration and destruction that results from military intervention. Let's hear from Robinson again, who notes:

> The day after Donald Trump's November 2016 electoral victory, the stock price of Corrections Corporation of America (CCA, which later changed its name to CoreCivic), the largest for-profit immigrant detention and prison company in the US, soared 40 per cent, given Trump's promise to deport millions of immigrants. Earlier in 2016, CCA's CEO Damon Hiniger reported a 5 per cent increase in first quarter earners as a result of "stronger than anticipated demand from our federal partners, most notably Immigration and Customs Enforcement," as a result of the escalating detention of immigrant women and children fleeing violence in Central America. The stock price of another leading private prison and immigrant detention company, Geo Group, saw its stock prices triple in the first few months of the Trump regime (the company had contributed $250,000 to Trump's inauguration and was then awarded with a $110 million contract to build a new immigrant detention centre in California). (Robinson 2018a: 9)

What is important to consider here is that the war against undocumented immigrants in the United States does not simply involve US firms. You don't need to be an American citizen to participate in the war against undocumented immigrants and asylum seekers in the United States. Robinson reports that

> Hundreds of private firms from around the world put in bids to construct Trump's infamous US-Mexico border wall. Every phase in the war on immigrants has become a source of profit-making, from services inside immigrant detention centres such as healthcare, food, phone systems, to other ancillary activities of the deportation regime, such as government contracting of private charter flights to ferry deportees back home. In its economic dimension, this war opens vast new outlets for unloading surplus, whilst in its political and ideological dimensions it turns immigrants into scapegoats for the disaffection of downwardly mobile,

disproportionately white, sectors of the working class. At the same time, given that such companies as CCA and Geo Group are traded on the Wall Street stock exchange, investors from anywhere around the world may buy and sell their stock, and in this way develop a stake in immigrant repression quite removed from, if not entirely independent, of the more pointed political and ideological objectives of this repression. (Robinson 2018a: 9–10)

And what about the profits that are augmented by the "war on terrorism" through militarization and repression? Robinson has outlined the bones of this program:

Military contractors such as Raytheon and Lockheed Martin report spikes each time there is a new flare-up in the Middle East conflict. Within hours of the 6 April 2017 US tomahawk missile bombardment of Syria, the company that builds those missiles, Raytheon, reported an increase in its stock value by $1 billion. As in the war on immigrants, we see in the "war on terrorism" an increasing fusion of private accumulation with state militarisation. Global weapons sales by the top 100 weapons manufacturers and military service companies increased by 38 per cent between 2002 and 2016. These top 100 companies across the globe, excluding China, sold $375 billion in weapons in 2016, generating $60 billion in profits, and employing over three million workers.35 In addition, private military and security (that is, mercenary) firms had outlays of over $200 billion in 2014 and employed some 15 million people.36 Whilst blackwater-Constellis Groups and G4S are the most well known, the Pentagon contracted some 150 such firms from around the world for support and security operations in Iraq alone. (Robinson 2018a: 10)

I cross the US-Mexican border frequently, and have done so for decades, since Instituto McLaren has expanded from Mexicali, to Tijuana, to Ensenada, to Michoacán, to Oaxaca, to Chiapas, and elsewhere throughout Las Americas. I make my way to Cuba from Mexico. To see the United States from the vantage point of Mexicana/os is difficult for a privileged white man, but I have tried my best. Significant sectors of the working class in the United States remains hostile to immigrants, and there are many reasons for this. Yet, at the same time, the working class remains crucial for putting an end to the value form of labor. There are more wage earners on the planet today than at any time in history, but the problem is that the progressive elements of the working class remain dispersed, distracted, and disconnected, and in a pitched battle with the vile forces of racism, misogyny, and homophobia.

PJ: Arguably, a large part of this battle is fought online. While we already talked a lot about digital media, challenges such as usage of personal data (Peters and Jandrić 2018a) and post-truth (Jandrić 2018c) are increasingly coming back to the fore.

PM: We are closer to creating a science of total manipulation; to creating fascist dictators scientifically through mass media. Some of this sounds mundane. If I purchase a shirt online, I will become the object of relentless advertising each time I search for something on the Internet. Let's say I purchase a brand-name pair of sneakers—advertisements for those sneakers will pop up while I am searching for information that might help my neighbor who is suffering from Alzheimer's. Or I will get distracted from a research assignment by a notice on my computer screen that Trump has made some outrageous political decision. Many people love being distracted from the terrible monotony and grinding familiarity of everyday life, from the daily physical and emotional pain of being fragile humans in a brutal world. Distraction is a drug. It gives us respite from drudging sameness, and we can temporarily forget our mortality and the existential threats that confront us as we eke out our survival.

I have some chronic physical ailments that demand distraction to prevent me from being overwhelmed by debilitating depression and I will pretty much welcome any distraction to keep my mind away from that kind of pain. But I also try to work through the pain by thinking through the difficult truths of our historical times and finding ways to address our collective inertia. It all boils down to strategies and tactics and building solidarity. And there is the fact that we love being entertained, even by reckless fools like Trump, if they can capture our attention and keep our emotional arousal high such that we hunger for the next episode of Crazyville. Some people who believe themselves to be human, just like the rest of us, love to watch others suffer as the world loses stability, and smile at the thought of all those Hollywood movie stars who lost their homes in the California wildfires. These people secretly feel a sense of satisfaction when an immigrant child dies in US border custody— that's what they deserve for trying to enter the United States and draining our economy. We don't want freeloaders here! There is an ugliness to humanity that we cannot avoid facing. Our own personal histories, our family histories, the history of the world, is chock full of horror, unimaginable hatred horror. But also of examples of courage in the face of such horror.

PJ: However horrible, death porn has always been popular . . . I still remember tourist agencies offering 'war tours' to Sarajevo, Vukovar, and other battlefields at the peak of the 1990s Balkan wars. Reading your words, however, I'm more interested in this combination of entitlement and *Schadenfreude*. How does it come about? Why do these people believe that they are better than others?

PM: A misunderstanding of how capitalism works inclines people to believe that they should all be rich if they work hard and that minority groups must be cheating or be involved in some criminal activity if they are better off financially than white folks. Or else they are the recipient of those damn liberal civil rights initiatives that enable them to get jobs that rightfully belong to white people! A naive belief in meritocracy creates the illusion that people in our democracy are being rewarded according to their worth to the social order and that the system must be blown up when white people are suffering economically while other racial groups—like those rich Chinese immigrants—are paying cash for their houses! These are echoes of the mimetic rivalry that I hope to discuss with you later. And yes, government leaders pandering to their greatness as a nation is something Hitler used and Trump uses to attract his white followers, especially those who feel nonwhite groups are unfairly overtaking them in numbers and/or financially. If only we could limit their numbers and create laws to keep them in their place!

White folks down on their luck, as they used to say, are targets of all kinds of ideological forces digitally at work throughout the mediaverse that exhort them to cling to their whiteness as some kind of prized possession that not even Lebron James can have with all his millions of dollars. I may be poor but at least I'm white! How pathetic. If I had a dime for each time I was accused of being a traitor to the white race by white supremacists, I'd already have enough to purchase one of Trump's signature chocolate desserts served at Mar-a-Lago to foreign dignitaries. But I'd rather invest the money in purchasing the collected works of Malcolm X.

The Christian Republic of American States

PJ: Among all this rising fascism and xenophobia, what is your biggest fear right now?

PM: What I fear the most at this moment in our turbulent legacy of self-movement we call history is the judgmental fascism currently pulsating through the airwaves, the courts, the schools, and the evangelical churches throughout the United States, the consecration of a purblind authoritarian populism in the election of Trump, bringing the entire public into an embattled stance in an inexorably privatized sphere. It's clear that we are in a prelude to increasing strife and dissension as the providential plot of the evangelicals' arcs toward theocracy. Should I be speaking in tongues and rolling my eyes like Rudy Giuliani to make my point?

No that's not necessary. Just witness the current push to overturn *Roe vs. Wade*, the white nationalist militia-minded neo-Nazis fueled by hate, trapped in the violence of a scapegoat mechanism of all against all in a Hobbesian scenario filled with lucid dreams of crackling A-15s and hirsute men in MAGA hats pulling the trigger on high school students. It is a violence that, especially these days, is directed against immigrants (recurrent accusations by the persecuting mob that they are rapists, murderers, and terrorists are projections of those engaging in the anti-immigrant violence and are used to justify persecuting them) and against people of color by white people. It is a violence punctuated by social media algorithms that help white supremacists find common cause and the immemorial custom among politicians of lacking self-dispossession that has peaked beyond imagination. It is amplified by Trump's craven, escalating, inflammatory, and shame-faced attack on Rep. Ilhan Omar, knowingly putting her life in danger; by the increasing rivalry that results from internal mediation (the subject imitates the model's desires and ends up desiring the same thing, in Girard's sense) and metaphysical desire (the desire to be other people, promoting resentment against others) that comes with living in an economic tinder box, in a capitalist society where the wealthy control the means of production and the rest fight each other to survive.

PJ: What are some possible signs of relief amidst this unceasing state of flux?

PM: According to the long-running survey of Americans' religious identity known as the General Social Survey (NORC at the University of Chicago 2019), for the first time in the past forty-four years, we are seeing record numbers of Americans defining themselves as not being affiliated with any organized religion. In fact there are more Americans defining themselves in this way (researchers call them "religious nones") than the number of Catholics and evangelicals combined. These "religious nones" constitute "a diverse group made up of atheists, agnostics, the spiritual, and those who are no specific organized religion in particular" (Monahan and Ahmed 2019). This has made the Christian right frantic in their search to turn the United States into a theocratic state, and if this conjures images of *The Handmaid's Tale* by Margaret Atwood (1986), you would not be exaggerating this threat. We have all been wringing our hands over the fake science of creationists and the fake history of American exceptionalism, but a current plot by the evangelicals called Project Blitz is set to make the United States a theocracy, not very different in principle from existing Islamic republics, that are officially ruled by Islamic laws, despite the fact that Jean-Jacques Rousseau and John Locke argued in very different ways against the idea of a religious state.

PJ: I find it really hard to imagine the United States as a theocracy—how could that happen?

PM: I can imagine Vice President Mike Pence salivating at the initiatives of the religious right's Project Blitz. I am certain that this religious hypocrite who serves as one of the most anti-Christian Christian Vice Presidents in US history would love to hold an exalted position in the future Christian theocratic state currently known as the United States of America, but likely to be renamed The Christian Republic of American States or something of that ilk, after the nation's second civil war ends with the South prevailing. The oily, smarmy purveyors of white Christian evangelical dominionism are indeed powerful and are fueled by a grave misunderstanding of the teachings of Jesus. In fact, everything about their actions goes against the grain of Jesus's teachings, turning them into pallid abstractions, into sound bites to serve their political agenda. It is as if they are paying homage to Christianity in order to pervert Christ's teachings. They are preparing the obsequies for teachings born of love. The worst crimes that Christians can commit are those undertaken in the name of Jesus. Congressional resolutions celebrating America's "Christian heritage" only adds fuel to their fire. The evangelicals responsible for Project Blitz are very savvy politically and know how to use senate bills in a canny way in order to slowly, step-by-step, achieve their religious agenda such as the freedom to discriminate as a fundamental right, that is, the right to exercise bigotry under the law.

PJ: Please say more about Project Blitz. We haven't heard much about it at this side of the ocean . . .

PM: The custodians of Project Blitz have been successful so far in helping to pass state legislation to protect their anti-LGBTQ discrimination. They have made an alliance with the American Legislative Exchange Council, or ALEC, a right-wing business organization. The central goal of Project Blitz is to enhance and protect their beloved white supremacist Christian ethno-state. Project Blitz introduced over fifty bills in at least twenty-three states in 2019. Paul Rosenberg (2019a) cites research by Frederick Clarkson of Political Research Associates, who has discovered the stealthily crafted and egregiously sinister playbook of these Christian dominionists. There are three tiers to their strategy. According to Clarkson,

> The first tier of Project Blitz aims at importing the Christian nationalist worldview into public schools and other aspects of the public sphere, the second tier aims at making government increasingly a partner in "Christianizing" America, and the third tier contains three types of proposed laws that "protect" religious beliefs and practices specifically intended to benefit bigotry. (in Rosenberg 2019a)

Category three has three parts, which Clarkson describes

> as having two main underlying intentions . . . [f]irst to denigrate the LGBTQ community, and second to defend and advance the right to discriminate. This is one way that the agenda of theocratic dominionism is reframed as protecting the right of theocrats to discriminate against those deemed second-class, at best. (in Rosenberg 2019a)

In order to advance their theocratic agenda, Project Blitz uses misleading language that "inverts common sense" such as deploying the term "religious freedom laws," which, in effect, only protect bigots and which at their core lies a homophobic discriminatory vision that reinvents freedom of religion as racism (in this case, exercising religious freedom is tantamount to being antigay, antisocialist, antiabortion, anti-immigrant, anti-Muslim). In effect, the language allows theocrats to define themselves as the victims and to discriminate against the oppressed. The second strategy called "goalpost moving" offers us another example of how this is accomplished. Rosenberg describes this as follows:

> The entire Project Blitz concept is premised on moving the goalposts. It's built into the very structure of its three-tiered playbook, as well as the logic of the supporting arguments. A similar strategy was involved in promoting vouchers in Arizona, beginning with a voucher for students with disabilities, then following up with bill after bill offering vouchers to more and more students, eventually all of them, with no guarantee protecting the first group of recipients from getting lost in the process. "Every single, little expansion, if you look at who's behind it, it is the people that want to get that door kicked open for private religious education," the mother of two children on the autism spectrum said. "All we (families with disabled students) are was the way for them to crack open the door." (Rosenberg 2019a)

Rosenberg describes the third strategy as "pre-emption":

> Project Blitz doesn't use the term "pre-emption," but since state-level law routinely pre-empts local laws—which often protect LGBTQ rights, for example—it's implicitly integral to their strategy. Model bills tracked by USA Today often focused on such pre-emption: *These laws, in effect, allow state legislators to dictate to city*

councils and county governing boards what they can and cannot do within their jurisdiction—including preventing them from raising the minimum wage, banning plastic grocery bags, and destroying guns. (Rosenberg 2019a) (italics in original)

PJ: This sounds frightening, Peter. Can you perhaps say more about the ideology behind Project Blitz?

PM: The wingnut Christians who are behind Project Blitz adopt a falsified history of America as a "Christian nation," which serves to dismantle the wall between church and state erected by the country's founders. As such supporters of Project Blitz "position themselves as the 'true Christians' and 'true Americans' suffering from government oppression" (Rosenberg 2019a) who hold the following convictions that must be protected under the law:

The sincerely held religious beliefs or moral convictions protected by this act are the belief or conviction that:

(a)   Marriage is or should be recognized as the union of one man and one woman;
(b)   Sexual relations are properly reserved to such a marriage; and
(c)   Male (man) or female (woman) refer to an individual's immutable biological sex as objectively determined by anatomy and genetics at time of birth. (Rosenberg 2019a)

Do these off-the-peg evangelical positions really warrant being classified as sincerely held religious beliefs? Or are they egregious betrayals of human decency? What if the range of religious beliefs could be stretched to perdition and beyond, to become fit meat for religious fanatics fueled by avarice and contempt? There is a point at which white nationalist Christian evangelism becomes militant irreligiosity in which retrieving our shared humanity becomes supremely unrealistic.

What if, for instance, such positions could be unthinkably applied to the execution of women who have abortions? Wait, that's already being considered by the Republican-controlled Texas legislature! We are already dancing on the edge of an abyss on this one! The legislature recently held a meeting to consider a bill that would ban abortion at any stage of pregnancy, would criminalize women who have abortions and medical professionals who perform them, even in cases of rape, human trafficking, or incest, and would expose women who have abortions to the charge of homicide—a crime that in the notoriously conservative state of Texas carries the death penalty. After New York state passed legislation making it possible for women to obtain abortions after twenty-four weeks if they are facing health risks or serious fetal complications, Trump in his usual demented, self-preening fashion ramped up the rhetoric with false accusations and conjured delusions that the Democrats were permitting "a baby to be ripped from the mother's womb moments before birth." Interesting words from a man who creates publicly sanctioned violence under his sacerdotal oversight. There seems to be a perfect storm brewing for Project Blitz's fascist vision to be realized. While there are a sufficient number of prominent legislators and judges who exercise enough influence on public policy at all levels of government to push the country further toward a fascist theocracy, the recent poll indicating a rise in the "religious nones" is, in fact, an encouraging counterpoint. And I say this as a Catholic. A Catholic who is not perfectly aligned with Catholic doctrine.

PJ: As a rule of thumb, all Christians are against abortion—and yet, abortion bans impose strong restrictions on women's freedoms. How do you, as a practicing Catholic, see the question of abortion?

PM: Inasmuch as I would like to see a society in which abortions are unnecessary except in cases where the mother's life is threatened, I believe that it is a woman's choice as to whether or not she should have an abortion. Of course, I am not in favor of abortion; I mean, who would actually want to promote abortion as a lifestyle? The very idea of encouraging women to have abortions as some kind of birth control habit is repugnant. While I respect my antiabortion sisters and brethren, I believe that more harm is done to women by criminalizing abortion. I also am aware that reproductive health care in this country is becoming more of a luxury for women from the ruling class. I do not advocate for abortion, yet I believe that the question of abortion is an issue that must be understood as one between women and their own conscience, and here I lean closer to feminist bioethics and cannot in good conscience condemn women who make a choice to have an abortion. Most embryos never reach personhood since among women who know they are pregnant, the miscarriage rate runs between 10 percent and 20 percent. And nearly half of all fertilized zygotes do not become persons since they do not survive the first two weeks. Around 50 percent of all fertilized eggs are lost before a woman misses her period. Still, we do need to continue to struggle with the bioethics surrounding, for instance, using "spare" embryos from *in vitro* fertilization for research purposes, and other uses of embryos such as *in vitro* creation of embryos in scientific experiments; the cloning of embryos, and the creation of hybrid embryos. The issue of research involving tetragametic chimerism or even heteropaternal superfecundation could also pose questions for ethicists to debate.

Legally, should a fertilized egg have equal rights as a mother if the mother is in need of a life-saving medical procedure that might possibly harm the fetus? These are very difficult, compulsively soul-searching decisions that require moral perspicacity. Lobbying for abortion restriction under the Christian banner of "saving lives" is impeccably unrealistic and positively anti-Christian in my view. Abortion restriction is killing many women who have nowhere to turn except to back alley doctors. If Catholics don't want abortions, then they need to push for comprehensive sex education and contraceptives and all the resources necessary for a healthy pregnancy. And furthermore, resources necessary to help their children after they are born. Why do many Christians seem to care more about the children who are unborn than they do about those who are already born? As a brutal, cold-blooded, belligerent, and irresponsible capitalist society, we abort children once they are born by not providing affordable housing, health care, and healthy environments where their "species being" (Marx's term) can flourish and a vision of self-determination can be cultivated and the idea of transcendence can be rescued. Those who defend capitalism, the pharmaceutical companies that jack up their prices for medications so much that people die as result of not being able to afford them, must assume responsibility for the fate of human life on this planet—if people want to criminalize abortion, then let anyone who opposes Medicare for all be put into prison.

Valerie Tarico (2018) has framed abortion issues in theological terms to challenge those infected by bibliolatry: God aborts 60 percent of fetuses and prescribes an abortion potion (Numbers 5:22-27); an infant becomes a person after birth (Levitius 27:6); the Bible doesn't define when life becomes a "living soul." What about the misogyny in the Bible? That women should keep silent (1 Cor 14:34); that a raped daughter should be sold to the rapist (Deut. 22: 28-29); that a woman is the property that a woman is the property of a man (Exodus 20: 17) or that female infants are twice as unclean as male infants (Leviticus 12: 1-8). But throwing competing biblical verses at one another—weaponizing the scriptures to suit one's agenda—is not the answer either. We need to approach the question of abortion with understanding and compassion, and follow our conscience, guided by love and an ethics of care. Science and religion need not work against each other—our country has never needed Freirean dialogue on this issue more than in these fractious times. Paulo, where are you? Noam Chomsky unzips the political history at play here:

> One should bear in mind the utter cynicism of the Republican Party since Reagan. Take their actual planks. One unbreakable commitment of the Republican party is anti-abortion. What's called pro-life. Where'd that come from? You go back to the 1960s. The leading republican figures, Ronald Reagan, George HW Bush, all the rest of them were what we call pro-choice. What changed? Well, in the 1970s, Republican strategist, Paul Weyrich, had the brilliant idea that if the Republicans pretended, I stress pretended, to be anti-abortion, they could pick up the evangelical vote and the northern working class Catholic vote. So they turned on a dime. They all became passionately anti-abortion. (Chomsky in Mehdi 2019)

PJ: The ideology and the practical consequences of Project Blitz seem so awful, that I cannot imagine their straightforward implementation without at least some resistance. Where do you see seeds of that resistance?

PM: I agree with my colleagues that we urgently need a contemporary Martin Luther King, a Henry Wallace, and a Eugene Debs to move us forward, not backward, in today's pathetic rehabilitation of the likes of James Forrestal, J. Edgar Hoover, and Joe McCarthy, so that we can serve the world, not dominate it. But we also need Karl Marx, Rosa Luxemburg, Hannah Arendt, Franz Fanon, Raya Dunyevskaya, Che Guevara, Grace Lee Boggs, Malcolm X, Camilo Torres, Paulo Freire, Ernesto Miguel d'Escoto Brockmann, Samuel Ruiz García, and the spirit of the North American Maryknoll missionary order. While the accomplishments that they effect reach far beyond what might seem their obvious range, it is likely that none of these historical figures could gain the necessary political or spiritual traction today to make a dent in the current digitally manufactured *Zeitgeist* and socially unifying political violence of today's spiritually tethered world. This is true for all kinds of reasons that I shall not elaborate here. But we are the beneficiaries of their experiences. We can admire the rich conjugation of theory and practice (praxis) in their writings and lived experiences, and can learn much from what they accomplished and how they accomplished it; they have forged trails overgrown with wisdom and regret and sometimes watered with their blood that can give us purpose and direction. And that's by no means spare change as we make our own paths so that we will no longer be alone together as we face mighty perils ahead.

PJ: What is the role of liberation theology as we make these new paths by walking?

PM: Let's not forget the crucial role that liberation theology must play in an increasingly secularized society. But at the same time, let's not rail against secularization in the manner that Mike Pompeo has been doing recently! Those raising their heads above the parapet who argue that science has done more than religion to bring about understanding regarding race, sexuality, intelligence, morality and hence has propelled us further along the road to civil rights and gender equality than religion are most assuredly correct. The religious authoritarian is more tempted to keep us in the Dark Ages citing biblical authority to, let's say, justify keeping women in the kitchen and gays and lesbians in the closet. Once you winnow out the freight of supercilious bollocks that frequently descends from the pulpit in fire and brimstone, you often find a streak of madness that wants to drive us into one religious war after another, to rent asunder both analysis and reason in a Trumpian tweetfest that makes the Newspeak of Oceania seem like critical theory in comparison. So yes, secularization has helped the social health of societies to grow—we no longer immolate socially reprobated citizens in lavish spectacles, unless we live in Saudi Arabia were bodies are sometimes crucified after beheadings. So, yes, I would not want to live in a religious state, Islamic, Christian, or otherwise. What we are left with is a choice either to abandon the notion of God altogether or to conceive of God in different ways than do many of our so-called religious authorities.

In Christianity, there is a vast history of interpretations of scripture, the hermeneutics of which can be understood in the contexts of national, international, and geopolitical events, social relations of production and historical conjunctures of various sorts, as well as paradigm shifts in science, cultural evolution—and the consequent evolution of our understanding of God, which we can take into account via anthropological, theological, eschatological, cultural, and psychological registers. Those who were subjected to the laboratory of death known as Auschwitz, or to the Spanish Inquisition, or to the US-trained death squads that ravaged Latin America in the 1970s and 1980s, can attest to the barbarism and depravity of humanity. Neither God nor science has assured me that such horrors will not again manifest themselves under resurgent fascist regimes, or even under the banner of American democracy. What I believe transcends such horror, such publicly sanctioned violence under sacerdotal oversight, are the teachings of the new covenant, which has been a revelation for me—that to escape the acquisitive mimesis and sundry animosities and the Golgotha of the scapegoat mechanism, we need a model whose history has been unburdened of the sins of this world and into whom we can assimilate our lives.

The impact of the "Christ event" on human history is something that is important in my understanding of the meaning of being human, and of working to become more fully human. For many campesinos working in the base communities in Latin America whose families were slaughtered by state militias throughout the 1970s, the power of death was broken as a result of the Christ event, but not the fact of death. I am not saying that we should mix a bit of Christianity in our revolutionary gruel, as we would add walnuts or chia seeds to our breakfast granola, but that the very heart of Christianity collapses its own ontological foundations when it turns away from those who suffer, those who are the most vulnerable of our society. Christianity can be otherworldly in its talk of eternal salvation, but it can also be otherworldly in its lack of heart, and unfortunately we have more than enough empirical proof of the latter to render this historical judgment. Liberation theology is able to offer salvation to the scandal of the church of empire, a church that routinely pretends to rediscover its original role of helping the poor yet appears cursed by an inability to foresee the future of the history it has already lived through time after time. Do some find God only in the foxhole during an artillery barrage? Yes. But others find God on the picket line, in the dampness of the jail cell, and in the march across the Edmund Pettus Bridge.

We Must Save Ourselves

PJ: Our discussions about fascism and Donald Trump, and the aforementioned attempts in turning the United States into a theocracy, obviously have a lot in common. What can we do from the position in and against (Holloway 2016) this state of affairs?

PM: It is quite clear that we are facing not simply the prospect of a global police state, but the vile reality that a global police state has already come into being, even if we find it at times to be somewhat out of focus. I cannot remember a single time during my life when the organized working class was as weak as it is today, far weaker than many other radical models prophesized. But it also has the potential to be unprecedently strong. It is not that fascism has been significantly absent over the past decades in the United States since World War II, but the pace at which twenty-first-century fascism has come upon us is due to the fact that twenty-first-century capitalism has become a self-fueling engine whose capacity to travel the globe has intensified dramatically over the last few decades. Speed here is mixed with scale. Hence, for those of us who have chosen a life of self-reference in the midst of historical uncertainty and the birth of new systems of panoptical surveillance weaponized to crush the human will to resist and designed to help generate in the citizenry a studied inattention to the perils of the marketing strategies created to depoliticize us—we must stubbornly continue to reflect upon the need to foreground the forces and relations of production as the medium of our most vital concerns if we are to break free from our shackles of alienation, lest we unsuspectingly betray our ontological vocation of becoming more fully human. Our aptitude and inspiration for becoming social justice educators must not remain simply in the form of abstract avowals of emancipation that remain prone to being crushed under the steel-toed jackboots of neo-Nazi ideology especially during this world-altering time of ignorance. I cannot even detect in today's factories of fearmongering—that is, the right-wing media—even a faint adumbration of optimism that is requisite for us to continue to live as moral beings, according to values that elevate and ennoble us rather than ethically impair us.

PJ: Perhaps we don't have much ground for optimism, but that should not lead us to defeatism! Where do you see opportunities for resistance to today's global rise of fascism?

PM: Changes in the material and sociocultural dimensions of society need to be made, but these can be attained only at the price of changing the entire social system. And we need to build new political parties and organizations to make this possible. Education can no longer serve to release us from the cruel instruments of capitalism that hold us forever in bondage. The fulfillment of our needs and the potential afforded by our human nature requires certain tasks—the decommodification of society being only one of many. Where we once looked to an enlightened public sphere to create the conditions of possibility for subsistence strategies and deracinated ontologies for human flourishing, we now stare in horror at the neoliberal transnationalization of the state. We suddenly wake up to the narcissistic slithering of a bully boy populist jibber-jabbering with delight at the transubstantiation of democracy into a global police state. There is nothing mystical about it! There has occurred a transvaluation of values through a reverse engineering of nazification and ideological moves that are intended to fructify fascism. This has been achieved with an uncanny precision, one that makes the entire process so applicable for containing today's volatile realities and succession of ethical immobilities because such toxic proclivities are as prevalent and natural as fast food—only this menu contains the capillaries of political strychnine! One of the leading authorities on the transnational capitalist state, William Robinson, writes the following:

> Both classical and current discussion on fascism also stresses national military expansionism. It is more analytically and conceptually accurate to talk of a *global police state*. The global order as a unity is increasingly repressive and authoritarian and particular *forms* of exceptional national states or national polities, including 21st century fascism, develop on the basis of particular national and regional histories, social and class forces, political conditions and conjunctures. Yet the militarization of cities, politics, and culture in such countries as the United States and Israel, the spread of neo-fascist movements in North America and Europe, the rise of authoritarian regimes in Turkey, the Philippines, and Honduras, are inseparable from these countries' entanglement in webs of global wars and the militarized global accumulation, or global war economy. The powers that be in the international system must secure social control and defend the global order in each particular national territory lest the global order itself becomes threatened. (Robinson 2018b)

I remember with crystal clarity September 11, 2001. I knew instantly what the political implications of that day would spell out, but I didn't realize the global police state would emerge so rapidly from the well-timed lexicon of torture, revenge, racism, imperialism, and the pharisaical calculus of a vengeful Christianity.

PJ: September 11 had a profound impact on everyone. . . . I vividly remember watching the news on television and thinking: this is the end of America as we know it. Yet, I watched the attack in my parents' home in Zagreb, Croatia, while you experienced it from the belly of the beast. What happened in the aftermath of the attack? How did it reflect to (public perception of) your work?

PM: Shortly after watching the terrorist attack on the Twin Towers on television, I was scheduled to give a talk at the elite private university, Dartmouth. After my keynote address, there was some mild applause but mostly silence. Here I was criticizing US foreign policy during a time that any criticism of the United States was deemed traitorous. Just days after 9/11. It took many months for the collective trauma to begin to attenuate among the US population. Shortly after my speech at Dartmouth, I was invited to speak at Evergreen University and I was so pleased to be there along with people I have long admired, Amy Goodman and Naomi Klein. I was so pleased to be invited to speak at this impetuously aberrant campus I had heard so much about. I gave the same talk as the one I gave at Dartmouth, but this time it was met with enthusiastic shouts and deep-throated roars of approval.

Later, in 2003, an Evergreen student, Rachel Corrie (I recall someone telling me that she might have attended my 2001 talk), was run over by an Israeli bulldozer as she tried courageously to prevent it from demolishing a Palestinian home. She was a voice of resistance, a spark that should have started a counterrevolution, but didn't. A play based on her life was flatly rejected by many theater owners throughout the country. This revealed to me how encysted we are in organized ideological hypocrisy. And things have only gotten worse. As Robinson writes:

> The "war on terrorism," with its escalation of military spending and repression alongside social austerity, has collateral political and ideological functions. It legitimates the new transnational social control systems and the creation of the global police state in the name of security. It allows states to criminalize social movements, resistance struggles, and "undesirable" populations. (Robinson 2018b)

Robinson pulls no punches, and his remarks are always backed up by empirical evidence. The broad sweep of global terror in the guise of humanitarian missions to democratize "failed" states and antihumanist forms of religious subjectivity cannot but engender a collective shudder among those who strive for sensuous living labor—what Charles Reitz refers to as "the elemental form of the human material condition." We cannot lose our "sensuous appreciation of our emergent powers," which includes bioecologically developed communities of cooperation and solidarity—in short, a commonwealth. This means advocating for "the survival power of partnership and cooperation" and "the categorical ethical advantages" of qualities such as "empathy, reciprocity, hospitality, and respect for the good in common" (Reitz 2018: 94).

PJ: Can you relate this critique to education?

PM: Let me try. Whether our morality derives from religious tenets or, like Reitz (2018), from our evolutionary kinship, we find that morality can be stretched to serve a number of ends, some worthwhile and some ignominious. Schooling was set up during industrial capitalism to warehouse students and teach them to fit into society and not complain on the assembly lines or in the office cubicles—in short, it was designed to create the conforming citizen. Neoliberal education is designed to enforce entrepreneurialism in the service of the consumer citizen. Critical pedagogy was designed to create the critical citizen but not necessarily to change the objective material conditions that would, in effect, make critical education obsolete. Critical education is dependent upon creating more "free agents" who can join the winning corporate teams without changing the rules of the game.

Revolutionary critical pedagogy has caught on straightaway to the fact that the game itself is rigged and it doesn't matter who wins or loses, or what the rules are, the game will still go on. Revolutionary critical pedagogy wants not only to shut down the game but replace the game of capitalism with freely associated labor. Revolutionary critical pedagogy recognizes the eschatological abyss that separates the capitalist elect from the proletariat damned, reinforcing the human tendency to overlook the comradeship that can obtain within the human community. The tendency of regarding some people as social ciphers and others as our brothers and sisters is only exacerbated by capitalism. We must stand at the edge of capitalism's moral abyss and stare down into it and not let vertiginous thinking get the better of us. We are not, like Candide, schooled by Dr. Peter Pangloss, to think that all is for the best in the best of all possible worlds. Yet as Marxists we are too often admonished as naive by our academic associates when we assert our moral imperative to change the world.

PJ: Thank you, Peter—this is probably the best definition of revolutionary critical pedagogy I've read to date!

PM: The enduringly scabrous circuits of militarized accumulation of which Robinson (2019: 183) speaks "coercively open up opportunities for capital accumulation worldwide, either on the heels of military force or through states' contracting out to transnational corporate capital the production and execution of social control and warfare." There are no discernably specific political objectives when it comes to "the generation of conflicts and the repression of social movements and vulnerable populations around the world" since these are primarily independent accumulation strategies that, tragically, lead to permanent global warfare that are of various intensities such as "'humanitarian missions,' 'drug interdiction operations,' 'anti-crime sweeps,' undocumented immigrant roundups, and so on" (Robinson 2019: 183). According to Robinson,

> In many states, public school students are now thrown into jail for tardiness and absences. According to a complaint filed with the US Department of Justice in June 2013, students in Texas have been taken out of school in handcuffs, held in

jail for days at a time, and fined more than $1000 for missing more than ten days of school. According to the complaint, school grounds are run like a police state, with guards rounding up students during "tardy sweeps," suspending them, and then marking their absences as unexcused even when students have legitimate reasons for absence, such as family emergency or illness. The Pentagon has supplied schools throughout the United States with military-grade weapons and vehicles and even with grenade launchers. Schools have spied on students in their home by supplying laptop computers with webcams that are activated by remote control. The surveillance state has invaded the public school system, especially poor, working class and racially oppressed communities, with closed-circuit television cameras, security checkpoints, full armed guards, and military recruiters. (2019: 157–58)

The criminal justice system in the United States has made a sweetheart deal with the school system. Both simultaneously fail to open a path for oppressed communities to become ontological antagonists against a system that claims to support them while at the same time engages in cynical attempts to "'prepare' students for prison and 'social death' rather than for a life of labor" (Robinson 2019: 158). Robinson cites Atilio Boron's famous study of the role of the World Bank in the neoliberalization of education, citing evidence that reveals that by 2008, 60 percent of all universities in Latin America were private. This was accompanied by the "deleterious deterioration in the quality of education at the public universities, together with defunding, rising student fees, a decline in instructor earnings, and a shift to part-time and contract instructors" (2019: 199). And so, life persists in a flatlined landscape without utterances, as if schooling were just a pretext to transform life into a looped soundtrack from Kenneth Anger's film *Scorpio Rising* (1963). Live your soundtrack, because it's the only thing that will keep a life of shards and fragments coherent to make you believe you might actually be on a path toward some worthwhile goal. But whenever you imagine this just might be a path to something productive it's turned into garish sentimentality, a path to oblivion in all of its transcendent beauty.

PJ: And these amazing soundtracks also happen to be global! What about the US public image of a defender of global democracy?

PM: Some countries see the United States as the champion of freedom and democracy, but much of the rest of the world sees the country as the most dangerous threat to world peace. You won't learn that by listing to Fox News, populated by a horrid cabal of hate-mongers like Sean Hannity, Tucker Carlson, and Laura Ingraham. These are shallow minds overpopulated by self-regard, clusters of tiny neurological apertures through which hate is refracted to an angry public thirsting for scapegoats to crucify in order to assuage their rage. Okay, I've written with sympathy about white folks in Appalachia and America's Rust Belt who are struggling against austerity capitalism. My own ancestors, some of whom were Irish tinkers or gypsies who immigrated to what's called Canada's Appalachia, could certainly identify with the plight of struggling white folk in the United States. Most of the rage you see among the small towns scattered throughout the United States is white rage resulting from poverty, opioid addiction, and lack of health benefits, all manufactured and carried out by a broken political system that is terminally infested with decay and graft, and steered by corrupt officials energized by an unquenchable thirst for power.

Such rage among the poor is understandable. But such rage can also serve as a toxic fuel to bolster fascist ideology, racism, homophobia, and white supremacy. The Tea Party, the alt-right, and evangelical Christians who preach the prosperity gospel, or who are willing to support a pathetic serial liar like Donald Trump because they believe he is bringing the world closer to the Second Coming, are doing the kind of work that the SS did for Hitler's Germany. Many of the prosperity preachers are millionaires that pretend to speak for the people as good, law abiding followers of Christ yet channel the collective hate of the country against immigrants, birthright citizenship, people of color, the LGBTQ community, and use fake news to create fake news. That's quite a trick. They create a hyperpatriotism enforced by the surveillance state. They function as neo-Nazis in silk suits.

PJ: The Frankfurt School has taught us about all that, and much more, almost a century ago . . .

PM: Indeed. Many parallels could be drawn from the heyday of the Frankfurt School, not the least its complex and nuanced relationships to fascism. The ideological mentors of Donald Trump view leftists as "cultural Marxists"—as the offspring of the Frankfurt School set up by Marxist intellectuals in Germany. Many of these intellectuals were Jewish and fled to the United States after the Nazi takeover of Germany. Today's alt-right Nazis and white nationalists blame the emergence of feminism, political correctness, the gay rights movement, multiculturalism, and incarnations of civil rights and social justice on "cultural Marxism." But they fail to recognize that the Frankfurt School theorists were critical of orthodox Marxism, shifted their focus away from classical Marxism's preoccupation with political economy, contributed landmark studies on the technocratic rationality of the culture industries of the United States, authoritarianism, anti-Semitism, and melded Marxist theory with psychology and social theory. It's the same old fascism versus communism divide with some new features and twists. The alt-right is fighting political correctness, which they see as tantamount to a socialist takeover of US culture.

It's easy to see how the current pro-Trump movement with its neo-Nazi hate groups in tow could feel threatened by critical theory that exposes their ties to fascism, authoritarian populism, and racism. Critical theory exposes the shallow consumer and advertising culture and narrow, sclerotic ideologies remastered and revivified through technological networks that are inextricably indentured to corporate capitalism. Everything that enables fascism and reproduces inequality and injustice is exposed. It is the kind of theory that lays bare the underpinnings of capitalist injustices and reveals that Emperor Trump has no clothes. They unveil the hate groups that have formed a protective shield for Trump's base, groups like the ill-begotten Proud Boys. The vilest and most pathetic rhetoric in US history is coming from Trump's pandering to his base. Trump's supporters have no problem with bloviating about chain migration while at the same time putting the children of asylum seekers in cages, all the while likening Trump to a harbinger of God. Fear is what they use in their insane arguments that decent, hard-working white people are being replaced by hordes of criminals from south of the border. That white people are now the new oppressed. Tell that to the indigenous populations of the United States! The sentiment would be funny if it weren't so tragic. Exalted Knights of the Ku Klux Klan, Auburn White Student Union, Borderkeepers of Alabama, the Daily Stormer, Soldiers of Odin, Faithful Word Baptist Church, Nationalist Women's Front, Vinlander's Social Club, Western Hammerskins, Tony Alamo Christian Ministries, David Horowitz Freedom Center, Soldiers of Odin, White Aryan Resistance—these are organizations whose ideologies, beliefs, and practices putrefy the seeds of freedom and liberty in a vile swampland of violence and hate.

PJ: Can we go back to opportunities for resistance, opportunities for hope? Our situation is dire, and these attempts are urgent!

PM: Even in the face of the nightmare of capitalist overaccumulation, of machines and technology replacing living labor with labor-saving devices, of the removal of barriers to the drive to augment value, of the specter of a chronic expansion of debt-driven consumption reaching the breaking point, of the widening gap between the productive economy and "fictitious capital," of communal disintegration and social upheaval— even in the face of all of these obstacles, the potential for rebellion among the global working class and surplus humanity is always already prohibitive in these times. One reason for this is that the logic of capital today works through a highly dispersed working class ill-equipped to challenge systems of warfare, social control, and repression that the transnational capitalist class uses a means of making profit and continuing to accumulate capital in the face of economic stagnation—what Bill Robinson refers to as "militarised accumulation, or accumulation by repression" (Robinson 2019: 183). In the foreseeable future it would be foolish to expect the international proletariat to achieve a success comparable to, say, Operation Bagration. Even with the help of superior numbers and using the maskirovka—"we're just a reincarnation of the peace-and-love hippies"—as a form of ideological subterfuge, the idea of mounting a Vitebsk-Orsha Offensive against the ranks and rants of the international ruling class would be tantamount to a rapturous underestimation of the power of capitalist ideology at this particular historical conjuncture. The weapons we currently have available would permit us to mount nothing more than, perhaps, a charm offensive. A viable alternative to capitalism needs to reach hegemonic ascendancy and we are a long way from that. But we are also much closer than we think if we factor in the risks we must be willing to take in achieving our goal.

Can socialism redound to the liberation of all? The worst of the unctuous, mealy mouthed, lickspittle, all-out twenty-first-century fascists, who rabidly disdain democracy, are not only nativist white supremacists with their high contrast undershaved hair topped by a greased back long quaff, who sport slick three-piece business suits or feral troglodytes celebrating national holidays on their Harleys, or a salubrious version of the Manson Family hiding in the San Fernando canyons with the Yeti. They are not only the stereotype of an ever-calculating cabal of white-haired bankers sitting on billions of uninvested cash; nor are they silver spoon investors or inside traders, oleaginous devotees of the cult of the "founding fathers" of our plutocracy with their barbaric demands for the powerless to acquiesce to the custodians of capital. Rather, some of them are actually tech-savvy millennials variously positioned within the contradictory continuum of alienation brought about by the commodification and domination that has swathed most of the planet in a prickly blanket of encrusted misery—what we know as an increasingly weaponized neoliberal capitalism. These particular millennials are growing up in a post-truth/pre-fascist landscape and are unable to escape the posttruth world. They are confronted with an ever-burgeoning tech sector described by Bill Robinson as "computer and electronic product manufacturing, telecommunications, data processing, hosting, and other information services, platforms, and computer systems design and related services" that is "now at the cutting edge of capitalist globalization and is driving the digitalisation of the entire global economy" (Robinson 2017a). Yet it is with this very same group of millennials that there is hope. Again, alienation runs along a contradictory continuum.

PJ: As we already discussed, contemporary capitalism is less and less dependent on workers. The promise of social progress through technology has definitely shown its ugly side. . . . Where should we seek solutions to this problem? Who should take the lead in these processes?

PM: You might be thinking of what strategies the transnational corporations might be considering given the heightened social tensions created by austerity capitalism. If you were thinking of the military-industrial complex and the surveillance state, you are correct. Robinson asks how the global economy is "based more and more on the development and deployment of these systems of warfare, social control, and repression simply as a means of making profit and continuing to accumulate capital in the face of stagnation"—what Robinson (2019: 183) refers to as "militarized accumulation, or accumulation by repression" leading to twenty-first-century fascism. He warns that "[a]s digitalisation concentrates capital, heightens polarisation, and swells the ranks of surplus labour, dominant groups turn to applying the new technologies to mass social control and repression in the face of real and potential resistance" (Robinson 2017a). In twenty-five years, the United States will lose 40 percent of all existing jobs (Peters, Jandrić, and Means 2019). Hasn't the life arc of global capitalism been incandescently forgetful of its lifeblood, the workers—from sausage makers to scientists—forgetful of all of those dependent upon a wage to survive? How much longer can workers survive as precarious, contract, and part-time labor shorn of benefits? Look what has happened in Latin America with indigenous populations moving from the countryside to the cities in search of work, once they were dispossessed of their land? Look at what is happening to peasants in China right now, leaving life in the countryside to share a tiny one-room apartment in Beijing? I meet them all the time in Changchun, Chengdu, Beijing. All of them—and us—face the specter of the surveillance state and the militarization of society. There is no singularity that is going to jump out of the chaos to save us (sorry Ray Kurzweil, you are full of deep fakery). We must save ourselves.

9

We Want What Others Want: Ayn Rand, René Girard and Acquisitive Mimesis

Ayn Rand: The Saint of Human Greed

PJ: I visited you at Chapman in 2015 for the opening of the Paulo Freire Archives. After the event, we took a collective photo next to Freire's bust, which is a few minutes walk from the Donna Ford Attallah College of Education Studies. Then you took me to the opposite side of the campus, which has busts of other people that the university considers important: Ayn Rand, Margaret Thatcher, and Donald Reagan. We finished the day with a cup of coffee and a discussion about this schizophrenic ideological mess behind honoring radically different people and worldviews. While our conversations have obviously focused to people from our own intellectual tradition such as Karl Marx and Paulo Freire, I would like to briefly turn our attention to the other side of the campus: to understand what we are fighting against, we need to look into works and legacy of these people. Let's start from arguably one of the greatest influences of the American right—the infamous Ayn Rand.

PM: The bust of the repugnant Ayn Rand that haunts a walkway on Chapman University's lush campus is a bitter reminder that universities have capitulated to the dark phlegm of her worldview as the philosopher of greed, hence they both serve and justify the privilege of the wealthy against the dignity of the wretched of the earth. In a cruel irony, her literary form, common to subway station newsstands, speaks to the very people most vulnerable to one day becoming the object of her derision—what she considers to be the undeserving poor and slothful middle-class underlings. How fitting that her bust stands transfixed on the students from financially stable families that pass her by on the way to their classes! It is as if her whispers follow the freshmen from classroom to dormitory, from her corpus of demonology to the malleable subjectivity of a young mind—on your road to financial success don't forget to brow-beat and kick the lazy moochers in the teeth who are blocking your path, for they serve not only as your enemy, but as the enemy of America!

The works of Rand, such as *The Virtue of Selfishness* (1964), cannot take refuge behind the prestige of the Bible since she was an atheist, but her ulterior motives, entombed in the misery of others, are offered protective shelter by the denoted barons of the academy who unwittingly serve as persecutors of humanity. I can think of another persecutor of humanity, Roland Freisler, president of the People's Court in

Nazi Germany, and featured performer in the hideous and farcical blood tribunals, who gleefully sent children and the aged to their death. While I do not consider Rand in the same category as Freisler, she remains on my list of loathsome personalities.

PJ: For readers less familiar with German history, can you just briefly introduce Roland Freisler and his legacy?

PM: Roland Freisler, Hitler's evil clown blood judge, who tied the tongues of Germany's accused with his piercing, pincer voice, stands out as one of history's most ardent defenders of fascism. The victims of Freisler's court almost always were put to death. Berthold von Stauffenberg, brother of Claus, who was part of a conspiracy to kill Adolf Hitler, was ordered by Freisler to be hung on a meat hook by piano wire and just before death to be resuscitated and then hung again, and this procedure was repeated three or four times and filmed for Hitler's personal viewing. Among Freisler's most famous victims were students from the University of Munich who were members of the White Rose group, who participated in nonviolent resistance against the Nazi regime. Freisler expelled the students from their own embodied selves, through execution, and made them incarnate. Yet their words and example of their lives are brought to life to challenge the demonic order of all fascist social systems. The members of White Rose had recognized the murderous fascism of the Third Reich as demonic and their Nazi overlords feared a mimetic escalation, and so members of White Rose were made scapegoats. As Girard notes:

> Under the effect of mimetic escalation, the internal division of every "satanic" community is exacerbated; the difference between legitimate and illegitimate violence diminishes, expulsions become reciprocal; sons repeat and reinforce the violence of their fathers with even more deplorable results for everybody; finally they understand the evil of the paternal example and curse their own fathers. (Girard 1986: 188)

PJ: Thank you so much. And what about Freisler's legacy today?

PM: Recently I attended the wedding of my friend Carl Boggs, and during the ceremonies, presided over by Ford Roosevelt, the grandson of Franklin Delano Roosevelt, the attendees were all gifted with a white rose in memory of the White Rose group of teenage German resistors to the Nazi regime and sentenced to the guillotine by judge Freisler. I often think of the core members of the White Rose, Sophie Scholl, her brother Hans Scholl, and Christoph Probst, all in their early twenties. On February 22, 1943, Freisler excoriated them mercilessly for several hours before convicting them of treason and sentencing them to death. Hours later they bravely faced the guillotine. Before his head fell, Hans cried out, "Long live freedom!" If students want inspiration, let them forego a visit to the busts of Ronald Reagan and Margaret Thatcher that adorn the walkways of Chapman University, and wander about on the road less traveled on the other side of the campus where the bust of Paulo Freire proudly sits. Or visit the busts of Martin Luther King, Jr., who once gave a speech at Chapman, or Benito Juárez, the sole indigenous President of Mexico, a land of indigenous peoples.

PJ: Freisler's terrible deeds were not just about punishment; more importantly, his victims were also stripped of any human dignity. That is not too far from Ayn Rand's attitude toward the poor …

PM: The work of Rand opposes Ernst Bloch's concept of *eudaimonia*, which he developed in his masterful *Natural Law and Human Dignity* (Bloch 1961 [1986]) and that revolves around the concept of human dignity. Rand represents the apotheosis of bourgeois natural law, its stammering quintessence, and equally the natural standard for the putrefying human degradation to which Bloch, one of our most lucid critics of bourgeois social life, opposes. Robert Spencer (2017) offers a distillation of Bloch's *eudaimonia* as "the possibility of self-flourishing," which is the quintessence of his rehabilitation of natural law. Spencer is worth quoting:

> Bloch accepts that an essential part of human happiness is the possibility of self-flourishing or eudaimonia, which a positive rather than a negative right but which cannot by definition cannot be chosen by one for others. The aim is not human happiness as such, which is how eudaimonia is sometimes translated into English. Human flourishing describes a life made meaningful through, for example, devotion to others, intellectual, imaginative or creative achievement, or the full exercise of one's potentialities and abilities. Accordingly, natural law for Bloch is oriented above all towards the abolition of human degradation. Without such standards or what is right and just, exploitation cannot be reproved and a qualitatively different future society cannot even be foreseen, let alone brought into being. (Spencer 2017: 130)

Spencer's capsulated description of *eudaimonia* points toward Bloch's implicit goal of a classless society. This is not something that can, however, be imposed. As Spencer points out:

> But human nature is not static for Bloch; it is not some standard to which individuals must aspire or be forced to conform. Rather, since human beings are diverse, mutable, self-created creatures, the goal of any authentically radical politics is to bring about (by definition, voluntary rather than forcibly) a world in which individuals dispose of the natural right to determine their own lives and in doing so unfold the various possibilities of their being. (Spencer 2017: 131)

PJ: Rand's work was not only about despising individual human beings for their "shortcomings"; she developed a whole value system where the marketplace is the king.

PM: The value of her work for humanists remains nugatory, except, perhaps, as a model for the capitalist id—and one that rivals our very own President Trump, which is no easy feat. While Rand hectored any and all who might put in a good word for socialism, and while she decried the welfare state with the most vehement rhetoric she could muster, she nevertheless received Social Security payments and Medicare benefits under her husband's name (Holland 2018). Damn any and all who might wish to intervene in the marketplace! Do not sully that pristine landscape with your filthy regulation! I imagine her ghost carrying miles of chains, a Dickensian image, as she lumbers down Wall Street arm-in-arm with Augusto Pinochet, Ronald Reagan, and Margaret Thatcher, bless them all! Rand absolutely hated to pay taxes and the idea that the government might redistribute some of the wealth from capital to labor made her fit to be tied. Anyone who could not achieve the means to survive after retirement was deemed a parasite. Her writings were filled with concordant details that fit the profile of the paradigmatic free market capitalist, Gordon Gekko. It doesn't take a consummate expert in *Verdinglichung* theory[1] to surrender Rand's work to the ash heap of history.

PJ: Rand's thinking might belong to the ash heap of history, but her views are reflected in many contemporary policies and seem to be on the rise again!

PM: Indeed—Rand's work remains the cornerstone of today's right-wing libertarians such as those infernal dunderheads that make up the American Tea Party. Joshua Holland (2018) writes:

> The degree to which Ayn Rand has become a touchstone for the modern conservative movement is striking. She was a sexual libertine, and, according to writer Mark Ames, she modeled her heroic characters on one of the most despicable sociopaths of her time. Ames' conclusion is important for understanding today's political economy. "Whenever you hear politicians or Tea Partiers dividing up the world between 'producers' and 'collectivism'" he wrote, "just know that those ideas and words more likely than not are derived from the deranged mind of a serial-killer groupie. . . . And when you see them taking their razor blades to the last remaining programs protecting the middle class from total abject destitution—Social Security, Medicare and Medicaid—and bragging about how they are slashing these programs for 'moral' reasons, just remember Rand's morality and who inspired her." Now we know that Rand was also just as hypocritical as the Tea Party freshman who railed against "government health care" to get elected and then whined that he had to wait a month before getting his own Cadillac plan courtesy of the taxpayers. (Holland 2018)

Holland's perspective certainly echoes my own. Political economists from mainstream political science programs throughout the United States seem to regard capitalism as an objective reality that cannot be shifted off its concrete pedestal—especially not shifted toward the left—since any discernible shift would amount to a seismic rift within democracy itself. This fails to take into account Marcuse's somber insight:

> Economic relations only seem to be objective because of the character of commodity production. As soon as one delves beneath this mode of production, and analyses its origin, one can see that its natural objectivity is mere semblance while in reality it is a specific historical form of existence that man has given

---

[1]   *Verdinglichung* theory, or theory of reification, is a theory of ideologies which attribute social relations to people's attributes. A typical case in the point is the statement: the poor are lazy.

himself. Moreover, once this content comes to the fore, economic theory would turn into <u>critical theory</u>. (Marcuse 1960: 281, emphasis original)

PJ: As you already mentioned, Rand's writing was not particularly consistent with her own practice . . .

PM: Rand's actions in accepting Social Security and Medicare were certainly hypocritical, but her hypocrisy is mirrored in by many mainstream Republicans. Does the following description by Holland sound familiar? Similar, perhaps, to your next-door neighbor?

> A central rule of the US political economy is that people are attracted to the idea of "limited government" in the abstract—and certainly don't want the government intruding in their homes—but they really, *really* like living in a society with adequately funded public services.
>
> That's just as true for an icon of modern conservatism as it is for a poor mother getting public health care for her kids. (Holland 2018)

Mark Ames notes that most countries have not embraced Rand's philosophy and provides a possible reason why.

> One reason most countries don't find the time to embrace Ayn Rand's thinking is that she is a textbook sociopath. In her notebooks Ayn Rand worshiped a notorious serial murderer-dismemberer, and used this killer as an early model for the type of "ideal man" she promoted in her more famous books. These ideas were later picked up on and put into play by major right-wing figures of the past half decade, including the key architects of America's most recent economic catastrophe—former Fed Chair Alan Greenspan and SEC Commissioner Chris Cox—along with other notable right-wing Republicans such as Supreme Court Justice Clarence Thomas, Rush Limbaugh and South Carolina Gov. Mark Sanford. (Ames 2010)

Ames here cites not simply the "right-wing attack-dog pundits and the Teabagger mobs fighting to kill health care reform and eviscerate 'entitlement programs'" (2010) but also a number of recognizable political figures who worship at the altar of Ayn Rand, strewn with skulls and crossbones and assorted Satanic paraphernalia. In fact one poll found Rand's novel, *Atlas Shrugged* (1992) [1957] to be the second most influential book of the twentieth century. The Bible was found to be the most influential.

From Praise for a Serial Killer to Socialism for the Rich

PJ: In *Atlas Shrugged* (1992) [1957], Rand fiercely cherishes a serial killer.

PM: The superhero of her novel, John Galt, was based on a real-life American serial killer, William Edward Hickman, who butchered and dismembered a twelve-year-old girl named Marion Parker in 1927. Rand's early notebooks contain "worshipful praise" of Hickman (Ames 2010). Rand intensely admired Hickman's sociopathic qualities. As she wrote in her notes: "Other people do not exist for him, and he does not see why they should" (Ames 2010). She also described Hickman as having "no regard whatsoever for all that society holds sacred, and with a consciousness all his own. He has the true, innate psychology of a Superman. He can never realize and feel 'other people'" (Ames 2010). If Rand considers serial killer William Hickman as a "genuinely beautiful soul" (Ames 2010) and inspiration, then we must pause and consider how far we have strayed from Bloch's natural law grounded in dignity. Was it Hickman's example that made Rand loathe altruism and worship greed and selfishness? Or was Hickman the culmination of her philosophy that she laughably called Objectivism?

PJ: We are definitely very far from any positive reference to human dignity, Peter. However, there is much to be learned from negative examples, and I do want to explore Rand's glorification of a serial killer in more depth. It is a truly fascinating case!

PM: The nineteen-year-old Hickman was the son of a paranoid-schizophrenic mother and grandmother. According to his classmates, he enjoyed strangling cats and snapping the necks of chickens. A college dropout, he engaged in a wild crime spree, robbing gas stations and drug stores across the Midwest and west to California. He was accused of "strangling a girl in Milwaukee and killed his crime partner's grandfather in Pasadena, tossing his body over a bridge after taking his money" (Ames 2010). Hickman traveled to California and kidnapped Marion Parker from Mount Vernon Junior High school in Los Angeles, and demanded a ransom from Marion's father, a prominent banker. Hickman was a narcissist, and considered himself a cunning crook, signing his letters "The Fox" (Ames 2010). The father wrote to Hickman that he suspected Hickman might deceive him, and after butchering Marion, Hickman wrote a letter back to Marion's father feigning being hurt at the father's suggestion that Hickman might be lying. At this point I want to share a description of Hickman's murder of Marion Parker, which Ames (2010) retrieved from several newspaper reports from 1927. And as you read it, please remember that this is the man that Ayn Rand lionized as her "superman":

> "It was while I was fixing the blindfold that the urge to murder came upon me," he continued, "and I just couldn't help myself. I got a towel and stepped up behind Marion. Then before she could move, I put it around her neck and twisted it tightly. I held on and she made no outcry except to gurgle. I held on for about two minutes, I guess, and then I let go. When I cut loose the fastenings, she fell to the floor. I knew she was dead. Well, after she was dead I carried her body into the bathroom and undressed her, all but the underwear, and cut a hole in her throat with a pocket knife to let the blood out." Another newspaper account explained what Hickman did next: Then he took a pocket knife and cut a hole in her throat. Then he cut off each arm to the elbow. Then he cut her legs off at the knees. He put the limbs in a cabinet. He cut up the body in his room at the Bellevue Arms Apartments. Then he removed the clothing and cut the body through at the waist. He put it on a shelf in the dressing room. He placed a towel in the body to drain the blood. He wrapped up the exposed ends of the arms and waist with paper. He

combed back her hair, powdered her face and then with a needle fixed her eyelids. He did this because he realized that he would lose the reward if he did not have the body to produce to her father.

Hickman packed her body, limbs and entrails into a car, and drove to the drop-off point to pick up his ransom; along his way he tossed out wrapped-up limbs and innards scattering them around Los Angeles. When he arrived at the meeting point, Hickman pulled Miriam's [*sic*] head and torso out of a suitcase and propped her up, her torso wrapped tightly, to look like she was alive—he sewed wires into her eyelids to keep them open, so that she'd appear to be awake and alive. When Miriam's father arrived, Hickman pointed a sawed-off shotgun at him, showed Miriam's head with the eyes sewn open (it would have been hard to see for certain that she was dead), and then took the ransom money and sped away. As he sped away, he threw Miriam's head and torso out of the car, and that's when the father ran up and saw his daughter—and screamed. (Ames 2010)

Rand wrote in her notebook that Hickman represented "the amazing picture of a man with no regard whatsoever for all that a society holds sacred, and with a consciousness all his own. A man who really stands alone, in action and in soul. Other people do not exist for him, and he does not see why they should" (Ames 2010). Michael Prescott (2005) presents some other bits of information on Rand's notebook as follows:

In her journal circa 1928 Rand quoted the statement, "What is good for me is right," a credo attributed to a prominent figure of the day, William Edward Hickman. Her response was enthusiastic. "The best and strongest expression of a real man's psychology I have heard," she exulted.

At the time, she was planning a novel that was to be titled The Little Street, the projected hero of which was named Danny Renahan. According to Rand scholar Chris Matthew Sciabarra, she deliberately modeled Renahan—intended to be her first sketch of her ideal man—after this same William Edward Hickman. Renahan, she enthuses in another journal entry, "is born with a wonderful, free, light consciousness—[resulting from] the absolute lack of social instinct or herd feeling. He does not understand, because he has no organ for understanding, the necessity, meaning, or importance of other people. . . . Other people do not exist for him and he does not understand why they should." (Journals 27, 21–22; emphasis hers.)

"A wonderful, free, light consciousness" born of the utter absence of any understanding of "the necessity, meaning, or importance of other people." Obviously, Ayn Rand was most favorably impressed with Mr. Hickman. He was, at least at that stage of Rand's life, her kind of man.

So the question is, who exactly was he?

William Edward Hickman was one of the most famous men in America in 1928. But he came by his fame in a way that perhaps should have given pause to

Ayn Rand before she decided that he was a "real man" worthy of enshrinement in her pantheon of fictional heroes.

You see, Hickman was a forger, an armed robber, a child kidnapper, and a multiple murderer.

Other than that, he was probably a swell guy.

I agree with Ames (2010) that Rand's ideas "are nothing more than a ditzy dilettante's bastardized Nietzsche." Former Central Bank chief Alan Greenspan, whose relationship with Rand dated back to the 1950s, took umbrage at a negative review of *Atlas Shrugged* and published a letter to the editor that ends: "Parasites who persistently avoid either purpose or reason perish as they should. Alan Greenspan" (Ames 2010). One of our more pathological political figures, GOP Congressman Paul Ryan, once declared: "Rand makes the best case for the morality of democratic capitalism" (Ames 2010). That is an interesting observation by Ryan, since, as Ames (2010) points out, Rand wrote that "Democracy, in short, is a form of collectivism, which denies individual rights: the majority can do whatever it wants with no restrictions. In principle, the democratic government is all-powerful. Democracy is a totalitarian manifestation; it is not a form of freedom." Those who worship Rand, like those who worship Trump, belong to a yeasty coterie of soul snuffing brigands, whose Janus-faced political bloodlust, blinkered rationality and complicity in dictator-centric nationalism has created the condition for a new and more vicious stage of state capitalism.

PJ: Rand's hypocritical actions in accepting Social Security and Medicare while preaching her every man for himself ideology are not mirrored only by the American Republican Party. Similar hypocrisy can also be found in many contemporary situations, such as large government bailouts of banks that happened during the economic crisis 2007–8. What are the general principles behind this hypocrisy?

PM: Paul Buchheit (2015) has pointed out that within the United States, "law enforcement, education, health care, water management, government itself—all have been or are being privatized. People with money get the best of each service." This is hardly a staggering insight. What is not so obvious is that proponents of privatization have no problem asking the government to bail them out when their financial schemes don't go as planned. This is what we can call socialism for the rich. The superrich demand freedom to privatize when it suits their interests but often rely on the government to help them, oftentimes on the premise that they are "too big to fail." Buchheit (2015) examines the premises used by the rich to justify their position on privatizing everything, from the land, to marine life, to outer space, and to the very air that we breathe. This reasoning follows the dictates of the Saint of Human Greed, Ayn Rand. Rand rejected the morality of altruism, with the conviction that financial success is accomplished by singular individuals; communal values are rejected, along with government institutions (except those that protect the superrich), and this echoes Ronald Reagan's assertion that it is "the government [that] is the problem" (Buchheit 2015). And we can't forget Margaret Thatcher's proclamation that "there is no such thing as society" (Buchheit 2015).

Each time I pass the statues erected to Rand, Thatcher, and Reagan on Chapman University's campus my stomach turns into knots to think that any respectable institution would revere these leaders. But they are lionized on many university campuses. Public transportation in California, for instance, was decimated by the auto industry. The lack of light rail and other public transportation systems has made California a living hell for commuters and has despoiled the environment in the process. Are rail systems, the postal service, and public education really examples of Soviet-style socialism? It sickens me to listen to the get-rich-quick crowd who are engaging in global marketing in their bedrooms and garages pride themselves as the real risk-takers who are driving the economy when the state operates on a much more massive scale, making greater risks in order to spark innovation, and this is especially true in technology and pharmaceuticals because "industry cannot justify applications that require 10 to 20 years of development and which demand a coordination of physics, chemistry, biology, medicine, engineering, and computer science" (Buchheit 2015). Given the "mind-boggling array of deductions, exemptions, exclusions, and loopholes" enjoyed by the rich, it is staggering that anyone could be sympathetic to their cries of "privatize everything" (Buchheit 2015). Marx talked about freely associated labor, and believed it was possible to challenge capitalism while developing a coherent alternative.

PJ: In "A schoolman's guide to Marshall McLuhan" John Culkin wrote: "We shape our tools and, thereafter, our tools shape us" (Culkin 1967: 70). Often wrongly attributed to McLuhan, this claim can also be applied to your last words. Whether we like it or not, physical infrastructures such as roads and railways and intangible "infrastructures" such as one's attitude to work determine our individual and collective behavior. Trapped within this dialectic, how can we go about creating sustainable alternatives?

PM: What I like about Peter Hudis' (2012) work on Marx's conception of an alternative to capitalism is his reflection on Marx's notes on the "Absolute Knowledge" chapter of Hegel's *Phenomenology of Spirit* (Marx 1970 [1843]). Here Marx focuses on Hegel's concept of self-movement through second negativity. Marx was able to see clearly the reasons behind why the products of human action come to dominate the subjects that produce them, and why human beings are largely oppressed by abstractions such as socially necessary labor time. When social phenomena take on a life of their own and dictate the behavior and actions of the social agents that are responsible for creating them, then they must be replaced by an alternative (see Hudis 2012: 207). What was needed in Marx's time, and what is needed today, is a transcendence of value made from the standpoint of its transcendence, not value as determined by socially necessary labor time. The early phases of socialism may be characterized by value determined by *actual* labor time, but not in a truly communist society. We need an alternative to value production that is viable, in which people can emotionally invest, so that they can take action in their own communities while remaining connected to national and transnational organizations fighting alongside them. It is the very struggles of the proletariat both locally and transnationally that will determine the specific form or forms of postcapitalist society.

These struggles need to be philosophically guided. This requires philosophical and theoretical labor on the part of each and every one of us, as Hudis affirms. Movements from theory must simultaneously become movements from practice, and it is in this dialectical interplay that real change will emerge. So in light of what Marx struggled to achieve, the phrase coined by Milton Friedman must be met with an indignant rebuke: "Underlying most arguments against the free market is a lack of belief in freedom itself" (Buchheit 2015). Real freedom means freedom of the markets? Seriously? Can we stop vomiting now? And Freidman's statue also adorns one of Chapman's lustrous campus walkways. Countering Friedman, I agree with Buchheit's (2015) comment that "this 'freedom' has generated the greatest inequality in nearly 100 years," and I condemn any libertarian troglodyte who asserts that some inequality is a good thing for the poor. Buchheit (2015) writes that "At least $2.2 trillion per year in tax expenditures, tax underpayments, tax havens, and corporate nonpayment go mostly to the very rich, the most brazen of whom make the astonishing claim that their hedge fund should be taxed at a much lower rate than a teacher's income." Further, Buchheit notes that

> [t]heir tax breaks are augmented by the payroll tax rate limit, which allows multi-millionaires to pay a tiny percentage compared to middle-income earners; by high-risk derivatives that are the first to be paid off in a bank collapse; and by a bankruptcy law that allows businesses, but not students, to get out of debt. (Buchheit 2015)

The government is moving so much wealth from labor to capital that the government is literally being defunded, making privatization seem like the only viable option. Let's put public schools in corporate hands, and let's use standardized tests that are biased toward middle-class white kids to defund the public schools! Private banks take one out of every three dollars that we spend through interest! It's not free market individualism that benefits the people, it's the public interest! Now I don't believe the public interest is served by capitalism, but shifting more resources from labor to capital in the name of freedom is one of the biggest scams perpetrated on the people, and it has to be met with sustained resistance. Buchheit (2015) appositely quotes George Lakoff who writes: "The Public provides freedom. . . . Individualism begins after the roads are built, after individualists have had an education, after medical research has cured their diseases . . ."

PJ: Thank you very much for this analysis, Peter! Now I've learned more about selfishness than I can take in one go. . . . Let's walk again to "our" side of the campus.

René Girard's Acquisitive Mimesis

PM: Allow me to draw attention to René Girard, the conservative French Catholic thinker to whose anthropological philosophy I am much drawn. He famously coined the term "acquisitive mimesis." We want what others want. The desire we have for something provokes others to want what we want because we want it. We imitate the desire of others and the more society becomes globalized, the more we want the same things—but in a world of the rich and the poor, when goods are coveted but not in abundance, what then? We fight each other, and this can be on an individual or even a national level. Look at the nationalism today in North America and Europe. But we fight not because of our differences but because of our similarities—we want the same things. So the more we fight, the more we resemble others with whom we are fighting. We white Anglophones want immigrant-free societies, white societies, so those oppressed whites, the *vox populi*, chose to make Hillary Clinton their favorite scapegoat, with the help of the alt-right media and hackers from other countries whose leadership felt they would fare better under Trump. Trump's rallies are lurid scapegoat spectacles where he chooses the next victims to be demonized by his base.

What causes people to long to be the person for whom our desire is modeled? Sometime this longing is crazed and turns into mad envy. We idolize people and imbue them with metaphysical qualities that we feel we sorely lack. We imagine our models have more fulfilling lives than we do. We desperately need to become more aware of how we scapegoat others, what happens to us when we are introduced to charismatic figures, why we join crowds, and what desires and models of our desire can hurt and harm us, not to mention hurt and harm others. We need good mimetic models who can transform our thinking and change our lives—for me that has been people such as Paulo Freire and Noam Chomsky. Donald Trump has become a model for many Americans—he's rich, has a beautiful wife, and is not afraid to make controversial statements about his opponents, neo-Nazis, women, and military leaders that would damn others if they dared say the same things. The *vox populi* have encouraged Trump to become more racist, xenophobic, and fascist, and Trump is all too eager to comply. Calling for Hillary Clinton and Joe Biden to be "locked up" restores social harmony for Trump's base, but only for the moment. But that doesn't bother Trump's base because every week Trump escalates the rhetoric even further and helps them choose another scapegoat.

PJ: Thinking of common ancestors I noticed an interesting correspondence: both Ayn Rand and René Girard seem to heavily draw from Friedrich Nietzsche. While we already established that Rand has significantly misinterpreted Nietzsche's thought (not unlike his Nazi aficionados during the Second World War), please connect Nietzsche's philosophy and Girard's acquisitive mimesis.

PM: According to Gil Bailie (2016), an important interpreter of Girard, Nietzsche's will-to-power was founded on an unexamined premise. Nietzsche was fascinated with the mechanism that drives the will. In *The Gay Science* (1882) Nietzsche refers to this as the will to strike a blow (see Bailie 2016: 287). Bailie correctly sees that the person who wills to strike a blow must be seen in relation to the counter-will of the rival, or double (using Girard's terms). Nietzsche failed to recognize that "such a will is but a crippled form of volition inasmuch as it is thoroughly predicated on the existence of an adversarial counter-will" (Bailie 2016: 288). Bailie echoes some prophetic insights of Girard, who noted that Nietzsche's popularity at the end of the nineteenth century was hardly coincidental, and that his thoughts were "destined to overtake a once Christian civilization" precisely when Christian influence on Western civilization was at a low point. Girard admired the fact that Nietzsche understood that gods and heroes who were sacrificed in pagan mythology were similar in form to the killing of Christ. But Nietzsche did not recognize the innocence of Christ, since for him it contradicted those important aspects of life's eternal return, which includes violence. According to Girard, Nietzsche

> thought Christianity's witness to the innocence of Christ was socially harmful and that the world needs the sacrifice of the victim as part of life's eternal return, which includes destruction. Nietzsche was the first to see this problem clearly, but he was perverse in choosing the violent lie instead of the peaceful truth of the victim. (Girard 1996: 272)

Nietzsche's Dionysus accommodates violence and destruction, and this is required for the emergence of a higher moral being. Violence should not be suppressed in the search for a higher type of being. The notion of innocence is anathema to Nietzsche. Nietzsche understood that Jesus was not a sacrificial victim, but a victim that stood against the very notion of sacrifice. However, such a view for Nietzsche objects to life itself—it represents a condemnation of the pagan order, and thus of human life itself. Girard writes:

> Nietzsche was the first thinker to see clearly that the singularity of Judeo-Christianity was that it rehabilitates victims that myths would regard as justly immolated. Of course for Nietzsche this was a dreadful mistake that first Judaism, then Christianity had inflicted on the world. Nietzsche chose violence rather than peace, he chose the texts that mistook the victim for a culprit. What he could not see was the scapegoat mechanism. (Girard 1996: 271–72)

PJ: These days, Peter, we can see this scapegoat mechanism all around us. However, looking for mystical scapegoats such as Jesus is very different from pointing to human scapegoats such as the poor.

PM: Today's Christian evangelicals sound more like Nietzsche than Jesus. They wail about socialism creating a culture of dependence. In this regard, Amanda Marcotte (2018) goes right to the heart of the matter. Christianity today is simply a "cover" or mask for conservative political policies. Evangelicals aren't even funny anymore, like Robert Tilton, the "farting preacher." As a young man I would howl in laughter at the screen when Tilton was preaching to his television viewers, speaking in tongues, and smiling ruefully, his facial contortions giving the game away, at least to me. Many evangelicals lie with the demons and beget ideological offspring who are so villainous that they do a disservice to Satan, who at least has a sense of humor, presumably. Christianity gives a religious cover to their political outlawry, a sheen of pious respectability to their shrill, self-righteous attacks on those who don't ascribe to their loathsome politics of hate. Marcotte writes:

> Without Christianity, the underlying mean-spiritedness of conservative policies is simply easier to spot. Without religion, you're stuck making libertarian-style

arguments that sound like things cackling movie villains would say, like Ayn Rand saving civilization should reject "the morality of altruism." Since Christianity teaches altruism and generosity, it provides excellent cover for people who want to be selfish, a sheep's clothing made of Jesus to cover up the child-starving wolf beneath. Since Christians are "supposed" to be good people, people who really aren't good are lining up to borrow that reputation to advance their agenda. (Marcotte 2018)

PJ: This is all too familiar, Peter . . . and can be seen in a widespread image of good old conservative Christian boys preaching social justice at their tea parties and taking the stand of moral superiority over the poor.

PM: Perhaps I should not refer to Girard as conservative but rather as dogmatic for he posits with stunning luminosity the uniqueness of Jesus, and the Bible, especially the gospels, with the fervor reserved for only the most devout Catholics. Girard proclaims: "As long as there is any chance of its success, the preaching of the Kingdom has no dark counterpart and is accompanied by no pronouncements that strike fear" (1978: 201). For Girard, there is no substitute for the Christian gospels as well as for both the Old Testament and New Testament. Girard believes myths speak to false revelation and are pagan, whereas Christianity cannot be considered a myth for it exposes the pagan illusions existent in all myths. For Girard, all that is relevant in his theories is torqued toward Christianity, and I realize this can be off-putting to many non-Christians. For Girard, the Old Testament prefigures the salvific mission of Jesus the Christ.

Girard, as previously noted, asserts that the outcome of mimetic contagion is the victim mechanism, the mechanism of scapegoating or "all against one" that is triggered during scandalous moments or moments of mimetic crisis, what Girard calls "mimetic snowballing" (2001: 146). The unmasking of the single victim mechanism by the Resurrection of Christ exposes the collective murder essential to the generation of all myths. According to Girard, "[t]he Cross enables the truth to triumph because the Gospels disclose the falseness of the accusation; they unmask Satan as an imposter" (2001: 138). In other words, "[t]he Crucifixion reduces mythology to powerlessness by exposing violent contagion, which is so effective in myths that it prevents communities from ever finding out the truth, namely the innocence of their victims" (Girard 2001: 138). Christ deprives the victim mechanism (which to Girard is synonymous with the Devil) of its illusory nature, darkness is made translucent, making it more difficult to hide the efficacy of the mimetic violence so that it can continue to wreak havoc upon human culture. So for Girard, the Christ deprives the victim mechanism of its power while at the same time reveals the collective murder at the heart of all culture.

PJ: As you said, the ritual of murder appears in all myths (with all due respect to Girard, here I also include Christianity). What is the social role of this ritual; why is it omnipresent?

PM: The founding or primordial murder of all civilization is trans-mythological, it is a concept discovered in Egypt, India, China, Germany, and many other cultures. Communities invariably recollect the founding murder in a similar fashion and create laws against murder, violence, etc. In this way the founding murder becomes "the matrix of all institutions" (Girard 2001: 84). The founding murder becomes repeated in rituals, and ritual sacrifice, which includes the single victim or scapegoat mechanism. Murder often satisfies the appetite for violence, and after the exile or execution of the scapegoat, the community believes they have rid themselves of someone who is responsible for all of their woes and troubles (Girard 2001: 87). The murder initially has a stabilizing effect and requires that the community believe the person murdered to have been guilty. The murder needs ritual reenactments and sacrifice to perpetuate its cultural institutions. Ritual reenactment of the founding murder is an *a priori* idea that reproduces cultural institutions and the key institution for Girard is religion, which he believes to be the universal basis of all culture. It is, in a word, indispensable.

All of our cultural institutions originate from ritual acts. The ritualization of myths through sacrifice is an attempt to bring calm to the storm of mimetic chaos or contagion that arises out of mimetic rivalry—our desire for the desire of the other. Ritualized sacrifices are an antidote to violent mimetic conflicts and attempt to moderate and attenuate the mimetic violence. When some scandal inflicts itself on a community (such as the current refugee crisis in the United States and Europe) ritual sacrifice is called in to moderate the chaos and restore equanimity (children of refugees coming from Central America are separated from their parents and placed in cages, while the parents are warehoused in obscenely crowded camps without access to toothbrushes and other basic amenities). All nation-states have a violent origin in the single victim mechanism; all state powers are rooted in collective violence and murder. These sacrifices were made not to become one with the evil they inflicted on others but to distance the persecutors from the evil. In Christian terms, the perpetrators of those sacrifices (which Girard sees as synonymous with Satan) were not attempting to become one with Satan but to keep Satan at a distance. But in the end they functioned as Satan's "tributaries" (Girard 2001: 98). The Crucifixion of Jesus exposes the underlying mechanism of violent contagion and therefore renders myth and ritual powerless. The scapegoat or "all against one" mechanism unleashed by mimetic contagion now can be traced to its founding murder. The purpose of myths and rituals is to prevent communities from discovering the "innocence" of their sacrificial victims. Living in such ignorance keeps humans in blissful chains, in a servitude "that has lasted since the beginning of human history, since the 'foundation of the world'" (Girard 2001: 138). Woe to us in North America who celebrate Columbus Day without recognizing the slaughter of the indigenous peoples of Las Americas with the arrival of this "explorer." Thankfully Columbus Day is being replaced in numerous cities and states in the United States with Indigenous Peoples' Day.

PJ: While keeping Satan at a distance, many a scapegoat has acquired at least some overtones of holiness (we worship our homelands born from the blood of those who fought for it) and sometimes even divinity (a typical case in this point is of course Jesus). Even totally atheist heroes, such as Jan Palach (who burned himself to death over the Soviet invasion in Czechoslovakia) and Aaron Schwartz (who committed suicide over the fear from long-term imprisonment for copyright infringement) carry traces of this aura of holiness. How do you make of this path from sacrifice to holiness?

PM: As we know, there is a "mimetic crisis" that brings about an upheaval of internal discord, and the persecution of the surrogate victim as a way of bringing about reconciliation. In today's United States, it is the immigrant and the migrant that are persecuted. In many countries throughout Europe, this is also the case. The aggravation of conflict through mimetic rivalry incites the scapegoat mechanism. Often there occurs a "double transference." First, the victim is imbued with the emotions provoked by the crisis and its resolution. Second, the conscious awareness that the participants have of the victim "is linked structurally to the prodigious effects produced by its passage from life to death" (Girard 1978: 100). This can be referred to as a sudden "liberating reversal" signaling that the process leading toward the sacred has begun and this process is what constituted the forerunner of our human culture. In fact, all past conflict is embodied in the figure of the reconciliatory victim. This is what Girard means by the violence of the sacred.

The Christian gospels put to rest the mythic gods that emerge from collectively inspired murder, from the unanimity of persecution, from mimetic contagion. For Girard, the gospels are manifestly unique because they reveal a truth hidden from humanity since the foundation of the world: that gods cannot be created by sacralized violence or by the collective contagion of worshiping many idols. By contrast, the gospels expose the "poisoned fruit" of polytheism and its pantheon of pagan gods. The gospels are unique because, unlike other religious traditions, they deny the divinity of the collective victim, such as in those religions who first demonize the victim of persecution than divinize the victim. To Girard, Christianity is not a myth and does not deal in the generative power of collective contagion. The single victim or scapegoat mechanism is bound to acquisitive mimesis, an innate feature of human beings, and is likely to have given birth to all the gods of all the religions. Yet the true divinity of Jesus annulled this (Girard 2001: 121).

PJ: I can see why Girard, as a devout Christian, believes that Christianity is not a myth. However, as you said earlier, ritual sacrifice does happen across cultures and religions, and denying the divinity of the collective victim does not seem to make too much of a difference. What is, then, the unique contribution of Christianity to the age-old scapegoat mechanism?

PM: The resolution of the biblical Yahweh in the divinity of Jesus as well as the Holy Spirit (as described in the Gospel of John) gave birth to a Trinitarian deity—and this has resulted in many attacks on the divinity of Jesus as simply a modification of prior myths related to pagan gods such as Osiris or Dionysus. Yet the mythic gods are repossessed by a persecutory unconscious—those who sacrifice in their name do the work of Satan while believing they are doing the right thing. Girard's central premise here is that the single victim mechanism, the scapegoat mechanism brought about by a scandal or mimetic crisis, can no longer be concealed by the "princes of this world" after the resurrection of Jesus as the Christ. Satan can no longer protect his realm, that is, he can no longer pull the wool over our eyes and hide the mimetic scapegoat mechanism beneath a veil of ignorance. It has been said that God used the cross of Jesus to dupe Satan. We should not, therefore, be surprised that we, ourselves, have been unable to identify the "mimetic circle" since, for Girard, mimetic contagion is the same thing as Satan. Girard writes that

> mythical-ritual societies are prisoners of a mimetic circle that they cannot escape since they are unable to identify it. This continues to be true today: all our ideas about humankind, all our philosophies, all our social sciences, all our psychological theories, etc. are fundamentally pagan because they are based on a blindness to the circularity of mimetic conflict and contagion. This blindness is similar to that of mythical-ritual systems. The Passion accounts, allowing us to understand the single victim mechanism and its mimetic cycles, enable us to find and identify our invisible prison and to comprehend our need for redemption. Since the "princes of the world" were not in common with God, they did not understand that the victim mechanism they unleashed against Jesus would result in truthful accounts. If they had been able to read the future, not only would they not have encouraged the Crucifixion, but they would have opposed it with all their might. (2001: 149–50)

Here it is imperative to pay attention to Girard's argument that myths (that we enact ritually) are in the thrall of mimetic contagion, so much so that those whose consciousness is saturated by them are unable to realize it. Girard directly and unflinchingly states: "No text can make allusion to the principle of illusion that governs it" (2001: 147). This is what Girard refers to when he talks about the "structuring power" of myth—those trapped within the victim mechanism and the power of illusion cannot suspect their own subjection, or the game is over. He further notes that

> To be a victim of illusion is to take it for true, so it means one is unable to express it as such, as illusion. By being the first to point out persecutory illusion, the Bible initiates a revolution that, through Christianity, spreads little by little to all humanity without being really understood by those whose profession and pride are to understand everything. This is one of the reasons, I believe, Jesus speaks the literal truth when he exclaims: "I thank you, Father . . . that you have hidden these things from the wise and clever and revealed them to babes" (Matt. 11:25). (Girard 2001: 147)

PJ: What are the main implications of Girard's theory of acquisitive mimesis for our contemporary condition?

PM: To grasp the fundamentals of Girardian theory, it is important to acknowledge how Girard conceives of myth. He writes:

> The myths are not aware of their own violence, which they project upon the higher transcendental level by demonizing and then deifying their victims. It is just this transfigured violence that becomes visible in the Bible. The victims are seen as true victims, no longer guilty but innocent. The persecutors are seen as true persecutors, no longer innocent but guilty. It is not merely our predecessors whom we unceasingly accuse who are guilty; we all stand in need of pardon. A myth is a lie in the sense that it is the deceptive nonprepresentation that mimetic contagion

and its victim mechanism generate by means of the community that becomes their instrument. The mimetic contagion is never objectified; it is never represented in the mythic narrative. It is its real subject, therefore, but it is always concealed as such. It is what the Gospels call Satan, or the devil. (2001: 148)

Again, gods cannot be created by sacralized violence and then mythologized, or by the collective contagion of having many idols to worship. This idea is forever exposed, undressed, and revealed by the cross as a false transcendence. By triggering the victim mechanism, Jesus was able to reverse the victim mechanism for all time. Satan no longer controlled the single victim mechanism—the cross "reversed like a glove" mimetic contagion and the victim mechanism once and for all. It does not reveal that Satan was actually tricked by God, but rather reveals "the inability of the prince of this world to understand the divine love" (Girard 2001: 152). Jesus did not bring persecutory unanimity; if anything he brought disharmony and division and such division, according to Girard, plays an important role in our world where "deprived of sacrificial safeguards, mimetic rivalries are often physically less violent, but they insinuate themselves into the most intimate relationships" (2001: 159). We no longer have sacrificial protection, and so even the most intimate relationships can transform into their opposite—into enemy twins who compete over the same things.

PJ: What are the consequences of this lack of sacrificial protection?

PM: The concern for victims in our contemporary cultures has become, according to Girard, "the secular mask of Christian love" (2001: 165) as it denounces its own laxity, its Pharisaism, its feigned humility and sincerity, and its morbid propensity to measure victimage statistically. This modern concern for victims is, for Girard, "unifying the world for the first time" (2001: 167) as the mimetic structure of persecution becomes more widespread. This is due to the way Girard's work is rapidly being taken up in a multitude of disciplines. And this victimage mechanism destroys the social order/structure/community founded upon it as it becomes clearer that the scapegoat mechanism is implicit in the ideological hegemony of the ruling powers. But making the sacrificial mechanisms more visible increases violence, since the mechanisms that keep chaos in check cannot survive such transparency. Here in the United States, for example, the more that women and minority groups are revealed to be victims of structural violence, the more that society tightens its grasp on the population. Fascism prevails. Girard reveals that the solution to mimesis is another mimesis and can be found in the anthropological substructure of the Passion. The last messenger who is murdered to resolve the scandal brought about by the incarnation is the Son of God.

PJ: While I am not too convinced by the religious aspects of Girard's work, he does make some important philosophical points. The scapegoat mechanism has indeed cleared up a lot of my thinking about some burning problems of today!

PM: I have some concerns with Girard's work, but I strongly feel that Girard must be taken seriously. What I find problematic is that his work raises doubts about the importance of mythic cosmovisions of indigenous peoples. Is mimetic desire and the resultant contagion at the core of all indigenous religions? I am not convinced. Do they not prefigure or reflect some of the teachings mirrored by the Christ? Yes, I believe that they do, most emphatically. At the same time I admire Girard's concern for the victim, and his articulation of mimetic desire, especially when scarcity brought by capitalist exploitation is throwing the world into mimetic crises on a global scale. Nearly all of the inhabitants of the so-called Third World are demanding the same lifestyles as those of the so-called First World. And who can blame them? The so-called underdeveloped countries of the world got that way by being overexploited by so-called First World countries.

I agree with Girard that the divinity of Christ is the truth of the scapegoat, the truth of the innocent victim. But is Jesus only one of many victims transformed by their execution into gods—Gandhi, Martin Luther King, Malcolm X, Che Guevara? According to Girard, only a God-man is fully capable of abandoning violent mimesis and thus able to free us from our entrapment in the mimetic predicament. Only someone who is both human and divine, for only God can be subjected to human desire and violence and overcome them. For Girard, it is the Resurrection of Christ that confirms that this is so. To agree with Girard you have to agree that only Christ has equaled God in the perfection of his love, and has achieved humanity in its most perfect form. Here you must be willing to embrace the idea of the incarnation—and thus, accordingly, to embrace our ontological vocation as the struggle to become more fully human by throwing off the chains of the violence that begat human culture. Our enslavement to violence, to transcendent violence, led to the crucifixion of God. Well, here we get into questions of faith and grace.

PJ: What about pedagogy?

PM: For me, the Girardian message is clear and requires a pedagogical intervention. As educators, we must refuse to cover up the violent and genocidal founding acts of US culture. Instead of romanticizing the victims, creating the image of the noble native decades after exterminating entire indigenous populations, for example, we need to acknowledge the acquisitive mimesis that is part of our human nature and struggle to overcome it. How many Americans know about the Elaine Massacre in Arkansas, in 1919, when more than 200 African Americans were tortured and then slaughtered by white mobs throughout Phillips County? Many of the victims of this massacre had served in World War I, were exploited as sharecroppers, and kept in perpetual debt by white landholders who had joined the Progressive Farmers and Household Union of America in order to redress their grievances of unfair wages and to protest white farmers cooking the books.

We need to remember that 200 Arapaho and Cheyenne people, mostly women and children, from Black Kettle's encampment, lost their lives in the horrifying Sand Creek Massacre near Fort Lyon, Colorado, on November 29, 1864, when 700 members of the Colorado Territory militia set out to crush the Indians. This murderous attack on an indigenous population (some witnesses report that they were flying the American flag over their encampment as a sign of peace) was led by Colonel John Chivington of the 3rd Colorado Cavalry Regiment, a Methodist preacher and freemason. Soldiers took human fetuses and male and female genitalia as trophies. Captain Silas Soule and Lt. Joseph Cramer refused to participate in the massacre, as Soule ordered his men in Company D of the First Colorado not to fire upon the tribes, and Kramer of Company K did the same. Today these two courageous men are honored by the Cheyenne and Arapaho peoples. Awareness of this early history of our nation should give us just cause to develop a more egalitarian community. If we wait for a transcendental guarantee of success from the Almighty Man in the White Beard who sits atop the clouds, we will be waiting forever.

PJ: And justice?

PM: We read in the gospels that God sent the Holy Spirit and to me this means humanity has an opportunity to overcome its mimetic predicament by creating forms of community where justice prevails—distributive justice, fairness, essential human rights, and a restorative justice where we are obliged to help others fulfill their basic human needs, and where we abandon retributive justice and adopt an ethics of caring. In the United States we have divorced human rights from a critique of political economy, as we have already, *a priori*, rationalized the despotism of the market. As Daniel Bensaid (2002) puts it, there is no theory of justice in itself, only justice relative to the mode of production, since capitalist exploitation is unjust from the standpoint of the class that suffers it. We decide not to redistribute the wealth of the rich, preferring instead to help the rich get richer, thereby increasing the size of the common cake. As long as the worst off are getting a few more crumbs, then we falsely assume that there is no exploitation taking place. Only when exploitation occurs to the detriment of the weakest is there said to be injustice. I believe we must break out of this charade that offers to legitimate exploitation in the name of democracy and follow instead Marx's storied injunction: From each according to his or her abilities and to each according to his or her needs. Here we do not utilize a rationalized metrics or moral code from which to pronounce ethical judgment over others but rather integrate ethics into the very constituent assemblages of communal life. Our approach, like that of Marx, is metaethical rather than suprahistorical.

Beyond the Crisis of Hopelessness

PJ: This conversation carries some deep undertones of hopelessness, Peter—and critical pedagogy is all about hope! What does liberation theology tell us about that?

PM: Clearly, Petar, we are facing a crisis of hopelessness. While in my writings for the past forty years, I have often spoken of the need for hope in the manner put forward by Paulo Freire, Ernst Bloch, and others, I want to approach the topic of hope and redemption from another angle (see McLaren and Jandrić 2019c). Now I am not retracting the support I have given over the years to the formulations of and discussions on hope by Freire and Bloch. Clearly this is important work. But it's also worth considering the challenge posed by Miguel De La Torre (2015) who argues that what we urgently need today is, in fact, a theology of hopelessness. To take up a theology of hopelessness requires that we jettison the dominant Western theology of substitution. Let me explain. De La Torre (2015: 145) writes:

> Although we are capable of deducting the causes of oppression, although we are capable of conceptualizing how oppression is institutionalized so as to privilege the few, although we are capable of hypothesizing upon the intersectionality of different oppressive social structures, still, we find in Jesus an individual who chose solidarity with our suffering and, thus through his example, provides a body of action to emulate. Jesus' importance is less for the philosophizing, theologizing or theorizing about why people are oppressed; rather, Jesus provides us with praxis-based survival strategies whose purpose is to bring about salvation/liberation via a more just social order.

God remains silent before our seeming unanswerable questions. The purpose of God, if God has a purpose, is certainly not to provide us with satisfactory doctrinal answers but, as De La Torre (2015: 145-46) notes, to "sustain us during the unanswerable questions" and to help us "remain faithful in the presence of a silent God" and furthermore, to teach us "how our undeserved sufferings, our rejection by those privileged by society, and our death become the suffering, rejection, and death of God." As far as hope is concerned, "hope seems to be mainly claimed by those with economic privilege as a means of distancing themselves from the unsolvable disenfranchisement most of the world's wretched are forced to face" (De La Torre 2015: 137). Using the example of the Mexico's wretched of the earth, "the least of the least," De La Torre (2015: 137-38) writes that the "oppressed of the world occupy the space of Holy Saturday, the day after Friday's crucifixion, and the not yet Easter Sunday of resurrection."

PJ: In this way, Peter, hope becomes a vehicle of oppression—and I'm sure that is not what De La Torre, or indeed you, have in mind.

PM: Hope can certainly serve as an excuse not to take action in and on the world because you often hope that God will make certain that all ends well without much participation by you personally. In the words of De La Torre (2015: 138), "hopelessness becomes the companion of used and abused people." He explains this further:

> The virtue and/or audacity of hope becomes a class privilege experienced by those protected from the reality of Friday or the opium that is used to numb that same reality until Sunday rolls around. Regardless of the optimism professed, the disenfranchised, their children, and their children's children will more than likely continue to live in an ever-expanding poverty. Sunday seems so far away. Waiting, *esperando*, becomes tiresome. The situation remains hopeless.

De La Torre (2015: 159) argues that "the Euroamerican Jesus will not save Hispanics, mainly because we remain complicit with the very neoliberal colonial venture that oppresses the world's marginalized, ignoring or providing justification for the prevailing structures of oppression that remain detrimental to Latino/as."

As I have written extensively in *Pedagogy of Insurrection* (McLaren 2015b), Jesus preaches against the economic system that allows some to be rich and some to be poor. In short, he is a communist. De La Torre (2015: 107) writes that, in the parable of the vineyard, Jesus "defines justice as ensuring that each worker obtains a living wage, regardless of the hours worked, so that all can share in the abundant life." Jesus is advocating a living wage that ensures each family can survive. In fact, argues De La Torre (2015: 110), "[a]nyone who claims power and privilege forfeits his or her claim to God's eschatological promise." De La Torre (2015) learned to communicate with the Orishas, the African Gods carried by African slaves to the Caribbean, Brazil, and the United States. He learned to speak from a Cuban *Santera*; I learned to speak to the Orishas from a *Pai-de-Santo* in Brazil. But that is another story.

PJ: That's another story indeed—and De La Torre, a successful real estate broker turned Southern Baptist minister, who wrote books on topics such as Santeria and sex, can definitely communicate in very different registers. What about the register of critical pedagogy?

PM: Can we, beyond all hope, believe in hope? Rather than advocate a hopelessness that "may temporarily soothe the conscious of the privileged," or that "gets in the way of listening and learning from the oppressed," De La Torre (2015: 138–90) develops a methodology that propels hopelessness toward praxis. He advocates that "followers of Jesus wishing to do liberative ethics must approach the task from a theology of hopelessness, where meaning and purpose is given to life in the struggle of implementing justice-based praxis." In other words, he advocates what I have been calling in my own work, revolutionary critical pedagogy.

Writing from the perspective of what he calls "a Hispanic political theology," De La Torre (2015: 146) informs us that while God appears absent to suffering and oppressed Latino/as, and creates feelings of hopelessness, because of Jesus' suffering and death on the cross they now know that God has experienced their own suffering and that He creates "solidarity with all who continue to be crucified today on the crosses of ethnic discrimination so that the privilege few can continue to have abundant life at the expense of poor, marginalized Latinas/os." This idea can pertain to all oppressed and disenfranchised peoples, regardless of ethnicity. Those who engage in the "politics of Jesus" face vilification and persecution from the state and from those who are held captive by the dominant Western triumphalist tropes surrounding Christian salvation, and from those who reject the politics of Jesus as a path leading to a transcendent power over injustice.

PJ: The idea of Jesus being crucified *for us* is very different from the idea of Jesus being crucified *in solidarity with us*. Contemporary Catholicism, at least in its version I was brought up in, seems to firmly stand with the first interpretation. . . . Is that what De La Torre's "theology of substitution" is about?

PM: Exactly Petar. That is my reading. Those who suffer see very little in a theology of substitution that speaks of redemption and atonement. This reflects serious problems that reside in dominant understandings of the theory of atonement that have grown out of the suffering, death, and resurrection of Jesus as the Christ. The "theology of substitution" basically heralds Jesus for taking the place of sinners on the cross. God punishes his only child for our sins, turning God into a divine abuser, "the ultimate oppressor who finds satisfaction through the domination, humiliation, and pain of God's child" (De La Torre 2015: 150). This theory of atonement has very little in common with a loving God. And this particular theology, popular among white Christian evangelicals, is responsible in part for so much violence done in the name of Jesus. If Jesus takes your place on the cross, then it was you who, in the first place, deserved such unthinkably vicious punishment. For those who reject Jesus as their personal savior, the most brutal form of violence awaits them—an eternity in hell. Violence against nonbelievers has become a hallmark of American culture—just think of the extermination of indigenous peoples, the enslavement of Africans, the invasion of Iraq, and the Islamophobia that has opened the veins of this country. De La Torre (2015: 151) writes:

> If crucifixion, rather than the goodness of humans, is the historical norm in which Christians (as well as believers from other faith traditions) willingly participate to protect their perverted definition of the good, then does not a substitution theological theory of a God who employs crucifixion to satisfy God's vanity only aid and abet all the crucifixions that have brought so much of life to a brutal and torturous end?

This is precisely why crucifixion must never glorify suffering inflicted unjustly throughout history.

De La Torre (2015: 151) also admonishes so many of us when he writes: "Nor should the cross become a paragon to be visited upon those who refuse to allow Jesus to be their substitute against a God who is angry because of our infidelity." We thus need to ask, alongside De La Torre (2015: 150):

> If the tortured Jesus on a cross before a silent, and seemingly uncaring God is replicated throughout history, as illustrated in numerous massacres of the innocent, uncountable carnage, and savage butchery, then should not the quest for today's crucified be to resignify the Jesus of the dominant Christian culture that is now the crucifier of the world's disenfranchised?

I would agree. Jesus must become resignified as the incarnated word that stands in solidarity with the oppressed, even those oppressed who have concluded that God cannot exist given such a history of unimaginable suffering.

De La Torre (2015: 155) rightly warns that "Jesus voices an eschatological admonishment on what is expected from those who would follow him." Because of the "hopelessness of vanquishing oppressive social structures," believers in Jesus can still find God's peace, which De La Torre (2015: 155) maintains is "a peace embedded in a messianic vision of a God that prepares a banquet for all people, where everyone, regardless of race, ethnicity, class, gender, ability, or gender preference is welcomed to feast on the finest wines and richest foods." This certainly doesn't sound like the Trump administration's policies regarding immigrants, nor even Trump's sumptuous Mar-a-Lago banquets where he would be flanked with one of his Roy Cohn "fixers," Michael Cohen or Rudy Giuliani. In sum, for De La Torre (2015: 123), we "are called to emulate Jesus' purpose statement by committing to struggle with and for the oppressed, as well as being able to learn about God from the oppressed."

PJ: How should we, according to De La Torre, go about this emulation of Jesus' purpose? Isn't it a bit too much to ask from us, regularly people, to be like Jesus?

PM: De La Torre (2015: 161) describes the practice of *jodiendo*, which means the process of screwing things up. He advocates it as a praxis of resistance. It's a practice of instability, of "upsetting the prevailing social order." It's a bit like becoming Exú, the trickster in Umbanda or Candomblé. This follows his idea of "Jesus the troublemaker, the bringer of conflict, the disrupter of unity." He explains that "*[j]oderones* are tricksters that lie so that truth can be revealed." In fact,

> When they lie, cheat, joke, and deceive, they unmask deeper truths obscured by the dominant culture's moralists. These means employed by the *joderones* in the struggle for liberation may not be considered moral by the dominant culture; nevertheless, such tricksters are ethical, and operating in a realm that moves beyond good and evil, beyond what society defines as being right or wrong. (De La Torre 2015: 163)

So Jesus Christ, the *joderon*, "screws with those who established themselves as the political and religious leaders of the people and from their lofty positions screw the very people they are entrusted to represent, support, and protect" (De La Torre 2015: 165). This, according to De La Torre, represents a praxis of love: "To *joder* is an act of love towards oppressors, designed to force them to live up to their rhetoric in the hope that confronting. Their complicity with oppressive structures might lead them toward their own salvation." However, De La Torre (2015: 161) warns that

> A liberative ethics *para joder* can be frightening to those who are accustomed to their power and privilege because hopelessness signals a lack of control. Because those who benefit from the present social structures insist on control, sharing the plight of being vulnerable to forces beyond control will demonstrate how hope falls short.

This idea is similar to what I wrote in my anthropological work on liminality, in particular my use of the term liminal servant (McLaren 1999), although I was applying it to the role of the teacher, not to the Son of God.

10

Siddhartha Meeting Jesus in the Desert of the Real: Christian Ecopedagogy in and for the Anthropocene

Ecosocialism and the Catholic Mystics Steering the Rainbow Warrior

PJ: Let's switch our attention to the crucial question of our times—the collective relationship between human beings and nature. While there are plenty of analyses of this relationship in fields from hard sciences to social sciences and humanities, I think that there is a lot to be learned by looking at them through the lens of liberation theology.

PM: Public intellectuals who are involved in critical approaches in the social sciences, the hard sciences, theology, literature, and the arts have often revealed that their work has an ecospiritual dimension. When we aspire toward and are guided by a form of ecospirituality, it is important that we do not in any way deemphasize the materiality and temporality of exploitation: that exploitation has an objective and tangible dimension and that it need not continue. Our world is teeming with abundance, but such unparalleled abundance needs to be liberated from capitalist relations, since we have the technological capabilities of supplying earthly necessities to everyone on planet Earth. But this is not happening. We need to ask why.

What does education truly mean if not to admonish our students to be critically engaged with Marx, with Freire, with ecopedagogy, with critical pedagogy, with ecospirituality, with a dialectical and materialist perspective? Because the very future of our biosphere is in great jeopardy. There will never be a reconciliation of alienated humanity with our Mother Earth unless we recover the emancipatory dimension of philosophy, pedagogy, and the social commons. This means an entire renovation of the media, focusing their pedagogical dimensions on challenging forces of oppression and domination. Given the gravity of today's metabolic rift—meaning "the generalized commodity dependency" that exists between the natural and the social world or "the interchange of matter and energy between humanity and nature through life-sustaining social structures"—it makes little sense to avoid discussing the creation of an alternative world system outside the social universe of value production (Reitz 2018: 41).

PJ: "In the age of metabolic rift, human identities are products of complex interchanges between our biological nature and labor—and closely linked to dominant capitalist ideology" (Jandrić 2017: 120). As you rightly point out, our technology (here I am using the word in the Ellulian sense, which includes not only machines but also our social organization) (Ellul 1964) simply cannot be thought of without its political economy (see Peters and Jandrić 2018a) and labor (Peters, Jandrić, and Means 2019).

PM: On this note, I very much like Charles Reitz's development of a labor theory of commonwealth, in which labor is postulated not only as an "ethico-aesthetic" sensibility but also as a "social-ecological" relationship. Reitz writes: "Commonwealth labor is not only a social and productive force, but also labor that is liberated, labor that is meaningful, labor even in aesthetic form" (2018: 41). This type of labor would be consonant with "the axial values of world's wisdom traditions" and dependent upon "the metabolic relation between human society and nature that Marx describes" (2018: 40). Further, the act of laboring would be governed by a "form of eco-humanist governmental stewardship of the proletariat" (2018: 40). It should be clear among those who value self-reflection that we won't have a future if we don't address the exhaustion of the earth created by the expansion of transnational capital:

> ocean acidification, pollution of the globe's freshwater supply, overexploitation of ground water in industrial food production, biodiversity loss, atmospheric aerosol loading, chemical pollution, the energy crisis from coal to oil, the climate/carbon metabolism crisis, i.e., climate change. (Reitz 2018: 42)

The path to William Blake's Golgonooza (1966) moves me away from the theistic orthodoxy of Rust Belt evangelicals, or, conversely, the pantheistic "all is God and God is all" of ancient shamans, right up to the cosmo-visioneers of the New Age present. My own understanding of God and the cosmos is not pantheistic but rather panentheistic—all is not God, one thing is not another, yet God is in all and all is in God, and creatures and God are irrevocably and everlastingly intertwined. It is both ecosocialism and the Catholic mystics steering the Rainbow Warrior; it is Siddhartha meeting Jesus in the desert.

PJ: I like the metaphor, Peter! Let's extend it with a reference to Žižek (2002): Siddhartha meeting Jesus in the desert of the real.

PM: That's an excellent extension, Petar. Reitz develops an ethics out of nontheistic humanist philosophy based on the human condition as living labor, that is, on the sensuous practical activities—the ontological ground of concrete and living labor of human beings and their potential to enhance and ultimately fulfill the dimension of what Marx referred to as our "species being." These include "our subsistence strategies, and our earliest forms of communal labor in egalitarian partnership societies" (Reitz 2018: 93). Essentially, it is an ethics of cooperation and partnership that involves "bioecologically generated economic, aesthetic, intellectual and moral standards gravitating toward the humanism of a communally laboring commonwealth" (2018: 94). I find Reitz's development crucial and absolutely necessary for our ecospiritual journey toward immanentizing the eschaton. Reitz grounds these characteristics on the "categorical ethical advantages" developed from our evolutionary history, such as "the power to subsist cooperatively" as well as "to create communicate, and care communally" (2018: 94). Here Reitz sets his ethics against congealed or dead labor that manifests itself as a result of our commodified economy and the dominative power of the transnational capitalist class to wield value augmentation in ways that serve its own interests.

PJ: What is the philosophical background of this ecospiritual journey?

PM: Liberation theologians such as Leonardo Boff have taken us on an ecospiritual investigation largely inspired by the work of Teilhard de Chardin. The Jesuit priest Pierre Teilhard de Chardin, a revered anthropologist and world-renowned spiritual thinker, developed scintillating insights into the profoundly intimate relationship between the evolutionary development of the material and the spiritual world, leading him to celebrate the sacredness of matter infused with the warp and weft of the cosmos, which he considered to be divine. His investigations led him to believe that the world itself shall become a living host, a liturgy. Believing the universe to be evolving toward a true cosmic liturgy, where the concentration of cosmic consciousness reaches its endpoint, the Omega Point, or the Christ, he posited that God is implicit in matter, and as matter develops into consciousness, it becomes more complexified and more concentrated over time. He maintained that God is infused in matter, in consciousness, and over time God's presence in the cosmos becomes more explicit. That creation is occurring, even now as we read these words. All of humanity is helping to finish this task by participating in the divine relationship between matter, the soul, and the Christ, arching toward the fullness of the Godhead, the Pleroma.

Here we can see that Teilhard de Chardin's vision is well discerned, even in the face of the calumnies he faced within the Catholic Church, which, at the time of this writing, still has refused to waive the *monitum* issued by the Holy Office in 1962 regarding the writings of Father de Chardin. We can interpret Father de Chardin's views as perceiving technology as assisting in this evolutionary voyage toward the Pleroma, by helping to create the Noosphere—a cosmic intelligence network. I would, however, be reluctant to assume that Teilhard de Chardin envisioned supercomputers creating a singularity and pushing all of humanity into some transhuman world, assisted by AI robots sporting white robes and halos. Here we must be careful not to spend our fund of speculation into a deficit, especially when we think we can catch God flat-footed, as He or She or He/She creates a new computer program. Even speculation has an exhaustible capacity. Surely we can know God through revelation but we cannot calibrate revelation using a supercomputer. Although I know some quantitative researchers who would have no problem trying to come up with some algorithms.

PJ: Teilhard de Chardin certainly did not imagine today's supercomputers—yet these supercomputers inevitably carry a strong imprint of Catholicism (Fuller and Jandrić 2019). In our postdigital world, this imprint reaches all the way to the question of what it means to be human.

PJ: Indeed, Petar. Leonardo Boff uses the example of the Trinity ("perfect dialectic") in his exegesis on the "theosphere"—a Trinity that enwraps the Father, Son, and Holy Spirit, "one in the other" in a "relational circularity" that avoids essentialism by perichoresis (communion and complete relationality), which Boff describes as a type of "inter(retro)relating." This formulation clearly reflects the logic of Teilhard de Chardin's "cosmogenesis." Where Boff and Reitz intersect is in their discussion of what it means to be human. Boff refers to human agency as "spirit." He writes that the human spirit is a force for socialization and communication, is a power of meaning, is a power of transcendence. He elaborates further:

> Conscious vitality is structured around a vital center, the conscious and unconscious self; it signifies the unity of all experience with which human beings come into contact, in communion with or rejecting the things affecting them, both on the phenomenological level and on the level of depth and archetype. Living means being about to bring things together continually in a dynamic and open way, without ever coming to a complete unity close in on itself. It is always an open, dialectically balanced system, relating to self, the other, mystery, and the all. (Boff 1997: 160–61)

This is basically an extension of Reitz's ontology of labor to the vital energy of the cosmos groaning to be liberated, traveling on route from cosmogenesis to christogenesis. However, you do not have to be alive "according to the Spirit" to understand the values embedded in the evolutionary history of our communal laboring. Sensuous labor does not need to be "eschatologized" in order to provide the loam of our understanding in terms of what is necessary to remain a viable species on a floundering planet. While it is true that "[e]verything is in a process of genesis and gestation; nothing is utterly finished, and anything is open to further acquisitions" (Boff 1997: 176), we need not believe that the cosmos is infused with God and Word, or follow the teachings of the Patron Saint of Ecology, Saint Francis.

Give to the Emperor the Things That Are the Emperor's, and to God the Things That Are God's

PJ: We definitely need some kind of a balance between godly matters (such as eschaton) and human matters (such as capitalist exploitation). Jesus said: "Give to the emperor the things that are the emperor's, and to God the things that are God's" (Mark 12:17). Can we take these words as a point for departure?

PM: I believe there is merit in viewing today's capitalist society as desacralized, as having been given over to Western technology and the commodification of human subjectivity. And further, there is merit in drawing on the potential wealth of polytheism. St. Francis "reclaimed the truth of paganism: this world is not mute, not lifeless, not empty; it speaks and is full of movement, love, purpose, and beckonings from the Divinity" (Boff 1997: 205). As a panentheist, not a pantheist, and as a Marxist humanist, I can appreciate this. Boff writes:

> Paganism gave expression to this spirit in polytheistic frameworks, but that does not invalidate the psychological and spiritual wealth that make it possible to fill human attitudes with the sacred and prevent life from being smothered in immanence or delivered to lonely despair. (Boff 1997: 205–6)

By immanentizing the eschaton, I am not trying here to return to the ahistorical "matterism" of the eighteenth century, equating materialism with "thingness" that makes experience the limit of knowing. Nor am I kneeling before the altar of discursive immanentism since both of these positions mask the social relations of production and claim that the material is really immaterial, since there is certainly a cause we can attribute of immiserated humanity—capitalist social relations!

The suffering that permeates capitalist society is not caused by some abstract failure to live up to our fully developed species being. I don't believe, in other words, that "*human extinction* is the only viable solution to anthropogenic climate change" (Cotter et al. 2016: 225). Humans exploit humans, and this exploitation has not stopped with capitalism, but has exponentially increased because of it. And thusly it is also collectively transformable. We must refuse the trap of "event-al thinking," which amounts to "the paralogic of singularities that rewrites history as an uninterrupted series of irruptions without causality" (Cotter et al. 2016: 228). The ecologically corrupted biosphere is not some multivalenced hyperobject that cannot be grasped—but first and foremost an historical relation of exploitation that can be overcome through socialism.

PJ: In order to grasp the biosphere, arguably, we must first grasp our own nature. In the age of digital (Haraway 1991 [1985]) and biochemical (Préciado 2013) cyborgs, powered by various combinations of digital and nondigital technologies (see Fawns 2019; Sinclair and Hayes 2019; Peters and Jandrić 2019a and b; Escaño, 2019), questions such as *What is life?* and *Who can be considered human?* acquire important new dimensions. How do you go about these questions?

PM: Those are very difficult questions, Petar. You are always pointing me to new directions and challenges, some of which I have been wrestling with but by no means am I confident in providing an answer. The theoretical advances of Jeremy England, who teaches at MIT, do not see life as accidental but necessary—as an inexorable acquisition of matter under specific conditions, since the universe has established self-organizing principles or features. England's multidisciplinary approach to evolutionary theory—which contains elegant mathematical formulas and theory-testing agendas—is "broader than life itself" and in this sense echoes some of the ideas of pre-Socratic natural philosophers (Rosenberg 2019b). England proposes that atoms that are driven external energy sources (such as the sun or chemical fuel) and surrounded by a heat bath (such as the ocean or atmosphere) and will restructure themselves gradually so that they can dissipate increasingly more energy. As Rosenberg summarizes:

> "[U]nder certain conditions" where life is *possible*—as it is here on Earth, obviously—it is also quite *probable*, if not, ultimately, *inevitable*. Indeed, life on

Earth could well have developed multiple times independently of each other, or all at once, or both. The first truly living organism could have had hundreds, perhaps thousands of siblings, all born not from a single physical parent, but from a physical system, literally pregnant with the possibility of producing life. And similar multiple births of life could have happened repeatedly at different points in time.

That also means that Earth-like planets circling other suns would have a much higher likelihood of carrying life as well. We're fortunate to have substantial oceans as well as an atmosphere—the heat baths referred to above—but England's theory suggests we could get life with just one of them—and even with much smaller versions, given enough time. (Rosenberg 2019b)

We end up with the idea that life is an inevitable consequence of thermodynamics. Given the right conditions, a random group of molecules will self-organize in a way that allows them to more efficiently use energy in their environment. This system improves over time its ability to absorb energy and begins to take on the features of life. The external energy source causes the molecules to arrange themselves in a shape that resonates with their environment.

PJ: Given enough time, even the smallest probabilities become inevitable—like in the proverbial story where a group of monkeys with typewriters will eventually produce all Shakespeare's plays. How does this relate to your argument, Peter?

PM: Not directly, but there are some interesting issues upon which we can speculate. Evangelical Christian creationists often cite the laws of thermodynamics to disprove evolution, but England's theory reveals that thermodynamics actually drives evolution. For instance, creationists will argue that according to experimental and physical observation, in any closed system the energy of the cosmos is constantly being degraded, leading to a random movement of molecules, disorder, and chaos—what we call entropy. This appears to contradict the claims of naturalistic evolutionism that requires that physical laws and atoms organize themselves into increasingly complex arrangements. Don't these pronouncements of the naturalistic evolutionists contradict the Second Law of Thermodynamics? England's view suggests, as Rosenberg (2019b) puts it, that "thermodynamics *drives* evolution, starting even before life itself first appears, with a physics-based logic that applies equally to living and non-living matter." But the Second Law of Thermodynamics is premised on closed systems. Life is not a closed system. Ilya Prigogine's work on energy flowing through self-organized dissipative structures, both living and nonliving, helps to explain why this is so. Order can arise from disorder—this is ubiquitous throughout the natural world—without an intelligent design. We know that living things interact with their environment so as to survive and replicate themselves. They have a function. Molecules and atoms have physical features that make this interaction possible.

England, himself a devout Jew, has been described as a fervent believer in God. Werner Heisenberg said that the first gulp from the glass of the natural sciences will turn you into an atheist, but God is waiting for you at the bottom of the glass. Heisenberg (1973) also said that "Where no guiding ideals are left to point the way, the scale of values disappears and with it the meaning of our deeds and sufferings, and at the end can lie only negation and despair. Religion is therefore the foundation of ethics, and ethics the presupposition of life." Of course, morality could have developed from interactions throughout our biological history as hominids—and even before that! But science can't tell us if humans developed as a random occurrence or whether we are here for a reason.

PJ: Whose reason, Peter? The reason of God, the reason of nature?

PM: Yes, that is the question, Petar. That is the very question. Unlike for many Christian evangelicals who read the Bible literally, for me science poses no threat to the idea that God exists. For me God represents the conditions of possibility that love manages to exist in a cruel and unforgiving universe. Why the universe is so wonderful and so cruel is a daunting puzzle, and we must look to both science and religion for answers to why there is so much suffering and hatred in the world. So many of the Christian evangelicals, such as Franklin Graham, try to redpill the public with their reactionary political views, and gaslight their followers with unguarded thoughts about gays, lesbians, immigrants, and feminists—all of this causes them to faceplant terribly—and then to hucksterize the public. Their hypocrisy becomes painfully blatant. We need a diversity of theories of creation as much as we need a diversity of atoms in the universe. Rigid totalizing theories are not salutary for the mind or for the soul. To explain everything based on a single principle or idea will not allow us to have sympathy or synergy for all things and the sacramental message that they echo, or for the marriage between Agape and Eros that St. Francis—the patron saint of ecology—achieved. But this does not leave Franklin Graham and the evangelicals off the hook.

PJ: Science poses no threat to the idea that God exists, but science also poses no threat to the idea that God does not exist. Why do you prefer the first part of this dialectic over the second?

PM: Yes, you can't prove a negative, and all of that, good question. Theologians can debate God and the Trinity, and well they should, but that is not part of my challenge. I cannot codify and quantify or even qualify the "immanent data" inherent in an economy of salvation. I cannot ascertain if God's revealed triunity advantages the noumenal Trinity or the economic Trinity, and I cannot be sure if such distinctions are more obfuscating than illuminating since theological axioms must be approached from theology and not from critical pedagogy, without, of course, ignoring theology's pedagogical dimensions. Suffice it to say that God can be conceived not as unipersonal but as a triune entity of both being and revelation, without separating the two aspects, and without forgoing the Threeness of Father, Son, and Holy Spirit, all existing together but not in some dependent hierarchy. They exist together as an act of commensurate grace, presenting to us the conditions of possibility for participating in a divine mission to achieve justice. This is an opportunity for participating in the enfleshment of divine love, for humans to mediate God's love as they embody the Holy Spirit as an act of self-giving. Of course, we can conceive of God in other terms, and refer to other modalities. I do not wish to split doctrinal hairs. Any term we use to capture the triune essence of God distracts us, and necessarily distorts the conceptual framework we use to make such claims about divine affiliations and covenants within salvation history and in doing so makes them unanswerable such that we can only speak of the triune God through paradoxes. There is no way we can avoid dividing the essence of God with all of our conceptual distinctions, except through eschatological complacency. So I prefer to focus on the divine mission of achieving justice. For me, Christ represents the possibility for love and social justice in the cosmos, and I feel the religion of Jesus should never have been turned into a religion, which is why I think many atheists make the best Christians.

Christian Ecopedagogy in and for the Anthropocene

PJ: Slowly but surely, humankind has entered the age of the Anthropocene where "social life can no longer be thought of as an autonomous sphere separate from its base and the material conditions of its existence" (Wark 2015; see also Wark and Jandrić 2016). This, as scientists have repeatedly pointed out, brings humanity to the brink of its own extinction.

PM: Do most of us worry that the Andromeda galaxy will collide with our own Milky Way galaxy 8 billion years from now, or that the Royal Astronomical Society predicts a powerful Magellanic Cloud—a black hole or neutron star—will probably collide with the Milky Way much sooner, perhaps in 2 billion years? People seem to react to climate disaster in a manner similar to thinking about these and similar issues, like worrying about our sun going through the planetary nebula stage and fading out in 5 billion years, almost all of the hydrogen in its core fusing into helium, causing the sun to collapse under its own weight and vaporizing the earth in the process. If there is no immediate crisis, we can put it all off. And this is why humans are likely to be long extinct before the earth is reduced to a simmering mist. The insecurity created by transnational capital has most of humanity focusing on the moment, on our immediate survival. We hope that government or university scientists will solve these larger problems for us through technological breakthroughs. We think: Isn't that what we pay them to do? And who can blame us? We condemn people who don't recycle their trash and often the very people we condemn are those depending upon our trash for their survival. Climate disaster isn't something we can shrug off like the inevitable extinction of our galaxy. We are already at the cusp of disaster.

PJ: In the Anthropocene everything is connected to everything else, and at fundamental levels. What is your take on that?

PM: Ervin László (2008) echoes Teilhard de Chardin when he views civilization as evolving toward what he calls Holos. This is a teleological perspective—civilization is becoming increasingly complex—but it is unclear if it will survive. We could, in fact, be entering into a dystopian, post nuclear holocaust moment anytime soon. László maintains that we are moving toward a holistic society, having evolved from mythic Stone Age civilizations where the universe was just some vast, luminiferous ether, through theocratic societies of old, and the current short-term, reason-based society under the control of Logos. László affirms that the United States is headed toward a holistic society based on partnership, cooperation, resource sustainability, renewable-energy technologies, organic food, alternative medicine, and the usual suspects you would talk about in your tantric yoga classes over mint tea and multigrained toast.

The ontological compass around which a new planetary morality is evolving is supposedly being fashioned for the new *Zeitgeist* by the theoretical insight that particles are entangled, nonlocally, throughout the biosphere. Go purchase your electric car now, comrade, or at least get a hybrid! Stop repressing the prior unity that inhabitants of oral cultures shared, get to your spiritual Pilates class, and stretch your metaphysical tendons! Recognize your entanglement in the cosmic plenum and get with the program! Matter, energy, time, and space all interact, get it? But I shouldn't wax so sarcastically about this, so I will pull back a bit.

The discovery of the wave nature of quanta does give us some potentially important ways of reengaging and repristinating the world. We have all had fun with Niels Bohr's complementarity principle, which claims that "a complete knowledge of phenomena on atomic dimensions requires a description of both wave and particle properties" (Encyclopaedia Britannica 2019). Now scientists are beginning to speculate that there exists a level below quanta and spacetime. It is thought that the actual origin of the universe that populates space and time is the very same medium that connects them. Nobody is quite sure what this deeper level of the cosmos might be, even those adept in the superstring theory. The fact that things in the world move really has to do with shapes, variations, and the curvatures of space. What about the medium that subtends space—what László and others refer to as the cosmic plenum? What are its properties? Are we talking about atemporal four-dimensional physical space consisting of both quanta and fields? What about the level of coherence necessary for biological organisms to evolve on this planet?

PJ: What is the relevance of theology to these questions?

PM: That's always the issue for me, Petar. We are persistent in our breathtaking desire to become enemies of nature (to coin a phrase by one of my heroes, Joel Kovel), to lead the race to world destruction, to initiate the mass extirpation program known as omnicide. We are in the Holocene epoch, or what has been called the time of the sixth extinction or Anthropocene extinction. As Chomsky (2017) has noted, we are destined to become the next asteroid to destroy the planet. Unprecedented changes in our social media are likely to push us to the brink—our social media platforms are now inundated with blogs, email-forward chains, clickbait sites, newsfeed algorithms, machine-learning algorithms—all designed to evoke "high arousal" emotions and limiting our attention spans so that we flip around like the moth larvae in Mexican jumping beans. We might wonder why the Bible would be useful in addressing this crisis, since many evangelical Christians—and not just troglodyte Republicans—deny that climate change exists or that humans have anything to do with it. In the Bible, especially the Book of Psalms, we see the first historical evidence of God taking the side of victims, victims who are being persecuted by enemies. The Bible reveals what is behind polytheism and all mythology—the mimetic scapegoat mechanism of "all against one."

PJ: How does this relate to (human) evolution?

PM: There is a relation, I think. For instance, Erwin László makes the point that the level of coherence necessary for biological organisms to evolve on this planet must take into account both the genome and the phenome. Unlike Darwin's hypothesis, the genome does not mutate in a purely random fashion, since it is a prisoner to the effect of the phenome. If this were not the case, genetic rearrangements for complex organisms to evolve would be practically impossible. It would simply take too long in Darwin's model for the appearance of mutations that are productive for the human species. A single mutation cannot produce viable organisms since human organisms are far too complex. As László puts it, "The parts of an irreducibly complex organism are interrelated in such a way that removing any part destroys the function of the whole" (2008: 104). This requires a level of precision not accounted for in Darwin's theory that rests upon the premise of random mutations.

The answer to human evolution may reside in our better understanding of the cosmic plenum and the manner in which complex systems have to be kept in a functional relationship with every other part of the system. So do we, as László implies, go off and explore the field domain, the relationship between the spacetime domain and the waves that carry information without carrying energy? Do we give priority to the field-based waves that create the entities of the spacetime domain, which can be considered the "hardware" of the universe? Or do we focus more on the waves that carry information, on what we could call the "software" of the universe? What were the constraints that were present in the cosmic plenum at the time the universe arose? László suggests the Big Bang was responsible for our unique universe, and not necessarily for the billions of other possible universes that may exist. The fact that our universe "is improbably fine-tuned to the evolution of complexity" (2008: 116) creates some interesting transcendental explanations that can be logically extrapolated (i.e. that are logically required) but not empirically verifiable.

PJ: What kind of explanations do you have in mind, Peter? It doesn't really seem that ancient scriptures are very well suited for these new developments!

PM: Exactly, Petar, and this very issue has given rise to a new theology. László describes this new theology as operating within both "top-down" and "bottom-up" forms of intervention. Top-down intervention would be a type of divine intervention that shifts "the probabilities of (otherwise random) quantum events on the assumption that variations at that level do not cancel out but produce amplified effects on macroscopic levels" (László 2008: 117). According to the new quantum theologians, God "influences the course of evolution without interfering with the laws of nature" (László 2008: 117). This form of deism "maintains that the information that guides the evolutionary process is generated in and by the universe itself" (László 2008: 117). Further,

> [i]f a creative act endowed the primordial cosmic plenum with the information that governs the interaction of the entities that emerge in the successive universes, the two domains of the cosmos, the energy-processing spacetime domain of actual entities and the information-conserving field domain, interact and give rise to the process and the products of evolution. (László 2008: 117)

The idea posited by László is that looking at the world holistically gives rise to a new planetary ethics by reconceptualizing the concept of freedom.

PJ: Freedom is indeed a central question here—and the one that requires our deeper engagement. What do you mean by freedom in this context, Peter?

PM: László conceives of freedom as deriving "from the energetic interaction of the actual entities of the universe with each other in the spacetime domain and with their in-formational interaction with the field domain" (László 2008: 118). We can, according to László, become aware of incoming energy and informational flows, and achieve a level of freedom that correlates with our level of evolution. We can acquire some kind of "internally guided selectivity" that can lead to two kinds of interactions— "self-determined selectivity in regard to energy flows in the spacetime domain and to 'information' through the field domain and the capacity to choose . . . responses to both" (László 2008: 119). The upshot of László's thinking here is to argue that we can be guided by minimum and maximum forms of moral behavior. The minimum code "requires that one's action should not conflict with the right of others to live and grow: Live so that others can also live" (László 2008: 121). The maximum code states: "Act so as to further the evolution of a humanly favorable dynamic equilibrium in the biosphere" (László 2008: 121).

So does viewing evolution through energy and information change the nature of the game for us? Does being able to account for the past within the present, and to speculate on how the future anterior creates the context for our evolutionary path to complexity and Teilhard de Chardin's Omega Point give us a new hope for creating a new world absent of the social relations of capitalist exploitation? Or is quantum mechanics something for academics to discuss at their wine and cheese soirees? Do we drastically need to develop a theory of mind/brain that moves beyond conventional physicalist terms? A guerilla war waged on conventional physicalist orthodoxy? Will the social sciences be cannibalized by the biological sciences and by neuropsychology? Will historical materialism and Marxism be regarded as antiquated leftovers from the nineteenth century? Will the idea of a World-Soul help or hinder our search for a politics of liberation? What will happen to the idea of the human being as a causally effective agent? Will the idea of the agent of history be overturned by the idea of a psychophysical, essentially subjective, self? These are questions that go beyond this book.

PJ: These questions do not merely reach beyond this book; arguably, and I think more importantly, they reach beyond our contemporary capacities as human beings. Having said that, we do know that freedom is dialectically intertwined with our idea of the self—who we are determines what we can do and vice versa. Furthermore, individual freedom can be defined in relation to our responsibilities as members of the society. . . . How can we connect things we know about freedom, things we know about the self, and things we know about our social relationships?

PM: What worries me is that the idea of the self will be diminished to a local autonomous subject, connected to others by some kind of quantum membrane, leaving the state and its apparatuses in the hands of the owners—the corporate bosses, those who augment value and keep living labor under the heel of dead labor. Achieving our goal will not be helped by reducing the self to, say, a collection of singularities that redetermines itself out of existential "angst," as much as waging war against the transnational capitalist class.

The danger with the new paradigm of mind/body made possible by "new age theory" is that it can become cannibalized by a cynical reasoning that presupposes that everything is ideological or discursive (therefore emancipation from capital as a social totality, as a set of social relations, is simply a form of mystification). Such reasoning thus over time becomes transformed into an infantilizing trope suggesting that the power of dialectical reasoning to remake history in challenging oppression and class exploitation is insufficient. So yes, read quantum physics and think green but take your copy of *Capital* with you to reread on the picket line.

PJ: What is the future of liberation theology in the Anthropocene?

PM: Will the era of the Anthropocene—or Capitalocene as Sam Fassbinder (2008) puts it—bring about new advances in liberation theology or vice versa? I think that the study of the psychology of consciousness that examines the interconnective and integral aspects of knowing, being, and becoming as they are manifested as a spaciotemporal whole will be a helpful area of study—as quantum mechanics and neuroscience develop. But how useful will this be if we lose historical materialist analysis in the process? I believe at this point we can concede the fact that we are all imprisoned by our limited psychoid structures and the constantly shifting eidetic forms of our archetypes working across different cultures make us feel that we are connected yet fundamentally separated from each other. So for me, the rampant dualism in Western cultures is ripe to be overcome by new approaches to understanding the relationship between matter and the psyche, which is why I have always been interested in rites and rituals of indigenous cultures. Do we have epistemic access to the unconscious? I believe that we do through archetypes, and of course we can use Jung as a reference point. However, as Laughlin notes, Jung remained a dualist in his distinction between instincts and archetypes. For Jung, spirit and matter interact at certain suture points, whereas I view spirit and matter as enfolded in each other as a totality. I think Jung essentially tried to express this but his attempt to avoid physiological reductionism led him into a dualist *cul-de-sac* (see Laughlin 1982: 315–16).

Archetypes mediate content differently, and there are personal, collective, and cross-culture variations within universal archetypes. Universal archetypes also include processes of transformation, sometimes conceptualized as stages in a wider process of individuation. Our mythological dreaming is in constant dialogue with our conscious ego. This is how people transform and develop into unique individuals. You know the old saying—ontology recapitulates phylogeny—it refers to that biogenetic law or embryological parallelism that we all learned about as teenagers in science classes. Using that phrase, we could say that archetypes are organs of the psyche, and they help us pass through developmental stages with no Omega Point or fixed terminus. The question raised by Laughlin and others has to do with the ontological status of archetypes. Are they embodied structures within the mind/brain and if so, do they also represent the domain of the spirit? I hold to a nondualistic conception of spirit and matter, which holds that the mental and the physical are two aspects of the same substance—and this substance is not some unfallen essence but an interactive relationship, a system of intelligibility, or mode of knowing, that has theurgical power when we try to understand it through images that leap from our unconscious like a breaching whale on the California coast.

Laughlin claims archetypes are inherent systems of neural circuitry. Well, does this rule out the spiritual? Not if we can consider quantum interactions between neural systems and the quantum universe, which will also include archetypal neural systems. Laughlin sees archetypes as "species typical structures made up of living cells that may well communicate with each other and with the universe at the level of quantum interactions" (Laughlin 1982: 317). To the extent that the Anthropocenic world explores and attempts to map and understand these forms of communication, and their meaning-making dimensions, I think there is reason to believe that the further study of mind-matter (psychophysical) correlations (and these could have infinite aspects to them) may prove fruitful for understanding religious experiences—that is, for learning more about how we and the cosmos are mutually constitutive and what conscious reality lies at the heart of the universe.

Cosmology, Consciousness and Their Politics

PJ: You are completely right to point out that questions such as human survival in the Anthropocene are not only political, technological, or even practical. Most importantly, these questions are deeply connected to human consciousness—which is a question of equal interest for science and religion. What is your take on nature and production of consciousness?

PM: I want to depart from speaking in granular detail about the production of consciousness not simply for expository convenience but because I am not well enough versed in the vernacular of the philosophy of the unconscious and key issues that involve, for instance, subliminal uprushes bursting through the staid and ordinary humdrum of everyday life, or communication between subliminal and supraliminal consciousness. Surely hypnagogic reveries and epiphanies—not to mention fits of cryptomnesia and preconscious mentation—are part and parcel of religious experience, or part of what we could call spirituality, but I have not studied these phenomena closely enough to provide substantive insights into this area. So I would caution readers that my ideas in this area remain provisional, open-ended, speculative, unresolved, unfinished. I can say, however, with some confidence, that as far as my own writing goes, I cannot remember the content of my work in my books, articles, or interviews, except in general themes. It often happens that I look at my computer screen and see brush strokes of words and ask myself—did I paint those words? I cannot remember the experience of writing except a lingering feeling that it was not me doing the writing but the ideas, metaphors, words, borrowing my fingers to make some point. Sometimes I feel there are spirits urging me to join other forces in a cosmic takedown the impetuous dullard,

Dumbo-Donnie, from his throne. Sometimes I need to just raise my rhetorical fist on a page. Sometimes I feel that my works are more like panoramas of feeling, rather than specific explanations for various phenomena.

I shy away from explanations that are quantifiable because they are often too statically fixed, or statically asphyxiated, entombed within discrete and segregated boundaries, and I tend more toward free association and realize that this is akin to trespassing into dangerous territory, even for a social scientist. I express myself through writing, using discursive and propositional forms of thought, but there are plenty of nonlinguistic symbolisms in the arts that fashion meaning with a cosmogonic force as powerful—if not more powerful—because they penetrate the deepest strata of the subliminal. I also play guitar, invariably the blues (even though here I don't understand what I'm doing and am not very technically proficient). But playing guitar for me is not a revolutionary politics but more of a politics of self-care. Most important is spending time on picket lines, debating in coffee houses, visiting favelas, and engaging in dialogue with the popular majorities—precisely because you need to embody your narrative and actually try to get things done. Politics for self-expression alone is not politics—it's narcissism. Writing can be a form of politics but it's the lived experiences that power your writing that are crucial.

PJ: Music acts on a primordial level and brings out our deepest feelings—your guitar and my bass are not only instruments of pleasure but also means for unveiling our hidden thoughts and intuitions. Our playing might not sound so pleasant to our listeners, because of our obvious lack of technical proficiency, but our readers might be thankful for thoughts and ideas inspired by these horrible sounds!

PM: Yes, Petar, and that brings me to the idea of consciousness, what it is, and what might shape it. An important work, *Irreducible Mind: Toward a Psychology for the 21st Century* by Edward Kelly, Emily Williams Kelly, Adam Crabtree, Alan Gauld, Michael Grosso, and Bruce Greyson (2007) is a good example of writings on consciousness inspired by F. W. H Myers and William James. Myers and James are iconoclastic thinkers whose works both encapsulate and foreshadow a nondualistic approach to consciousness. This book very much captured what I have intuitively grasped, but not with the expertise afforded in their pathbreaking works. Such works are fundamental to developing a psychology of consciousness for the twenty-first century. Kellys' work on moving beyond a non-Cartesian dualist-interactionist model provides the sweet loam for comprehending the development of consciousness. The key challenge for future educators is to explore relations between mind and brain and quantum nonlocality and attempt to fathom how all of these are currently captured, but not unanimously, in structured hierarchies of exploitation and oppression.

We get so caught up in our search for a theory-that-explains-everything that we fail to situate ourselves as researchers, theoreticians, artists, mystics, entrepreneurs—within the capitalist system. We take the system for granted and it becomes invisible to us. Everything we do is affected by capitalism—where and when we conceive our children, what financial support we can give to our families, where we live, what schools our children attend, how we provide shelter for ourselves and our loved ones, and how we make sense of our everyday lives. Our personalities are shaped by capitalist social relations and so we need to understand why so many personalities turn out to be authoritarian, minted for tyrants such as Trump. And how some personality structures are able to break free. But breaking free from fascism isn't enough. We need to have alternative models—not just of individual beings, including beings such as Jesus that some people might choose to call divine and others might choose to see primarily as a good moral role model, but models for a sustainable environment, for solidaristic interconnections between our families, our "talking circles," our neighborhoods, our countries, and the rest of the world. These models need to be socially shared and therapeutically oriented and thus coherent when it comes to understanding how capitalist economies work.

That's a tough task—bringing all of this together so that our theories of consciousness are connected to theories of solidarity, empathy, love, and grace—and liberation from systems of mediation that reproduce social relations entombed in structured hierarchies. That's why we are social justice educators. What must be kept at the center of our exploration of consciousness is the realization that social consciousness grows out of certain productive, economic relationships. And this necessarily creates a certain social being. It is this social being that determines their consciousness. This is precisely what Marx said. Our social being determines the very questions that we ask about consciousness in the first place, and why we ask those questions. Let's begin with recognizing the forces and relations of production that shape our social being and provoke that being to ask questions in certain ways, with certain interests in mind that can be connected to the ruling ideas of the ruling class.

PJ: Capitalism is indeed foundational to our human condition. Yet our present is just a small, and some would say insignificant, window in human history. Can you perhaps historicize—and politicize—human consciousness of today?

PM: We are approaching a more integrated and integrating picture of consciousness that is reconcilable within new paradigms of being and becoming and that possesses some type of culturally conditioned consensual validation—we, the people, the popular majorities, must be able to invest affectively in a new vision of the future and believe it can be realized. And this means ideological warfare. I consider all my work propaganda for a new future. I hope it helps to create a consensus for the importance for struggling for a socialist future! At present, as Chomsky notes (Herman and Chomsky 1988), the media by and large culturally condition and manufacture consent for a capitalist ideology that is hospitable to the fascist hieroglyphics of Trump and his minions. But let's not throw out the baby with the bathwater. The social gradient of anxiety and alienation in our society is due to a social gradient of the exploitation of human labor, the selling of our collective labor power for a wage, and not even a living wage at that!

Today we are still living in prehistory as Marx saw it. The institutions of capitalist society—more specifically the bourgeois modes of production—can be considered prehistorical, because, according to Marx, capitalism is historically specific and therefore its variability makes it fundamentally changeable. Alternative theories must be intelligible within a coherent descriptive framework and must be able to correct the defects of capitalism. We can no longer live sane lives within the constraints imposed by capitalism. We must adapt to the constraints imposed by the nature of our species being, but we must also adapt to the demands of today's fiercely interconnected and multiversal global society.

We do this through the archetypal structure of the self, as Laughlin points out, but also as Marx points out, through collective class struggle—a struggle that now must be transnational since we are dealing with the development of transnational capitalist class. If we move toward a more polyphastic comprehension of consciousness, we have to challenge the postindustrial false consciousness of monophasic capitalism endemic to our current politico-economic system (Laughlin 2011: 481). Can we organize our dreamwork toward achieving this aim as we do for organizing our strikes against the corrupt union-bashing bosses? I would argue this challenge is also imperative for the left. Because I believe that the way we organize our society economically has causal primacy over the cultural conditioning of consciousness (Laughlin 2011: 482)—which, contra Laughlin, does not necessarily make me an Althusserian. Together with asking our friends—What's your politics?—we also need to ask: What's your cosmology?

PJ: This sounds like a completely rational, almost natural conclusion—yet it is extremely rare in our sciences and research methods. What is your take on links between cosmology and consciousness?

PM: That's difficult for me to discern. Let me try. I am sure almost every reader who is interested in the topic of consciousness has read the famous essay by David J. Chalmers "Facing Up to the Problem of Consciousness" (1995). I don't believe there has been much progress in cracking the nut of consciousness since this essay first appeared. Chalmers argued that in order to understand conscious experience we need to move *beyond* problems about the performance of functions. Chalmers writes:

> To see this, note that even when we have explained the performance of all the cognitive and behavioral functions in the vicinity of experience—perceptual discrimination, categorization, internal access, verbal report—there may still remain a further unanswered question: *Why is the performance of these functions accompanied by experience?* (Chalmers 1995)

Explaining the functions of cognitive behavior does not answer this question. He further notes:

> This further question is the key question in the problem of consciousness. Why doesn't all this information-processing go on "in the dark," free of any inner feel? Why is it that when electromagnetic waveforms impinge on a retina and are discriminated and categorized by a visual system, this discrimination and categorization is experienced as a sensation of vivid red? We know that conscious experience *does* arise when these functions are performed, but the very fact that it arises is the central mystery. There is an *explanatory gap* (a term due to Levine 1983) between the functions and experience, and we need an explanatory bridge to cross it. A mere account of the functions stays on one side of the gap, so the materials for the bridge must be found elsewhere. (Chalmers 1995)

Chalmers is not denying that experience *has* no function. Maybe experience does play an important cognitive role. But experience has to be more than explanation of its function. He writes that "There is no cognitive function such that we can say in advance that explanation of that function will *automatically* explain experience." We need to move beyond the usual explanatory methods of cognitive science and neuroscience since they are *only* equipped to explain the performance of functions. Chalmers correctly argues that "to account for conscious experience, we need an *extra ingredient* in the explanation" (Chalmers 1995). Even when we search the hinterlands of chaos and nonlinear dynamics, or neurophysiology, or quantum mechanics, and become experts in nonalgorithmic processing we are still unable—at least up to this point—to find anything close to the key to this mystery.

PJ: Our experience of consciousness is individual, yet consciousness clearly develops in relationship to our environment—including but far from limited to other (human) beings. My recent work with Michael Peters on collective intelligence shows that individual consciousness cannot be thought of without group consciousness, and group consciousness is directly connected with ways we communicate, which these days brings us to connections between consciousness and (digital) technology (Peters and Jandrić 2018a). But first things first: what do you think of group consciousness?

PM: I very much enjoy the work you are doing with Mike Peters. Tam Hunt and Jonathan Schooler have developed a resonance theory of consciousness—employing the idea of synchronized vibrations—which they claim is "at the heart of not only human consciousness but also animal consciousness and of physical reality" (Hunt 2018). This sounds like the kind of talk I had with Timothy Leary when we dropped acid together in 1968. So is the answer to nondistorted communication (not in the Habermasian sense, surely) to be found in vibrational resonance in underlying fields in various scales? Hey, man, send me some good vibes! We still say, "Hey man, that guy gives me bad vibes" and remain guided in our political decision-making by our "gut feelings" of resonance with other people. Will we be able to purchase made-to-resonance robot partners with whom we can share our lives? How will the lords of Silicon Valley program for resonance? We know that when certain objects come together they vibrate at the same frequency through what Hunt and Schooler (Hunt 2018) call spontaneous self-organization. Sounds a bit like Rosa Luxemburg when she talks about anarchist movements, doesn't it? So we are talking about "synching up" and there are, according to Hunt (2018), all types of examples of "synching up" from physics, biology, neuroscience, and chemistry that involve fireflies, lasers, and the moon's orbit around the earth. According to Hunt (2018), "[n]euroscientists have identified sync in their research, too. Large-scale neuron firing occurs in human brains at measurable frequencies, with mammalian consciousness thought to be commonly associated with various kinds of neuronal sync."

Other scientists have shown how various electrical patterns sync in the brain to produce different types of human consciousness, involving gamma, beta, and theta waves. So will we go on dating websites and provide preferences for our favorite neuronal wavelengths? According to research on wave frequencies,

Gamma waves are associated with large-scale coordinated activities like perception, meditation or focused consciousness; beta with maximum brain activity or arousal; and theta with relaxation or daydreaming. These three wave types work together to produce, or at least facilitate, various types of human consciousness, according to Fries. But the exact relationship between electrical brain waves and consciousness is still very much up for debate. . . . Synchronization, in terms of shared electrical oscillation rates, allows for smooth communication between neurons and groups of neurons. Without this kind of synchronized coherence, inputs arrive at random phases of the neuron excitability cycle and are ineffective, or at least much less effective, in communication. (Hunt 2018)

If this sounds like panpsychism—it is. All matter, in this view, has some associated consciousness. I happen to agree with Hunt that consciousness did not emerge at some point during evolution but has always associated with matter. But as matter becomes more complex—that is, more interconnected—so does consciousness, and here we are back to some of the fundamental questions raised earlier in our discussion of Teilhard de Chardin. So why are biological structures more "conscious" than nonbiological structures? Hunt writes:

Biological organisms can quickly exchange information through various biophysical pathways, both electrical and electrochemical. Non-biological structures can only exchange information internally using heat/thermal pathways—much slower and far less rich in information in comparison. Living things leverage their speedier information flows into larger-scale consciousness than what would occur in similar-size things like boulders or piles of sand, for example. There's much greater internal connection and thus far more "going on" in biological structures than in a boulder or a pile of sand. (Hunt 2018)

Human beings are therefore more conscious entities than, say, lumps of coal, which would be conscious at the atomic or molecular level only. The secret, apparently, is in the combinations of microconscious entities that together create a higher level macroconscious entity.

So shared resonance among many smaller constituents and the speed of the resonant waves that are present become the "limiting factor" that determines the size of each conscious entity from moment to moment. Is the answer to building a new world creating more "gamma synchrony" between capitalists and workers? Will these theories of consciousness help teachers produce larger-scale critically conscious students? Perhaps, yes. But the point that we shouldn't forget in our voyage into the postdigital world of consciousness is that we don't need to resonate at the level of gamma waves to understand how capitalism is destroying the world. Reading Marx and the Marxist literature is sufficient to establish an explanatory framework. But our theories need to resonate with others' explanatory frameworks. So we need to talk to each other, and try to understand what makes certain theories "synch up" with some people, and create static interference with others.

PJ: All this talk of shared resonance strongly reminds me of my experiences in various walks of life, from music and theater to fatherhood. In a recent book, I wrote:

> Jamming, or jam-sessioning, is a form of musical interaction where people play together without set rules—everything, from melody to rhythm, is based on improvisation. Now how do you tune in 3–6 musicians? The answer is simple: we communicate our feelings, intents, and planned changes in rhythm and tonality, through music. . . . Theatre and music used to be the most primordial forms of dialogue I ever experienced—and then I fathered my son Toma. Now there is this little creature who cannot tell you what he wants or feels, but if you tune to his body and soul, both you and him will know all you need to know. (Jandrić 2017: 362)

Please describe your own experiences of "synching up." How do they connect with your work?

PM: My thoughts on consciousness haven't been put forward, except in this book. I haven't tried to link any of this systematically to my previous work. It's more in the tradition of a McLuhan probe. I'm interested in various theories pertaining to consciousness and I want to understand where they might fit within a Marxist critique of political economy, if at all. In the realm of education, my own work shares some affinity with British Marxist educators such as Dave Hill, Paula Allman, Mike Cole, and Glenn Rikowski, the work of Maltese educator Peter Mayo, sociologists Carl Boggs and Bill Robinson, and Marxist philosopher Peter Hudis. I don't have much of an opportunity to share my work on liberation theology with others, since few of my friends and colleagues are familiar with this tradition—and some find my connection to Catholicism quite macabre, as they view the church, quite rightly if you look at the right wing of the church, as they would a medieval torture chamber. For me, it is a journey that is far from over. Over the years there have been horrible, often infantile splits between individuals and groups, usually a result of mimetic rivalry (see our discussions about René Girard), and it is vitally important to be able to find one's own voice, one's own path, yet recognize at the same time the multiple affinities that you share—or that it is possible for you to share—with others. Listening to Seamus Heaney read his work, or listening to a recording of Dylan Thomas reading his poem "Lament," is unbearably beautiful to me. When I watch the films *Cool Hand Luke*, *Land and Freedom*, *Romero*, or *Zorba the Greek*, I cannot be contained. Not everyone will resonate with these experiences as I do. Some will. I call these my comrades, my *camaradas*.

PJ: And what about the philosophical background of your experiences? Coupled with your insisting on political economy of injustice, contained in capitalism, what you just said brings about a tension between Hegel and Marx.

PM: That gets tricky, Petar. Well, like Charles Laughlin, and others after him, I adhere to a monistic and radically empiricist perspective that posits pure experience as a sensorium preexisting cognitive acts, which overlay what Laughlin refers to as the experiential epoch. I see technologies as mental models created by the brain used to better understand the minds that built these technologies. Reality always transcends these models because these models are mechanisms of mediation and there is always more reality that needs to be mediated than the structures of mediation themselves. Gatebox, the company that created a hologram of Miku, a Japanese cartoon character, has issued more than 3,700 marriage certificates to people who want to wed a hologram. For those who will marry Miku, she will never grow old and die. When holograms of cartoon characters are sought after as marriage partners, it should give us pause— how much reality today is too much? And in what ways do our neuropsychological, sociohistorical, and cultural systems and social relations of production interface with our experiential epoch?

Finally, Petar, does my interest in consciousness make me a Hegelian? Hegel, after all, believed that "idea" or "consciousness" was the essence of the universe and fundamental for the interminable reproduction of civilization. By contrast, Marx held that the ultimate cause that determines the whole course of human history is the economic development of society. Because they observed real objective social relations, Marx and Engels considered the social relations prevailing at any stage of historical development to be determined by the economic conditions. Of course I am interested in the mode of production—that is, the relations and forces of production, and the dialectical relationships between ideas that have achieved hegemonic ascendancy. I am interested in that discursive locus of prevailing rationality that enchains the masses to the ruling ideas of the ruling class and social relations of production, but I am also interested in ideas that speak not only idiomatically but universally the language of freedom outside the traditional caveats used by liberals to place themselves somewhere in a dead zone between reformism and a militant leftism—a zone of self-grounded and self-validating truths that percolate through the dark relay of ignorance. That is why revolutionary critical pedagogy is centered around the idea of praxis. And that is why moonlight shines bright over Kangding Town.

Postdigital Revolutionary Critical Pedagogy in and for the Anthropocene

11

Postdigital Science and Education

Petar Jandrić

Not only is the Universe stranger than we think, it is stranger than we can think.
Werner Heisenberg (1974)

Since childhood I had an equal interest in natural and social sciences, arts and humanities, philosophy, and mythology. As a student of physics I annoyed my teachers with questions about the nature of being; as a journal editor in philosophy of education I seem to create a lot of discomfort by asking authors how they *feel* about own research; as an aficionado of arts and culture I receive blank stares when I ask about the epistemic implications of artwork. Always against the hegemony of disciplinary boundaries, always perceived as an *enfant terrible*, it took me a while to realize that this battle is not only mine. Inspired by mid-twentieth-century development of cybernetics, with a group of like-minded people[1] I started to explore "the essential unity of the set of problems" (Wiener (1948) [1961]: 11) pertaining to human knowledge, learning, and technology. Our work has departed from an inspiring article by Nicholas Negroponte, who boldly claims:

> Face it—the digital revolution is over. . . . Its literal form, the technology, is already beginning to be taken for granted, and its connotation will become tomorrow's commercial and cultural compost for new ideas. Like air and drinking water, being digital will be noticed only by its absence, not its presence. (Negroponte 1998)

From here, we started developing a theory that accepts the shift from twentieth-century primacy of physics to twenty-first-century primacy of biology; we examined the conceptual shift from continuous analog technologies (such as gramophone) to discrete digital technologies (such as CD); we looked into the contemporary human condition drawing from various posthumanist traditions from Donna Haraway until today; and we examined the contemporary educational reality "where the social

---

[1] The core of this group consists of six people gathered around the journal *Postdigital Science and Education*: Jeremy Knox, Tina Besley, Thomas Ryberg, Juha Suoranta, Sarah Hayes, and Petar Jandrić. Journal webpage: https://www.springer.com/education+%26+language/journal/42438. The journal now also has its associated Postdigital Science and Educaton Book Series: https://www.springer.com/series/16439.

and the material worlds come together—where the human teacher's agency comes up against the workings of data to conduct another, and different, kind of teaching which is neither human not machinic but some kind of gathering of the two" (Bayne in Jandrić 2017: 206).

Looking at terminology we decided that existing research approaches such as e-learning, technology-enhanced learning, networked learning, and others project heavy (philosophical) biases. Therefore, we decided to start anew. Faced with a similar challenge, Norbert Wiener and his group "have been forced to coin at least one artificial neo-Greek expression to fill the gap" and have called their work cybernetics (Wiener (1948) [1961]: 11). We decided to follow the other common path taken by diverse traditions in philosophy, social sciences, and the humanities (such as postmodernism, futurism, accelerationism) and sought inspiration in the arts. In early 2000s literature in diverse artistic fields including music (Cascone 2000) and fine arts (Pepperel and Punt 2000) we found complementary ideas under the name of postdigital.[2] We decided to adopt and adapt the concept: published a "mission statement" article about our ideas (Jandrić et al. 2018), founded the journal *Postdigital Science and Education* and the associated book series, invited a wider group of like-minded researchers, and initiated broader dialogue (see Arndt et al. 2019; Cormier et al. 2019). Developing a new concept in a heavily cluttered research space has already provoked some resistance (e.g., Levinson 2019); on the bright side, it signals our refusal to engage in academic turf wars and provides an opportunity to develop a new research community that has the potentials to build bridges and connections between theories and methodologies.

So what, then, is the postdigital? In an early attempt to describe the postdigital, we wrote:

> The postdigital is hard to define; messy; unpredictable; digital and analog; technological and non-technological; biological and informational. The postdigital is both a rupture in our existing theories and their continuation. . . . the contemporary use of the term "postdigital" does describe human relationships to technologies that we experience, individually and collectively, in the moment here and now. It shows our raising awareness of blurred and messy relationships between physics and biology, old and new media, humanism and posthumanism, knowledge capitalism and bio-informational capitalism. (Jandrić et al. 2018: 895)

Since we wrote these words, the concept of the postdigital has been criticized on various grounds. Paul Levinson writes: "I do not disagree that we are in a postdigital age. I disagree that we are first entering it now" (Levinson 2019: 14). Andrew Feenberg similarly claims: "In reality, these terms 'digital' and 'postdigital' seem artificial. If the terms have something like the content I am ascribing them, then the postdigital preceded the digital and should be called the predigital instead" (Feenberg 2019: 9). Other authors, such as Sinclair and Hayes, see things a bit more optimistically: "The postdigital throws up new challenges and possibilities across all

---

[2] As far as we are aware, the word postdigital was first mentioned in Kim Cascone's article "The aesthetics of failure: 'post-digital' tendencies in contemporary computer music" (Cascone 2000).

aspects of social life. We believe this opens up new avenues too, for considering ways that discourse (language-in-use) shapes how we experience the postdigital" (Sinclair and Hayes 2019: 119). At the moment, the postdigital condition is the elephant in the room. While most people will agree that "[a]ll teaching should take account of digital and non-digital, material and social," it is much more difficult to critique own philosophical positions and accept that "ideas like 'digital education' are useful insofar as they encourage people to look closer at what is happening, but become problematic when used to close down ideas or attribute instrumental or essential properties to technology" (Fawns 2019: 142). Along these lines, Peters and Besley (2019) advocate for development of a critical philosophy of the postdigital. As I write these words, more critiques of the postdigital are written and produced in *Postdigital Science and Education* and elsewhere (see Arndt et al. 2019; Cormier et al. 2019; Hrastinski et al. 2019; Knox 2019b, c; McLaren 2019b; Malott 2019; Rikowski and Ford 2019; Lewis 2019; Matias and Aldern 2019).

Around 2015 the correspondences between Peter and I have taken a strong turn toward liberation theology. While I always prided myself for rejecting disciplinary borders, I could not grasp relevance of concepts such as the Holy Trinity for the postdigital condition. To add insult to injury, my lack of understanding was anything but humble. Being a proud atheist, anarchist, and iconoclast, I inadvertently succumbed to the academic sin of thinking about the world through the lens of my own worldview and trapped myself into my own little epistemic cocoon which firmly excluded myth, belief, and religion. Near the end of preparing this book's manuscript, however, I finally woke up from this self-indulgent dream. I realized, paraphrasing the Poet, that there are more things in heaven and earth than are dreamt of in my philosophy—whether I like it or not, the postdigital condition cannot be thought of without myth, belief, and religion. After years of disconnected engagement in postdigital theory and liberation theology, in this concluding chapter I offer a preliminary synthesis.

Postdigital theory rightfully emphasizes that the digital revolution is over; that biology has become more important than physics; that the digital cannot be thought of without the analog; that contemporary meaning of what it means to be human needs to involve some sort of sociomaterialist correspondence between human and nonhuman actors; that the age of the Anthropocene now requires us to think and work at a planetary level; that processes driving all these phenomena are dialectically intertwined with contemporary capitalism; that we need to approach these questions far beyond traditional disciplines; and much more. By now, however, postdigital theory has largely failed to grasp that humans are not only beings of logic and emotion—we are also beings of myth and faith (see Cormier et al. 2019; McLaren and Jandrić 2019d; Jandrić, forthcoming 2020a). We want what others want, we seek purification through ritual sacrifice, we are prone to various archetypes, we are puzzled by duality between mind and matter, and we ask, in Peter's words, "if humans developed as a random occurrence or whether we are here for a reason." We seek the eschaton of freedom and justice, although we know that we will never get there. We know that people and machines need to work together, but we cannot agree how—even when it comes to our own survival as a species. So how do we even try to reach beyond academic ivory tower and seek real change?

In response to this question, I situated my work at the postdisciplinary intersections between technologies, pedagogies, and the society (Jandrić 2012, 2014a, 2016, forthcoming 2020b, Jandrić and Hayes forthcoming 2020). "In 2011, when I first met Peter McLaren at the Second International Critical Conference on Critical Education in Athens, I boldly asked: You wrote 50 books on education—and you never addressed the question of technology. Would you like to give me an interview on the topic?" (Jandrić 2017: 160). After almost a decade of working with Peter, I can only confirm that the task of developing a new critical pedagogy for the Anthropocene is more urgent than ever. This new critical pedagogy has three important prongs—and these prongs roughly follow the structure of this book. The first part, "Revolutionary Critical Pedagogy Meets Digital Technology," claims that contemporary critical pedagogy is due for another reinvention in and for our high-tech society. The second part, "Revolutionary Critical Pedagogy Meets Liberation Theology," emphasizes the importance of myth, faith, and belief. The third part, "Revolutionary Critical Pedagogy in, against and beyond Transnational Capitalism," brings these insights together to analyze pressing problems of today from emerging global fascism to the environment.

Born by "the wretched of the Algerian suburbs, the oppressed of the Brazilian favelas, the precarious of American and European inner cities, the exploited of the post-communist China, and the victims of the school-to-prison pipeline," revolutionary critical pedagogy is a local and global struggle against capitalism, hegemony, and all sorts of oppression, which "reinvents itself in numerous contexts and circumstances, and offers diverse opportunities for living with the world" (Jandrić 2018b: 199). Building on these shoulders, and many others, in this book we outline some initial contours of a new postdigital revolutionary critical pedagogy in and for the Anthropocene. Our theories are full of unanswered questions, and transnational capitalism, authoritarianism, and fascism are *en route* to develop unimaginable new forms of postdigital slavery and environmental decay. However, postdigital revolutionary critical pedagogy offers a tiny straw of hope—and I do hope that our little straw will grow stronger and stronger in the years to come.

This growth will inevitably arrive at a high price. In our age of Anthropogenic climate change, the Four Horsemen of the Apocalypse have ridden out of their stables. The first horseman has already gone a long way. Pestilence, or Antichrist, represents the siren call of capital over humanity, probably best summarized in the phrase attributed to Frederic Jameson and often used by Slavoj Žižek: "It is easier to imagine an end to the world than an end to capitalism" (Fisher 2010). The second horseman, Famine, is pretty much around the corner. Climate experts unanimously agree that our lands will become too hot, too cold, or sink below sea surface; water will be polluted; people will starve. To add insult to injury, these changes will not hit all parts of the earth equally—some areas will be affected only mildly, while others will become literally uninhabitable. As hundreds of millions of people will turn into climate refugees, the third horseman—War—will get its twenty minutes of fame. It is hard to say whether we will destroy the planet in one blow, or the world will become a military zone where the haves will oppress the have-nots by military power. In both scenarios, however, the last horseman—Death—patiently waits for a large percentage of human population.

The Four Horsemen of the Apocalypse are riding, but the Humankind is riding as well. Our horsemen are Knowledge, Wisdom, Politics, and Love. Our swords are science, art, technology, critical pedagogy, storytelling, myth, faith, religion, and other great developments of human civilization. Our shields are love, tolerance, agreement, and the ability to predict natural and social phenomena. The Four Horsemen of the Apocalypse are strong, but the Humankind does stand a fair chance for winning this probably most important battle in our history. However, our collective battle—The Humankind vs. the Four Horsemen of the Apocalypse—cannot be further from grandiose, epic battles depicted in Hollywood blockbusters (see Jandrić 2019c). There is no individual David who can fight the Goliath of the rising seas; there is no individual Luke Skywalker who can fight the monster of capitalism, and there is no individual James Bond who can arrest the key mafioso and behead ruthless corporate polluters who, paraphrasing Peter, would profit from the tears of the poor if they knew how to market them effectively. In our age of the Anthropocene, individual heroes have given way to collective action—now we are all Davids, Luke Skywalkers, and James Bonds. Revolutionary critical pedagogy needs to be lived and loved every day, at work and at home, in our waking hours and in our dreams. We need to open a postdigital horizon of possibility for the survival of human race, and we need to do it now. Yesterday would have been better; tomorrow might be too late.

12

Reclaiming the Present or a Return to the Ash Heap of the Future?

Peter McLaren

Years ago, when I was a professor at UCLA, I was invited by a medical researcher at UCLA's Ronald Reagan School of Medicine to train researchers to undertake ethnographic studies as part of the human genome project. Tempted by a promise of augmenting my modest professor's salary with much-needed funding, I flatly refused to have anything to do with the project, since at that time there were molten discussions around the question of ownership over the genetic codes being investigated—would they belong to the so-called preliterate peoples being studied in, for instance, Panama, or would the ownership belong to the principal investigators of the project? With the architectonics of physics being replaced by a shift toward biology, bio-knowledge, bio-capitalism, I neither embrace nor disavow the notion that we live in a postdigital age since the systems of intelligibility used to avow or disavow our digital landscape are constructed out of the very same mechanisms and machinations of choice—and the same systems of intelligibility—used to construct the very concept of postdigital, not to mention the subjective conditioning and worldview of those employing the term. The postdigital challenge is all around us (Jandrić et al. 2018), I agree, but the postdigital was not just jolted into life at the point of conception. There are all kinds of social, political, geopolitical, and ethical implications surrounding the term postdigital.

Postdigital messaging travels faster than the speed of history and enables us to remember the future and forget the past in ways unimaginable only a century ago. The saturation of our social universe in postdigital hieroglyphics requires a postdigital pedagogy. Postdigital pedagogy seeks to examine critically how our taken-for-granted digital technologies generate and reproduce our existential and objective worlds, as we create ecologies of computation that are asynchronous, geopolitically specific, culturally various and that mediate our lives ideologically in social, political, ontological, epistemological, ethical, and aesthetic ways. The speed at which these technologies travel reduces them oftentimes to signifiers without referents, endless databases that can be repurposed for the commodification of our subjectivity in whatever niches make sense to our cultural guardians, and where variety or the lack thereof is used to elicit and effect forgetfulness in the production of a monochromatic world of pure contemporaneity. The resulting surfeit of messaging endlessly postpones reality until it can be captured by capital and put into the service of new networks of value production and surveillance. We have become ensepulchured in the viral dissemination of image board memes, where the pixel has become the equivalent to a God's particle. The new present created by transnational capitalist computational logistics can only be addressed in the past. The future has already happened. The present has yet to arrive. The postdigital world is a world of pure anticipation without arrival. We live in our bedrooms surrounded by prescription medications in anticipation of diseases that never appear, that is, until they do appear, and then we panic. And then we fetishize our panic and turn it into an avant-garde theory and become the first to write about it. After we have emptied ourselves of our ideas, we realize we've let the world pass us by. But we cover that up nicely by becoming professional melancholics. We then swan into the role of academic 'elder' and realize after it is too late that our aerosol world of postmodern transgression (tattoos and retro fashion and dropping some swear words into our keynote speeches) and aqueous collegial bonds is no match for countering either the Trump-loving neo-Nazi groups such as Stormfront, Fascist Forge, Atomwaffen Division and The Base, who brazenly share online military tradecraft such as explosives usage and promote 'lone wolf' terrorist tactics or FBI First Amendment abusers and their sophisticated forms of militarized political surveillance of leftist intellectuals and activists.

Recently I received a series of videos from a brilliant young scholar friend of mine, who teaches in China. She is in her late thirties, is regarded by many (including myself) as a classic beauty, and she teaches at a university in the northeast of the country, not far from North Korea. As an experiment, she was able to find someone to employ a generative adversarial network technique to create an image synthesis based on artificial intelligence that superimposed her face on elegiacal scenes from popular movies. The videos transported my friend as the lead protagonist into popular contemporary cinematic clips and bite-sized historical dramas with a stunningly realistic effect. This technique is known as a "deep fake." But we both worry about the dark side of such deep fake techniques. Seeing is no longer believing.

Can the term postdigital help us to re-understand the values that emerged from our analog forbears? Are we forever fated to be empretzeled in Wittgenstein's language games or have the new digitalized technologies give rise to a new Wittgensteinian platform of language games that replace the entire sense of what Wittgenstein meant by a language game? Explaining the world via a biological membrane or as a digital screen of numerical computations will certainly have implications beyond our expectations. So have we gone into a full tilt paradigm shift in the sense of Thomas Kuhn's notion of arriving at a new scientific consensus, where we are encountering a way of understanding media and technology in a manner that we, perhaps, would never have considered valid before? In other words, has our scientific field undergone a new postdigital "paradigm shift" in the Kuhnian sense or is it slouching along in the multilinear footsteps of some scientific community consanguineous with scientology or with a cluster of sofalizing trolls rather than, say, bearing a resemblance to a communal gathering of software geeks from Google? Will collective enthrallment with the postdigital animate our universe with ideas better equipped to normalize exploitation and oppression by creating a new, superintelligent global brain? If so, what will be its prototype, classic exemplar, or touchstone? Global intelligence as the lodestar for cognitive performance or make the case for the creation of an intelligently passive human multitude? Or perhaps, given the geopolitical and sociocultural conditions of the times in which we live, will we choose to create an uncritical, angry mob, styled after Hitler's Brownshirts or Trump's burly gammons? Capitalism's technological enforcers have been appointed to make us forget that we possess the capacity to alter or change our world. Will our postdigital universe emerge carelessly from the griffonages of a soggy-brained professor, afflicted with dysania, or from some bio-powered hard drive afflicted by a crapulent program created by some cocaine-addicted technician working a second job in a meth lab? Will it help us to refunction our idea of praxis, by conjoining negatively with "experience" as the event horizon of the real? Or will our postdigital world bring us challenging new ways to engage and transform oppressive social forces minted by history? Will the postdigital future commute the death sentence on the planet by repristinating our Mother Earth through technologies fostering sustainable ecosystems? Or will those technologies simply continue to reify a fetishized praxis of the pseudoconcrete?

After all, the conditions for the possibility of change, and for change itself—what we call praxis—cohabit the world alongside oppression. While analogue and digital seem to be incommensurable languages, both are constitutively necessary to explain reality and to understand what forces and relations shape the human condition. But are there not more dimensions to reality than those that can be explained as analogue and digital? Or postdigital? Having rejected its Marxist antecedents, is the postdigital in constant danger of being grasped one-sidedly, that is, as the "inside of consciousness" rather than the "outside" of economic forces and relations of production? Viewed as historically conditioned action systems defined by their relationship to historical contingencies, does the idea of an emancipatory postdigital reality require abolishing the conditions which require it—capitalist exploitation? To what does the postdigital society aspire? What will happen when 80 percent of jobs worldwide become automatable within the next few decades? Are we talking about creating a viable counter-hegemony to the capitalist present—a concrete utopia? Or some intricately elaborate and abstract pseudo utopia? Are we talking about a postdigital politics of mere resistance or a politics of transformation? What kind of sociohistorical human agent do we wish to nurture in a postdigital society? One whose computational capacity and recursive self-improvement is enhanced genetically? A being that is emulatable by postdigital materials and powered by evolutionary algorithms? Can we face the fact that our claims about human intelligence or human agency can only be ideological? These are fundamental questions that must be addressed. We can never realize the full potential of this agency within a postdigital culture or society, we can only anticipate postdigital society in all of its glory in the absence of such a society, and we can only understand it through the prison house of our concepts and/or our experiences.

None of this escapes ideology. None of this escapes the fact that knowledge is created out of our social existence, as Marx has taught us. As Marx (1977) put it: "It is not the consciousness of men that determines their existence, but their social existence that determines their consciousness." Denying the centrality of the basic forces and relations of production as iterated by Marx guarantees that postdigital capitalist formations will not make exploitation obsolete. Because it is very likely postdigital materialism will be devoid of the historical materialism of which Marx spoke, and instead will rewrite class in terms of some kind of subjectivizing role, a feature of subjective relations, a type of autonomous and self-generating autopoiesis. Does anybody think that dehierarchized technology will be able to hide the ideological dimension? And do you think that by drawing attention to this dilemma in the lecture hall, you will be contributing to building a new world? Do you think you can outsmart your techno-mediated brain by fetishizing, libidinalizing, and ideologically weaponizing your postdigital materialities? Do you think you can retreat into a Spinozean ethics of embodiment or escape into the "structures of feeling" arguments introduced decades ago by the Birmingham Center for Contemporary Cultural Studies? Sorry, nostalgia will not help in this case. The disavowed other of class exploitation, of settler colonialism, will now be dressed in a new mask. Whether it takes the form of steampunk goggles of brass and leather, or whether it's made from new sheets of artificial skin used to cover your favorite tattoo, or from a cluster of singularities orbiting a vortex, it still ignores the reality that social being determines consciousness, as Marx would put it, and not the other way around. This is akin to trying to immanentize the postdigital eschaton, as if the digital in some kind of sublated residue belonging to a newly discovered postdigital ur-force of incommensurable power suddenly becomes the object of our focus. So you think you can expunge contradictions between labor and capital and ditch the historical totality of capitalist social relations by rewriting the binary logic of history with some new rhizomatic discourse hidden in the metaphors of biology? Hats off to the technoculture gurus moving from astrophysics to the genetic code. But you are still mystifying technology as an affectively autonomous force, as the impersonal inscription of human flesh in a new codex spawned from an imaginary space that will prevent us from recognizing that the causes of human suffering are embedded in the socioeconomic forces and relations that have produced us.

Will the quickening impulse of our technoadventurers, as they forage through the hinterlands of a postdigital milieu, tap into some subliminal reservoir of luminosity while sucking into their digitalized lungs the effulgence of our evolutionary splendor like some cosmic vape, or merely rebirth their interiority and be overcome by the mimetic power of some new designer identity, as if some divine power bequeathed to them a cosmic e-cigarette? Just try to imagine Bogart and Bacall with e-cigarettes dangling from their lips? So what is behind, in front of, or beside this quest for the postdigital world? A digitalized intoxication with what is outside our intelligible world? A form of techno-gluttony? A search for some unsullied, undivided essence with or without casting aside considerations of evidential quality? Does it all boil down to a new search for a theory of mind? Does the brain produce mind or does the brain permit various expressions of mind? Are we not returning to the age-old question of whether or not consciousness preexists the brain? Are we not on a quest to break down further the boundaries of the supraliminal, subliminal, subjective, and objective? Before we decide which visual systems dominate, who has epistemic access to various cosmovisions, what causes the disparities between various psychological processes, or which populations of our collective neurons are privileged over others and under what conditions, we need to make sure the human population receives enough food and medical care.

US fascism, as Carl Boggs (2018) notes, feeds upon the seamless merger of total administration (or what we call totalitarianism or a rationalized domination of the masses), a process that is generated and protected by the technological rationality that is endemic to new forms of capitalism such as the move from global capitalism to transnational capitalism, and which serves to legitimate reactionary populist ultranationalism, the rise of white male evangelical and testosterone-driven Christian warriors in the thrall of a frenzied messianism and ready to defeat the Muslim hordes, the criminalization of abortion, the demonizing of gay, lesbian, and transgender youth, the proliferation of neoidentitarian movements, the rationalization of the warfare state, the militarization of the police, the atomizing of the public sphere, the steady expansion of the surveillance state, the defense at all costs of US superpower hegemony, militarized state capitalism, the creation of hundreds of military bases around the world that are the size of small cities, and the increasing power of the transnational corporate sector. Trump sits upon we, the people, as if we are his toilet. Only we are not gold-plated. Cannot you hear his bowels churn above our heads as he drops his putrefying nationalism, his moral manure, into the holes that Fox News, and Breitbart, and InfoWars have drilled into our heads? All of this has, of course, been enabled by his cult of personality that encourages millions of his followers who enjoy his lurid antics to pledge alliance to fascism: making fun of the disabled, grabbing women by their sex organs, condoning violence at his rallies, labeling immigrants as rapists and murderers, and supporting neo-Nazis as "very fine people." His penchant for lying blatantly about everything and anything has become normalized discourse now among the alt-right. This constellation of tyranny is succored by a society that retains the façade of liberal democracy with its systems of checks and balances. But this system of checks and balances is itself embedded in an ideology of political disengagement among the masses, insinuated into a technological society that distracts the population with a politics of political disingenuousness, with weapons of mass distraction, and with surfeit of choices that enables us to entertain ourselves to death. If digital technologies have provided new affordances for dialogue, what will postdigital dialogue (Jandrić et al. 2019) look like and what sociotechnical imaginaries will power them? What will postdigital reason look like? Will materialism, as Marx imagined it, be erased by a new postdigital ideological front for matterism, in the same way that poststructuralism eclipsed social forces and relations of production with an emphasis on culture and experience, obscuring and maintaining systemic class inequality and exploitation? These are the questions that must guide us as we make our way tremulously into the postdigital era.

Critical pedagogy in the postdigital age needs to serve more than a balm for bondage but as a light pointing past the limit situation of capitalism, toward the future as an untested feasibility (to coin Freire), where socialism is allowed to materialize in the hearts and minds of the people (and not simply remain looped into their computer hard drives) so that it can become coterminous with the revolutionary dialectics of economic transformation and collective governance. If you think I'm giving a more souped-up version of bringing heart and head together after technology has digitally unzipped them, you would not be wrong. But you wouldn't be getting the full picture. That requires not just a Christology from above, or from below, but from the inside. That is, after all, where the universe resides—in our guts.

Afterword

After All the Words: Faith and Action

Michael Adrian Peters

Revolutionary critical pedagogy reflects the intellectual and emotional impetus for all individuals on the planet to grasp in economic, cultural, and political terms, the downward slide of a system of capitalism that has become ever more reified, abstract, and formal so that people's lives and livelihoods can be washed away in the new algorithms without disturbing anything in the one-percent first world where ownership is regarded as a right. The now soon-to-be trillion-dollar Big Tech corporations in the United States constitute large logicosemiotic systems that seek to integrate everyone into the circuitry, to use our personal data freely, and to labor ceaselessly as users to participate in the digital process where we willingly surrender our agency, our humanity, and our souls.

This is one reason why the McLaren and Jandrić dialogues serve such a crucial purpose: to change our conditions of existence, away from impending serfdom, digital cloning, and ecological disaster.

Peter McLaren and Petar Jandrić, who have been friends and colleagues now for some years, have accomplished nothing less than revolutionizing the tradition of critical pedagogy as we have come to know and appreciate through the years. They have accomplished this through their further engagement with liberation theology and its humanist Christology—a distinctive element refined by Peter—in an age dominated by digital technology (a terrain well traversed by Petar in a variety of publications). But more than a mere cobbling together of themes, which at first blush may seem mutually excluding, such elements have been woven together, often in gleaming poetic cadences, through the personal narratives of the authors.

The synergy between McLaren and Jandrić has produced a set of dialogues that are rife with iconoclastic insights into our present human predicament. It bravely and brazenly demonstrates how dialectical materialism and Christian spirituality offer an immense reservoir of resources, strategies, and tactical initiatives against contemporary capitalism's politics of exploitation.

This is an unusual book, given its thematic content and the breathtaking range of theoretical insights brought to bear on planet Earth's history of human carnage. But it is also a hopeful and a distinctive treatise that combines humanist philosophies and theologies in an age of digital capitalism at a period in our history when the digital seems all-encompassing, all-powerful, and all-knowing. In a system of contemporary digital capitalism that rents our spirituality, and tracks and hacks our bodies and mind, taking the place of god, McLaren and Jandrić make room for a spiritual humanism, or a humanism that is based in both Marx and Christianity. There will be many readers who will take heart at this marriage, a path already well traveled by Freire, liberation theologists in Latin American, and Black liberation theologists in the United States, but a path creatively reconsidered by these authors in an age made increasingly forbidding by the rise of authoritarian populism and fascism.

McLaren and Jandrić's new dialogical work gives hope but also direction—also an action agenda, a form of resistance, a humanist politics, that revolutionary critical pedagogy infused by a postdigital science and theology from below offers us a way of reclaiming the present. It is a book designed to read the word and the world by drawing together disciplinary knowledges that up to the present time have not yet been considered together. This makes it a book not only of these times but for these times.

References

Aarons, M., & Loftus, J. (1998). *Unholy Trinity: The Vatican, the Nazis and the Swiss Banks*. New York: St. Martin's Griffin.

Adorno, T. W., Frenkel-Brunswik, E., Levinson, D. J., & Sanford, R. N. (1950). *The Authoritarian Personality*. New York: Harper and Row.

Alexander, M. (2010). *The New Jim Crow: Mass Incarceration in the Age of Colorblindness*. New York and London: The New Press.

Allman, P. (1999). *Revolutionary Social Transformation: Democratic Hopes, Radical Possibilities and Critical Education*. Westport, CT: Bergin & Garvey.

Allman P. (2001). *Critical Education against Global Capitalism: Karl Marx and Revolutionary Critical Education*. Westport, CT: Bergin & Garvey.

Althusser, L. (2008). *On Ideology*. London: Verso.

Ames, M. (2010). Ayn Rand, hugely popular author and inspiration to right-wing leaders, was a big admirer of serial killer. *AlterNet*, February. https://www.alternet.org/story/145819/ayn_rand%2C_hugely_popular_author_and_inspiration_to_right-wing_leaders%2C_was_a_big_admirer_of_serial_killer. Accessed May 14, 2019.

Anderson, A. H. (2019). Pentecostalism and social, political and economic development. Unpublished paper delivered at the Pentecostal Pastors' Conference, Stockholm, Sweden, 9 January. https://www.academia.edu/38124371/Pentecostalism_Sociopolitical_Engagement_and_Development. Accessed May 14, 2019.

Anderson, K. (2010). Overcoming some current challenges to dialectical thought. *International Marxist-Humanist*, 18 August. http://www.internationalmarxisthumanist.org/wp-content/uploads/pdf/anderson-overcoming-some-current-challenges-to-dialectical-thought-20100818.pdf. Accessed May 14, 2019.

Anger, K. (1963). *Scorpio Rising* [Motion picture]. New York: Puck Film Productions.

Araujo Freire, A. M. (2000). Foreword. In P. McLaren, *Che Guevara, Paulo Freire, and the Pedagogy of Revolution* (pp. xii–xvii). Lanham, MD: Rowman & Littlefield.

Arndt, S., Asher, G., Knox, J., Ford, D. R., Hayes, S., Lăzăroiu, G., Jackson, L., Mañero Contreras, J., Buchanan, R., D'Olimpio, L., Smith, M., Suoranta, J., Pyyhtinen, O., Ryberg, T., Davidsen, J., Steketee, A., Mihăilă, R., Stewart, G., Dawson, M., Sinclair, C., & Peters, M. A. (2019). Between the blabbering noise of individuals or the silent dialogue of many: A collective response to 'postdigital science and education' (Jandrić et al. 2018). *Postdigital Science and Education*, 1(2), 446–74. https://doi.org/10.1007/s42438-019-00037-y.

Assange, J., Appelbaum, J., Müller-Maguhn, A., & Zimmermann, J. (2012). *Cypherpunks: Freedom and the Future of the Internet*. New York: OR Books.

Atasay, E. (2013). Ivan Illich and the study of everyday life. *The International Journal of Illich Studies*, 3(1), 57–78.

Atkin, E. (2014). TransCanada buys town's silence on tar sands pipeline proposal for $28K. *Nation of Change*, 7 July. https://thinkprogress.org/transcanada-buys-towns-silence-on-tar-sands-pipeline-proposal-for-28k-4a59cf2bbd97/. Accessed May 14, 2019.

Atwood, M. (1986). *The Handmaid's Tale*. Boston, MA: Houghton Mifflin Harcourt.

AVPC (2016). Home. http://avpc.tvz.hr/welcome/. Accessed May 14, 2019.

Azarian, B. (2018). This complete psychological analysis reveals 14 key traits that explain Trump supporters. *RawStory*, 12 November. https://www.rawstory.com/2018/11/complete-psychological-analysis-reveals-14-key-traits-explain-trump-supporters/. Accessed May 14, 2019.

Badash, D. (2019). Priest who urged women to cover their shoulders to protect men's 'purity' calls Twitter 'demonic'—wipes account. *RawStory*, 10 June. https://www.rawstory.com/2019/06/priest-who-urged-women-to-cover-their-shoulders-to-protect-mens-purity-calls-twitter-demonic-wipes-account/. Accessed May 14, 2019.

Bailie, G. (2016). *God's Gamble: The Gravitational Power of Crucified Love*. New York: Angelico Press.

Barbrook, R. (2014). *Class Wargames: Ludic Subversion against Spectacular Capitalism*. Wivenhoe, New York, Port Watson: Minor Compositions.

Barbrook, R., & Cameron, A. (1996). The Californian ideology. *Science as Culture*, 6(1), 44–72.

Battles, M. (2011). *The Sovereignties of Invention*. Brooklyn, NY: Red Lemonade.

Bauman, Z. (2007). *Liquid Modernity*. Cambridge, MA: Polity Press.

Bauman, Z. (2012). *Liquid Times*. Cambridge, MA: Polity Press.

Bayne, S., & Ross, J. (2011). 'Digital native' and 'digital immigrant' discourses: A critique. In R. Land & S. Bayne (Eds.), *Digital Difference: Perspectives on Online Learning* (pp. 159–69). Rotterdam: Sense. https://doi.org/10.1007/978-94-6091-580-2_12.

Bensaid, D. (2002). *Marx for Our Times: Adventures and Misadventures of a Critique*. London: Verso.

Best, S., Kahn, R., Nocella, A. J., & McLaren, P. (Eds.) (2011). *The Global Industrial Complex: Systems of Domination*. Lanham, MD: Lexington Books, Rowman & Littlefield.

Bird, S. E. (2009). The future of journalism in the digital environment. *Journalism*, 10(3), 293–95. https://doi.org/10.1177/1464884909102583.

Black, D. (Ed.) (2014). *Helen MacFarlane: Red Republican: Essays, Articles and Her Translation of the Communist Manifesto*. London: Uncant Publishers.

Blake, W. (1966). *Blake: Complete Writings*. Edited by Geoffrey Keynes. Oxford: Oxford University Press.

Bloch, E. (1961) [1986]. *Natural Law and Human Dignity*. Cambridge, MA: MIT Press.

BlueServo (2019). Home. http://www.blueservo.com/vcw.php. Accessed May 14, 2019.

Boal, A. (2008). *Theatre of the Oppressed (Get Political)*. London: Pluto.

Boff, L. (1982). *Francis of Assisi: A Model of Human Liberation*. Translated by J. W. Diercksmeier. Maryknoll, NY: Orbis Books.

Boff, L. (1986). *Ecclesiogenesis: The Base Communities Reinvent the Church*. Maryknoll, NY: Orbis Books.

Boff, L. (1987). *Passion of Christ, Passion of the World: The Facts, Their Interpretation and Their Meaning Yesterday and Today*. Translated by Barr R. Maryknoll, NY: Orbis Books.

Boff, L. (1997). *Cry of the Earth, Cry of the Poor*. Translated by Philip Berryman. Maryknoll, New York: Orbis Books.

Boggs, C. (2018). *Fascism Old and New: American Politics at the Crossroads*. London and New York: Routledge.

Bojesen, E. (2017). Special Issue: Pedagogies of Insurrection. *Policy Futures in Education*, 15(5).

Bowers, C. A. (2014). Writings on education, eco-justice, and revitalizing the commons. http://www.cabowers.net/. Accessed May 14, 2019.

Brown, C. (1987). Literacy in 30 hours: Paulo Freire's process in Northeast Brazil. In I. Shor (Ed.), *Freire for the Classroom: A Sourcebook for Liberatory Teaching* (pp. 215–31). Portsmouth, NH: Boynton/Cook.

Buchheit, P. (2015). Our Ayn Randian dystopia: Here's the secret five-step plan to privatize everything. *RawStory*, 1 December. https://www.rawstory.com/2015/12/our-ayn-randian-dystopia-heres-the-secret-five-step-plan-to-privatize-everything/. Accessed May 14, 2019.

Burris, S. (2016). Donald Trump's 'spiritual advisor' sells eternal life for $1,144 by stealing from Harry Potter. *RawStory*, 11 July. https://www.rawstory.com/2016/07/donald-trumps-spiritual-advisor-sells-eternal-life-for-1144-by-stealing-from-harry-potter/. Accessed July 10, 2019.

Burris, S. (2019). Trump's personal pastor thinks everywhere she stands is sanctioned as holy—including the White House. *RawStory*, 8 July. https://www.rawstory.com/2019/07/trumps-personal-pastor-thinks-everywhere-she-stands-is-sanctioned-as-holy-including-the-white-house/. Accessed July 10, 2019.

Butt, R. (2009). Pope claims condoms could make African Aids crisis worse. *The Guardian*, 17 March. https://www.theguardian.com/world/2009/mar/17/pope-africa-condoms-aids. Accessed May 14, 2019.

Câmara, D. H. (2009). *Dom Hélder Câmara: Essential Writings*. Maryknoll, NY: Orbis Books.

Čapek, K. (2001) [1920]. *R.U.R. (Rossum's Universal Robots)*. New York: Dover.

Carr, N. (2011). *The Shallows: What the Internet Is Doing to Our Brains*. New York: W. W. Norton.

Cascone, K. (2000). The aesthetics of failure: 'Post-digital' tendencies in contemporary computer music. *Computer Music Journal*, 24(4), 12–18. 10.1162/014892600559489.

Castells, M. (2001). *The Internet Galaxy: Reflections on the Internet, Business, and Society*. Oxford: Oxford University Press.

Chalmers, D. J. (1995). Facing up to the problem of consciousness. *Journal of Consciousness Studies*, 2(3), 200–19. 10.1093/acprof:oso/9780195311105.001.0001.

Chaudary, A. (2007). On religion and politics: Noam Chomsky interviewed by Amina Chaudary. *Islamica Magazine*, 19 (April–May). https://chomsky.info/200704__/. Accessed May 14, 2019.

Chomsky, N. (2017). The end of history. https://youtu.be/Vg3gOFWfpck. Accessed May 14, 2019.

Christina, G. (2019). 7 ideas completely lost on people who are 'fiscally conservative but socially liberal'. *RawStory*, 21 January. https://www.alternet.org/2019/01/7-things-people-who-are-fiscally-conservative-but-socially-liberal-dont-understand/. Accessed May 14, 2019.

Collier, A. (2001). *Christianity and Marxism: A Philosophical Contribution to their Reconciliation*. London: Routledge.

Coltrane, J. (1965). A love supreme. https://youtu.be/ll3CMgiUPuU. Accessed May 14, 2019.

Cone, J. H. (2010). *A Black Theology of Liberation*. Maryknoll, NY: Orbis Books.

Cormier, D., Jandrić, P., Childs, M., Hall, R., White, D., Phipps, L., Truelove, I., Hayes, S., & Fawns, T. (2019). Ten Years of the Postdigital in the 52group: Reflections and developments 2009–2019. *Postdigital Science and Education*, 1(2), 475–506. https://doi.org/10.1007/s42438-019-00049-8.

Cornell University Media Relations Office (2014). Media statement on Cornell University's role in Facebook 'emotional contagion' research, June 30, 2014. http://mediarelations.cornell.edu/2014/06/30/media-statement-on-cornell-universitys-role-in-facebook-emotional-contagion-research/. Accessed May 14, 2019.

Cotter, J., DeFazio, K., Faivre, R., Sahay, A., Torrant, J. P., Tumino, S., & Wilkie, R. (2016). The 'event-al' logic of disaster and 'left' extinctionism. In J. Cotter, K. DeFazio, R. Faivre, A. Sahay, J. P. Torrant, S. Tumino, & R. Wilkie (Eds.), *Human, All Too (Post) Human: The Humanities After Humanism* (pp. 223–36). Lanham, London and New York: Lexington Books.

Couldry, N. (2010). *Why Voice Matters: Culture and Politics after Neoliberalism*. London: Sage.

Culkin, J. M. (1967). A schoolman's guide to Marshall McLuhan. *The Saturday Review*, 51–53, 70–72.

Cymet, D. (2011). *History vs. Apologetics: The Holocaust, the Third Reich, and the Catholic Church*. Minneapolis, MN: Lexington.

Dalea, R., & Robertson, S. (2004). Interview with Boaventura de Sousa Santos. *Globalisation, Societies and Education*, 2(2), 147–60. https://doi.org/10.1080/14767720410001733629.

Davis, C. (2015). An interview with a revolutionary, Professor Peter McLaren. *Huffington Post*, 3 August. https://www.huffingtonpost.com/creston-davis/an-interview-with-a-revol_b_6825766.html. Accessed May 14, 2019.

De La Torre, M. (2015). *The Politics of Jesús: A Hispanic Political Theology*. Lanham: Rowman and Littlefield.

Dean, J., Medak, T., & Jandrić, P. (2019). Embrace the Antagonism, Build the Party! The New Communist Horizon in and Against Communicative Capitalism. *Postdigital Science and Education*, 1(1), 218–35. https://doi.org/10.1007/s42438-018-0006-7.

Dear, J. (2006). Ita, Maura, Dorothy and Jean. *National Catholic Reporter*, 5 December. https://www.ncronline.org/blogs/road-peace/ita-maura-dorothy-and-jean. Accessed May 14, 2019.

Debord, G. (1994) [1967]. *The Society of the Spectacle*, Translated by Donald Nicholson-Smith. New York: Zone Books.

Duchrow, U. (1999). Europe and global economic justice. In: A. Morton & J. Francis (Eds.), *A Europe of Neighbors? Religious Social Thought and the Reshaping of a Pluralist Europe* (pp. 125–40). Edinburgh: The University of Edinburgh.

Duigan, J. (1989). *Romero* [Motion picture]. Los Angeles: Warner Bros.

Dunayevskaya, R. (1958). *Marxism and Freedom: from 1776 Until Today*. New York: Bookman Associates.

Dunayevskaya, R. (1978). *Marx's 'Capital' and Today's Global Crisis*. Detroit, MI: News & Letters.

Eagleton, T. (2009). *Reason, Faith and Revolution: Reflections on the God Debate*. New Haven, CT and London: Yale University Press.

Ellacuría, I. & Sobrino, J. (Eds.) (1993). *Mysterium Liberationis: Fundamental Concepts of Liberation Theology*. Maryknoll, NY: Orbis Books.

Ellul, J. (1964). *The Technological Society*. New York: Random House.

Encyclopaedia Britannica (2019). Complementarity principle. https://www.britannica. com/science/complementarity-principle. Accessed May 14, 2019.

Eryaman, M. (Ed.) (2009). *Peter McLaren, Education, and the Struggle for Liberation*. New York, NY: Hampton Press.

Escaño, C. (2019). Biopolitical commons in the postdigital era. *Postdigital Science and Education*, 1(2), 298–302. https://doi.org/10.1007/s42438-019-00041-2.

Etelson, E. (2014). Is modern technology killing us? *Truthout*, 19 September. http://www. truth-out.org/opinion/item/26295-is-modern-technology-killing-us. Accessed May 14, 2019.

Evans, T. L. (2012). *Occupy Education: Learning and Living Sustainability*. New York: Peter Lang.

Fanon, F. (2001). *The Wretched of the Earth*. London: Penguin.

Fassbinder, S. (2008). Capitalist discipline and ecological discipline. *Green Theory and Praxis*, 4(2), 87–101.

Fassbinder, S. C., & McLaren, P. (2006). The 'dirty thirty's' Peter McLaren reflects on the crisis of academic freedom. *MRonline*, 6 April. https://mronline.org/2006/04/06/the-dirty-thirtys-peter-mclaren-reflects-on-the-crisis-of-academic-freedom/. Accessed May 14, 2019.

Fawns, T. (2019). Postdigital education in design and practice. *Postdigital Science and Education*, 1(1), 132–45. https://doi.org/10.1007/s42438-018-0021-8.

Feenberg, A. (1991). *Critical Theory of Technology*. New York: Oxford University Press.

Feenberg, A. (2019). Postdigital or predigital? *Postdigital Science and Education*, 1(1), 8–9. https://doi.org/10.1007/s42438-018-0027-2.

Fejes, A., & Nicoll, K. (2008). *Foucault and Lifelong Learning: Governing the Subject*. London: Routledge.

Fischman, G., Sunker, H., Lankshear, C., & McLaren, P. (Eds.) (2005). *Critical Theories, Radical Pedagogies, and Global Conflicts*. Boulder, CO: Rowman & Littlefield.

Fisher, M. (2010). *Capitalist Realism: Is There No Alternative?*. Winchester: Zero Books.

Ford, D. R. (2016). Review of Peter McLaren (2015) Pedagogy of insurrection: From resurrection to revolution. *Texas Education Review*. https://review.education.utexas. edu/wp-content/uploads/2016/04/Ford_Final_pedagogy-of-insurrection-review:4-14. pdf. Accessed May 14, 2019.

Ford, D. R., & Jandrić, P. (2019). The public intellectual is dead, long live the public intellectual! The postdigital rebirth of public pedagogy. *Critical Questions in Education*, 10(2), 92–106.

Foucault, M. (1995). *Discipline and Punish: The Birth of the Prison*. New York: Vintage.

Freeman, M. (1998). Mythical time, historical time, and narrative fabric of the self. *Narrative Inquiry*, 8(1), 27–50. https://doi.org/10.1075/ni.8.1.03fre.

Freire, P. (1970). *Cultural Action for Freedom*. Cambridge, MA: Harvard Educational Review.

Freire, P. (1972). *Pedagogy of the Oppressed*. Harmondsworth: Penguin Education Specials.

Freire, P. (1973). Education, liberation and the Church. *Study Encounter*, 9(1): 1–16.

Freire, P. (1978). *Pedagogy in Process: Letters to Guinea-Bissau*. New York: The Seabury Press.

Freire, P. (1995). Preface. In P. McLaren (Ed.), *Critical Pedagogy and Predatory Culture* (pp. ix–xi). London: Routledge.

Fuller, S., & Jandrić, P. (2019). The postdigital human: Making the history of the future. *Postdigital Science and Education*, 1(1), 190–217. https://doi.org/10.1007/s42438-018-0003-x.

Gadotti, M. (1994). *Reading Paulo Freire: His Life and Work*. Albany, NY: State University of New York Press.

Girard, R. (1978). *Things Hidden Since the Foundation of the World*. Translated by Stephen Bann and Michael Metteer. Stanford, CA: Stanford University Press.

Girard, R. (1986). *The Scapegoat*. Translated by Yvonne Freccero. Baltimore: The Johns Hopkins Press.

Girard, R. (1996). *The Girard Reader*. Edited by James G. Williams. New York: The Crossroad Publishing Company.

Girard, R. (2001). *I See Satan Fall Like Lightning*. Translated with a Foreword by James G. Williams. Maryknoll, NY: Orbis Books.

Giroux, H. (1999). Preface. In P. McLaren, *Schooling as a Ritual Performance: Toward a Political Economy of Educational Symbols and Gestures* (3rd ed., pp. ix–xiv). Lanham, MD: Rowman and Littlefield.

Giroux, H. A., & McLaren, P. (Eds.) (1989). *Critical Pedagogy, the State, and Cultural Struggle*. Albany, NY: SUNY Press.

Giroux, H. A., & McLaren, P. (Eds.) (1994). *Between Borders: Pedagogy and the Politics of Cultural Studies*. New York, NY: Routledge.

Goodman, P. (1973). *Compulsory Miseducation*. Harmondsworth: Penguin Education Specials.

Gorin, J. (2010). Mass grave of history: Vatican's WWII identity crisis. *The Jerusalem Post*, 22 February. http://www.jpost.com/Features/In-Thespotlight/Mass-grave-of-history-Vaticans-WWII-identity-crisis. Accessed May 14, 2019.

Green, E. (2016). What are the most-cited publications in the social sciences (according to Google Scholar)? http://blogs.lse.ac.uk/impactofsocialscien ces/2016/05/12/what-are-the-most-cited-publications-in-the-social-sciences-accor ding-to-google-scholar/. Accessed May 14, 2019.

Grosfoguel, R. (2008). Transmodernity, border thinking, and global coloniality. *Eurozine*. http://www.eurozine.com/pdf/20080704-grosfoguel-en.pdf. Accessed May 14, 2019.

Gutiérrez, G. (1988). *A Theology of Liberation: History, Politics, and Salvation*. Translated by C. Inda and J. Eagleson. Maryknoll, NY: Orbis Books.

Habermas, J. (1970). *Towards a Rational Society*. Boston: Beacon Press.

Habermas, J., & Ratzinger, J. (2005). *Dialektik der Säkularisierung: über Vernunft und Religion*. Freiburg: Herder.

Haraway, D. (1991) [1985]. *Simians, Cyborgs, and Women: The Reinvention of Nature*. New York: Routledge.

Harcourt, B. E. (2015). *Desire and Disobedience in the Digital Age*. Cambridge, MA: Harvard University Press.

Hardt, M., & Negri, A. (2001). *Empire*. Cambridge, MA: Harvard University Press.

Harron, M. (2000). *American Psycho* [Motion picture]. Vancouver: Lions Gate Films.

Hart, I. (2001). Deschooling and the Web: Ivan Illich 30 years on. *Educational Media International*, 38(2–3), 69–76. https://doi.org/10.1080/09523980110041449a.

Harvey, D. (1990). *The Condition of Postmodernity: An Enquiry into the Origins of Cultural Change*. Cambridge, MA: Blackwell.

Hayek, F. (1948). *Individualism and Economic Order*. London: Routledge.

Hayes, S. (2018). Learning in the age of digital reason, Petar Jandrić. *Policy Futures in Education*, 16(3), 372–74. https://doi.org/10.1177/1478210317736436.

Hayes, S. (2018). Widening participation and social mobility applies to university staff as well as students. *WONKHE*. https://wonkhe.com/blogs/widening-participation-and-social-mobility-applies-to- university-staff-as-well-as-students. Accessed May 14, 2019.

Hayes, S. (2019). *The Labour of Words in Higher Education: Is It Time to Reoccupy Policy?* Leiden: Brill Sense.

Hayes, S., & Jandrić, P. (2014). Who is really in charge of contemporary education? People and technologies in, against and beyond the neoliberal university. *Open Review of Educational Research*, 1(1), 193–210. https://doi.org/10.1080/23265507.2014.989899.

Hedges, C. (2018a). *America: The Farewell Tour*. New York: Simon & Schuster.

Hedges, C. (2018b). Neoliberalism's Dark Path to Fascism. *Truthdig*. 26 November. https://www.truthdig.com/articles/neoliberalisms-dark-path-to-fascism/. Accessed May 14, 2019.

Heidegger, M. (1977). *The Question Concerning Technology and Other Essays*. New York: Garland.

Heisenberg, W. (1973). Naturwissenschaftliche und religioese Wahrheit. Frankfurter Allgemeine Zeitung, 24 March, pp. 7–8. (Speech before the Catholic Academy of Bavaria, on acceptance of the Guardini Prize, March, 23 1974).

Heisenberg, W. (1974). *Across the Frontiers*. New York: Harper & Row.

Henkin, D. (2006). *The Postal Age: The Emergence of Modern Communications in Nineteenth-Century America*. Chicago: The University of Chicago Press.

Herman, E., & Chomsky, N. (1988). *Manufacturing Consent*. New York: Pantheon.

Hern, M. (1998). *Deschooling Our Lives*. Philadelphia: New Society.

Herzog, W. (1994). *Parables as Subversive Speech: Jesus as Pedagogue of the Oppressed*. Louisville: Westminster John Knox Press.

Hill, D., McLaren, P., Cole, M., & Rikowski, G. (Eds.) (2002). *Marxism against Postmodernism in Educational Theory*. Lanham, MD: Lexington Books, Rowman & Littlefield.

Hinnem, N. (2013). Marx and the Bible. *The Oxford Left Review*, 11, 31–37.

Holland, J. (2018). Ayn Rand raged against government benefits—but grabbed Social Security and Medicare when she needed them. *RawStory*, 25 November. https://www.rawstory.com/2018/11/ayn-rand-raged-government-benefits-grabbed-social-security-medicare-needed/. Accessed April 1, 2019.

Holloway, J. (2016). *In, Against, and Beyond Capitalism: The San Francisco Lectures*. Oakland, CA: PM Press/Kairos.

Holst, J. D. (2002). *Social Movements, Civil Society, and Radical Adult Education*. Westport, CT: Praeger.

Hrastinski, S., Olofsson, A. D., Arkenback, C., Ekström, S., Ericsson, E., Fransson, G., Jaldemark, J., Ryberg, T., Öberg, L.-M., Fuentes, A., Gustafsson, U., Humble, N., Mozelius, P., Sundgren, M., & Utterberg, M. (2019). Critical Imaginaries and Reflections on Artificial Intelligence and Robots in Postdigital K-12 Education. *Postdigital Science and Education*, 1(2), 427–45. https://doi.org/10.1007/s42438-019-00046-x.

Hudis, P. (2000a). The dialectical structure of Marx's concept of "revolution in permanence." *Capital & Class*, 24(1), 127–43. https://doi.org/10.1177/030981680007000106.

Hudis, P. (2000b). Can capital be controlled? *News & Letters*. http://newsandletters.org/4.00_essay.htm. Accessed May 14, 2019.

Hudis, P. (2012). *Marx's Concept of the Alternative to Capitalism.* Leiden and Boston: Brill.

Hudis, P. (2015). *Frantz Fanon: Philosopher of the Barricades.* London: Pluto.

Hunt, T. (2018). Consciousness might be a result of basic physics, say researchers. *The Conversation*, 10 November. https://www.sciencealert.com/consciousness-could-all-come-down-to-the-way-things-vibrate. Accessed May 14, 2019.

Huxley, A. (1932). *Brave New World.* London: Penguin.

Illich, I. (1971). *Deschooling Society.* London: Marion Boyars.

Illich, I. (1973). *Tools for Conviviality.* London: Marion Boyars.

Illich, I. (1982). *Medical Nemesis: The Expropriation of Health.* New York: Pantheon.

Industrial Workers of the World (1916). *Industrial Workers of the World Songs or "The Little Red Songbook."* London: W. Oliver. http://www.musicanet.org/robokopp/iww.html. Accessed April 15, 2019.

International Journal of Educational Reform (2001). Special Issue: The Revolutionary Pedagogy of Peter McLaren. *International Journal of Educational Reform*, 10(2).

International Marxist-Humanist Organization (2019) Main Page. http://www.internationalmarxisthumanist.org/. Accessed May 14, 2019.

Isacson, A., & Olson, J. (1999). *Just the Facts: A Civilian's Guide to U.S. Defense and Security Assistance to Latin America and the Carribean.* Washington DC: Latin American Working Group.

Jandrić, P. (2010). Wikipedia and education: Anarchist perspectives and virtual practices. *Journal for Critical Education Policy Studies*, 8(2), 48–73.

Jandrić, P. (2011). In and against radical monopoly: Critical education and information and communication technologies. *Problems of Education in the 21st Century*, 35(1), 70–84.

Jandrić, P. (2012). The question concerning anti-disciplinarity. In K. Štefančić (Ed.), *Eastern Surf: Kernel Panic Control* (pp. 108–19). Velika Gorica: The Open University of Velika Gorica.

Jandrić, P. (2013). Academic community in transition: Critical liberatory praxis in the network society. In T. Issa, P. Isaías, & P. Kommers (Eds.), *Information Systems and Technology for Organizations in a Networked Society* (pp. 88–106). Hershey, PA: Idea Group.

Jandrić, P. (2014a). Research methods are made by questioning: The postdisciplinary challenge of networked learning. In S. Bayne, C. Jones, M. de Laat, & T. Ryberg (Eds.), *Proceedings of the 9th International Conference on Networked Learning 2014* (pp. 162–69). Lancaster: University of Lancaster.

Jandrić, P. (2014b). Deschooling virtuality. *Open Review of Educational Research*, 1(1), 84–98. https://doi.org/10.1080/23265507.2014.965193.

Jandrić, P. (2015). Deschooling virtuality 2.0. *Concept*, 6(2), 1–10.

Jandrić, P. (2016). The methodological challenge of networked learning: (post) disciplinarity and critical emancipation. In T. Ryberg, C. Sinclair, S. Bayne, & M. de Laat (Eds.), *Research, Boundaries, and Policy in Networked Learning* (pp. 165–81). New York: Springer. https://doi.org/10.1007/978-3-319-31130-2_10.

Jandrić, P. (2017). *Learning in the Age of Digital Reason.* Rotterdam: Sense.

Jandrić, P. (2018a). Peter McLaren: Portrait of a revolutionary. *Rassegna Di Pedagogia*, 76(1–2), 139–58. https://doi.org/10.19272/201802102010.

Jandrić, P. (2018b). The challenge of the internationalist critical pedagogue. In McLaren, P. & Soohoo, S. (Eds.), *Radical Imagine-Nation: Public Pedagogy & Praxis.* New York: Peter Lang.

Jandrić, P. (2018c). Post-truth and critical pedagogy of trust. In M. A. Peters, S. Rider, M. Hyvönen, & Tina Besley (Eds.), *Post-Truth, Fake News: Viral Modernity & Higher Education* (pp. 101–11). Singapore: Springer. https://doi.org/10.1007/978-981-10-8013-5_8.

Jandrić, P. (2019a). The three ages of the digital. In D. R. Ford (Ed.), *Keywords in Radical Philosophy and Education* (pp. 161–76). Leiden: Brill/Sense. 10.1163/9789004400467_012.

Jandrić, P. (2019b). The postdigital challenge of critical media literacy. *The International Journal of Critical Media Literacy*, 1(1), 26–37. https://doi.org/10.1163/25900110-00101002.

Jandrić, P. (2019c). We-Think, We-Learn, We-Act: the Trialectic of Postdigital Collective Intelligence. *Postdigital Science and Education*, 1(2), 275–79. https://doi.org/10.1007/s42438-019-00055-w.

Jandrić, P. (forthcoming, 2020a). Critical consciousness against Armageddon: The end of capitalism vs. the end of time. *Educational Philosophy and Theory*.

Jandrić, P. (forthcoming, 2020b). The postdigital challenge of critical educational research. In R. L. Allen & C. Mathias (Eds.), *Critical Theoretical Research Methods in Education*. New York: Routledge.

Jandrić, P., & Boras, D. (2012). *Critical e-Learning: Struggle for Power and Meaning in the Network Society*. Zagreb: FF Press & Polytechnic of Zagreb.

Jandrić, P., & Boras, D. (Eds.) (2015). *Critical Learning in Digital Networks*. New York: Springer.

Jandrić, P., & Hayes, S. (2018). Who drives the drivers? Technology as ideology of global educational reform. In A. Means & K. Saltman (Eds.), *Handbook of Global Educational Reform* (pp. 307–22). Hoboken, NJ: Wiley Blackwell. https://doi.org/10.1002/9781119082316.ch15.

Jandrić, P., & Hayes, S. (2019). The postdigital challenge of redefining education from the margins. *Learning, Media and Technology*. https://doi.org/10.1080/17439884.2019.1585874.

Jandrić, P., & Hayes, S. (forthcoming, 2020). Postdigital we-learn. *Studies in Philosophy of Education*.

Jandrić, P., Knox, J., Besley, T., Ryberg, T., Suoranta, J., & Hayes, S. (2018). Postdigital science and education. *Educational Philosophy and Theory*, 50(10), 893–99. https://doi.org/10.1080/00131857.2018.1454000.

Jandrić, P., Knox, J., Macleod, H., & Sinclair, C. (2017). Special issue: Learning in the age of algorithmic cultures. *E-learning and Digital Media*, 14(3).

Jandrić, P., Ryberg, T., Knox, J., Lacković, N., Hayes, S., Suoranta, J., Smith, M., Steketee, A., Peters, M. A., McLaren, P., Ford, D. R., Asher, G., McGregor, C., Stewart, G., Williamson, B., & Gibbons, A. (2019). Postdigital dialogue. *Postdigital Science and Education*, 1(1), 163–89. https://doi.org/10.1007/s42438-018-0011-x.

Jandrić, P., Sinclair, C., & Macleod, H. (2015). Special issue: Networked realms and hoped-for futures: A trans-generational dialogue. *E-learning and Digital Media*, 12(3–4).

Johnson, E. A. (2002). *She Who Is: The Mystery of God in Feminist Theological Discourse*. New York: Crossroad.

Johnson, E. A. (2018). *Creation and the Cross: The Mercy of God for a Planet in Peril*. Maryknoll, NY: Orbis Books.

Johnson, S. (2019). White evangelicals are least likely to say U.S. should accept refugees. *The Washington Post*, 19 July. https://bigthink.com/culture-religion/evangelicals-immigration. Accessed May 14, 2019.

Johnston, J. (2003). Who cares about the commons? *Capitalism Nature Socialism*, 14(4), 1–42. http://dx.doi.org/10.1080/10455750308565544.

Kahn, R. (2010). *Critical Pedagogy, Ecoliteracy, and Planetary Crisis*. New York: Peter Lang.

Kahn, R., & Kellner, D. (2007). Paulo Freire and Ivan Illich: Technology, politics and the reconstruction of education. *Policy Futures in Education*, 5(4), 431–48. https://doi.org/10.2304/pfie.2007.5.4.431.

Kelly, E. F., Crabtree, A., & Marshall, P. (Eds.) (2015). *Beyond Physicalism: Toward Reconciliation of Science and Spirituality*. Lanham, MD: Rowman & Littlefield.

Kelly, E. F., Kelly, E. W., Crabtree, A., Gauld, A., Grosso, M., & Greyson, B. (2007). *Irreducible Mind: Toward a Psychology for the 21st Century*. Lanham, MD: Rowman & Littlefield.

Kincheloe, J. (2000). Foreword. In P. McLaren, *Che Guevara, Paulo Freire, and the Pedagogy of Revolution* (pp. ix–xii). Lanham, MD: Rowman & Littlefield.

King, M. L. (1963) [2003]. I have a dream. http://news.bbc.co.uk/2/hi/americas/3170387.stm. Accessed May 14, 2019.

Kirylo, J. D. (2011). *Paulo Freire: The Man from Recife*. New York: Peter Lang.

Knox, J. (2019a). Book review: Learning in the age of digital reason. *Educational Philosophy and Theory*, 51(1), 128–29. https://doi.org/10.1080/00131857.2017.1410475.

Knox, J. (2019b). What does the 'Postdigital' mean for education? Three critical perspectives on the digital, with implications for educational research and practice. *Postdigital Science and Education*, 1(2), 357–70. https://doi.org/10.1007/s42438-019-00045-y.

Knox, J. (2019c). Postdigital as (Re)Turn to the Political. *Postdigital Science and Education*, 1(2), 280–82. https://doi.org/10.1007/s42438-019-00058-7.

Kolhatkar, S. (2014). Orwell's Dystopian future is almost here: A conversation with Glenn Greenwald. *Truthdig*, 3 July. http://www.truthdig.com/report/print/orwells_dystopian_future_is_almost_here_a_conversation_20140703. Accessed May 14, 2019.

Kosinski, M., Stillwell, D., & Graepel, T. (2013). Private traits and attributes are predictable from digital records of human behavior. *Proceedings of the National Academy of Sciences* (PNAS). http://www.pnas.org/content/110/15/5802.full. Accessed May 14, 2019.

Kovalik, D. (2013). US still fighting 'threat' of liberation theology. *Counterpunch*, 5 March. http://www.counterpunch.org/2013/03/05/us-still-fighting-threat-of-liberation-theology/. Accessed May 14, 2019.

Kramer, A. D. I., Guillory, J. E., & Hancock, J. T. (2014). Experimental evidence of massive-scale emotional contagion through social networks. *Proceedings of the National Academy of Sciences of the United States of America*, 111(24), 8788–90. https://doi.org/10.1073/pnas.1320040111.

Lanier, J. (2011). *You Are Not a Gadget*. London: Penguin.

Lankshear, C., & McLaren, P. (Eds.) (1993). *Critical Literacy: Politics, Praxis, and the Postmodern*. Albany, NY: SUNY Press.

Lankshear, C. & McLaren, P. (1994). *Politics of Liberation: Paths from Freire*. London: Routledge.

László, E. (2008). *Quantum Shift in the Global Brain: How the New Scientific Reality Can Change Us and Our World*. Rochester and Vermont: Inner Traditions.

László, E. (2014). *The Self-actualizing Cosmos: The Akasha Revolution in Science and Human Consciousness*. Rochester, VT and Toronto: Inner Traditions.

Laughlin, C. D. (2011). *Communing with the Gods: Consciousness, Culture and the Dreaming Brain*. Brisbane, Australia: Daily Grail Publishing.

Laughlin, T. (1982). *Jungian Theory and Therapy*. Los Angeles: Panarion Press.

Lebacqz, K. (1986). *Six Theories of Justice: Perspectives from Philosophical and Theological Ethics*. Minneapolis, MN: Augsburg.

Leech, G. (2012). *Capitalism: A Structural Genocide*. London: Zed Books.

Leonard, P., & McLaren, P. (Eds.) (1993). *Paulo Freire: A Critical Encounter*. New York, NY: Routledge.

Levinson, P. (2019). Needed: a 'Post-Post' Formulation. *Postdigital Science and Education*, 1(1), 14–16. https://doi.org/10.1007/s42438-019-0031-1.

Lewis, T. E. (2019). Everything You Always Wanted to Know About Being Postdigital but Were Afraid to Ask a Vampire Squid. *Postdigital Science and Education*. https://doi. org/10.1007/s42438-019-00082-7.

Lowy, M. (1993). Why nationalism? *Socialist Register*, 29. https://socialistregister.com/ index.php/srv/article/view/5626. Accessed May 14, 2019.

MacCannell, D. (1984). Baltimore in the morning . . . after: On the forms of post-nuclear leadership. *Diacritics*, Summer, 33–46.

MacLeod, A. (2019). Noam Chomsky: The real election meddling isn't coming from Russia. *Truthdig*, 21 June. https://www.truthdig.com/articles/noam-chomsky-the-real-election-meddling-isnt-coming-from-russia/. Accessed October 14, 2019.

Macrine, S., McLaren, P., & Hill, D. (Eds.) (2009). *Revolutionizing Pedagogy: Education for Social Justice Within and Beyond Global Neo-Liberalism*. London: Palgrave Macmillan.

Malaparte, C. (1944) [2005]. *Kaputt*. New York: New York Review Books.

Malott, C. (2019). The Sublation of Digital Education. *Postdigital Science and Education*. https://doi.org/10.1007/s42438-019-00083-6.

Marcotte, A. (2018). Here's how philosophers of selfishness came to use christianity as their cover story. *RawStory*, 24 November. https://www.rawstory.com/2018/11/heres-philosophers-selfishness-came-use-christianity-cover-story/. Accessed May 14, 2019.

Marcuse, H. (1960). *Reason and Revolution*. Boston: Beacon Press.

Marcuse, H. (2011). The role of religion in a changing society. In D. Kellner & C. Pierce (Eds.), *Psychology, Psychoanalysis and Emancipation: Collected Papers of Herbert Marcuse, Volume 5* (pp. 182–88). Oxon and New York: Routledge.

Martin, G., Houston, D., McLaren, P., & Suoranta, J. (Eds.) (2010). *The Havoc of Capitalism: Publics, Pedagogies and Environmental Crisis*. Rotterdam: Sense.

Marx, K. (1955). *The Poverty of Philosophy—Answer to the Philosophy of Poverty by M. Proudhon*. Moscow: Progress.

Marx, K. (1970) [1843]. *Critique of Hegel's Philosophy of Right*. Translated by A. Jolin and J. O'Malley. Cambridge: Cambridge University Press.

Marx, K. (1976). Theses on Feuerbach. In Marx-Engels-Collected-Works (MECW), Volume 5. http://marxists.anu.edu.au/archive/marx/works/1845/theses/original.htm. Accessed May 14, 2019.

Marx, K. (1977). *A Contribution to the Critique of Political Economy*. Moscow: Progress Publishers.

Marx, K. (1981). *Capital, Vol. III*. New York: Vintage.

Marx, K., & Engels, F. (1848). The Communist Manifesto. https://www.marxists.org/ archive/marx/works/1848/communist-manifesto/index.htm. Accessed May 14, 2019.

Matias, C. E., & Aldern, J. (2019). (Un)Common White Sense: the Whiteness Behind Digital Media. *Postdigital Science and Education*. https://doi.org/10.1007/s42438-019-00076-5.

McDonald, F. (2019). The moon landings have a nazi problem. *RawStory*, 24 June. https:// www.rawstory.com/2019/06/the-moon-landings-have-a-nazi-problem/. Accessed July 14, 2019.

McKenna, B. (2013). The predatory pedagogy of online education. *Counterpunch*, 3 June. http://www.counterpunch.org/2013/06/03/the-predatorypedagogy-of-online-education/. Accessed May 14, 2019.

McLaren, P. (1980). *Cries from the Corridor*. London: Methuen.

McLaren, P. (1995). *Critical Pedagogy and Predatory Culture: Oppositional Politics in a Postmodern Era*. New York, NY: Routledge.

McLaren, P. (1997a). *Revolutionary Multiculturalism: Pedagogies of Dissent for the New Millennium*. Boulder, CO: Westview Press.

McLaren, P. (1997b). Paulo Freire's Legacy of Hope and Struggle. *Theory, Culture & Society*, 14(4), 147–53. https://doi.org/10.1177/026327697014004007.

McLaren, P. (1999). *Schooling as a Ritual Performance: Towards a Political Economy of Educational Symbols and Gestures*. Lanham, MD: Rowman & Littlefield.

McLaren, P. (2000). *Che Guevara, Paulo Freire, and the Pedagogy of Revolution*. Boulder, CO: Rowman & Littlefield.

McLaren, P. (2005a). *Capitalists and Conquerors: A Critical Pedagogy against Empire*. Lanham, MD: Rowman & Littlefield.

McLaren, P. (2005b). *Red Seminars: Radical Excursions into Educational Theory, Cultural Politics, and Pedagogy*. Cresskill, NJ: Hampton Press.

McLaren, P. (Ed.) (2006). *Rage and Hope: Interviews with Peter McLaren on War, Imperialism, and Critical Pedagogy*. New York: Peter Lang.

McLaren, P. (2013). Reflections on love and revolution. *International Journal of Critical Pedagogy*, 5(1), 60–68.

McLaren, P. (2015a). Self and social formation and the political project of teaching: Some reflections. In B. J. Porfilio and D. Ford, *Leaders in Critical Pedagogy: Narratives for Understanding and Solidarity* (pp. 127–40). Rotterdam: Sense.

McLaren, P. (2015b). *Pedagogy of Insurrection: From Resurrection to Revolution*. New York: Peter Lang.

McLaren, P. (2016). *Life in Schools: An Introduction to Critical Pedagogy in the Foundations of Education* (6th ed.). New York: Routledge.

McLaren, P. (2019b). *Breaking Free: The Life and Times of Peter McLaren, Radical Educator*. Illustrated by M. Wilson. Gorham, ME: Myers Education Press.

McLaren, P. (2019a). Reclaiming the present or a return to the ash heap of the Future? *Postdigital Science and Education*, 1(1), 10–13. https://doi.org/10.1007/s42438-018-0015-6.

McLaren, P. (2019b). God and governance: Reflections on living in the belly of the beast. *Postdigital Science and Education*, 2(1), 311–34. https://doi.org/10.1007/s42438-019-00050-1.

McLaren, P., & Farahmandpur, R. (2004). *Teaching against Global Capitalism and the New Imperialism: A Critical Pedagogy*. Lanham, MD: Rowman & Littlefield.

McLaren, P., & Fassbinder, S. (2013). His work, his visit to Turkey and ongoing popular struggles: Interview with Peter McLaren. *CounterPunch*, 11 June. http://truth-out.org/news/item/16903-his-work-his-visit-to-turkey-and-ongoing-popular-struggles-interview-with-peter-mclaren. Accessed May 14, 2019.

McLaren, P., Hammer, R., Sholle, D., & Reilly, S. (1995). *Rethinking Media Literacy: A Critical Pedagogy of Representation*. New York, NY: Peter Lang.

McLaren, P., & Jandrić, P. (2014a). Critical revolutionary pedagogy is made by walking—in a world where many worlds coexist. *Policy Futures in Education*, 12(6), 805–31. https://doi.org/10.2304/pfie.2014.12.6.805.

McLaren, P., & Jandrić, P. (2014b). Kultura borbe protiv neoliberalnog kapitalizma. *Zarez*, 398–99(16), 8–9.

McLaren, P., & Jandrić, P. (2015a). Critical revolutionary pedagogy in and for the age of the network. *Philosophy of Education*, 14(1), 106–26.

McLaren, P., & Jandrić, P. (2015b). Revolutionary critical pedagogy is made by walking— in a world where many worlds coexist. In P. McLaren, *Pedagogy of Insurrection: From Resurrection to Revolution* (pp. 255–98). New York: Peter Lang.

McLaren, P. & Jandrić, P. (2015c). The critical challenge of networked learning: Using information technologies in the service of humanity. In P. Jandrić & D. Boras (Eds.), *Critical Learning in Digital Networks* (pp. 199–226). New York: Springer. https://doi.org/10.1007/978-3-319-13752-0_10.

McLaren, P. & Jandrić, P. (2017a). Revolutionary critical pedagogy is made by walking—in a world where many worlds coexist. In P. Jandrić, *Learning in the Age of Digital Reason* (pp. 159–94). Rotterdam: Sense.

McLaren, P., & Jandrić, P. (2017b). From liberation to salvation: Revolutionary critical pedagogy meets liberation theology. *Policy Futures in Education*, 15(5), 620–52. https://doi.org/10.1177/1478210317695713.

McLaren, P., & Jandrić, P. (2018a). Karl Marx and liberation theology: Dialectical materialism and Christian spirituality in, against, and beyond contemporary capitalism. *TripleC: Communication, Capitalism & Critique*, 16(2), 598–607. https://doi.org/10.31269/triplec.v16i2.965.

McLaren, P., & Jandrić, P. (2018b). Peter McLaren's liberation theology: Karl Marx meets Jesus Christ. In J. S. Brooks and A. Normore (Eds.), *Leading Against the Grain: Lessons for Creating Just and Equitable Schools* (pp. 39–48). New York: Teachers College Press.

McLaren, P., & Jandrić, P. (2018c). Paulo Freire and liberation theology: The Christian consciousness of critical pedagogy. *Vierteljahresschrift für wissenschaftliche Pädagogik*, 94(2), 246–64. 10.30965/25890581-09402006.

McLaren, P., & Jandrić, P. (2019a). Revolutionary critical rage pedagogy. In M. F. He & W. Schubert (Eds.), *Oxford Encyclopedia of Curriculum Studies*. New York: Oxford University Press.

McLaren, P., & Jandrić, P. (2019b). Revolucionarna kritička pedagogija ostvaruje se u hodu: u svijetu gdje mnogi svjetovi supostoje. In P. Jandrić, *Znanje u digitalnom dobu. Razgovori s djecom jedne male revolucije*. Zagreb: Jesenski i Turk.

McLaren, P., & Jandrić, P. (2019c). Postdigital cross border reflections on critical utopia. *Educational Philosophy and Theory*.

McLaren, P. & Jandrić, P. (2019d). The fellowship of the crooked cross: Trump's evangelical hounds of hell. *Postdigital Science and Education*. https://doi.org/10.1007/s42438-019-00074-7.

McLaren, P., & Kincheloe, J. L. (Eds.) (2007). *Critical Pedagogy: Where Are We Now?*. New York, NY: Peter Lang.

McLaren, P., McMurry, A., & McGuirk, K. (2008). *An Interview with Peter McLaren*. Waterloo: University of Waterloo. http://english.uwaterloo.ca/PeterMcLareninterview.pdf. Accessed May 14, 2019.

McLaren, P., & Rikowski, G. (2001). Pedagogy for Revolution against Education for Capital: An e-dialogue on education in capitalism today. *Cultural Logic*, 4(1).

McLaren, P., & Smith, V. (2017). What unites us. https://blogs.chapman.edu/magazine/2017/03/15/what-unites-us/. Accessed May 14, 2019.

McLaren, P., & SooHoo, S. (Eds.) (2018). *Radical Imagine-Nation: Public Pedagogy & Praxis*. New York: Peter Lang.

McNally, D. (2001). *Bodies of Meaning: Studies on Language, Labor, and Liberation*. Albany, NY: State University of New York Press.

McSherry, J. P. (2005). *Predatory States: Operation Condor and Covert War in Latin America*. Lanham, MA: Rowman & Littlefield.

Mehdi, H. (2019). Deconstructed Special: The Noam Chomsky Interview. *The Intercept*, 31 October. https://theintercept.com/2019/10/31/deconstructed-special-the-noam-chomsky-interview/. Accessed November 4, 2019.

Miranda, J. P. (1974). *Marx and the Bible: A Critique of the Philosophy of Oppression*. Maryknoll, NY: Orbis Books; Oxon and New York: Routledge.

Miranda, J. P. (1977). *Being and the Messiah: The Message of St. John*. Maryknoll, NY: Orbis Books.

Miranda, J. P. (1980). *Marx against the Marxists: The Christian Humanism of Karl Marx*. Translated by J. Drury. Maryknoll, NY: Orbis Books.

Miranda, J. P. (2004). *Communism in the Bible*. Translated by R. R. Barr. Eugene, OR: Wipf & Stock.

Monahan, N., & Ahmed, S. (2019). There are now as many Americans who claim no religion as there are evangelicals and catholics. *CNN News*, 13 April. https://www.cnn.com/2019/04/13/us/no-religion-largest-group-first-time-usa-trnd/index.html. Accessed May 14, 2019.

Morozov, E. (2014) The rise of data and the death of politics. *The Observer*, 20 July. http://www.theguardian.com/technology/2014/jul/20/rise-of-data-death-of-politics-evgeny-morozov-algorithmic-regulation. Accessed May 14, 2019.

MRZine (2019). *Main Page*. New York: Monthly Review. http://mrzine.monthlyreview.org/. Accessed May 14, 2019.

Neary, M., & Rikowski, G. (2000). The speed of life: The significance of Karl Marx's concept of socially necessary labour-time. British Sociological Association Annual Conference 2000, 'Making Time - Marking Time'. York: University of York.

Negroponte, N. (1998). Beyond digital. *Wired*, 12 January. http://www.wired.com/wired/archive/6.12/negroponte.html. Accessed May 14, 2019.

Nelson, J. (1991). *The Perfect Machine: Television and the Bomb*. Toronto: New Society.

Nietzsche, F. (1882). *The Gay Science*. https://librivox.org/the-joyful-wisdom-by-friedrich-nietzsche/. Accessed May 14, 2019.

Noble, D. (2001). *Digital Diploma Mills: The Automation of Higher Education*. New York: Monthly Review Press.

Nocella, A., Best, S., & McLaren, P. (Eds.) (2010). *Academic Repression: Reflections from the Academic-Industrial Complex*. Oakland, CA: AK Press.

NORC at the University of Chicago (2019). General Social Survey. http://gss.norc.org/. Accessed May 14, 2019.

Orwell, G. (1949). *Nineteen Eighty-Four: A Novel*. London: Secker & Warburg.

Paris, E. (2011). *Genocide in Satellite Croatia, 1941–1945: A Record of Racial and Religious Persecutions and Massacres*. Whitefish, MT: Literary Licensing, LLC.

Pepperell, R., & Punt, M. (2000). *The Postdigital Membrane: Imagination, Technology and Desire*. Bristol: Intellect.

Peters, M. A., & Besley, T. (2019). Critical philosophy of the postdigital. *Postdigital Science and Education*, 1(1), 29–42. https://doi.org/10.1007/s42438-018-0004-9.

Peters, M. A., & Jandrić, P. (2018a). *The Digital University: A Dialogue and Manifesto*. New York: Peter Lang.

Peters, M. A., & Jandrić, P. (2018b). Peer production and collective intelligence as the basis for the public digital university. *Educational Philosophy and Theory*, 50(13), 1271–84. https://doi.org/10.1080/00131857.2017.1421940.

Peters, M. A., & Jandrić, P. (2018c). Neoliberalism and the university. In D. Cahill, M. Cooper, M. Koenings, & D. Primrose (Eds.), *SAGE Handbook of Neoliberalism* (pp. 553–64). London: Sage.

Peters, M. A., & Jandrić, P. (2019a). AI, human evolution, and the speed of learning. In J. Knox, Y. Wang, & M. Gallagher (Eds.), *Artificial Intelligence and Inclusive Education: Speculative Futures and Emerging Practices* (pp. 195–206). Springer Nature. https://doi.org/10.1007/978-981-13-8161-4_12.

Peters, M. A., & Jandrić, P. (2019b). Posthumanism, open ontologies and bio-digital becoming: Response to Luciano Floridi's Onlife Manifesto. *Educational Philosophy and Theory*, 51(10): 971–80. https://doi.org/10.1080/00131857.2018.1551835.

Peters, M. A., Jandrić, P. & Hayes, S. (2019). The curious promise of educationalising technological unemployment: What can places of learning really do about the future of work? *Educational Philosophy and Theory*, 51(3), 242–54. https://doi.org/10.1080/00131857.2018.1439376.

Peters, M. A., Jandrić, P., & Means, A. J. (Eds.) (2019). *Education and Technological Unemployment*. Singapore: Springer.

Pew Research Center (2011). Global christianity a report on the size and distribution of the world's christian population. https://web.archive.org/web/20131101114257/http://www.pewforum.org/files/2011/12/Christianity-fullreport-web.pdf. Accessed May 14, 2019.

Pignataro, A. (2019). Chapman Professor Mclaren Reflects on Fascism in Orange County. OCWeekly, 14 October. https://ocweekly.com/chapman-professor-mclaren-reflects-on-fascism-in-orange-county/. Accessed October 18, 2019.

Polanyi, K. (2001). *The Great Transformation: The Political and Economic Origins of Our Time*. Boston: Beacon Press.

Postone, M. (1996). *Time, Labor and Social Domination: A Reinterpretation of Marx's Critical Theory*. Cambridge: Cambridge University Press.

Pozo, M. (2003). Toward a critical revolutionary pedagogy: An interview with Peter McLaren. http://facpub.stjohns.edu/~ganterg/sjureview/vol2-1/mclaren.html. Accessed May 14, 2019.

Préciado, B. (2013). *Testo Junkie: Sex, Drugs, and Biopolitics in the Pharmacopornographic Era*. New York, NY: Feminist Press.

Prensky, M. (2001). Digital natives, digital immigrants. *On the Horizon*, 9(5), 1–6. https://doi.org/10.1108/10748120110424816.

Prescott, M. (2005). Romancing the stone-cold killer: Ayn Rand and William Hickman. http://michaelprescott.freeservers.com/romancing-the-stone-cold.html. Accessed May 14, 2019.

Pruyn, M., & Charles, L. M. H. (Eds.) (2005). *De la pedagogía crítica a la pedagogía de la revolución. Ensayos para comprender a Peter McLaren*. New York, NY: Peter Lang.

Pruyn, M., & Charles, L. M. H. (Eds.) (2007). *Teaching Peter McLaren: Paths of dissent*. New York, NY: Peter Lang.

Rand, A. (1964). *The Virtue of Selfishness*. New York: New American Library.

Rand, A. (1992) [1957]. *Atlas Shrugged* (35th anniversary ed.). New York: Dutton.

Reimer, E. W. (1971). *School Is Dead: Alternatives in Education*. London: Penguin.

Reitz, C. (Ed.) (2013). *Crisis of Commonwealth: Marcuse, Marx, McLaren*. Lanham, MD: Lexington Books, Rowman & Littlefield.

Reitz, C. (2015). *Philosophy & Critical Pedagogy: Insurrection & Commonwealth*. New York: Peter Lang.

Reitz, C. (2018). *Ecology and Revolution: Herbert Marcuse and the Challenge of a New World System*. London and New York: Routledge.

Ritzer, G., Jandrić, P. & Hayes, S. (2018). Prosumer capitalism and its machines. *Open Review of Educational Research*, 5(1), 113–29. https://doi.org/10.1080/23265507.2018.1546124.

Rikowski, G., & Ford, D.R. (2019). Marxist Education Across the Generations: a Dialogue on Education, Time, and Transhumanism. *Postdigital Science and Education*, 1(2), 507–24. https://doi.org/10.1007/s42438-018-0028-1.

Rivage-Seul, M. (2008). *The Emperor's God: Imperial Misunderstandings of Christianity*. Radford, VA: Institute for Economic Democracy Press.

Rivage-Seul, M. (2016). Chomsky on U.S. war vs. liberation theology. https://mikerivageseul.wordpress.com/2012/04/28/chomsky-on-u-s-war-vs-liberation-theology/. Accessed May 14, 2019.

Robinson, W. I. (2004). *A Theory of Global Capitalism: Production, Class, and State in a Transnational World*. Baltimore, MD: Johns Hopkins University Press.

Robinson, W. I. (2014). *Global Capitalism and the Crisis of Humanity*. New York: Cambridge University Press.

Robinson, W. I. (2016a) Sadistic capitalism: Six urgent matters for humanity in global crisis. *Truthout*, April 12. http://www.truth-out.org/opinion/item/35596-sadistic-capitalism-six-urgentmatters-for-humanity-in-global-crisis. Accessed May 14, 2019.

Robinson, W. I. (2016b). Reform is not enough to stem the rising tide of inequality worldwide. *Truthout*, January 1. http://www.truth-out.org/news/item/34224-reformis-not-enough-to-stemthe-rising-tide-of-inequality-worldwide. Accessed May 14, 2019.

Robinson, W. I. (2017a). Debate on the new global capitalism: Transnational capitalist class, transnational state apparatuses and global crisis. *International Critical Thought*, 7(2), 171–89. https://doi.org/10.1080/21598282.2017.1316512.

Robinson, W. I. (2017b). Trumpism, 21st-century fascism, and the dictatorship of the transnational capitalist class. *Social Justice*, January 20. http://www.socialjusticejournal.org/trumpism-21st-century-fascism-and-the-dictatorship-of-the-transnational-capitalist-class/. Accessed May 14, 2019.

Robinson, W. I. (2018a). The next economic crisis: Digital capitalism and global police state. *Race & Class*, 60(1), 77–92. https://doi.org/10.1177/0306396818769016.

Robinson, W. I. (2018b). Accumulation and the global police state. *Critical Sociology*. http://www.soc.ucsb.edu/faculty/robinson/Assets/pdf/Accumulation%20Crisis%20and%20Global%20Police%20State%20pdf%20published.pdf. Accessed May 14, 2019.

Robinson, W. I. (2019). Global capitalist crisis and 21st century fascism: Beyond the Trump hype. *Science & Society*, 83(2), 155–83. https://doi.org/10.1521/siso.2019.83.2.155.

Rohr, R. (2016). The path of descent. Center for action and contemplation, 16 October. http://centerforactionandcontemplation.cmail19.com/t/ViewEmail/d/A2C391CB09818C45/12E9998DA07E136EC67FD2F38AC4859C. Accessed May 14, 2019.

Rosen, M. (2000). The Marxist critique of morality and the theory of ideology. In E. Harcourt (Ed.), *Morality, Reflection and Ideology* (pp. 21–43). Oxford: Oxford University Press.

Rosenberg, P. (2019a). The Christian right has a plan to turn the us into an oppressive theocratic state—and they have already started. *RawStory*, April 13. https://www.rawstory.com/2019/04/christian-right-plan-turn-us-oppressive-theocratic-state-already-started/. Accessed May 14, 2019.

Rosenberg, P. (2019b). The brilliant science that has creationists and the Christian right terrified. *Rawstory*, January 19. https://www.rawstory.com/2019/01/brilliant-science-creationists-christian-right-terrified/. Accessed May 14, 2019.

Ross, E. W. (2016). Peter McLaren, *Life in Schools: An Introduction to Critical Pedagogy in the Foundations of Education* (1988). In J. L. DeVitis (Ed.), *Popular Educational Classics: A Reader*. New York: Peter Lang.

Sanders, B. (1995). *A Is for Ox: The Collapse of Literacy and the Rise of Violence in an Electronic Age*. London: Vintage.

Sanders, B., & Illich, I. (1989). *ABC: The Alphabetization of the Popular Mind*. London: Vintage.

Sandlin, J. A., & McLaren, P. (Eds.) (2009). *Critical Pedagogies of Consumption: Living and Learning in the Shadow of the "Shopocalypse."* New York, NY: Routledge.

Sennett, R. (2012). *Together, the Rituals, Pleasures and Politics of Cooperation*. New Haven, CT: Yale.

Shackelford, K. (2014). Jeremy Begbie: What can Jazz teach us about being a christian? All about Jazz, October 16. https://www.allaboutjazz.com/jeremy-begbie-what-can-jazz-teach-us-about-being-a-christian-jeremy-begbie-by-k-shackelford.php. Accessed May 14, 2019.

Shea, M. (2018). Biblical basis for war. https://www.documentcloud.org/documents/5026577-Biblical-Basis-for-War.html. Accessed May 14, 2019.

Shirky, C. (2011). *Cognitive Surplus: Creativity and Generosity in a Connected Age*. London: Penguin.

Sigman, A. (2007). *Remotely Controlled: How Television Is Damaging Our Lives*. London: Ebury Press.

Sinclair, C., & Hayes, S. (2019). Between the post and the com-post: Examining the postdigital "work" of a prefix. *Postdigital Science and Education*, 1(1), 119–31. https://doi.org/10.1007/s42438-018-0017-4.

Smith, L. T. (1999). *Decolonizing Methodologies*. London/Dunedin: Zed Books/University of Otago Press.

Smith, T. (2009). *Globalization: A Systematic Marxian Account*. Chicago: Haymarket.

Sobrino, J. (2001). *Christ the Liberator*. Maryknoll, NY: Orbis Books.

Sotiris, P. (2013). Thoughts on the political significance of the Turkish movement. http://theirategreek.wordpress.com/tag/syntagma/. Accessed May 14, 2019.

Spencer, R. (2017). Postcolonialism is a humanism. In D. Alderson & R. Spencer (Eds.), *For Humanism: Explorations in Theory and Politics* (pp. 120–62). London: Pluto Press.

Standing, G. (2011). *The Precariat: The New Dangerous Class*. London: Bloomsbury. http://dx.doi.org/10.5040/9781849664554.

Standing, G. (2014). *A Precariat Charter: From Denizens to Citizens*. London: Bloomsbury.

Standing, G. & Jandrić, P. (2015). Precariat, education and technologies: Towards a global class identity. *Policy Futures in Education*, 13(8), 990–94. https://doi.org/10.1177/1478210315580206.

Stetsenko, A. (2002). Vygotsky's cultural-historical activity theory: Collaborative practice and knowledge construction process. In D. Robbins and A. Stetsenko (Eds.), *Vygotsky's Psychology: Voices from the Past and Present*. New York: Nova Science Press.

Suoranta, J., & Vadén, T. (2010). *Wikiworld*. London: Pluto.

Tarico, V. (2018). How to effectively confront anti-abortion zealots with Bible verses. *RawStory*, June 8. https://www.rawstory.com/2019/06/how-to-effectively-confront-anti-abortion-zealots-with-bible-verses/. Accessed May 14, 2019.

Teilhard de Chardin, P. (1959). *The Phenomenon of Man*. New York: Harper and Row.

Teilhard de Chardin, P. (1964). *The Future of Man*. New York: Harper and Row.

Teilhard de Chardin, P. (1965). *The Appearance of Man*. New York: Harper and Row.

Teilhard de Chardin, P. (1966a). *The Vision of the Past*. New York: Harper and Row.

Teilhard de Chardin, P. (1966b). *Man's Place in Nature*. New York: Harper and Row.

Teilhard de Chardin, P. (1968). *Science and Christ*. New York: Harper and Row.

Thomas, D. (2010). Lament. https://youtu.be/h1xLuTbBdrA. Accessed May 14, 2019.

Todd, J. (2012). From deschooling to unschooling: Rethinking anarchopedagogy after Ivan Illich. In R. H. Haworth (Ed.), *Anarchist Pedagogies* (pp. 69–87). Oakland: PM Press.

Tolkien, J. R. R. (2012). *The Lord of the Rings*. Boston: Mariner Books.

Tomasevich, J. (2001). *War and Revolution in Yugoslavia, 1941–1945: Occupation and Collaboration*. Stanford, CA: Stanford University Press.

Turkle, S. (2012). *Alone Together: Why We Expect more from Technology and Less from Each Other*. New York: Basic Books.

Turner, D. (1983). *Marxism and Christianity*. Oxford: Blackwell.

USA Today. (2011). Sinaloa cartel gives blessing to newest Mexican drug ballads. December 21. http://usatoday30.usatoday.com/news/world/story/2011-12-21/Alfredo-Rios-narcocorrido-Sinaloa-drug-ballad/52146296/1. Accessed May 14, 2019.

van Dijk, J. (1999). *The Network Society*. London: Sage.

Vials, C. (2017). Adorno's The authoritarian personality. *Solidarity*, March–April. https://solidarity-us.org/atc/187/p4900/. Accessed May 14, 2019.

Victoria, B. D. (2006). *Zen at War*. Lanham, MA: Rowman & Littlefield.

Wark, M. (2015). *Molecular Red: Theory for the Anthropocene*. London: Verso.

Wark, M., & Jandrić, P. (2016). New knowledge for a new planet: Critical pedagogy for the Anthropocene. *Open Review of Educational Research*, 3(1), 148–78. https://doi.org/10.1080/23265507.2016.1217165.

Watts, A. (1966). *The Book: On the Taboo Against Knowing Who You Are*. New York: Pantheon.

Whyte, C. (2019). Green New Deal proposal includes free higher education and fair pay. *New Scientist*, February 12. https://www.newscientist.com/article/2193592-green-new-deal-proposal-includes-free-higher-education-and-fair-pay/. Accessed May 14, 2019.

Wiener, N. (1948) [1961]. *Cybernetics: Or Control and Communication in the Animal and the Machine*. Cambridge, MA: MIT Press.

Wikipedia (2019a). Peter McLaren. http://en.wikipedia.org/wiki/Peter_McLaren. Accessed May 14, 2019.

Wikipedia (2019b). *E-learning*. https://en.wikipedia.org/wiki/E-learning. Accessed May 14, 2019.

Williams, R. (2014). *Bonhoeffer's Black Jesus: Harlem Renaissance Theology and an Ethic of Resistance*. Waco, TX: Baylor University Press.

Winn, M. (2002). *The Plug-in Drug: Television, Computers, and Family Life*. London: Penguin.

Youyou, W., Kosinski, M., & Stillwell, D. (2015). Computer-based personality judgments are more accurate than those made by humans. *Proceedings of the National Academy of Sciences* (PNAS). http://www.pnas.org/content/112/4/1036.full.pdf. Accessed May 14, 2019.

Žižek, S. (2002). *Welcome to the Desert of the Real: Five Essays on September 11 and Related Dates*. London and New York: Verso.

Žižek, S. (2012). *Less Than Nothing: Hegel and the Shadow of Dialectical Materialism*. London and New York: Verso.

Index